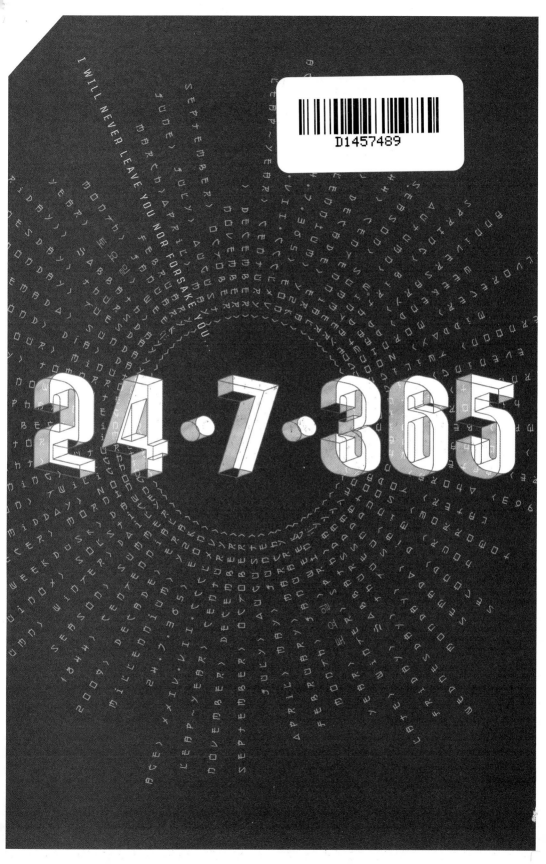

Other books by Dwain Neilson Esmond:

Beyond the In-a-Pinch God
Can You Hear Me Now?

To order, call
1-800-765-6955

Visit us at
www.reviewandherald.com
for information on other Review and Herald® products.

For more 24.7.365, visit
www.DwainEsmond.org

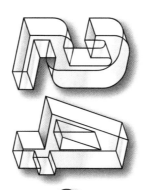

/// ONE YEAR IN THE WORD

DWAIN NEILSON ESMOND ///

REVIEW AND HERALD® PUBLISHING ASSOCIATION

Since 1861 | www.reviewandherald.com

Review and Herald® titles may be purchased in bulk for educational, business, fund-raising, or sales promotional use. For information, e-mail SpecialMarkets@reviewandherald.com. The Review and Herald® Publishing Association publishes biblically based materials for spiritual, physical, and mental growth and Christian discipleship.

The author assumes full responsibility for the accuracy of all facts and quotations as cited in this book.

Unless otherwise noted, all texts in this book are from the *Holy Bible, New International Version.* Copyright © 1973, 1978, 1984, International Bible Society. Used by permission of Zondervan Bible Publishers.

Texts credited to Message are from *The Message.* Copyright © 1993, 1994, 1995, 1996, 2000, 2001. Used by permission of NavPress Publishing Group.

Texts credited to NKJV are from the New King James Version. Copyright © 1979, 1980, 1982 by Thomas Nelson, Inc. Used by permission. All rights reserved.

Bible texts credited to NRSV are from the New Revised Standard Version of the Bible, copyright © 1989 by the Division of Christian Education of the National Council of the Churches of Christ in the U.S.A. Used by permission.

Verses marked TLB are taken from *The Living Bible,* copyright © 1971 by Tyndale House Publishers, Wheaton, Ill. Used by permission.

This book was
Edited by Penny Estes Wheeler and JoAlyce Waugh
Copyedited by James Cavil
Designed by Ron J. Pride
Cover photos © 2008 Jupiterimages Corporation
Interior designed by Heather Rogers
Typeset: Bembo 10/11.5

PRINTED IN U.S.A.
12 11 10 09 08   5 4 3 2 1

Library of Congress Cataloging-in-Publication Data
Esmond, Dwain, 1971-   .
  24-7-365 : a year in the Word / Dwain Neilson Esmond.
    p. cm.
  1. Bible—Reading. 2. Bible—Meditations. 3. Devotional calendars—Seventh-day Adventists. 4. Seventh-day Adventist teenagers—Prayers and devotions. I. Title.
BS617.E86 2008
220.071—dc22
                    2008023416

ISBN 978-0-8280-2336-8

FOR MY SON

My son is 5 months old right now—from the date of conception, that is. He's still growing in his mother's womb. I've attended two ultrasound photo shoots so far, and the sight of him—the little feet, the fluttering valves of his heart, the eyes that peer into my soul—does things to me. I have but one sacred wish for my son and this is it: that he will love the Lord Jesus Christ with all his heart, soul, mind, and strength, and that he will cherish God's Word and live it.

It's the same wish that I have for you.

The Bible is perhaps the most misunderstood, misquoted, and mishandled book of all time. Yet it is biggest bestseller the world has ever known. That's not a coincidence. The Bible is much more than ink stains on paper; it contains the very thoughts of God as given to men and, as such, it is unlike any other book that was ever written.

As you read *24-7-365*, remember that it can never replace the priceless treasures hidden in the Bible. Make the reading of God's Word the first thing you do each day. Ask God's Holy Spirit to help you understand what you're reading. Meditate on it. Pray about it—and you will be transformed.

ACKNOWLEDGMENTS

I couldn't have produced this volume without the able help of some of the most talented people anywhere—the Review and Herald Book Division, led by Mario Martinelli. I first want to express my deepest appreciation for Jeannette Johnson, the acquisitions editor who has continued to believe that I have something to say that's worth printing. Jeannette, you are special!

Penny Estes Wheeler, you took my discordant notes and made them sing. You are a joy to work with. I thank you!

James Cavil, the best copy editor working anywhere in the world today, it was an honor to have you work on my book. Who would've thought that a Cowboys fan could love a Redskins fan? I love you, man! Thanks so much.

And to my Lord and Savior, Jesus the Christ. What can I say about You? I give You my life.

──> "MR. NOTHING, MEET MR. SOMETHING" <

In the beginning God created the heavens and the earth. The earth was without form, and void; and darkness was on the face of the deep. Genesis 1:1, 2, NKJV.

ey! It's 2009. Uh, duh! You knew that, right? You watched the ball drop in Times Square last night. You got the headache and stomachache to prove it. (Actually the new year began at sunset on December 31, you know, for "the evening and the morning were the first day" [Genesis 1:5, KJV], but let's leave that alone.)

You've been on earth for more than a minute now, so chances are you're a pro at the whole New Year's thing. It never gets old, does it? Ever wonder how the angels in heaven and the unfallen worlds viewed the birth of earth that very first New *World's* Eve?

God stepped out into total darkness, total absence of anything—the most nothing that has ever been—and simply began to speak. I imagine trillions of planets with their beautiful beings bent low, watching God's hands, listening to God's voice, trusting God's heart.

There were no New World parties headlined by Fall Out Boy or T.I. at the birth of earth. No police on horseback to keep people in line. No SWAT teams patrolling out of sight to prevent terrorists from turning the New Year's celebration into a New Year's nightmare. No boozed-up crowds, no balloons or streamers, no Dick Clark, and no ball. God was about to do the impossible, and every unfallen world stood transfixed, immobile, waiting to see what God would dream up this time.

As God stepped into the darkness and began to speak, nothing was introduced to something, and not just any something. This something—earth—would mean everything to God. No wonder God looked at it all and declared that it was "very good" (Genesis 1:31).

As you read through God's Word this year, He will transform you into something beautiful—and this time He's got a lot more than nothing to work with. Get your read on!

/////// HOT READ ///////

Read Genesis 1-3 today. God didn't do a shoddy job of creating earth and its inhabitants. How much care will you put into what you do this year?

──> ALL SWOLLED UP! <

Then the Lord said unto Cain, "Why are you angry? Why is your face downcast?"
Genesis 4:6.

ongratulations! You made it to day two. You did read Genesis 1 to 3 yester-day, right? If you did, then you know God dropped some verses on nothing and up came earth, a perfect paradise. When I get to heaven, I'm heading straight for God's mouth. I want to see what else He's got in there, don't you? Day one's reading had me celebrating God's creation, but it also introduced me again to Satan's destructive power.

The fallout from Adam and Eve's bad choice didn't end with their sin. Fast-forward to Genesis 4, and you'll see Cain all "swolled up" at Abel. What's his beef? Well, you read it. God accepted Abel's sheep offering and rejected Cain's offering of fruit. What's God got against fruit? Nothing, really. But God required from Cain and Abel a lamb sacrifice, because the lamb symbolized Jesus, who would one day come to earth and die for the sins of the world. Cain knew this, yet he chose to offer fruit. So the only one he should have been mad at was himself.

Cain reminds me a lot of myself when I was a teenager. When I caught chicken pox, I got all "swolled up" at my kid sister because I thought she gave it to me. I couldn't get to God, who had failed to protect me from the dreaded scourge. I couldn't take out my anger on my older brothers. (They'd take theirs out on me.) So I had to take it out on the only person in the house I could beat up—my sister. Some tough guy I was back then, huh?

Misplaced anger can lead us to make very poor decisions. In the case of Cain, it led him to do the unthinkable: kill his little brother, an act that drove him from God's presence (Genesis 4:16). How you deal with your anger can either bring you closer to God or drive you far from Him. If something makes you upset today, talk to God about it. Pray. Nothing is too small to discuss with God. Don't pull a Cain.

///////// HOT READ ///////

Today as you read, don't miss Genesis 6, the story of the Flood. Focus on verse 6. Is there something that you are currently doing that is making God cry?

——> HIGH MAINTENANCE? <

Then Noah built an altar to the Lord and, taking some of all the clean animals and clean birds, he sacrificed burnt offerings on it. Genesis 8:20.

My wife says that I'm hard to please—that I'm high maintenance—but I don't believe it for a minute. She always points to the countless things I do before I sit down with her to eat a meal. I confess—I do have a ritual. I arrange my plate a certain way. If anything is missing or out of place, then I've got to get up and make it right. Once I start, however, there's no stopping me.

The food thing is nothing compared to my before-bedtime ritual, though. I gotta wash my face, pour warm water in my ears, take out a perfectly sturdy Q-tip, and you know what comes next. Let the big dig begin!

These are but two of my many quirks. Don't laugh; you've got some too. I once had a friend who loved to get athlete's foot just so he could have the pleasure of picking at it. Hey, whatever floats your boat, right? (OK, that's just straight-up filthy.) Anyway, I don't think I'm high maintenance at all. A little quiet time with my Q-tip at night and I'm good.

"High maintenance" is a charge that's not just leveled at ear-pickers like me, though. People say it about God all the time. "He's too hard on us." "His commandments can't be kept." "He's gonna burn people up in hell!" Is God really hard to please? Noah helped me answer that question today as I read Genesis 8.

When Noah and his family walked out of the ark on dry land following the Flood, the first thing that Noah did was to build an altar and make a thanksgiving sacrifice to God. He acknowledged God—first. Here's God's response to Noah's act of love: The Lord smelled the pleasing aroma and said in his heart: "Never again will I curse the ground because of man. . . . And never again will I destroy all living creatures, as I have done" (Genesis 8:21). Noah acknowledged God's goodness, and that pleased God.

///////// HOT READ ////////

Don't miss God's solemn covenant with Noah in Genesis 9, the "ites" of Genesis 10, or the builders in Genesis 11. These are major setup chapters for what comes next.

——> WANNA GET AWAY? <

Leave your country, your people and your father's household and go to the land I will show you. Genesis 12:1.

akinah Booker had no idea just how much her 9-year-old son, Semaj, hated living in Tacoma, Washington. One day the four-foot-nine-inch fourth grader stole a neighbor's Acura and was spotted by police while attempting to get on a nearby freeway.

You'd think the sight of cops yelling from their cars for him to pull over would scare the 9-year-old, but not this kid. Semaj led police on a high-speed chase that ended when he took a wrong exit, blew out the car's engine, and hit a tree.

Because of his age, no juvenile detention center would admit him, so he was sent home. By 6:00 a.m. the next day he was gone again. When police finally caught up to little Mr. Booker this time, he was coming off of a Southwest Airlines flight in San Antonio, Texas. You read that right! He had somehow run away from home again, made his way to the airport, passed through security checkpoints at two separate airports, boarded flights with no boarding passes, and found his way to San Antonio. Why did Semaj go to all this trouble? He desperately wanted to get to his dream destination—Dallas, Texas. Sometimes you just gotta get away!

What happens when you're comfortable right where you are, but God wants you to make like a banana and split? That's what He told Abram—whose name God would later change to Abraham. God told him to leave his home, his land—everything that he knew—for a place that God would eventually show him. That's right—unlike Semaj, Abram had no idea where he was going. What was God up to?

Well, you read yesterday about Babel. The people after the Flood had become so evil, so bent on doing their own thing, that God decided to raise up a nation that would obey Him and serve as an example of righteousness to a wayward world. The man who would become the father of this nation was Abram. But in order to obey God and receive God's blessing, Abram had to leave what was comfortable to him behind. What was that blessing? Check out Genesis 12:1-3. Now, is that an awesome promise or what?

/////// HOT READ ///////

Abram was called by God, but he was not perfect. Read Genesis 12:10-20.

——> IF YOU'RE NOT GOING TO DANCE . . . <

Abram lived in the land of Canaan, while Lot lived among the cities of the plain and pitched his tents near Sodom. Now the men of Sodom were wicked and were sinning greatly against the Lord. Genesis 13:12, 13.

was getting my groove on. I had waited for years for a party like this, and my day had finally come. I'd been to "get-togethers"—you know, what Christians call their parties—but this was no get-together. We were all Christians, but you wouldn't have known it that night. Heads jerked back and forth as we did the wop and cabbage patch, popped and uprocked. (I know, I know. What's that? Never mind.)

The whole shindig was planned on the low. My friend's parents were going to be out of town, so her house was the spot. Since I hadn't been to a real party before, I was kind of scared to get on the "dance floor"—a tiny living room floor, actually. But everyone was getting down, including the honeys who were wearing painted-on jeans and tight tops.

I didn't plan to get my swerve on, but when a cute girl grabbed my hand and led me to the floor, well, you know what happened next. Later I regretted that night, not because I caught a VD or something crazy like that, but because my relationship with God had taken a direct hit!

That's probably how Lot felt after he and his daughters barely escaped the destruction of Sodom. (You'll read about that two days from now.) When Lot first looked at the beautiful, fertile rolling hills near Sodom, he never expected to get caught up in its lifestyle, but he did.

It's never a good idea to get close to sin, no matter how spiritually strong you think you are. Lot's life would have been very different had he chosen to remain close to the positive spiritual influence of Abraham. I hadn't planned to do much at the party, but it wasn't long before I'd joined in and was doing everything.

If I wasn't planning to dance, I shouldn't have gone to the party.

///////// HOT READ ///////

Check out Proverbs 4:14 for some good advice that just might save your life. I sure wish I had obeyed those words.

---> HURRY UP AND WAIT <

So after Abram had been living in Canaan ten years, Sarai his wife took her Egyptian maidservant Hagar and gave her to her husband to be his wife. Genesis 16:3.

f the Bible were a soap opera, today's reading would make for good television. It's all here: a promise from God that old Abe and Sarai would have a son after a lifetime of being unable to have children; a beautiful servant named Hagar in the prime of her childbearing years; a plot to make it all happen; and a huge mess when the plan goes horribly wrong.

Abram and Sarai had been in Canaan—the land that God had promised to show Abram (Genesis 12:1)—for 10 years. The Bible doesn't say whether or not during those 10 years God had reiterated His promise to give them an heir. One thing's for sure, however; they were getting antsy—especially Sarai.

"The Lord has kept me from having children. Go, sleep with my maidservant; perhaps I can build a family through her," Sarai told Abram (Genesis 16:2). Hear the frustration in her voice? She wanted a family so badly that she was willing to let her husband sleep with another woman. Back then men often had concubines, but that was still pretty desperate, wasn't it?

But Sarai wasn't the only desperate person in the tent. Abram doesn't come back with "Baby, what've you been smokin'? Let's just trust God. I love you too much to do that."

The old man says, "Well, sweetheart, if you insist! It's really gonna hurt me to do this, but if I have to . . ." Where was the man whose belief in God was counted to him for righteousness (Genesis 15:6)?

Abram and Sarai's plan to produce an heir tells us this truth about human nature: desperate people do desperate things. Maybe there's something that you've been waiting on for what seems an eternity. Don't be tempted to do a "wrong" to bring about a "right" outcome. Abram and Sarai waited another 14 years before the son God promised was born, but he was—and great suffering resulted from their decision to fulfill God's promise themselves.

////// HOT READ //////

Why did God change Sarai's name (Genesis 17:15, 16)? Do you think it had anything to do with the Hagar incident?

——> SODOMGATE <

"My lords," he said, "please turn aside to your servant's house. You can wash your feet and spend the night and then go on your way early in the morning."
Genesis 19:2.

If you haven't read today's Scripture, let me warn you—it's definitely R-rated: for violence, adult language, and mature sexual themes. Genesis 18-21 had my eyeballs popping, y'all. In Genesis 21 Baby Boy finally shows up, and he's cute to boot. The birth of Isaac leads to the "DIS-missal" of Hagar and Ishmael. Can you say "BABY, MAMA DRAMA"?

I started to tackle "Hagargate," but "Sodomgate" was way too deep to overlook. Can you imagine it? Two weird strangers roll up in Sodom. They don't smile. They don't greet anyone. They barely speak. Lot recognizes something special about them. Fearing for their safety, he intones, "Trust me. You really don't want to stay out here tonight."

The strangers are more than capable of taking care of themselves, but after Lot keeps insisting, they go to Lot's house. They aren't there very long when "the men of the city," old and young, come out to Lot's ranch and surround his property (Genesis 19:4). Their demand: "Bring out those two strangers. We want to have sex with them." What happens next is even more bizarre than this request.

Lot tries to reason with the men by offering them his two daughters, who are virgins. (What kind of father would do such a thing? I digress—back to the perverts at Lot's door.) Lot's gesture backfires. The men become incensed and try to kill him. Just in the nick of time the angels snatch him back inside, saving his life and later the lives of his entire family when God destroys Sodom and Gomorrah.

It is clear from this biblical episode that God does not condone homosexuality, though He loves all people, including homosexuals. God loves us too much to leave any of us just the way we are. Anger was one of my biggest challenges, but God took that from me. I remember the porn trap that entangled me. God had to take that before it destroyed me and those I love. If you plan to follow God, prepare to be changed!

/////// HOT READ ///////

You won't believe why God spared the lives of Lot and his children. Read Genesis 19:29 and find out.

——> A TALE OF TWO A'S <

Then God said, "Take your son, your only son, Isaac, whom you love, and go to the region of Moriah. Sacrifice him there as a burnt offering on one of the mountains I will tell you about." Genesis 22:2.

pril 2003. Aron Ralston, an experienced mountain climber, decided one Sunday to go out for a little hike. Ralston was so sure that he would be in no danger that he didn't tell anyone where he was going. While climbing, he encountered an 800-pound boulder. As he climbed around the boulder, it shifted, wedging his arm between the boulder and the wall of the canyon. His right hand was immediately crushed, and he was trapped where no one could hear or see him—literally, between a rock and a hard place.

Five days later, out of water and food, Ralston faced this decision: lose the hand or lose his life. He chose hand. He carefully removed a pocketknife he had with him and hacked his way through his crushed arm until he was free. Never underestimate the power of the human spirit when it wants to survive.

As painful as it must have been for Ralston to cut off his hand, his pain could not come close to Abraham's when God told him, "Take Isaac up to Mount Moriah and sacrifice him as an offering to Me." I bet Abraham would have gladly traded his dilemma for Aron's.

As sick as it must have been to saw through a limb, having to kill someone you love beyond words—someone who smiles like you, wants to be you, someone whom you waited for your whole life—must be worse. That's the decision Abraham faced, and like the other guy in today's devotion whose name begins with A, Abraham passed the test.

Here's my favorite part of this story: Early the next morning Abraham got up and saddled his donkey. He took with him two of his servants and his son Isaac. When he had cut enough wood for the burnt offering, he set out for the place God had told him about (Genesis 22:3). No hesitation. No protestation. No procrastination. Just obedience.

Abraham loved God more than he loved Isaac, the gift that God had given him.

/////// HOT READ ///////

Abraham loses the love of his life, Sarah (Genesis 23). Baby Boy gets the girl of his dreams (Genesis 24).

——> SLIM SHADY <

Jacob replied, "First sell me your birthright." "Look, I am about to die," Esau said. "What good is the birthright to me?" Genesis 25:31, 32.

or him it was just a game. First $50, then $100—it was all chump change to the "idiots" who fell for it. The "it" they fell for was a scam run by a 15-year-old named Hue.

Already a computer whiz at a very young age, Hue opened up shop on the auction pages of Yahoo and eBay. The laptops he advertised as the fastest around weren't fast at all, but that was a minor technicality. He bought junk, and simply marked up the price. No need to complicate his sales promotions with a little thing we like to call, uh, TRUTH!

Before his sixteenth birthday Hue had conned online buyers out of more than 5,000 of their hard-earned dollars. The scam really was not that complicated.

Hue is a lot like a certain famous Bible character who, shall we say, had a major honesty problem. You were introduced to him in Genesis 25:27-34. You know the story well. Esau, his older brother, returns from a hunting trip hungry and exhausted, and begs Chef Jacob for a taste of his lentil stew.

"Sure, you can have a taste," Jacob replies, "but it's gonna cost you, E."

"What?" Esau shouts. "I'm dying here. Why you gotta go Slim Shady on me all the time, J?"

"I want your birthright. Promise me that, and you've got the food" is Jacob's sly offer. (Just like a little brother, right?)

"OK, man! Whatever. You got it."

Taking advantage of one moment of hunger-induced amnesia, Jacob swindled Esau out of the double portion of their father's inheritance that traditionally went to the eldest son. The Bible then says, "So Esau despised his birthright" (Genesis 25:34). Translation: Esau didn't think his birthright was worth his time, so he sold it cheaply. In one careless moment Esau made a choice he'd regret for the rest of his life. In an equally careless moment Jacob, too, got suffering for the rest of his life. If you're thinking about going "Slim Shady" to get something you really want, better count the cost before you sell out.

/////// HOT READ ///////
Not sure how Jacob learned to be Slim? Read what his dad did in Genesis 26.

17

──> SO FINE YOU BLOW MY MIND <

Then Jacob kissed Rachel and began to weep aloud. Genesis 29:11.

ome girls have made me want to cry, but I have never cried over one. Guys, you know what I mean, right? I did cry at my wedding, but that was not due to the sheer "finery" that I beheld walking down the aisle to take my hand. When I looked at Ms. Kemba, I had nothing but love in my eyes and passion in my heart. I still love her!

Me and my telltale heart were fine until the I do's. That's when I looked at my father. Bad move. He broke down in tears—of joy, I hope. So here we were, two grown men, crying in each other's arms. OK, it's cheesy, but that's my man, so stop laughing. Just wait until your wedding day.

I've cried over the death of loved ones, such as the day my cousin was killed in a drive-by shooting. I cried once when the Pine Forge Academy choir sang "O for a Faith," one of my favorite hymns. I was going through some personal challenges, and that song caught me in a moment of weakness. (Note to self: Guys don't cry, sir!).

Genesis 29 tells us that Jacob broke down in a full-fledged wail over a chick named Rachel. Now, she was fine. No question about it. She was both shapely and easy on the eyes (verse 17). And she was not a video vixen. She was beautiful inside and out.

You read the story. Jacob, a.k.a. "Slim Shady," was on the run from Esau, heading in the direction of Uncle Laban's house. While chilling at a nearby well with some shepherds, they pointed to a shepherd girl bringing her father's flock to the well. As she came closer, Jacob left the other shepherds, removed the heavy rock that covered the well, poured water for her sheep, and did the unthinkable. (Close your eyes, this is R-rated.) He grabbed Rachel and kissed her. (Don't even think about doing this. You're way younger than Jacob was at that time, and God never told you to put your lips on anyone. Keep your lips and everything else to yourself—please!)

Jacob started "leaking." Jacob wept loudly for Rachel for much more than her beauty. God had just led him to the love of his life, and he was thankful. He was also a lot older than you are right now, so don't go crying over anyone just yet.

/////// HOT READ ///////
You cannot NOT read Genesis 29:13-30. Slim gets some of his own medicine.

———> FAMILY REUNION <

> *But Esau ran to meet Jacob and embraced him; he threw his arms around his neck and kissed him. And they wept. Then Esau looked up and saw the women and children. "Who are these with you?" he asked.* Genesis 33:4, 5.

oes your family get together for family reunions? My family doesn't. Don't even ask. It's complicated! We love each other, but we never really come together and show it with all the food, the weird and wacky relatives, and, of course, the reunion t-shirt. My family is so lame!

A few months ago I was talking with a really crazy friend of mine who always has the zaniest tales of family drama. When his family comes together for a re-union, it's not uncommon for more than 200 people to show up. He told me about one of his cousins who has not been seen by the family in quite some time. There's a search party looking for him at every reunion.

Everyone in the family wants to see him, but not because they miss him. In fact, if he ever showed up, he'd need his own private army. My friend told me that this black sheep of the family has swindled several aunts out of thousands of dollars. (Note to said black sheep: Your fam in Philly have a major beatdown waiting for you. Travel there at your own risk.)

Unlike my friend and his family in Philly, Esau was on a collision course with the black sheep of his family, Jacob. And he'd waited 20 years for this moment.

For those 20 years he stewed over the birthright that his twin had swindled from him and the blessing he had stolen from their father. Now, finally, he was going to serve Jacob a cold helping of revenge. But something happened to Esau's heart before he reached Jacob. Jacob had asked God to forgive the sins of his past and heal the relationship with his brother. As Esau approached, Jacob bowed low before Esau seven times begging for his forgiveness. Esau jumped off his horse, lifted Jacob from his knees, and kissed him as they both began to cry. There would be no drama at this reunion, because God was there. If you've got drama in your family, tell God about it. He can fix it.

///////// HOT READ ///////

Don't miss Jacob's UFC debut with God (Genesis 32:22-31). This moment changed Jacob's name and character.

January 12 • *Genesis 34-36*

—> THE RAPE OF DINAH <

When Shechem son of Hamor the Hivite, the ruler of that area, saw her,
he took her and violated her. Genesis 34:2.

f you've been reading the Bible along with me so far, you'd have to say that the rape of Dinah, found in Genesis 34, is one of the saddest episodes to date. The fall of Adam and Eve, Cain's murder of Abel, God's destruction of the world by a flood—all of those are at the top of my list of human failures after Creation.

But the story of Dinah makes me just plain crazy. Can you picture it? A young girl decides to take a walk to visit some older women in her community when along comes a rich playboy who grabs her, drags her into a corner, and rapes her. Perhaps Shechem said hello and she didn't respond. Maybe he grabbed her arm and she brushed it off, unlike the girls he'd "touched." We really don't know either way, but it's obvious that Shechem simply wouldn't take no for an answer. He violated Dinah, and then had the temerity—look that word up—to have his dad ask for her hand in marriage.

Maybe it's just me, but that's not how the marriage thing is supposed to work, is it? You don't rape first and propose second. You don't rape at all—ever! Dinah's violation was especially painful for Simeon and Levi to handle. She was their full sister, and merely a half sister to Joseph, Benjamin, Gad, Asher, Naphtali, and Dan. So they hatched their plan and executed it. Simeon and Levi killed every male in the local province where Shechem lived—including Shechem and his dad.

Serves 'em right? That's certainly how I felt—at first. But Simeon and Levi were wrong. Their anger was legit, but the way they handled it was wrong.

What should they have done? They should have talked to their father about their frustrations and trusted his judgment. But Simeon and Levi didn't trust their dad to restore Dinah's honor. Care to guess why?

//////// HOT READ ////////

Whose daughter was Dinah (Genesis 34:1)? Which of his wives did Jacob love most (Genesis 29:30)? Simeon and Levi didn't trust their dad's love for them, their mother, or their sister.

——> JUST DO IT <

> *The warden paid no attention to anything under Joseph's care, because the Lord was with Joseph and gave him success.* Genesis 39:23.

ude, I'm so stoked over today's Bible passage. (Wait, I sound like a surfer. What's happening to my inner thug?). Did you see Joseph pull his Mr. Bigstuff routine in Genesis 37? He was crusin' for a bruisin', wasn't he? And what about all that "hateration" from his brothers? Who hasn't thought of offing a sibling or two? Hands high!

Then there's the whole Potiphar's wife episode, complete with older woman/younger guy theme, sexy seduction, and a mock rape scene. Now, that's hot! All that's hitting me, but I'm really feeling the end of Genesis 39. Our hero is thrown into prison after being convicted on trumped-up rape charges, after being sold into slavery by his brothers, after being thrown into a well by, uh, his brothers. He's batting like .185 in July, to put it in baseball terms, but hang on. It's only spring. The fall is coming, and this rookie's gonna break out of his slump with a bang.

Through all his suffering Joseph had two things going for him: his God, and a killer work ethic. Young Joe did his work so well that when he finished, there was no one who could do it better. If you've got God on your side, a willingness to work hard at honest labor, and a humble spirit, God will exalt you. You will be successful!

I found this out in a small way when a college friend of mine named Mike called me up several years after we had graduated. He said, "Dwain, I just want to thank you for helping me with my writing way back in college." I kept listening. "Man, you don't know it, but what you showed me helped me pass my classes, and it's still helping me today in my career. You really blessed me, D. Thank you." Dude, I was speechless.

Mike's compliment really humbled me. I did my best to teach him what I knew about writing, and God blessed my efforts. From that experience I found out that if you do your best right where you are, God will bless everything you touch—everything!

/////// HOT READ ///////

Do not miss the saga of Judah and Tamar, his daughter-in-law. Remember, Jesus is a direct descendant of Judah.

——> OOPS! I FORGOT <

Then the chief cupbearer said to Pharaoh, "Today I am reminded of my shortcomings." Genesis 41:9.

t was dreams that got Joseph into trouble with his brothers. Why he would even listen to two guys who had dreams after all he went through is beyond me. If I were Joe, I would've probably said, "Quit dreaming, fellas. Get comfortable. You're gonna be here awhile."

But I'm not Joe. Joseph's trials had drawn him closer to God instead of souring him on the world. And when you get closer to God you tend not to turn down opportunities to help people. That's what Joseph did when the king's two attendants were placed under his supervision in the pen (Genesis 40).

They spoke of clusters of grapes and loaves of bread, hardly the stuff that dreams are made of, but these dreams had serious implications. In three days one guy would be restored to his former job and the other would be sentenced to die. These dreams were important.

Through Joseph, God had interpreted their dreams, and everything happened as Joseph said. In return for his help, Joseph simply asked the cupbearer to say a good word to the king on his behalf (verses 14-16). Did the cupbearer remember Joseph when he got out of jail? Well, kinda sorta.

He remembered Joe a whole two years later when Pharaoh had a troubling dream that no one could interpret. The cupbearer enjoyed his freedom so much that he forgot the one through whom God had given him hope. How ya like dem apples?

Truth is, if you live long enough, you're going to help people who'll soon forget what you did for them. People did it to Jesus. Think all the people watching Jesus get crucified were folks He didn't help? Think again.

Jesus said, "If you love those who love you, what credit is that to you? Even 'sinners' love those who love them. And if you do good to those who are good to you, what credit is that to you? Even 'sinners' do that" (Luke 6:32, 33).

//////// HOT READ ////////

You've completed two weeks in God's Word. Give yourself a big hand. Looking back on what you've read, where have you seen God's grace so far?

⟶ FULL CIRCLE <

So then, it was not you who sent me here, but God. Genesis 45:8.

ou can't read today's Bible passage without feeling a little weepy. The brothers who'd sold Joseph into slavery were caught in a life-threatening situation. Their homeland was engulfed by a famine, and the only aid agency handing out food was in Egypt. Headed by Joseph.

Do you remember the impeachment of a certain William Jefferson Clinton, former president of the United States? (You were little more than a baby back then, so you probably don't.) He'd carried on an affair with a young White House intern, and when he was caught his political enemies circled him and pounced. They dragged the affair out before the whole world and voted articles of impeachment against him, a punishment that is usually saved for those who commit "high crimes and misdemeanors."

You can imagine the utter fear that Mr. Clinton felt. He was wrong. He was caught, and there was nowhere to hide. But then a funny thing happened. Some of the people determined to ruin President Clinton had their lives turned upside down in the process.

While Mr. Clinton was being destroyed for lying about his affair, some of his chief accusers were committing the same sins. One by one they began to be exposed. Their bad behavior had come full circle, and boy, did it bite them.

Joseph had the right to destroy his brothers, to deny them his help and support. He could have had them killed. When a son-in-law of Saddam Hussein's— you remember the dead Iraqi dictator, don't you?—returned home after being pardoned by Saddam for treason, Hussein ordered his execution. Joseph could have done the same, but Joseph knew something that Saddam Hussein did not: Even the evil things that are done to us have to be approved by God. God sees and weighs it all.

Joseph told his brothers, "I forgive you. You meant to hurt me, but God led me here to save you."

Never repay evil for evil (Romans 12:21). Doing so will only destroy you.

///////// HOT READ ////////
Check out Israel's reunion with his son Joseph (Genesis 46:28-34). Sweet!

23

——> THE END <

Then Jacob called for his sons and said: "Gather around so I can tell you what will happen to you in days to come." Genesis 49:1.

The scene was classic. Joseph and his 11 brothers had been summoned to the land of Goshen in Egypt. Through Joseph, God had blessed his entire family with safety and prosperity. Their numbers multiplied, their wealth doubled and tripled—so much so that they began to be called Israelites, all descendants of Abraham as God had promised (Genesis 12). Dude, God keeps His promises!

Why did God go to all the trouble to call out a special group of people? After the Flood, God wanted a people who could serve as an example to the rest of the world by the way they acted, dressed, walked, talked, ate, lived, etc. He chose Abraham to be the father of this spiritual generation. And guess what? When you accept Jesus Christ as your Savior, you too become a part of this group.

We have come to the end of Genesis, and, sadly, the end of Jacob and Joseph's lives. If you're afraid of death, Jacob is one of the best examples in all of Scripture on how to die gracefully. When I read Genesis 49, I couldn't help re-membering a marriage seminar I attended with my wife a few months after we got married. While there we were asked this question: If you were going to die today, what would you say to your mate?

It wasn't long before couples started to tear up. Many couples had gone years without telling their significant others how much they loved and appreciated them. That activity changed the way I look at my wife and the people I love.

As Jacob approached the end of his life, he pronounced a special blessing on Joseph and his sons, Ephraim and Manasseh. Then he called together all his boys. One by one he shared with them their destiny. God had showed Jacob the path that each of their lives would take, Jacob told it to them, and then he blessed each of them. It was a fitting end to a great life. If you want to die right, live right. Live so that you'll have no regrets on that day.

///////// HOT READ ////////

After the death of Israel (Jacob), Joseph's brothers were still afraid of him. How did Joe respond to their fears (Genesis 50:15-21)? That's forgiveness!

——> JOE WHO? <

Then a new king, who did not know about Joseph, came to power in Egypt.
Exodus 1:8.

hen a person does something really great, people tend to remember them. In the nineteenth century a French chemist discovered that diseases were caused by germs rather than spontaneous generation. Before his discovery scientists believed that living organisms could miraculously come from nonliving organisms. Sounds wack now, doesn't it? It wasn't such a crazy idea until Louis Pasteur's experiments proved otherwise. Pasteur went on to develop a process we now call pasteurization, by which food is heated to destroy disease-causing microorganisms. You have him to thank for the absence of diseased microorganisms swimming in your milk. (Yuck!)

Suppose there was a scientist who did not know Mr. Pasteur. Suppose through some twist of fate he became head of the Food and Drug Administration. You know, the group that is supposed to protect citizens' food supply from disease—and terrorists. What if as FDA chief he moved to outlaw all pasteurization processes based on his own research? Do you think he'd get the Congress of the United States to go along with him?

Not! He'd have a better chance of being eaten by a bullfrog. At least I hope so, anyway. Yet something just like my fake scenario really happened in Egypt many years after Joseph's death. You remember, don't you, that it was Joseph whom God used to save the Egyptians and the then-known world from certain starvation during a worldwide famine (Genesis 41:57). Kind of unforgettable, don't you think?

Not for Egypt's new sheriff. Joseph had been long gone, and the monuments to him were old and rusty. As long as the Egyptians remembered Joseph, the Israelites were safe. When their memory failed, the Israelites were doomed. For the next 430 years the Egyptians enslaved the people of God.

Never forget or downplay the contributions of people who came before you—people who sacrificed so you could be successful.

////// HOT READ //////

Please read Exodus 2 today. No matter how bad your situation may be right now, God is going to deliver you, just as He sent Moses to deliver Israel.

——> MOI? <

But Moses said, "O Lord, please send someone else to do it." Exodus 4:13.

uys, I struggled to find something to write about today. There's just so much God all over today's reading that I couldn't make up my mind. I thought about tackling Pharaoh's bricks without straw law (Exodus 5:6-14), a task that was almost impossible for the Israelites. Straw was used to help the clay dry faster and bond better. Pharaoh was literally saying, "Produce the same amount of brick, and gather straw yourself! We won't help you!"

Ever had your computer eat an important assignment? Mine once ate the better part of a 25-page college paper. I was forced to redo it in a single night—talk about bricks without straw! I could tell you more about that horrific tale, but Moses just won't let me.

Next to Jesus, Moses is considered the greatest leader in all the Bible. But he didn't start out that way. When God tapped Moses to deliver his suffering people from Egypt, Moses started asking God questions.

"Moses said to God, 'Who am I?' (Exodus 3:11). Moses really didn't consider himself worthy for such a heroic task. After all, he'd been run out of Egypt 40 years earlier. He was *so* not ready to go back. God's answer: "Moe, I will be with you. Chilax!" (OK, God didn't say Chilax, but that's what He meant!)

"What shall I tell them?" Moses asked (verse 13). Moses knew that the Israelites weren't just going to say, "Sure, Moe, let's be out. All 2.5 million of us." Moses was appealing to God's authority. God heard and responded, "Tell them I AM sent you." Only God could get away with an answer like that. That's so cool.

Moses wasn't through questioning God. "What if they don't believe me?" he asked. When it became clear that God wasn't giving up, he broke out in full beg: "O Lord, please send someone else to do it" (Exodus 4:13). Moses simply did not want to go.

Ever been asked to do something for God? Did you ask "Why not someone else?" God knows your fears, and just as He was patient with Moses, He will be patient with you. God sees your potential. That's why He has prepared a special mission for you.

////// HOT READ //////
Exodus 6:1 is one of the "muscle" scriptures in the Bible. Claim it!

——> THE ONE <

And the Egyptians will know that I am the Lord when I stretch out my hand against Egypt and bring the Israelites out of it. Exodus 7:5.

ey, guys, where do we begin today? Wow, talk about fireworks! God's pulling out all the stops to free His people from Pharaoh's grip, isn't He?

There's something else in these chapters, though, that you may not have seen. We see the first plague, blood, in Exodus 7, and the seventh plague, hail, closes chapter 9. Some of the plagues God sent on Egypt were aimed specifically at some of the Egyptian gods.

In the first plague, God turned the waters of the mighty Nile River and all the water throughout Egypt into a bloody goo. The Egyptians considered the Nile a powerful god because it fertilized their fields and provided water with which to drink, bathe, and cook. In one swoop God devastated their belief in this god.

The Egyptians also worshipped Heqet, the frog goddess. After frogs covered every inch of Egypt, care to guess what they thought of Heqet? The Egyptians had two cow gods called Hathor and Apis. When the fifth plague wiped out most of the Egyptian livestock (horses, cows, donkeys, camels, cattle and sheep), Hathor and Apis were strangely silent.

Two years ago I went to see the great King Tut exhibit. You've heard of him, haven't you? He's the Egyptian boy king whose tomb was found and uncovered by archaeologist Howard Carter in 1922. Tut's tomb held many gods that the Egyptians believed would help him in the afterlife. The ancient Egyptians worshipped more than 80 different gods—one for just about every need in their lives. All created by them.

As the years passed, the Israelites there adopted some of these beliefs, worshipping the gods of their Egyptian masters. So God wanted both Pharaoh and the Israelites to know that He was the Lord, the one true God, and that there was no other god like Him.

Is God the only God in your life?

//////// HOT READ ////////

Don't miss the critical role that Aaron, Moses' older brother, is playing in Israel's deliverance.

27

——> WHAT'S IT GONNA TAKE? <

Do you not yet realize that Egypt is ruined? Exodus 10:7.

he September 10, 1982, entry of *Today in the Word,* a daily devotional from the Moody Bible Institute, carried this funny but true story.

Former heavyweight boxer James "Quick" Tillis is a cowboy from Oklahoma who fought out of Chicago in the early 1980s. He still remembers his first day in the Windy City after his arrival from Tulsa. "I got off the bus with two cardboard suitcases under my arms in downtown Chicago and stopped in front of the Sears Tower. I put my suitcases down, and I looked up at the tower and I said to myself, 'I'm going to conquer Chicago.' When I looked down, the suitcases were gone." James Tillis was quick, but so were the thieves in Chicago.

If you take the pride and hubris James Tillis showed in front of the Sears Tower in Chicago and multiply it by, say, a thousand or so, you'd just about get to the level of pride that Pharaoh had. Call me chicken, but I just can't see myself holding on to the people of God after bloody water, frogs, flies, and locusts. I'm not gonna get by the frogs, friends. That would be the last straw for me. I hate frogs!

Yet Pharaoh seemed unmoved. After each plague he promised to let God's people go, but once the plague subsided, he went back to his old ways and refused. The Bible tells us in several places that God "hardened" Pharaoh's heart so that he would not comply with Moses' requests. What exactly does that mean, though? Was God forcing Pharaoh to hold out when He could have broken him after the first plague and taken the Israelites out of Egypt?

The great writer Ellen White helps to clarify the matter: "There was no exercise of supernatural power to harden the heart of the king. God gave to Pharaoh the most striking evidence of divine power, but the monarch stubbornly refused to heed the light. Every display of infinite power rejected by him rendered him the more determined in his rebellion" (*Patriarchs and Prophets*, p. 268). Pharaoh's pride and rejection of God had hardened his heart. Don't ever let pride blind your eyes to God's leading in your life.

/////// HOT READ ///////

Check out 1 Samuel 6:6. Even other nations knew that Pharaoh had hardened his own heart against God.

——> FREE <

The Lord will fight for you; you need only to be still. Exodus 14:14.

f there had ever been a time to panic, this was it. Pharaoh and his mighty army were coming. The children of Israel could see the dust from their chariots off in the distance.

"How could you bring us out here to die," they shouted at Moses. "You idiot! We never should have left Egypt!" In a few short days they had already forgotten God. But Moses had an answer: "Just stand still and watch what God's about to do" (see Ex. 14:13).

You know the rest of the story. God slid His cloud between Pharaoh's army and His people, blew His breath, and opened the Red Sea, and His people passed through on dry land. Pharaoh's army followed them into the sea, and they all perished when the water came crashing down on them.

Here's something important to take away from God's deliverance of Israel: God can and will deliver you from the trials you face. But you must allow God to do this.

The final plague God used to free His people was the death of every firstborn male in Egypt, including cattle. God gave the Israelites strict instructions to follow in order to save their firstborn from this plague (Exodus 12). They were to slaughter an unblemished lamb and spread some of its blood on the top and sides of their doorposts. When the angel of God saw the blood, he would "pass over" that home.

The great "pass over" of the Israelites' homes points directly to Jesus' death on the cross for our sins. When we accept Jesus as our Savior, death, the punishment of God for our sins (Rom. 6:23), is placed on Christ. He is the spotless lamb whose blood must symbolically cover us, so that God's punishment for sin passes over us.

In a very real way, God worked through Jesus to deliver us from the slavery of sin (2 Cor. 5:19), just as He worked to free ancient Israel from Egyptian bondage. There's nothing we can do to earn salvation. It is God's gift to us, just as Israel's salvation was God's gift to them. How do you show your appreciation for God's awesome gift to you?

####### HOT READ #######

Read Romans 6:1-14 to find out how to live your gift every day.

——> SHADOW ECONOMY <

Then the Lord said to Moses, "I will rain down bread from heaven for you. The people are to go out each day and gather enough for that day." Exodus 16:4.

entlemen of Handy Hall, come and get your sacks." With those words, all hell would break loose in the men's dorm at Pine Forge Academy in the ancient days when I was there.

Droves of guys stampeded to the office area in the front lobby, jostling each other for a spot in line. There was rarely even a chance that anyone would fail to receive a sack, but that didn't stop us from running over, under, or around each other to get a good spot. Every Friday afternoon—the running of the bulls!

And what did we half kill each other for? A way-too-tiny drink—which most of us inhaled on sight—a "phony baloney" sandwich, two oatmeal or chocolate-chip cookies, potato chips, some lettuce and tomato slices, and a few condiments. It was nothing to write home about, and it was never, ever—I mean forever *never*—enough!

As dicey as it was to get a sack, what happened after we got them was even more crazy. Guys who didn't like the sandwich traded it for an extra juice drink or dessert cookie. The drinkers would work the halls until they'd amassed enough juice drinks to fill a pitcher. The cookie fiends would troll the halls until they got their sugar fix.

As I look back on it now, I can't help wondering why we acted as if we were never going to be fed again. A good explanation for our behavior is probably that guys are just plain greedy, but I think it was more than that. Truth is, we just didn't believe we'd survive the night on just the stuff in our sacks. (Guys get this way about food!)

That's probably how the Israelites felt when God sent them manna, bread from heaven. Food was so scarce in the desert that they panicked, sort of like we guys did every Friday afternoon in Handy Hall. We knew that we'd get another meal, but the Israelites had lived so long in slavery that they weren't sure they could trust God to care for their needs day after day. God did just that, though. He fed them throughout their sojourn in the desert.

Stressed out about something? Trust God to take care of you—today!

////// **HOT READ** //////

How long did God feed the Israelites in the wilderness? (See Exodus 16:35.)

——> SEEING GOD <

I am the Lord your God, who brought you . . . out of the land of slavery.
Exodus 20:2.

few years ago I watched *The Queen,* a movie that focused on how Queen Elizabeth and the rest of the monarchy responded to the death of Princess Diana. OK, you probably don't remember Princess Diana dying in a violent accident as she and her boyfriend sped away from a horde of paparazzi. Trust me, it was a very sad time.

Watching the movie, I was struck by how carefully people behaved in the queen's presence. If you were an official guest, the queen would summon you. Once in her presence, you were to bow. You never turned your back to her. Even the current prime minister of the United Kingdom, Gordon Brown, must obey these rules of royal etiquette.

If a mere queen has rules for entering her presence, imagine how terrifying it must have been for Moses to go see God. The Israelites were now out of Egypt, and it was time for God to give them the rules by which they should live. God knew that they'd picked up some really bad habits and behaviors from the Egyptians, so God had to reeducate them. But before He appeared to them, God insisted that they prepare.

First Moses had to dedicate the people. Then everyone had to carefully wash both their clothes and themselves. Then God told them to erect a fence around the base of Mount Sinai and to be sure that no one crossed it, or even touched the foot of the mountain. That was for their protection, for whoever touched it would die (Exodus 19:12). Pretty serious, huh?

Why was God so uptight about how the Israelites approached His presence? Here's what I think. God is not just holy; He is sinless, and His presence is a consuming fire to all who are sinful. (Approach His visible presence at your own risk.) Furthermore, God's moral law, the Ten Commandments, which He was about to share with the Israelites, is the foundation on which the earth was built *and* the foundation on which heaven is built. It's sort of God's constitution document. It's who He is. God wanted the Israelites then—and us now—to know that He is holy and His law is holy.

####### HOT READ #######

Did you catch the other laws that God gave Moses on Sinai (Exodus 21:12-20)? Be nice to your folks!

31

——> SHOW YOUR LOVE <

No one is to appear before me empty-handed. Exodus 23:15.

ou think Jesus was poor? He never rode an old donkey He rode a new donkey. I don't want an old car. I want a new car—one where my butt is the first to
touch the seat!"

I couldn't believe my ears. Never mind that several butts touch a car seat before the buyer's ever does, this preacher wanted his members to know that he
wanted a *new* car. (Don't worry, it's not your pastor. I saw this guy on TV.)

I'm still not sure what other point he was making, but it had to do with the
members giving him more money. That's how the whole 'Jesus rode new donkeys' thing got into the message. As he continued to yell at his congregation, a little girl walked up to the pulpit, reached out her hand, and handed him some
money. He thanked her and kept on preaching—or shaking down the members
for their money, you really couldn't tell. Now, that was an odd picture on the
screen: a preacher with a Bible in one hand and a fistful of dollars in the other.
(Insert joke here!)

Today you've been reading about all the laws that God gave Moses to develop the Israelite community. God gave clear commands regarding property, social responsibility, justice and mercy, and, of course, the Sabbath. One of the many
things that God stipulated was that no one was to come into His presence empty-
handed. The Israelites were to attend three annual festivals, and at each one they
were to bring an offering, but not just any offering: "Bring the best of the first-
fruits of your soil to the house of the Lord your God" (Exodus 23:19).

Did God know that He was going to run out of groceries and therefore
needed the Israelites to hook Him up? No. These gifts were designed to help the
Israelites to remember the One who had delivered them, who provided for their
every need—the One who loved them more than everything. The gifts were a
measure of their love.

Next time you go into God's presence, show your love. Bring the best offering you have and give it to God.

/////// HOT READ ///////

**Moses spent 40 days and 40 nights with God (Exodus 24:18). Now, that's
QT with God! Talk to God silently throughout your day. Turn off everything.**

──> SORRY, I GOTTA GO <

Then have them make a sanctuary for me, and I will dwell among them. Make this tabernacle and all its furnishings exactly like the pattern I will show you.
Exodus 25:8, 9.

met Gerry at the Just Claim It prayer conference held in Dallas, Texas, a few years ago. At that time he was a studying to be a youth pastor, and you could tell he loved God just by looking at him. As we talked, he told me about the time, not too long before, his parents stopped going to church. He was about 16 then, barely able to drive. His parents had been active members of their church for many years, but that all changed when they were accused of wrongdoing.

Later an investigation determined that the accusations were false. Gerry's parents had done nothing wrong, but the damage was done. They wanted nothing to do with church—ever again. But Gerry couldn't turn his back on church. He kept going all by himself, Sabbath after Sabbath. After almost a year his parents did the unthinkable. One Sabbath morning they decided to go with him. Now they're faithfully serving God again, thanks to the unflinching example of their then-teenage son.

When the Israelites were delivered from slavery in Egypt, God longed to be with them again in worship. This was reason number one that God went to such trouble to free His people. Up until then, the Israelites had not had a formal worship system. The tabernacle would change all of that. It would be God's way of dwelling with them.

The tabernacle served another purpose, though. God knew that if the Israelites did not make a habit of worshipping Him, they would follow the practices of surrounding pagan nations who worshipped false gods. So coming to the tabernacle and offering sacrifices in worship was meant to protect them from going astray.

Though Gerry's parents stopped going to church, his faith remained strong because he had made a habit of being in God's house on Sabbath. This practice of weekly worship helped to protect him from leaving God.

No matter how bad things get at home or at church, never stop hanging out with God at His house.

////// HOT READ //////

As you read Exodus 25-27, why do you think God was so specific and careful about how the sanctuary should be built? How should we treat God's house?

33

—> WANNA KNOW? <

Then I will dwell among the Israelites and be their God. They will know that I am Lord their God, who brought them out of Egypt so that I might dwell among them. I am the Lord their God. Exodus 29:45, 46.

here isn't much I remember about elementary school. I don't remember the names of my friends or my teachers. I barely remember the school I attended, though one tutor comes to mind. Her name was Sister Bobsemple. Yep, that really was her name. She taught me my ABCs and how to read. She'd be proud of me today, I hope.

I have just one strong memory from my days in elementary school. I remember my dad coming to my school just to visit me from time to time. I wasn't in trouble or anything. (If I got into any trouble he'd wait until I got home to pull out his belt and, well, you know.) My father would buy me lunch, usually a drink and sandwich. It wasn't much, and he didn't stay very long, but it was always cool to see my dad show up at school. If anyone doubted whether or not I belonged to somebody, whether or not anyone loved my droopy eyes, big nose, and nappy head, my father was exhibit A that somebody loved me in all my ugliness.

When God commissioned Moses to build a sanctuary so that He could dwell with the Israelites, He was doing something very similar to what my father did when he visited me at school. If your parents never showed up to meet with your teachers, counselors, and principal, the adults at school would start to wonder whether or not you had people who loved and cared about you. God wanted the Israelites, and the surrounding nations, to know that He was the "Godfather" of the Israelites. He was the one who delivered them from slavery. They would know that He was their God because He would make His home with them. He claimed the Israelites then, and He wants to claim you now.

But there was one catch. The Israelites had to make a place for Him, and it had to be special. That's why God was so particular about the building of the tabernacle and the consecration of the priests—Aaron and his sons. Is there room in your life for God?

///////// HOT READ ////////

Why did God go to such trouble to design special garments for the priests (Exodus 28)?

34

——> THE VIEW FROM UP THERE <

Aaron answered them, "Take off the gold earrings that your wives, your sons and your daughters are wearing, and bring them to me." Exodus 32:2.

ometimes it's tough to see something in its entirety until you look down on it from above. Ralph, one of my boys, found this out when he went to Hawaii on a recent vacation.

Ralph and his wife, Gisela, cruised around the Hawaiian Islands, stopping off here and there to buy stuff, take pictures, chill—you know, all the stuff you dream about doing when you're a teenager. During one of their getaways they decided to take a helicopter ride to see one of Hawaii's live volcanoes.

Ralph had seen volcanoes before in hi-def—TV, of course—so how much more was there really to see? Well, as it turns out, a whole lot. "Dwain, it was un-believable, man. Once the helicopter got over the volcano, dude, the color was like nothing I have ever seen before," Ralph's voice rushed on. "The guide told us the lava temperature was like 4,000 degrees, yo! On the side of the mountain the lava would hit a tree and poof—the tree was gone!" The view from up there was completely different from the view from earth.

If you read Exodus 32, the heart of today's reading, you were introduced to the other side of Aaron, Moses' older brother, the guy who did all the talking for Moses. When Moses went up to visit with God on Mount Sinai, he left Aaron to care for the people. Bad move. When Moses tarried, listening to God's specs for the tabernacle, the Israelites grew restless and asked Aaron to make them gods. Moses was obviously gone forever—they thought. Guess what? Aaron did it.

Ironically, while Aaron was leading the Israelites into idol worship, God was telling Moses about the sacred high-priestly role that He had reserved for Aaron. Read it again in Exodus 28 and 29. God had special gear for him, even a personal communication system that was for only him and God. God's purpose for Aaron was infinitely higher than what Aaron desired for himself. If Aaron had waited a little longer for Moses to return, he would have heard just how special he was in God's eyes. You may not think much of yourself right now, but don't sell out. Get the view from up there—heaven!

/////// HOT READ ///////

Note the special relationship Moses had with God (Exodus 33:12-23).

——> WHAT YOU SEE IS WHAT YOU GET <

*And he passed in front of Moses, proclaiming, "The Lord, the Lord, the compas-
sionate and gracious God, slow to anger, abounding in love and faithfulness, main-
taining love to thousands, and forgiving wickedness, rebellion and sin."*
Exodus 34:6, 7.

K, I think Exodus 34 just made it into my top five best chapters in the Bible.
I am so "amped" after reading this chapter that I just might pull an Enoch and
vanish. God's Word is blazin' Hot!

I started to feel the heat when I read Exodus 33:7-11. Moses had pitched a
tent far away from the Israelite camp—a tent that he dubbed the tent of meeting.
There he would meet with God to get his marching orders for the day. It made
me want to set up a spot in my life where I could meet with God uninterrupted
by cell phones, iPods, TV, the Internet, family, friends—everything.

Moses yearned to be closer to God—you would too if you were trying to
steer millions of people through a desert with no restrooms and no AC. As if the
whole tent of meeting thing wasn't enough, Moses said: "Now show me your
glory" (Exodus 33:18). And guess what? God did just that (verses 19-23). UN-
REAL!

What did God show him? His goodness. As He passed by Moses, God told
Moses His name, then the attributes that make Him who He is. "I am compassionate," said God. "I am gracious, slow to anger, and I've got more love than you
know what to do with. I am faithful. I love to forgive, no matter what you've
done. I am just. The guilty will be punished one day."

Of all the things that God could have shown Moses, He chose to show Moses
His character. God was saying to Moses, "You can't see My face and live, but this
is the essence of who I am, and what you see is what you get."

////////// HOT READ ////////

**Dude, God is really into details. Check out Exodus 35:30-35. Where do
your talents come from? Do you use them for God?**

——> THE LITTLE THINGS <

The Israelites did everything just as the Lord commanded Moses. Exodus 39:32.

've always been fascinated by space travel. I don't know if it was the old *Star Trek* reruns or what, but one thing's for sure—I'm into space travel.

It's weird, but I enjoy watching the space shuttle lift off, the massive thrusts from its booster rockets propelling it into the sky, defying gravity's pull. It's an awesome spectacle. Every time I see a successful launch and landing, I am reminded that thousands of people come together to make that shuttle mission successful, thousands of people performing minute little tasks, each of which could cause a catastrophe if not done right.

The importance of getting the little things right among all branches of NASA became frighteningly clear on January 28, 1986. One minute into flight, the shuttle *Challenger* exploded into a million pieces, killing its entire crew. It was one of the saddest days of my life, and people all around the world mourned our loss. The cause of the crash? A faulty O-shaped ring designed to create a seal between two parts of the shuttle's solid rocket booster. NASA engineers had failed to test the O-rings adequately in bitterly cold weather. Because they failed, a multimillion-dollar ship and its crew were lost, because of a faulty part that cost lest than 50 cents.

When God commissioned the building of His sanctuary, no detail of His building plan was to be left undone. He told Moses what wood to have the builders use, the precious metals to be molded, and who should do the work. He even specified the color of the thread to be woven into the priestly garments. No expense was to be spared, and no task was to be left undone. The tabernacle was meant to be a sort of shuttle, a place that would lift the Israelites closer to God through the atonement of their sins and obedience to God's laws. To avoid disaster, the work was to be done with the utmost care.

Today's reading teaches us that our God is big on "the little." He believes that if a job is worth doing, it's worth doing well—especially when He asks us to do it for Him. Always follow God's plan, and always do your best. You can begin today!

///////// HOT READ /////////

What was the final piece of clothing created for Aaron and his sons (Exodus 39:30, 31)? What made this piece so important?

——> WHAT YA GOT AGAINST ANIMALS? <

He is to slaughter the young bull before the Lord, and then Aaron's sons the priests shall bring the blood and sprinkle it against the altar on all sides at the entrance to the Tent of Meeting. Leviticus 1:5.

e honest. Leviticus is off to a bloody beginning, don't you think? If you're like me, you're wondering, "Uh, God, what's with all the mass murdering of animals? I thought You liked animals." There's more blood being spilled in the first three chapters of Leviticus than there is at a year's worth of Marilyn Manson concerts. As you'll soon find out, if you keep reading this challenging book of the Bible, God and Marilyn Manson spill blood for different reasons.

For one, Leviticus is God's instruction book to the nation of Israel back in the fifteenth century B.C. The Israelites were still fresh off their deliverance from Egyptian slavery, so God introduced Himself and His way of doing things. More than that, God wanted them to know that He had a special, sacred, holy purpose for their lives. But they could never be what God created them to be unless they understood, respected, and obeyed His laws.

The most sacred room in the sanctuary that God told Moses to build was the Most Holy Place. The most sacred item in the Most Holy Place was the ark of the covenant, and inside the ark were the Ten Commandments, written by God's own hand. God's commands were then, and are now, so sacred that to break them is to sin (1 John 3:4), and the punishment for sin is death (Romans 6:23).

Because God does not want anyone to die because of sin (2 Peter 3:9), He created a way for all of us to be forgiven. But that forgiveness comes with a price—the shedding of blood (Hebrews 9:22). Sounds a lot like what Jesus did for us at Calvary, doesn't it?

As you read Leviticus, remember that its sacrifices all point to Jesus, the Lamb of God who died once for all sin. Leviticus shows us God's way of repairing His relationship with the ancient Israelites, and He works the same way today.

///////// HOT READ ////////

Why do you think God specified that only animals without defects could be sacrificed?

──→ STOP SNITCHIN'? <

If a person sins because he does not speak up when he hears a public charge to testify regarding something he has seen or learned about, he will be held responsible. Leviticus 5:1.

I was at my friend's house when he hooked me with one of his crazy tales. "Dwain, let me tell you, man. Wall-to-wall people, sandwiched in the bar like sardines. The place is so tiny that you could barely move an inch. But yet, nobody saw anything. It's ridiculous."

My friend is Paul, an old Philadelphia cop who has seen the best and the worst of humanity. Once he went undercover to help bust a notorious criminal gang, only to wind up handcuffed and about to be thrown off the roof of a building. Just then a police siren off in the distance scared away the gang, and they left Paul there in handcuffs as the cop cars sped by, off to another crime scene. But God used them to save Paul's life.

Today Paul is telling me about a shooting he worked in a small neighborhood bar. Everyone saw it, but no one would speak up.

If the patrons at the bar that night lived in ancient Israel, they would have a really big problem—with God! God told Moses to tell the people that if a person fails to speak up about something they witnessed, then they would be held responsible for their silence. If someone committed such a crime, they would have to bring a female lamb or goat to the Lord as an offering to be sacrificed for their sin. (Poor animals!)

Today we live in a society in which crime seems to pay, especially for the criminals who intimidate their neighbors into silence. God's command to speak up was a means of teaching the Israelites to value each other, to care for their community, and to help make wrongs right. This was a part of what it meant to be holy, to live a pure life.

Believe it or not, God requires the same standard of care for our neighbors and communities that He required of the Israelites. When you and I see a wrong being done, we need to ask God for strength to do the right thing: Speak up!

/////// HOT READ ///////

How can God hold someone responsible for something did unintentionally? What were they to do when they found their wrong (Leviticus 5:17-19)?

——> "OH, NO! NOT THE KICKS!" <

> *Then Moses took some of the anointing oil and some of the blood from the altar and sprinkled them on Aaron and his garments and on his sons and their garments. So he consecrated Aaron and his garments and his sons and their garments.*
> Leviticus 8:30.

t happened at camp meeting. I'll explain, but first some background. Every year I pack up my wife and make my annual trek into the Pennsylvania countryside to the campus of Pine Forge Academy. The weekend of this particular camp meeting was one of the few with no showers in the forecast, so I decided to pull on some suede kicks I'd been dying to wear. They were a "smoove" beige/gray color, and I was gonna rock 'em with my white linen shirt and some tight khaki joints (uh, pants). Do I need to translate for you?

I started onto the campus grounds, when I was hit by a tornado—a kid from my church. When she saw me, she yelled, "Dwwwwwaaaaiinnnnnnnnnn!" and headed straight toward me. She was definitely an F5. Her feet looked like huge plows chewing up the grass and dirt with each step. When she got close, she jumped to hug me, and you wouldn't believe where her dirt-covered feet landed. Yep, right there—you know where. (Sorry, but I need some tissue.)

When I read the beautiful ceremony God organized for the anointing of Aaron and his sons as priests of Israel, call me shallow, but I recoiled in horror at the thought of oil being sprinkled on brand-new, perfectly tailored linen garments. Why would God tell Moses to commit such a fashion no-no? Oil on the head— sure. But on clothes?

The answer is fairly simple. God wanted the priests and the people looking on to know that not only were they to dedicate themselves to Him—everything they wore was to be dedicated to Him as well. The priests were special, and everything about them cried "Holy."

Guess what God's followers today are called (Revelation 1:5, 6).

The kinds of clothes we wear from day to day should glorify God and not ourselves—even if they are the "smoovest" pair of kicks ever. What do your clothes say about God?

/////// HOT READ ///////

Check out Leviticus 9:5, 6. What was God going to do after Moses ordained Aaron and his sons? How are you preparing for God's soon return?

──> DON'T EVEN CRY <

Then Moses said to Aaron and his sons Eleazar and Ithamar, "Do not let your hair become unkempt, and do not tear your clothes, or you will die and the Lord will be angry with the whole community." Leviticus 10:6.

id you know that you have three types of tears? Basal tears lubricate your eyes and keep them free of dust. Reflex tears clean your eyes when they're irritated by foreign particles. But you cry *psychic* tears from severe emotional stress. If you saw two of your family members die in a massive explosion, you'd probably cry for days—possibly years. What if the explosion happened and someone walked up to you and told you that you must not cry—not now and not ever? That's sort of what God said to Aaron after the death of his sons Nadab and Abihu.

You read about how they offered "strange fire" to the Lord, and how God responded, right? The Bible says that "fire came out from the presence of the Lord and consumed them" (Leviticus 10:2). But God didn't stop there. He told Aaron and Ithamar not to cry!

If you've ever watched the aftermath of a terrorist bombing in, say, Iraq, the mourners grab their heads and cry for all they're worth. Some even tear their garments. God told Moses to tell Aaron that no such expressions would be tolerated.

How could God be so cold?

God punished Nadab and Abihu severely because they carelessly disregarded an explicit command. The fire they offered to God was "ordinary fire," which God forbade them to offer Him. They were to put their censers in the fire from the altar of burnt offering, which God Himself had started and which was holy. What they did instead was kindle fire from a different source. They were also punished harshly because they were leaders who had been taught what to do and shown what was right, yet they chose to do what they wanted instead. Sound familiar?

But why not let Aaron mourn? Because it was Aaron's example of "lazy" obedience—when he led the Israelites in idol worship (Exodus 32)—that taught his sons to be careless with God's commands.

/////// HOT READ ///////

Backslide to Exodus 19:22. What did God say would happen to any priest who wasn't totally consecrated to God?

---> SPOTLESS SPOT <

You must keep the Israelites separate from things that make them unclean, so they will not die in their uncleanness for defiling my dwelling place, which is among them.
Leviticus 15:31.

hile browsing the Internet one day, I found one of the coolest sites. It's called howtocleananything.com. It's bookmarked in my favorites, because when my inner clean freak needs a good workout, this site can help me clean just about anything.

Right now I've got an old gunked-up keyboard with several keys glued down hard by some juice I spilled on it. Several friends told me to give it the dishwasher treatment, but I'm not feelin' that advice.

Enter howtocleananything.com. What advice did they give? "If the keyboard has an old or dried spill, you must first saturate the dried liquid. This means submersing it (yes, completely underwater) in a pan of water for a few hours; press any sticky keys to help loosen the dried material. When the dried spill has dissolved into the pan of water, or if the spill is fresh, rinse off the keyboard with distilled water. Use distilled water, as tap water contains minerals that can affect performance even after it is dry. Allow the keyboard to air-dry for at least a day or two." Sounds a lot like the dishwasher treatment, doesn't it? I think I'm going to give it a try, now that I've heard from a source I trust.

Dirty keyboards don't work right, and we don't either when we're dirty. In today's Bible passage, God gave the Israelites clear instructions to help them avoid infectious diseases and other pollutants that could destroy the nation. But God had another reason for His warnings. Because He would be living among them, everything about them had to be clean. God is a clean freak.

There's a reason you should pick up clothes thrown around your room, two-week-old pizza scraps under your bed, and that half candy bar under your pillow: GOD WANTS TO DWELL WITH YOU, AND HE WANTS TO COME TO A CLEAN PLACE. A gunked-up life is a lot like a gunked-up keyboard; it just doesn't work right. Keep your spot spotless for God!

/////// HOT READ ///////

Why did the Israelites have to go to the priest to get cleaned up?
Why didn't God give them a doctor to handle such issues?

——> I WANT YOUR SEX <

Keep my requirements and do not follow any of the detestable customs that were practiced before you came and do not defile yourselves with them. I am the Lord your God. Leviticus 18:30.

By the time you read this devotional message, Britney Spears, Paris Hilton, and Lindsay Lohan may be long forgotten. (I sure hope so.) But I'm writing this in 2007, and their escapades dominate the news every day. Never mind the wars and natural disasters claiming thousands of lives each week—many seem only to care about whether Britney wears underwear or not.

Illicit sexuality is not new. From the descendants of Cain up to the present day, people have broken God's laws concerning sex and, in so doing, broken themselves. There is no clearer chapter in all of the Bible on how God expects us to conduct ourselves sexually than Leviticus 18. Did you read it? If you haven't, stop right now and read it.

If you're reading from the New International Version of the Bible, count how many times God uses the "Do not have sexual relations . . ." phrase. I counted 19.

God wanted the Israelites to know that their sexuality was a gift, but that it would destroy them if they failed to heed His warnings against forbidden sexual experiences. Remember, Israel was on its way to the Promised Land after hundreds of years in Egyptian bondage. While they were in Egypt many harmful sexual practices had become common to them, so God needed to teach them a new, holy standard of sexual expression.

"Ick," you say. "I'd never do anything mentioned in Leviticus 18." Sure, you may never do them, but would you watch them? Do you watch movies with suggestive or explicit scenes? Do you download pornographic movies or pictures from the Internet? Do you have sexually explicit conversations with friends? If you do, ask God to help you stop all of these practices now. Such behaviors will defile, corrupt, and ruin your life. Just as God wanted Israel to be pure sexually, He wants the same from each of us today.

The best sex you'll ever have is that which comes when you follow and obey God's rules for good sex. Anything else can destroy you.

///////// HOT READ ///////

Ever wonder why Jews eat kosher foods? The answer is found in Leviticus 17:10-12.

——> SOMETHING FOR EVERYONE <

When you reap the harvest of your land, do not reap to the very edges of your field or gather the gleanings of your harvest. Do not go over your vineyard a second time or pick up the grapes that have fallen. Leave them for the poor and the alien. I am the Lord your God. Leviticus 19:9, 10.

ou probably know little about the country of North Korea. Don't feel too bad. Most people in the world don't. The nation is ruled by an eccentric dictator who has a special taste for fine wines, a very large movie collection, and a desire to produce nuclear weapons.

A few decades ago we fought a war against what is now North Korea, and technically speaking, that war is still not over. It ended with a truce, not a treaty. But it's not only North Korea's leader or its pursuit of nukes that troubles the world. It's also the fact that most of its people are starving to death. Poor peasants have resorted to eating leaves, grass, and tree bark.

Enter Karl Szmolinsky, a German farmer who, by the way, won an award for raising Germany's largest rabbit. Yep, his German gray giant weighs in at a whopping 23 pounds. (If you're into bunnies, you might not want to read the next line.) And Szmolinsky has offered to raise rabbits to help feed the North Korean population. Might not be what you or I would do, but at least Karl Szmolinsky is doing something.

God has a plan for feeding the homeless and the poor among us. Wanna hear it? *Share what you have.* That's it. God told ancient Israel that when your fields produce crops, don't glean it all for yourselves. Don't go over your vineyards several times to get every grape. Leave some for the poor and the aliens.

Maybe you've got no vineyards—I know I don't—but there's still much we can do to help those in need. Find a soup kitchen or a food pantry in your town. When you or your parents go shopping, buy a few extra cans of food. At the end of the month you'll have food to share with those in need in your area. You may not feed North Korea, but you'll be carrying out God's plan for the poor in your world.

/////// HOT READ ///////

Thinking about that tattoo? Check out Leviticus 19:28. Want to know how to treat legal and illegal aliens? See verses 33-37.

——> CELEBRATION TIME, COME ON! <

These are my appointed feasts, the appointed feasts of the Lord, which you are to proclaim as sacred assemblies. Leviticus 23:2.

God is into celebrations—really big, audacious, hairy celebrations.

As the Israelites prepared for a new life with God, He commanded that certain special feasts were to be observed each year. You read about some of them today, right (Leviticus 23)? Notice that the special day God wanted the Israelites to observe and keep holy was the Sabbath. Kind of significant, don't you think? The Sabbath comes once each week. It wasn't like they were going to forget to keep it holy—or were they? God didn't want them to let the Sabbath's frequency change how special it truly is. Then there was the Passover Feast and the Feast of Unleavened Bread. Remember what the Passover was all about? OK, I'll tell you again. When Pharaoh refused to free the Israelites, God sent His death angel through Egypt, and every firstborn male, human and animal, died. The Israelite males were saved by having the blood of a slain lamb smeared on the doorposts of their homes. Guess who was represented by those slain lambs? Christ, of course. He too was slain so that we might be saved from the penalty for our sins, which is death. Guess when Christ died? (Read it for yourself in John 19:14.)

The Feast of Unleavened Bread reminded the Israelites of that difficult night that they left Egypt so fast that they could not even put yeast in the bread they'd baked for the journey. So when they ate the unleavened bread at each Passover celebration, they remembered the hardship of their captivity and the fact that God delivered them with a mighty hand.

Through these ancient feasts God is also speaking to you. He wants you to know that He still delivers His children from bondage. No matter what you've done, no matter how far you've gone, God still loves you, and He wants to save you.

Is there something enslaving you—some attitude, some situation, some habit? Claim the power of God to deliver you. Ask God to do it for you right now, and you'll have a whole lot to celebrate.

////// HOT READ //////

Leviticus 24:10-23 is a disturbing bit of Scripture. It teaches us how careful we ought to be in how we use God's name. God's name is holy!

——> LET'S MAKE A DEAL <

If you follow my decrees and are careful to obey my commands, I will send you rain in its season, and the ground will yield its crops and the trees of the field their fruit.
Leviticus 26:3, 4.

e've come to the end of the book of Leviticus, and I hate to see it go. I was a little unsure of what Leviticus would be about, but I learned so much about God's holiness, the sanctuary services, and a whole lot more. And that's not all. Leviticus ends with a bang!

As I read chapter 25, I learned about God's way of handling property. Did you notice that the people were forbidden to farm every seventh year? This was a sabbath year for the land to rest, just like each Sabbath day is an opportunity for us to rest. Also, every fiftieth year land would revert to its original owners. This was God's way of making sure that none of the Israelites would end up homeless or destitute. God is a genius!

Just when I thought Leviticus couldn't get any better, along came chapter 26. In this awesome bit of scripture, God makes Israel an offer that they couldn't refuse. You can sum it up in two simple sentences: Obey Me, and I will bless you beyond your wildest dreams. Disobey Me, and you will suffer. That's it—plain and simple.

The blessings God promised were second to none: crops bursting from the ground, peace and safety, victory in battle, and countless offspring. These may seem small to us in America who have so much, but a few years ago I visited a small town in the mountains of Peru. The villagers lived in small houses, farmed the land, and seemed not to have much, but their needs were all supplied and they were thankful. And, I might add, they were generous. God promised to supply Israel's needs and then some!

Then He said this: "I will put my dwelling place among you, and I will not abhor you" (verse 11). That was the greatest blessing of all. God Himself would build a home in their neighborhood and never move out. His presence would bring the blessing.

Obeying God is never a gamble. God does not change, and neither do His promises (Malachi 3:6).

/////// HOT READ ///////

Did you read the list of punishments Israel would face for disobeying God? See Leviticus 26:14-38. Now read verses 40-45. God always gives us a chance to change.

——> A WHOLE BOOK ABOUT, UH, NUMBERS? <

Take a census of the whole Israelite community by their clans and families, listing every man by name, one by one. Numbers 1:2.

That's the first question that popped into my head years ago when I first tried to read through my Bible and failed. (I got distracted, but it's easier to blame Numbers.)

Truth is, this book is really one of the most fantastic books in all of Holy Scripture. For one, there's more to it than just a collection of numbers, of which there are plenty. The book is narrated by Moses, and recounts many of Israel's struggles in the wilderness as they wound their way to the Promised Land. It's sort of like a travelogue with a "grip" full of details.

The theme of holiness permeates Numbers, but there's another theme that comes through: the dangers of unbelief, or refusing to believe, in God and what He has said. When God promises something, He makes it happen, but even God cannot overcome our failure to believe in Him. But back to the numbers.

You know, you can learn a lot from numbers or the absence of them. Try subtracting 2 from 2 without the number 0. Good luck. Ancient Babylonians found this out around 400 B.C. and came up with zero as a place holder, a nothing space in a series of numbers. Without 0 you couldn't really distinguish between $34 and $340. Numbers matter!

In the first three chapters God told Moses to perform a census of the Israelites. It was God's way preparing a military force to protect the people. It was also a means of showing the Israelites—and us today—just how orderly God is. The Israelites were to place the tabernacle at the center of their encampment. Then the Levites' tents were to surround the tabernacle, and the other tribes around them. This arrangement reminded the Israelites to keep God at the center of their lives. Is God at the center of your life?

/////// HOT READ ///////

Where did the tribe of Judah camp? Numbers 2:3. Judah is the tribe through which Jesus came, and guess from what direction He'll be coming back? See Matthew 24:27.

---> STANDING OUT <

If a man or woman wants to make a special vow, a vow of separation to the Lord as a Nazirite, he must abstain. Numbers 6:2, 3.

ost people have no urge to stand out from the crowd, and most of those who have such an urge, want to stand out for all the wrong reasons. Cornelius Horan, 57, an Irish ex-priest, belonged the latter group, and he picked a big stage to make his big splash.

The year was 2004. The event? The Summer Olympics in Athens, Greece. The marathon is the race that defines the Summer Olympics because it demands the most of its participants. It is always the final event of the games. In 2004 Brazilian runner Vanderlei de Lima was leading the race a mere three miles from the finish line when a crazed man dressed in a kilt and green socks up to his knees suddenly burst out of the crowd and headed toward him.

Cornelius Horan grabbed Vanderlei de Lima and forced him to the side of the road, stopping him for what seemed like an eternity before fans and authorities could free the runner. Shaken by what happened, Lima finished third. Cornelius Horan got what he wanted: He stood out.

In ancient Israel, God offered a way for Israelites to stand out from the larger Israelite community, but it had nothing to do with self-adulation. If an Israelite wanted to be set apart, totally consecrated to God's service, they had to observe the Nazirite code.

For the period of their dedication, Nazirites could not drink anything fermented, go near a dead body, or cut their hair. It was a tough code to follow, but it was voluntary. Nazirites were holy, and their lives showed it. They stood out by standing up for God.

Samson was a Nazirite from birth, set aside for a holy purpose. But as we all know, Samson chose to use his special gifts to please himself and not God. If you want to stand out from the crowd, all you have to do is give your life to God and live for Him. You'll stand out—for all the right reasons!

HOT READ

Did you read Numbers 4? If God commanded such care for His ancient tabernacle, how does He expect you and me to treat the church in which we worship?

——> I WANNA KNOW <

Whenever the cloud lifted from above the Tent, the Israelites set out;
wherever the cloud settled, the Israelites encamped. Numbers 9:17.

Ever feel like God's not hearing you? Well, I've got some hope for you, and it's found in today's reading, Numbers 7, 8, and 9. But first a little background. By the time you hit Numbers 7, the children of Israel have been traveling for about a year on their journey to Canaan—the Promised Land. They have just completed building the wilderness tabernacle, which housed the sacred Most Holy Place. In this sacred place was the ark, which held the Ten Commandments written on stone by the finger of God. Numbers 7 and 8 capture some of the beautiful dedication ceremony for the tabernacle. Don't skip over these chapters. They are worth your time.

When the Israelites finished setting up the tabernacle, a cloud settled over it. They'd seen this cloud before, for it had accompanied them for more than a year. At night it came alive, glowing like fire. There was something else special about the cloud, though.

When the Israelites camped in a certain area, the cloud settled over the tabernacle. As long as the cloud was there, they were to stay put. When it moved from above the tabernacle, they were to break camp and roll out. They never knew where they would be going or how long they'd be staying once they got there. They could be in one location for a day or a year. They had to trust God. They had to have faith.

When you feel as if God's not hearing you, do you look for His signs? You may not see a cloud, but God will often speak to you through your family, through spiritual mentors, or sometimes even total strangers. For a long time I remember feeling really unsure about writing this book, about whether teens would want to go through the Bible with me for a year.

Then God spoke to me through a teenager who had gotten hold of part of the book. "I really like your new book," she said. "It's interesting." That's all she said, and that's all I needed to hear. She was the cloud I needed to see. I knew then that God was telling me to move out—to keep writing. Ask God to guide you, and watch for signs of His leading in your life today.

HOT READ

Read Numbers 9:1-8. Moses refused to answer the people until he had checked with God. Do you take your dilemmas to God?

——> GRACE <

If this is how you are going to treat me, put me to death right now—if I have found favor in your eyes—and do not let me face my own ruin. Numbers 11:15.

e's tired, son," my mom retorted sternly. "Be patient with him. He's just a kid." So I backed off. This was Mom's oldest grandchild. (My mom is no joke!)

My patience with him—my then-8-year-old nephew—had worn down to the nub. He was ruining a perfectly good day with all his crying. This was no ordinary cry, mind you. The little demon screamed nonstop for about 40 minutes, hardly pausing to breathe. Things didn't start out that way. We had been at the park most of the day. We watched huge carp play in the lake, ran a little B-ball, wore out the swings—you know, all the stuff you do at a park. I thought we were cool, but then something changed.

So I decided to do what any good uncle would do in a similar situation—drown him in the lake. OK, I dreamed about it, but prying him loose from his grandmother's arms would have been very tricky. So I settled for the next-best thing. If he was going to yell, then I was going to yell right back at him. It was an ugly scene—Springer-esque.

My mother, great woman that she is, had raised five children and understands that kids go a little bonkers when they're tired. God knows the same secret about us, too. That's how He tolerated the way Moses dissed Him in Numbers 11:15. Moses basically said, "Hey, God, You stuck me with Your people, and now You're going to let me fail. Just kill me now." Translation? "God, You really messed up my life!"

But God understood that Moses didn't mean what he had said. God knew that Moses' words came more from fatigue and frustration than from any hate he had for Him. So God chose not to respond to what Moses' mouth was saying. Rather, God listened to his heart and heard, "Father, I need help. I am overwhelmed."

Moses needed God's grace, and my little nephew needed some grace from me. Look for opportunities to share God's grace with someone today.

//////// HOT READ ////////

Numbers 12 is also filled with God's grace. What was God going to do to Aaron and Miriam? Who interceded to spare their lives? When you get grace, give grace.

——> GO BIG! <

And they said to each other, "We should choose a leader and go back to Egypt."
Numbers 14:4.

cookie store is a bad idea. Besides, the market research reports say America likes crispy cookies, not soft and chewy cookies like you make." That's what someone told Debbi when she pitched her idea for a cookie store. Time and again Debbi walked into banks trying to get a loan to start her dream business, but there was always some reason she couldn't get the money. She was always too young, or too inexperienced, or too poor, or too whatever.

Unwilling to give up her dream, at the tender age of 20 Debbi single-handedly convinced a bank to fund her unproven idea. And so Mrs. Fields Chocolate Chippery opened on August 16, 1977, and the rest, they say, is history. Today Debbi's little idea has ballooned into more than 700 Mrs. Fields company-owned and -franchised stores around America and in 11 other countries. Not bad, huh?

No matter how much you believe in your dreams, no matter how sure you are that you will be successful, there will always be people to doubt you. That must have been how Caleb and Joshua felt when they returned from spying out the land of Canaan—the Promised Land (Numbers 13). They weren't scared off by the giants who lived there or the powerful armies. They were ready to take God at His word. He said the land would be Israel's, and they believed Him.

But 10 other spies who also took the trip brought back a negative report, and they spread their fear to all the Israelites. When the Israelites heard about the powerful nations who lived in Canaan, they began to weep. They yearned to return to the slavery of Egypt, rather than embrace their destiny in the Promised Land.

Negative people can have a powerful impact on us if we choose to listen to them. God says that with His strength and His power we can do great things for Him. Don't allow anyone to steal your dreams. Share them with God to get His guidance. And when God tells you to go, don't "come up small." GO BIG! Go possess your destiny.

///////// HOT READ ////////

How did God react to the Israelites' unbelief? What punishment did He pronounce upon them? Numbers 14:20-24.

——> GREEN'S NOT YOUR COLOR <

Then the Lord said to Moses, "Say to the assembly, 'Move away from the tents of Korah, Dathan and Abiram.'" Numbers 16:23, 24.

e got all the pub—that's all the publicity, the accolades, the cheese. And he deserved it. Anthony was the fastest guy I'd ever run with during track and field.

We were two parts of a 4 x 100 relay team, and we were the fastest in our city. We had a great starter and a strong second leg. I ran the third leg to set up Anthony for the finish. If we were close to the leaders when I handed the baton to Anthony, we knew that we would win. Anthony was a great finisher. He would be mobbed at the end of just about every race, for we won most of our races because of Anthony.

The rest of the team would feel "some type of way" toward Anthony because of all the attention he got, unless we understood that each of our roles were important to our team's success. Anthony couldn't win without us, and we couldn't win without him.

If there ever was a group of guys in the Bible who didn't get the whole "roles" thing, Korah, Dathan, and Abiram were those guys. They felt that they could lead the nation of Israel better than Moses, that they should be high priests instead of Aaron—never mind that God gave Moses and Aaron their jobs. They weren't about to let a little detail like that stop them from taking over Israel and getting all the glory.

Korah and his henchmen had one really BIG problem. God wasn't down with their program. So God told Moses to have Korah, Dathan, Abiram, and the 250 wannabe priests assemble outside the tent of meeting—you know, the place where God spoke to Moses. (Earth to Korah and friends: DON'T GO!) Against their better judgment, the next day the threesome met Moses and Aaron with the entire Israelite gallery looking on.

You read the rest of the story, didn't you? God told the Israelites to move away from the tents of Korah, Dathan, Abiram, and their families. The earth opened up and swallowed them—all of them. Then a great fire consumed the 250 wannabe priests.

What's the lesson? Accept the role that God gives you and do what pleases Him.

///////// HOT READ ////////

Take a look at how God affirmed Aaron as high priest. See Numbers 18.

52

──> TEARS OF LOVE <

And when the whole community learned that Aaron had died, the entire house of Israel mourned for him thirty days. Numbers 20:29.

I t's Valentine's Day. Cuddly red teddy bears, red roses, red everything. There's precious little about death that fits into the whole love theme of Valentine's Day, but death can teach us much about love. Can you say—uh—Jesus?

The death of Aaron (Numbers 20:22-29) was a sad moment in the history of Israel. Aaron was the voice of God to the Israelites. This was the way it worked— at least at the beginning of Israel's journey through the wilderness. God spoke to Moses, who then would tell Aaron, who then would tell the Israelites.

The people had grown accustomed to Aaron's voice. Perhaps they liked him because he wasn't afraid to say or do what the Israelites wanted. Remember, he was the guy who built a golden calf out of jewelry because the people wanted a god that pleased them. Yep, Aaron made some big mistakes.

But God had chosen Aaron, Moses' older brother, in spite of his faults, to speak on behalf of his younger brother and, more important, to serve as the nation's spiritual leader. God loved Aaron despite his mistakes, but that didn't mean he didn't suffer for his moments of disobedience.

One such moment happened at a place called Meribah. The Israelites were angry that Moses and Aaron had led them to a place where there was no food and no water. When Moses and Aaron asked God what they should do, the Lord told them to call the Israelites together in front of a huge rock. "Speak to that rock before their eyes and it will pour out its water," the Lord said (Numbers 20:8). The next day Moses and Aaron did as God told them, but they failed to obey one crucial command. Instead of speaking to the rock, they struck it (verse 11), and the water came pouring out—as did God's anger.

The punishment for their error was swift. Neither Moses nor Aaron would lead the children of Israel into the Promised Land. Both were strong leaders, and to whom much is given, much is required. God must have cried at Meribah.

////// HOT READ //////
What other tragedy had hit the family of Moses? Numbers 20:1-3.

⟶ BALAAM'S BLUNDER <

Even if Balak gave me his palace filled with silver and gold, I could not do anything great or small to go beyond the command of the Lord my God. Numbers 22:18.

t all sounded great. Balaam had responded flawlessly to Balak's indecent proposal. "I can't curse God's people," he said. "I can't go beyond anything that God tells me to say." But Balaam wasn't through talking, and what he uttered next was way more important than what he'd said before.

"Now stay here tonight," began Balaam, "and I will find out what else the Lord will tell me" (Numbers 22:19). Balaam had no reason to wait on word from God. God had already told him that he was not to curse the Israelites as Balak desired (verse 12). In his head Balaam knew that God would not change His mind, but in his heart Balaam wanted the money.

People will do anything for money—even a little money. Joe Marano, of Brooklyn, New York, found that out the hard way. Joe decided to put up flyers around his neighborhood advertising his dog-walking business. One day he was horrified to see a woman tearing down all of his ads. When he asked her what she was doing, she said that she was taking down her signs because she was leaving the business. Surprised, Joe said, "But those are my signs!" That's when she admitted that she was desperate for the business and didn't want any competition.

How much were they competing for? Oh, $10 to $18 for a half-hour walk. They weren't exactly walking Paris's little mutt! OK, so it's a decent bit of cheddar, but is it worth climbing a lamppost to tear down a rival's flyers? Aren't there enough dogs to go around?

Balaam said all the right things, but his actions exposed his love of money, which outweighed his love for God. It took a talking donkey to save his life.

What will it take to save you from the love of money?

///////// HOT READ ///////

Check out Balaam's prophecy concerning Israel (Numbers 23:18-25). Balaam didn't stop there, either. Each time he opened his mouth God forced him to bless Israel (Numbers 24).

——> SLIPPERY SLOPE <

While Israel was staying in Shittim, the men began to indulge in sexual immorality with Moabite women, who invited them to the sacrifices to their gods. The people ate and bowed down before these gods. Numbers 25:1, 2.

ackie never intended to be alone with her boyfriend. They were just going to hang out after school at her house while she waited for her parents to come home. Rock—that's what everyone called Jared, the bulky senior—was the guy she'd liked since freshman year. He'd "holla" at her every now and then, but now they were together. There was no way that they were going to hook up, Jackie had decided.

She loved God; she went to church every Sabbath—not to mention that her parents would go ballistic if they found out she was even hanging with Rock. She had no intention of, well, doing anything out of bounds. It couldn't happen to her.

But it did. It started when Jackie told her parents that she was going to chill with Trish, but she flipped it and met up with Rock. He had held her hand, then his hands traveled to her waist, and each time he seemed to press harder. She liked him a lot, and she liked the attention that he gave her. So there they were, alone, in an empty house. They hugged, they kissed, and then they . . .

Even people with high standards, strong morals, and godly values can become victims of sexual immorality. The Israelites did. They had seen God's hand lead them throughout their wilderness journey, and now they were just a few miles from Canaan, the Promised Land. *Nothing could stop us now*, they thought, but they were wrong.

The Midianites failed in getting Balaam to curse the Israelites, but they had a secret weapon—gorgeous Midianite women. The men of Israel, young and old, saw them and had to have them. And so they not only surrendered their purity—they traded the true God for a false one.

Here's something that all of us must know: sexual immorality leads to spiritual apostasy. Translation? You can't commit sexual sin and love God at the same time.

Never sacrifice your purity for sexual pleasure.

/////// HOT READ ///////

Did you read Numbers 27? Sometimes God is accused of "hating" women. What does Numbers 27:1-11 tell you about God?

——> YOU GOT A DEAL! <

This is what the Lord commands: When a man makes a vow to the Lord or takes an oath to obligate himself by a pledge, he must not break his word but must do everything he said. Numbers 30:1, 2.

If you skipped over Numbers 28 and 29—God's directions concerning the feasts that the Israelites were to observe and the sacrifices required—you missed some great stuff. If you've been keeping up with your reading, you probably read the same stuff before in Leviticus and also earlier in Numbers. What does the fact that God keeps repeating these instructions tell you about how important worship is to Him?

As good as the first two chapters of today's reading are, I was struck by the opening verses of Numbers 30. Vows made to God were so serious that to enter into an agreement with God meant that you had to be really serious. Have you ever tried to make a deal with God? How about when you did something wrong and got caught? Did you promise God never to do it again if He intervened to free you? I have.

Once I stole some of my dad's gum and, wonder of wonders, he found out about it. My sister also took some. She'd faced "the wrath" before and lived to tell about it, so I figured it wouldn't be that bad. But I was sooooo wrong! My dad was one of those "spare the rod, spoil the child" sort of parents. So he believed in "wuppins," beatings, torture, tanning your hide, and just about every other form of punishment known to humanity. He's changed a lot since those days, but back then he was worse than OBL (Osama bin Laden).

I prayed earnestly to God begging for forgiveness, asking Him to save me from my enemy—my father. Perhaps God was asleep. He sure didn't hear my prayer. I got the "rod of correction," and the truth is I deserved it. My dad had forgiven me several times before this final straw broke the camel's back. I guess God turned down the deal I offered Him.

God wants us to think seriously about the promises we make to Him, and we shouldn't wait until we're in trouble to make them.

HOT READ

In Numbers 28 and 29 the aroma that comes from the sacrifices pleases the Lord. Why did God say He was pleased by the smell of burning sacrifices?

—> NO "I" IN TEAM <

*Let this land be given to your servants as our possession. Do not make us
cross the Jordan.* Numbers 32:5.

The year was 2007. The event? The Women's World Cup of Soccer. I rarely
follow soccer, but once every four years when the World Cup rolls around, I get
excited. Soccer is a beautiful game—even if it's not as physical as football.

But back to the Women's World Cup. The U.S. women had made it to the
semifinals, where the Brazilian team waited for them. The Brazilian team was very
good, especially a woman named Marta, whose ball skills were spectacular. In the
end the Brazilians won 4-0, and the score could have been worse.

As depressing as the game itself was for the American team, no one was prepared for the game of finger-pointing that followed. The U.S. coach had made a
last-minute decision to replace goalie Hope Solo with Briana Scurry, the star goal-
keeper on an earlier World Cup team. Solo was upset.

"It was the wrong decision, and I think anybody that knows anything about
the game knows that," she said. "There's no doubt in my mind I would have
made those saves." Her comments shredded her already-hurt team.

The Israelites could be compared to a team made up of 12 different players.
Each player had his role and function to help possess the Promised Land. You can
imagine the surprise Moses felt when two of his most important players decided
not to play. That is, instead of helping the other Israelites take the Promised Land,
the Reubenites and Gadites wanted to stay right where they had camped. It was
a selfish request. They were comfortable, and that's all that mattered to them.

Moses probably felt like giving them a piece of his mind, but he didn't. He
reminded them that the Israelites were to stick together until the whole team won,
until all the tribes were settled (Numbers 32:6-23). God expects us to love and
support each other. Start today.

HOT READ

**Did you notice all the violence in Numbers 31? Think about what you've read
before. Why was God so angry with the Midianites? (Hint: Numbers 25.)**

——> A L M O S T   H O M E <

These are the commands and regulations the Lord gave through Moses to the Israelites on the plains of Moab by the Jordan across from Jericho. Numbers 36:13.

he most dangerous period of any journey occurs when one gets close to home. If you recently received your permit to drive or just got your driver's license, the whole driving thing is still cool. When I first started driving, I wanted to drive everywhere. I'd reverse two feet down a driveway to pick up the newspaper, pull up, and park again. Friend, I enjoyed just sitting in the driver's seat.

But after you've been driving for a while, the buzz wears off. You begin to hate fighting traffic, you roll through a stop sign here or there, and you stop slowing down at yellow lights. These poor driving habits really come to the forefront when you get close to home. It's normal to let your guard down, to relax because you're just a few miles away from food and shelter. This is the reason studies show that most accidents happen within 15 miles of a person's home or intended destination.

Perhaps this is the reason the Israelites fell prey to the sexual immorality and apostasy of the Midianites. They were just a few miles from the Promised Land. They could see it across the Jordan River; they could taste its watermelon-sized grapes. They let their guard down.

God knew that if the Israelites were going to possess their destiny successfully, they would need a land code to help them divide the land fairly, legal codes to address criminal activities such as murder, and places the accused, innocent or guilty, could find refuge until trial.

Why did God do this? He didn't want the Israelites to come so close to their inheritance and then crash and burn because of disobedience or ignorance. Remember, they were about to possess land that God had promised to Abraham, their father, hundreds of years before. This was a big deal.

You too are nearing the heavenly Promised Land. Now is not the time to throw away God's laws. Be obedient until the end, and God will reward you greatly. Be faithful!

//////// HOT READ ////////

Read Numbers 35:6-33. Do you see any similarities to our laws today?

——> NEVER FORGET <

In the fortieth year, on the first day of the eleventh month, Moses proclaimed to the Israelites all that the Lord had commanded him concerning them. Deuteronomy 1:3.

ecember 26, 2004, saw one of the most tragic events in earth's history. A huge earthquake deep in the Indian Ocean sent massive 100-foot waves toward Sumatra, Indonesia, devastating much of the coasts of Southern and Southeast Asia. The earthquake measured 9.1 on the Richter scale and lasted between eight to 10 minutes. In that brief period an avalanche of water was unleashed that claimed more than 230,000 lives. That it happened on the day after Christmas seems an extra-cruel twist of fate.

While the earthquake destroyed countless lives, one group of poor villagers survived—in fact, everyone in their villages survived! The Moken, known as sea gypsies by some, live on the Surin Islands off the coast of Thailand. They have no written language, so knowledge is passed on from generation to generation through the retelling of their history. They have awesome memories.

No earthquake had hit their region for more than 500 years. Yet through storytelling the Moken had passed down an important warning: When the waters of the ocean recede rapidly [as in a tsunami], flee immediately to higher ground. Generation after generation, for 500 years, this message was passed on. And when the tsunami of 2004 began, the Moken remembered the teaching of their elders, and immediately fled to the highest point they could, 113 feet above sea level. Their villages were destroyed, but all of them lived.

The book of Deuteronomy is God's oral warning to the ancient Israelites and to us today. In this book Moses recounts the leading of God in Israel's past, and he warns the Israelites to always obey God in the future. (Today, in Deuteronomy 1-3, you began reading Moses' oral history of Israel's journey.) God did not want the Israelites to repeat their past mistakes, and He doesn't want you or me to do so either. Never forget the past and how God has led you. The lessons of the past can save us in the present and future if we learn them well.

////// HOT READ //////

Deuteronomy 1:39 reminds us that the young, the descendants of the original Israelites, entered the Promised Land. How are you preparing for heaven?

——> THE ONE <

Hear, O Israel: The Lord our God, the Lord is one. Love the Lord your God with all your heart and with all your soul and with all your strength. These commandments that I give you today are to be upon your hearts. Deuteronomy 6:4-6.

'm sorry, family, but today's reading almost brought me to tears. I feel like I'm right there on the banks of the Jordan listening to Moe. I can see his wise, compassionate face, his graying hair. I hear his powerful yet quiet voice, but I also see sadness in his eyes. God's people were finally heading to the Promised Land, but he was not (Deuteronomy 4:22).

In his farewell speech Moses reminds the Israelites always to obey God's commands. He repeats this warning several times in the three chapters you will read today. And of all the things Moses warned them about, idol worship was tops on his list and God's. "Do not follow other gods, the gods of the peoples around you; for the Lord your God, who is among you, is a jealous God and his anger will burn against you, and he will destroy you from the face of the land" (Deuteronomy 6:14, 15). Serious, huh?

I've read these scriptures before, but I understood them better when a teenage friend came to talk to me one day. I asked him what he was up to, and he whipped out his cell phone and showed me a picture. I expected a picture of his pet, or some girl that he liked. Not! It was a photo of his computer.

"What are you doing with that on your phone?" I asked incredulously.

"That's all I need in this world, man," he brightened. "I play World of Warcraft from the time I get up until I go to bed the next morning. All I need is food and my computer."

Dudes, I couldn't believe my ears. It was summer, and he was spending *all* his time playing video games. He was really telling me that his CPU was his god! I was so concerned that I stopped right there and prayed with him, asking God to help him to put God first in his life. I'm happy to say that a few weeks later he came to me and told me that he was letting go of video games to focus more on his schoolwork. I could see him beginning to change.

Your life is big enough for only one God. Make Him the love of your life.

HOT READ

What promise did God make to those who obeyed Him?
See Deuteronomy 5:32, 33.

——> DON'T GET IT TWISTED <

After the Lord your God has driven them out before you, do not say to yourself, "The Lord has brought me here to take possession of this land because of my righteousness." Deuteronomy 9:4.

y boy Forrest called me up one night. We laughed and talked together as usual about how crazy life is, and how great God is. We were almost through with our conversation when he told me that he had just lost his job.

Forrest wasn't sad or angry. He'd told me several times that his manager kept pressuring him to work on the Sabbath, and he had always refused. When Forrest was hired, they had agreed that he didn't have to work from sunset Friday evening to sunset Saturday evening. Now they were changing the agreement.

"Dwain," Forrest began, "I told them that I have not worked on a Sabbath in more than eight years and that I wasn't about to start now. I just can't do it." (Forrest had been an Adventist for about eight years at that time.) The boss called him in and told him to clear out his truck. It was over. The boss added that he'd make it so that Forrest couldn't get unemployment money while he waited for a new job.

But when Forrest called the unemployment office to inquire about money to support his family while he searched for a new job, the office manager questioned him. "You mean that you left your job over a day of worship?"

"Yes," Forrest stated, then explained the situation.

"Well, sir, you don't have to worry. I'm going to make sure that you get everything coming to you. When you file your papers, put my name on the documents." She was so moved by his testimony that she decided to help him personally.

There is something that all Christians gotta understand. Everything we have—good grades, clothes, jobs, nice cars, homes, etc.—comes from God. This was the message in Deuteronomy 9 that Moses wanted the Israelites to understand. They had done nothing to deserve the land they were about to inhabit. It was all a blessing from God, because of a covenant He had made with their ancestors.

Never forget that all you have comes from God and belongs to God!

//////// HOT READ ////////

Facing a tough situation? Read Deuteronomy 7:17-24. Take courage!

——> EVEN THE IMMIGRANTS >

He defends the cause of the fatherless and the widow, and loves the alien, giving him food and clothing. And you are to love those who are aliens, for you yourselves were aliens in Egypt. Deuteronomy 10:18, 19.

ight now in the United States there is a big hullabaloo about illegal aliens living among us. Most are of Mexican descent. There are about 12 million undocumented people living and working in America, and many Americans want them out.

It's a passionate issue for many. A leader of a group called The Minutemen has a band of heavily armed "citizen soldiers" at Arizona's border with Mexico. They hunt "illegals" trying to enter the country. Many believe that illegal immigrants should have no access to the U.S. health-care system, or be allowed to live or work in its communities. Some have even argued that those already in the country should be rounded up and sent back to their countries of origin.

I believe that those who enter our nation should do so legally. They, and everyone else, should obey the nation's laws. But they are here now, and while the nation may feel like kicking them out or treating them poorly, that's not what we are supposed to do as Christians. At least, that's not what the Bible teaches. Let me explain.

When the Israelites left Egypt following the plagues, some Egyptians went with them. A mixed multitude fled Egypt (Exodus 12:37, 38). Egyptians were not Israelites—God's people—yet God accepted them and sought to help them. God knew that as the Israelites journeyed to and lived in the Promised Land, many "aliens" would seek to live among them because of how blessed they were. God insisted that they not be mistreated. In fact, He goes even further: He says, "Love those who are aliens" (Deuteronomy 10:19).

God reminded the Israelites that when they were aliens in Egypt, they were mistreated and abused, but God rescued them. They were to do the same for others. Our nation's leaders will pass laws, build fences, and do whatever possible to prevent illegal immigration. So be it. God, however, is calling us to a higher standard of mercy.

If we love God, then we must love all His children—including illegal aliens.

///////// HOT READ ///////

If you've ever struggled with whether or not to obey God, read Deuteronomy 11:8-17.

——> WANNA BE A ROCK STAR? <

At the end of every seven years you must cancel debts. Deuteronomy 15:1.

ver owed someone a whole bunch of money and then had them say, "You know what? Don't even worry about paying me back, dude. It's all good!" Well, there have been times that I lent money to people who promised to pay me back but never did. After a while I just told them not to worry about paying me back, because the more I thought about the money I was owed, the more upset I got. Now, I never lend money; I give money, and I ask nothing in return. It's a tough policy, but it keeps me sane.

In the ancient Israelite economy God devised a perfect scheme for dealing with debts. Every seventh year all debts were to be forgiven. Some would try to game the system, of course. They'd borrow money and refuse to pay it back because they knew the cancellation year was coming, but God still urged lenders to help those in need. Here's what He said, "Be careful not to harbor this wicked thought: 'The seventh year, the year for canceling debts, is near,' so that you do not show ill will toward your needy brother and give him nothing" (Deuteronomy 15:9).

Now, what does any of this have to do with rock stars? I'm glad you asked. A popular rock star is known for trying to get rich countries to forgive debts owed to them by poor countries. His name is Bono, and he's the frontman for an old rock group named U2. I'm not into their music at all, or anything else they're doing, but I am feeling Bono's passion for the poor.

Because of shady deals between dictators and unscrupulous Western financiers, many dirt-poor African and Central American nations incurred debts to large Western nations. The rich made the deals, and the poor got stuck paying them off. In many cases, poor nations cannot even buy medicines for curable diseases because so much of their resources go to paying off debts to nations that don't even need the money. Bono works tirelessly to correct this wrong. He's also helping to fight AIDS worldwide.

Boy, do we need a year for canceling debts. If someone owes you something, why not give them the gift of forgiveness? If you do, God promises to bless you! Do a Bono!

####### HOT READ #######

Why did God tell the Israelites to eat certain foods and not others?
Deuteronomy 14.

——> ALL ABOUT ME >

Be sure to appoint over you the king the Lord your God chooses. He must be from among your own brothers. Do not place a foreigner over you, one who is not a brother Israelite. Deuteronomy 17:15.

ome nations are ruled by men who think that they are gods. When a leader forces the people of the nation to all but worship him or her, a personality cult develops. The names of rivers, lakes, mountain ranges, buildings, etc., are changed to his or her name. Many personality cults have existed in the world, but few like the one that occurred in China several decades ago.

Mao Zedong and his supporters liberated the Chinese people from the long and brutal rule of the Kuomintang party. Almost immediately the people aimed all their admiration at Zedong, the leader of the revolution that toppled the Kuomintang.

Mao Zedong's government passed strict rules preventing anyone from criticizing his regime. His picture adorned every official building in China. When his brutal rule led many to commit suicide, Mao callously remarked, "People who try to commit suicide—don't attempt to save them! . . . China is such a populous nation, it is not as if we cannot do without a few people." His policies led to the deaths of hundreds of thousands, possibly even millions, of Chinese people.

God understands human beings. He knows that when too much power is concentrated in hand of one person, that person often becomes corrupted by power. God knew that Israel would one day crave a king, so He made rules for kings to follow. First, the king was to be chosen by God Himself. The king was not to amass great wealth or marry many wives. In fact, the king would have to read and obey God's commands governing his kingship, or he and his descendants would not be blessed with long terms in power. These warnings were designed to protect the Israelite nation from pain and suffering, which, unfortunately, they would experience many times in the future as ungodly rulers oppressed them.

When God chooses a leader, He chooses people of character, people who listen to and obey Him.

/////// HOT READ ///////

Can't live without checking your horoscope? Better read Deuteronomy 18:9-12. God is so not into astrology of any kind.

⟶ SACRED VIOLENCE? <

Do not leave alive anything that breathes. Deuteronomy 20:16.

news story captured my attention a few years ago. A young father was at home with his infant daughter when the baby began to cry—and cry and cry! He soon grew frustrated and did the unthinkable. He threw the baby out the window. Yep, you read that right. But the story arrested my attention because of one other detail—the baby lived. A tree directly under the window broke her fall.

We feel sad when anyone suffers, but much more so when an innocent child is hurt. It is this innate emotional response to children's pain that makes me wonder how God could tell the Israelites to kill "anything that breathes" in the nations that occupied Canaan. It is hard for me to understand how a loving God could order such killing. But God had a reason, and while I may not understand it, I trust that God knows what He is doing, and I accept His decisions.

God did not want the Israelites to imitate the behavior of the Hittites, Amorites, Canaanites, Perizzites, Hivites, and Jebusites (Deuteronomy 20:17, 18). What behaviors did God worry about? The behaviors found in Leviticus 18, for starters. Read the chapter again. It's worth a second look. Not only that—these nations worshipped by sacrificing their children to their gods. Like Sodom and Gomorrah, their wickedness was so great that God decreed that they be totally destroyed.

Many today use God's mandate to destroy Canaan's wicked inhabitants to justify destroying people who do bad things today. They believe that they are acting for God. We must remember that at the time, God was the leader of Israel. He was speaking directly to them, outlining His purposes. No civil laws governed them outside of the laws that God prescribed. Today we have civil laws set up by the government, and we must obey them when they do not go against God's laws.

Furthermore, it's best to let God judge whether or not a person should be put to death for wrongs they've done. God will explain Himself to us one day soon.

////// HOT READ //////

Read Deuteronomy 20:1-4. Are you afraid of something right now? Why not claim this promise?

65

——> BLURRING THE LINES <

A woman must not wear men's clothing, nor a man wear women's clothing, for the Lord your God detests anyone who does this. Deuteronomy 22:5.

few years ago I was watching MTV—for research purposes, of course. I caught them during their annual spring break coverage—you know, scantily clad bikini babes, guys with no shirts, the whole parade of flesh. Between the music videos and enticing beach scenes, they showed clips from a beach contest hosted by none other than Jerry Springer.

Here's how the contest worked: Random guys and girls were selected from the audience and paired together. When a horn sounded, each pair would rush madly behind a curtain, where they quickly exchanged clothes. The guy would give up his shorts and T-shirt (if he was wearing one). The girl would give him her—whatever she was wearing. They had 30 seconds to make the switch and get dressed. The fastest changers won.

As you can imagine, the crowd went totally berserk when they appeared again. That was probably the last time that I really watched MTV's spring break coverage. The idea of girls going behind a sheet and getting undressed was way too enticing for me.

I'm glad I quit watching, because there was much more wrong with that contest than just the fact that flesh was everywhere. Guys were dressing in girls' clothing, and vice versa. It wasn't until I read Deuteronomy 22 that I understood just how wrong their behavior was. God created us male and female, and He wants us to keep those distinctions clear.

At the time, it was customary in other nations for men and women to swap roles and clothing. God rejected this behavior because it was an abomination to Him—something He disliked intensely. Cross-dressing was one of the by-products of practicing homosexuals, a sin that God warned the Israelites against (Leviticus 18 and 20).

Today some designers blur sexual differences in their clothing designs. Stay away from them. Be who God created you to be—a holy and honorable child of God.

/////// HOT READ ///////

As you read today's Bible passage, remember that the laws governing marital violations, for instance, had a specific connection to the times in which the Israelites were living.

⟶ SO MUCH FOR TROUBLE? <

When you have finished setting aside a tenth of all your produce in the third year, the year of the tithe, you shall give it to the Levite, the alien, the fatherless and the widow, so that they may eat in your towns and be satisfied. Deuteronomy 26:12.

Leona Helmsley. Does that name ring a bell with you? It probably shouldn't, for you weren't around when she first became famous, but allow me to fill you in.

During the eighties—yes, there was life before the nineties—Mrs. Helmsley was one of the richest women in all of New York. She had made her fortune in real estate. Unfortunately, she was also known as one of the biggest slumlords in all of New York City. She owned apartment buildings that she didn't keep up. Her run-down, roach-infested apartments soon attracted the attention of city regulators, and she got into a lot of trouble.

Investigations by the IRS led to convictions on tax-evasion charges. She was thrown into prison. She'd once quipped, "Only the little people pay taxes," but found out that that she was not exempt. Most of the people who worked for her hated her, because of the way she treated working-class people. She had little use for them.

Many Helmsley watchers saw a change in her when she donated several million dollars to help the Louisiana victims of Hurricane Katrina. But whatever came over her at that moment didn't last long. When she died, Leona Helmsley left more money for her dog, Trouble, than she did for any one of her grandchildren. Two grandchildren received nothing; two others got a whopping $5 million in trust and $5 million outright. And Trouble? Well, the little demon walked away with $12 million. Even in death she was mean!

Through Moses, God told the Israelites that every third year they were to collect a tenth, or tithe, of every crop produced in the land. This tithe was to be given to the poor, the widowed, the Levites (priests), and the immigrants who lived among them, "so that they may eat in your towns and be satisfied."

In a world in which dogs live better than human beings, it's great to know that God still cares for the needs of people—all people. We are in His hands, and what He gives us we are to share with those in need.

///////// HOT READ ///////

God is into graffiti! Don't believe me? Read it for yourself: Deuteronomy 27:1-8.

——> DEAL OR NO DEAL? <

This day I call heaven and earth as witnesses against you that I have set before you life and death, blessings and curses. Now choose life, so that you and your children may live. Deuteronomy 30:19.

If you read Deuteronomy 28-30, you probably need to take a deep breath right now. Wow! Now, that's what I call laying it all out in black and white. There's one thing we must know about God: He always gives us clear warnings before He punishes us.

In Deuteronomy 28 God was clear that Israel would be blessed for their obedience. They would be blessed in their cities and in their fields; blessed when they went out and when they came in; their crops and their cattle would be blessed. God would defeat their enemies and establish them as His holy nation. Not only that, but God would open the storehouse of His bounty and rain blessings on them. I'm not sure anyone could ever get tired of being blessed, but if anyone could, it was the Israelites.

These blessings represented one half of God's covenant with Israel, the same one He made with them 40 years earlier at Mount Sinai after He busted them out of their Egyptian jail. Israel controlled the other half of the covenant. They simply had to obey God's commands, and given what they'd been through in Egypt, obeying God should have been a piece of cake. If they failed to do so, however, they would feel the pain (Deuteronomy 28:15-68).

God was offering the Israelites the deal of a lifetime. Moses understood the stakes more than any one of them. After he relayed God's commands to the people, he spoke to them from his heart. What God wants to give you, he told them, is not something far away. It's not the heavens, and it's not across the seas. You don't have to go chasing after it. All these blessings are right here, right now. Make the choice to serve God today!

All of heaven listened to hear what the Israelites would say. The answer would determine whether they lived a long life of prosperity or died in infamy.

Today God is asking you and me to choose between life and death. I choose life!

///////// HOT READ ///////

God refuses to totally forget us when we mess up. Look at what He promised to do for the Israelites if they were willing to repent: Deuteronomy 30:1-10.

——> GOING <

Then Moses climbed Mount Nebo from the plains of Moab to the top of Pisgah, across from Jericho. There the Lord showed him the whole land. Deuteronomy 34:1.

e've come to end of Deuteronomy. What a wild ride it's been! We watched as the Israelites pitched their tents in Moab. Just over the Jordan River lay Canaan—the Promised Land. We listened as Moses reminded the people of where they'd come from (Deuteronomy 1-4). Then Moses dealt with their present state (Deuteronomy 5-26), laying out all the commands God had given them. Finally Moses told them about the blessings they could anticipate in the Promised Land if they remained obedient to God, and the curses that would fall on them if they did not (Deuteronomy 28-30).

Even as Moses prepared the Israelite nation to enter the Promised Land, God was preparing to put him to sleep. Moses accepted that he would die before God brought the Israelites into the Promised Land. The reason? Years earlier he disobeyed God, striking the rock at Meribah instead of speaking to it as God told him to do.

"I am now a hundred and twenty years old and I am no longer able to lead you," Moses began. "The Lord has said to me, 'You shall not cross the Jordan'" (Deuteronomy 31:2). Perhaps Moses should have been upset. Why couldn't God forgive him for his momentary fit of anger? Why couldn't God let bygones be bygones? And after all the flack that Moses had taken from the Israelites, surely he had a right to go to the Promised Land. Not to mention that this whole get-out-of-Egypt-march-through-the-desert thing was God's idea anyway, Moses might have reasoned.

Whatever his thoughts, we have no record of Moses being upset at his punishment. Instead, after pronouncing blessings on each tribe, Moses calmly walked away from the Israelites. He climbed the hill to Mount Nebo, where God said he would die. But before he died, God gave him a glimpse of the place he had worked so hard to reach. "This is the land I promised on oath to Abraham, Isaac and Jacob," said God (Deuteronomy 34:4). It was God's way of saying goodbye to a friend He loved dearly. Then Moses closed his eyes.

Amen.

///////// HOT READ /////////
Wouldn't you want God to say this about you? Deuteronomy 34:10-12.

——> INTRODUCING: JOSHUA <

Moses my servant is dead. Now then, you and all these people, get ready to cross the Jordan River into the land I am about to give to them—to the Israelites.
Joshua 1:2.

Longtime radio commentator Paul Harvey tells this true story. One warm summer morning a man by the name of Ray Blankenship was getting his breakfast when he looked out the window. To his horror, he saw a little girl struggling in the rain-flooded drainage ditch beside his home. Downstream the ditch rushed underneath a road, then emptied into the main culvert.

Ray ran out the door and raced along the ditch, trying to catch up to, and then get ahead of, the little girl. At last he hurled himself into the deep, roaring water. He was able to grab hold of the child's arm, and they tumbled end over end as Ray frantically reached out to grab hold of—anything. They were only about three feet from the culvert—and disaster—when Ray's free hand felt something sticking out from one bank. In a heartbeat he grabbed hold of it, desperately hanging on as the rushing water tore at them both. *If I can just hang on until help comes,* he thought desperately. But he did better than that. By the time the fire department rescue squad arrived, he'd heaved the little girl out on the bank. Both of them were treated for shock.

For his daring rescue, Ray Blankenship was awarded the Coast Guard's Silver Lifesaving Medal. The award is fitting, for Ray was at even greater risk to himself than most people knew. You see, Ray Blankenship cannot swim.

The book of Joshua is one of most amazing books you'll ever read. Like Ray Blankenship, Joshua faced deep waters as he prepared to lead the armies of God into battle against the powerful giants who lived in fortified cities in Canaan. He would need supernatural power to survive the mighty waters before him. He needed courage.

God refused to send Joshua to battle unprepared. First He told him, "As I was with Moses, so I will be with you; I will never leave you nor forsake you" (Joshua 1:5). Next He said, "Be strong and courageous" (verse 6), or "Don't wimp out!" Then God told the Israelites to obey the laws that Moses gave them, and to feast on His words. They were never to let His words depart from their lips (verses 7 and 8). Now, that's what I call a send-off!

//////// HOT READ ////////

What special item led the Israelites into battle? Joshua 3:1-8.

──> STONES? >

Each of you is to take up a stone on his shoulder, according to the number of the tribes of the Israelites, to serve as a sign among you. Joshua 4:5, 6.

There's nothing that people won't collect. There's a guy on the World Wide Web who calls his collection The Man Behind the Doll. Instead of Barbie dolls, he collects Ken dolls. (Need I say more?) Then there's the really eccentric guy who collects his naval fluff and leaves it in his bathroom for all his visitors to see. NO COMMENT!

Not only the weird and slightly insane have a hankering to amass stuff; the rich and famous collect with reckless abandon, and some of them have the bucks to do it right. Ralph Lauren, for instance—yeah, that guy with all the clothes that bear his name—is a diehard collector of vintage automobiles. He has a 1933 Bugatti Type 59 Grand Prix and a 1996 McClaren F1, a 1958 Ferrari Testa Rossa and a 1938 Bugatti Type 57 SC Atlantic Coupe. Ralph Lauren's car collection is so rare that the Boston Museum of Fine Arts asked to do an exhibit of 15 of his cars.

You know what? God is into collecting too. Today's reading proves it. As the Israelites prepared to enter Canaan, the Jordan River lay between them and their dream. God told Joshua to have the priests take the ark down to the bank of the river and step into the waters. When they did, the waters parted and rose up in a heap on each side, with dry land straight over to Jericho. The priests moved to the center of the river and stood there until all the people had crossed over. So that the Israelites would never forget this miracle, God told Joshua to have the leaders of the 12 tribes gather 12 stones from the center of the river where the priests were standing. Why?

"In the future, when your children ask you, 'What do these stones mean?' tell them that the flow of the Jordan was cut off before the ark of the covenant of the Lord" (Joshua 4:6, 7). Did you get that? God wanted the Israelites never to forget what He had done at the Jordan River. He wanted their children to know about Him. When God blesses you, what do *you* do to remember His goodness?

///////// HOT READ /////////

Read Joshua 6:1-10. Why did God choose to conquer Jericho in such a strange way—marching around it and blowing horns?

———> UNDERCOVER BROTHER <

> *The Lord said to Joshua, "Stand up! What are you doing down on your face? Israel has sinned; they have violated my covenant, which I commanded them to keep."*
> Joshua 7:10, 11.

oughnut Thief Sentenced to 30 Years. That was the title of the e-mail. You can see why it got my attention. What kind of nut would steal a doughnut and then be put in prison for 30 years? I had to read it now.

Scott A. Masters was really hungry and he couldn't afford the 52 cents to buy the doughnut, so he arranged a five-finger discount. Most shoplifters, the article noted, favored cold medicines and packaged meats. That's where the "Shoplifters Will Be Prosecuted" sign hung. But fresh fried doughnuts? Irresistible!

When a store clerk attempted to stop him from pilfering the sweet, Mr. Masters pushed the worker out of the way and continued out the store. For this little escapade the city prosecutor has charged him with strong-arm robbery, which carries a possible 15-year prison term. Add to that the 5 to 15 years he could get for stealing the doughnut, and we're up to a possible 30 years in prison. Plus that prior criminal record of his is not going over well either. As you read this, Mr. Masters is somewhere in a prison in Farmington, Missouri.

Stealing is never a good idea, especially when God tells us not to do so. God had made clear to the Israelites that once they captured Jericho, everything was to be destroyed, especially any items used for idol worship. But that message was lost on a guy named Achan. He stole "a beautiful robe from Babylonia, two hundred shekels of silver and wedge of gold weighing fifty shekels" (Joshua 7:21). He disobeyed God for a nice robe, a little more than six pounds of silver, and less than two pounds of gold.

Achan thought he would get away with it, but his sin affected the entire Israelite community. Israel lost its first battle with a city called Ai because the presence of God had left them because of Achan's sin.

Can one person's sin affect an entire community? Absolutely. If there's a sin in your life that you're covering, confess it and ask God to forgive you. Do it now.

//////// HOT READ ////////

Do you think that God was right to kill Achan's entire family when Achan was the one who sinned?

⟶> FORCED TO FIGHT <

The Gibeonites then sent word to Joshua in the camp at Gilgal: "Do not abandon your servants. Come up to us quickly and save us! Help us, because all the Amorite kings from the hill country have joined forces against us." Joshua 10:6.

he Gibeonites are some of the biggest fakers in the Bible. They belong at the top of the list next to Judas, who cleverly played the role of Jesus' disciple without truly being one. Both Judas and the Gibeonites must have learned their tricks from Satan himself, whose deception in the Garden of Eden was the greatest hoax ever pulled off.

You remember the Gibeonites from yesterday's reading, don't you? They heard that the Israelites had successfully defeated every nation in their path, so they decided not to wait for the inevitable. They dressed up like bums and headed in the direction of the Israelite camp. When the Israelites intercepted them, they told their clever, made-up story.

"We come from a far distance away, and we are poor. We have nothing to eat," they cajoled. "Please give us some food. And, by the way, we know how great you are. We know how great your God is, and we don't want any war with you. Since we live so far away, would you mind signing a peace treaty with us?" (See Joshua 9:8-13.)

Then the Bible says, "The men of Israel sampled their provisions but did not inquire of the Lord" (verse 14). Joshua made a treaty with the Gibeonites, and three days later he found out that the Gibeonites lived very near to them. They were neighbors. This was the first time in Joshua's leadership of Israel that he had forgotten to check with God. The Israelites later regretted the treaty made with the Gibeonites, because when five major Amorite kings rose up to fight the Gibeonites, the Israelites were forced to defend them. They had to honor the treaty they had made. Forced to fight for an enemy!

Sometimes we make hasty decisions and build friendships with the wrong people. When they get in trouble, we sometimes end up in trouble. Ask God to help you choose those you hang out with. Hang with friends who are honest, trustworthy, loving of God.

/////// HOT READ ///////

Read Joshua 11 carefully. If God was fighting for the Israelites, why did He ask them to fight for themselves? Why didn't He just destroy the inhabitants of Canaan with a plague and let the Israelites march into Canaan unbothered?

——> 85 YEARS YOUNG <

So here I am today, eighty-five years old! I am still as strong today as the day Moses sent me out; I'm just as vigorous to go out to battle now as I was then. Now give me this hill country that the Lord promised me that day. Joshua 14:10-12.

ou've probably heard about the two teens from Florida caught on a surveillance camera beating a homeless man with a bat. The man had done nothing to them. They were out to bash some bums. And who could forget the search two years ago for a man who videotaped himself sexually abusing a young child?

As sad as child abuse and vagrant abuse is, elder abuse happens more often than each of the other two. That's right, senior citizens are far more likely to be physically abused, and family members are most often the culprits.

The Bible teaches us to respect the elderly, and this thread weaves its way through the book of Joshua. When the Israelites had just about defeated every nation in sight, an 85-year-old came to Joshua, pointed to a huge hill covered with giants, and said, "Give me this hill." He wasn't just any senior citizen, though. He was Caleb.

Caleb was one of only two spies who had brought back a positive report to Moses after spying out the land of Canaan. Joshua was the other. The other 10 spies said that there was no way the Israelites could defeat the people of Canaan. So when Caleb approached Joshua, Joshua remembered his faithfulness and the promise made to him by Moses (Numbers 14:24).

Caleb wasn't about to let old age stop him from living in the land that was promised to him. "I am still as strong today as I was back then," he told Joshua, "With God's help I'll drive out the giants that live on that hill." And he did (see Joshua 15:14).

Joshua could have said to Caleb, "Old man, let it go! You're way too old for such a big task. Why not find a good nursing home, a comfortable rocking chair, and take it easy?" No, Joshua didn't say that. He respected the faithfulness of his old friend.

The Bible says, "Then Joshua blessed Caleb son of Jephunneh and gave him Hebron as his inheritance" (Joshua 14:13).

Always respect and cherish older people. They are really special to God and to us!

///////// HOT READ ///////

What word describes how Caleb obeyed God? Joshua 14:8, 9, 14.

──> THE BIG FINISH <

The people of Joseph replied, "The hill country is not enough for us, and all the Canaanites who live in the plain have iron chariots, both those in Beth Shan and its settlements and those in the Valley of Jezreel." Joshua 17:16.

Anything that's worth doing is worth doing _____? Care to fill in the blank? Here's a hint. Your parents have probably said this phrase to you several times.

I'm big on starting projects. Unfortunately, I'm not too big on finishing them. I know you don't do that, but I do. I've already told you about the many times that I started to read the Bible through, only to fall short. (This time I'm going to make it to the end! I kind of have to. This book sort of requires it, don't you think?)

Once I started building a home gym because I was gonna get "big," "cut," and "diesel." Seven years and two houses later it's finally done—only my dream of getting big is still just a dream. (Cut and diesel? Not!) Then there was the time I decided to stop drinking with my meals. Drinking with your meals hinders digestion, not to mention that it helps to widen your gut. I did great for a while, but slowly I started drinking with my meals again. (I'm still working on this.)

After reading Joshua 16-18 today, I'm feeling a little better. I'm not the only person who struggles with finishing what I start—doing the job right. The Israelites had the same problem. When you read today's passage, did you notice that the tribes of both Ephraim and Manasseh failed to finish what they started? Both tribes, descendants of Joseph, a guy who always finished what he started, failed to push the Canaanites from their land.

What excuse did they give? "The Canaanites have chariots of iron!" Translation? They were scared to fight the dudes in their territory, so they wanted Joshua to hook them up. Give them more land, preferably land with no one on it to fight.

"You guys are strong enough to drive them out," Joshua responded. "Don't let their iron chariots scare you. God is with you. You can do this!"

Do you think Ephraim and Manasseh listened to Joshua?

####### HOT READ #######

How did Joshua try to push the Israelites to possess their inheritance? Joshua 18:1-7.

——> LAST IN LINE <

*When they had finished dividing the land into its allotted portions, the Israelites gave
Joshua son of Nun an inheritance among them, as the Lord had commanded.*
Joshua 19:49, 50.

sad saga is playing out today as I write this entry. It's occurring in a country called Myanmar, also known as Burma. A small band of military leaders took power several decades ago and have ruled the country with an iron fist for more than 19 years.

In September 2007 the nation rose up against them in protest. They were led by Buddhist monks who are very respected by the people. The demonstrators marched peacefully for several days—then disaster. The dictators unleashed their military and police forces on them, killing at least 10 people and imprisoning hundreds more. Those are the numbers of dead and wounded as reported by Burma's government. Other reports from inside the country put the number of dead or wounded in the hundreds. It's hard to get any accurate information because the government controls all media, even shutting down the Internet when videos of the crackdown started showing up on YouTube.

While the people of Burma suffer, their leaders live a rich and comfortable life. They have shut the nation off from the rest of the world and treated its meager wealth like their own private candy store.

That's how it is in many places in our world today. National leaders often look out for themselves at the expense of their people. But that's nothing new. Back when Israel was conquering Canaan, all the surrounding nations had kings who lived lavishly and ruled absolutely. But God never intended for the Israelites to operate that way.

How do we know? Well, check out the example of Joshua. For several years Joshua had successfully led Israel into battle. He led the military campaign to clear the Promised Land. But Joshua was the last to receive his inheritance after the land was totally divided. Furthermore, Joshua understood that the true leader of Israel was God.

Great leaders sacrifice their personal ambitions for the good of people. That's what Jesus did for us at Calvary.

//////// HOT READ ////////
What did the tribe of Judah do for the tribe of Simeon? See Joshua 19:8, 9.

> FAMOUS FAREWELLS <

But if serving the Lord seems undesirable to you, then choose for yourselves this day whom you will serve, whether the gods your forefathers served beyond the River, or the gods of the Amorites, in whose land you are living. But as for me and my household, we will serve the Lord. Joshua 24:15.

have found it impossible to carry the heavy burden of responsibility . . . without the help and support of the woman I love." Those words were part of the famous farewell speech given by King Edward VIII of England in 1936 as he prepared to give up his throne to marry Wallis Simpson, a divorced American woman with whom he'd "fallen" in love.

Edward knew that the British public would not accept a twice-divorced American woman as their queen. So before his official coronation ceremonies he addressed the British people by radio, telling them that he would leave the throne behind for the woman he loved. At the time, Edward's abdication was a national scandal, real tabloid material. As farewells go, Edward's words remain some of the most famous of all time.

In the Bible Joshua's farewell to Israel is surpassed only by Moses' last words and, of course, the last words of our dying Savior, Jesus. His speech was not overly poetic. It was simple. It was the speech of a guy who had loved God with his whole heart for his whole life.

The heart of the speech is Joshua's plaintive request to Israel. "If you find it too difficult to serve God, choose today whom you will serve," he said. "Don't play with God. If you're not feelin' God, then stop faking. Follow your own gods." But Joshua didn't stop there. He wanted all Israel to know that he had made up his mind. He and his family would serve God faithfully to the end—no matter what Israel chose to do.

You will be called to take a stand for God while others are in the valley of decision. When you take your stand, others will be led to take theirs. Be faithful and stand for God today—no matter what others do.

/////// HOT READ ///////

Why was Joshua so concerned about Israel's future in the Promised Land? Joshua 24:23. Hidden sins (gods) prevent us from fully experiencing God's blessings.

——> THE BIG PICTURE, VOL. 1 <

I will never break my covenant with you, and you shall not make a covenant with the people of this land, but you shall break down their altars. Yet you have disobeyed me. Why have you done this? Judges 2:1, 2.

If you've been reading the Bible through thus far, Judges signals a change in God's relationship with His people. From the time God created Adam and Eve to when Israel finally entered the Promised Land, God was trying to rescue humanity from the power of sin. This is why God singled out Abraham and promised to make of him a great nation—Israel, as they would later be called when God changed Jacob's name. God wanted "peeps" who would show the world how to live a holy life. The world needed a witness, and Israel was to be it.

God rescued his crew from Egyptian slavery with the most astonishing natural disasters the world had ever seen. Why? Because God wanted His people to be free to worship Him, free to be one with Him. Then He gave them the Ten Commandments to teach them the standards that they were to live by. Through Moses He built a sanctuary to teach them how much God hates sin and how they could get back into a right relationship with Him.

By the time we get to Judges, the Israelites had successfully defeated almost all their enemies. If they had MTV back then, their houses would have been on *MTV Cribs*. They'd become so successful that they traded *the* God for the gods of the sinful nations that they failed to drive from Canaan.

Big mistake!

In the book of Judges God gets very fed up with Israel, so He withdraws His blessing from them. (That's the one thing that you never want God to do to you.) But Judges is not just about God judging His people; it's also about God's loving forgiveness of His people. The name of the book refers to the special leaders God raised up to save Israel from their enemies. Samson was one of those leaders.

The book of Judges teaches us that hidden sins bring terrible consequences, but it also lets us know that God will not forget us when we mess up. He loves us!

////// HOT READ //////
To understand Judges, you've gotta read Judges 2:10-19.

——> GIRLS ARE WEAK? <

Barak said to her, "If you go with me, I will go; but if you don't go with me, I won't go." Judges 4:8.

irls are weak. That's what's I thought when I was in junior high. We guys could run faster, jump higher, and do just about all things physical better than the girls. Of course, they were cuter, so we didn't brag too much.

Guys are physical by nature. You don't generally see girls slapping each other around, sliding down rails on skateboards, and generally beating each other into submission on a football field. At least that was my opinion until I met Hillary.

She was a girl, but then she wasn't. Like some guys, she lived for contact sports, such as basketball and football. She was no "girlie girl." Hillary had another talent, though, that surpassed all her other "skillz." She punched like a guy. We guys would sometimes push girls around—something we had no business doing—but it took only one or two of Hillary's haymakers to convince all to stay clear of her. And boy, did we ever!

I have no clue what the prophet Deborah looked like, but I am certain that she didn't have Hillary's "guns." Yet a rough-and-tumble four-star general refused to go to battle without her. What did she have that made her so tough? She trusted in God, and she obeyed Him. Because General Barak refused to fight the Canaanites without Deborah, she told him, "I will go with you. But because of the way you are going about this, the honor will not be yours, for the Lord will hand Sisera over to a woman" (Judges 4:9).

You heard Deborah right. A woman would kill one of the most fearsome enemies of the Israelites. Her name was Jael. Like Deborah, she was brave and ready to be used of God. When God trounced the Canaanites, Sisera, the general of the Canaanite forces, escaped. When he got tired, he stopped in a nearby tent to rest and hide from the Israelites—Jael's tent. The rest, as they say, is history. If you missed how the story ends, read the rest of Judges 4.

Girls are strong, especially when they follow God.

//////// HOT READ ////////

If you've ever struggled to know whether God is calling you to do something or not, please read Judges 6. Gideon was a lot like you. God is patient.

——> THAT'S "GANGSTA!"<

He went to his father's home in Ophrah and on one stone murdered his seventy brothers, the sons of Jerub-Baal. Judges 9:5.

bimelech. If there ever was an OG (original gangsta) in the Bible, that guy was Abimelech. Rappers rap about it, "playas" dream about it, but Abimelech? He got his "street cred" the hard way. He earned it. How? Read on.

He was Gideon's boy. Yes, sir, the son of Jerub-Baal, the man whom God used to destroy an army of 135,000 men. But Abimelech had one black mark by his name. He was the son of one of Gideon's concubines from Shechem, not one of Gideon's wives' children. The Bible doesn't say it, but you can be sure that Abimelech hated his second-class status. He knew that he'd never inherit his father's riches. He'd never be honored like his brothers—there were 70 guys ahead of him. So he decided to skip the line.

He raised an army of "reckless adventurers" of Shechemites, rode to the town in which Gideon's boys lived, and slaughtered them one by one. It was worse than the drive-by that killed Tupac, worse than the ambush that laid Biggie low, worse than anything writers for the old *Sopranos* show could dream up. The people of Shechem declared him king, but not before Jotham, the only brother to escape, made a fearful prediction: Abimelech will destroy them, and they will destroy him.

Jotham was right. Gaal, a man from Shechem who was just as ambitious as Abimelech, plotted to destroy Abimelech. The fickle people of Shechem, many of whom had supported Abimelech earlier, now supported Gaal. When Abimelech got wind of Gaal's treachery, he planned a surprise attack on Gaal and the people of Shechem. Abimelech killed all the people of Shechem. Not content to stop there, he pressed his attack against the citizens of Thebez who had locked themselves in a tower. When Abimelech approached the tower to set it on fire, a woman dropped a huge stone from the roof of the tower. The stone found its mark. It cracked Abimelech's skull and led to his death.

What goes around comes around. Abimelech's reign began in blood and ended in blood—his own. It's never a good idea to tear others down to raise ourselves up.

///////// HOT READ ////////
What big mistake did Gideon make before his death? Judges 8:22-27.

⟶ "DO IT AGAIN, PLEASE!" <

Go and cry out to the gods you have chosen. Let them save you when you are in trouble! Judges 10:14.

y now you may have picked up the pattern in Judges. Israel forsakes God for heathen gods made from wood and stone; God allows their enemies to conquer them; the Israelites cry out to God for deliverance; and God sends a deliverer to free them. This pattern repeats itself seven times in Judges.

Along with the awesome theme of grace—God's willingness to forgive us when we mess up—there's also this: Sin that is not overcome gets worse. In the first few chapters of Judges we see Israel worshipping a heathen god or two here and there. But in Judges 10 the gods have multiplied. "They served the Baals and the Ashtoreths, and the gods of Aram, the gods of Sidon, the gods of Moab, the gods of the Ammonites and the gods of the Philistines" (Judges 10:6). But hang on. It gets even weirder.

The Israelites chose to worship the gods of their oppressors. Once one generation went through the "sin-grace cycle," the next generation not only seemed to forget the lesson of obedience to God—they forgot who it was that enslaved them. But this time would be different.

God "sold" them to the Philistines and the Ammonites, who shattered and crushed them (Judges 10:7, 8). The Philistines ruled over the Israelites on the eastern side of the Jordan River. When they cried out to God for deliverance, He replied, "Ask the gods you've been serving to help you." God is cold sometimes, isn't He?

What's more, the Israelites were forced to reach out for help to a great, God-fearing warrior named Jephthah. Now, they'd run him out of town because his mother was a prostitute. Yet God used Jephthah to deliver Israel—again!

The grace, or goodness, of God is meant to lead us to repent of our sins and with His help put those sins away forever (Romans 2:4). If God has forgiven you of something, ask Him for strength never to do it again. Sin grows stronger with each indulgence, but so does the power to overcome each time you choose to obey God.

////// HOT READ //////
Who started "hating" Jephthah after God helped him defeat the Ammonites? Judges 12:1-4. God's family was now fighting each other.

——> SUPERMAN RISING <

The angel of the Lord appeared to her and said, "You are sterile and childless, but you are going to conceive and have a son." Judges 13:3.

e was the world's strongest man. He won the strength contest in 2002, 2003, 2005, and 2007. I'm referring to Mariusz Pudzianowski of Poland.

Mariusz Pudzianowski is blessed with the body of a god. Powerful legs, a skinny waist, logs for arms, and a will to win that few competitors can match. He is simply the complete package. When other strongmen collapse in pain, Pudzianowski keeps on going. The secret of his strength? No secret, really. Year-round Mariusz Pudzianowski trains like a champion. Most of his Strongman wins came in the gym, long before the competition.

Mariusz P. may be the world's strongest man, but long before he showed up, another mesomorph dominated the planet. His name was Samson, and his strength came directly from God. I doubt that Mr. Pudzianowski could take a lion by the jaws and tear it apart (Judges 14:6), but Samson did. With a donkey's jawbone he killed 1,000 Philistine soldiers. No man will ever pull that off again.

Samson's strength came from God, and it was to be used for God. God raised him up to deliver the Israelites from the hand of the Philistines after—get this— Israel "did evil in the eyes of the Lord" *again* (Judges 13:1). Samson's birth and development was unlike any of the earlier judges (deliverers). An angel from heaven appeared to his mother and told her that she would become pregnant with a baby boy who would begin to deliver Israel from the Philistines.

The angel told his mother and father what he could and could not eat, how he ought to dress, even how he must wear his hair. Samson was to be a Nazirite (Numbers 6), someone who took a sacred vow to dedicate his life to God for a specific, holy purpose. Samson was in a special club, one to which John the Baptist would later belong.

////// HOT READ //////

What act of God accompanied Samson's feats of strength? Judges 14:6; 14:19; 15:14, 15; etc. Is God's Spirit active in your life?

──> SUPERMAN'S KRYPTONITE <

He awoke from his sleep and thought, "I'll go out as before and shake myself free."
But he did not know that the Lord had left him. Judges 16:20.

amson is likely the strongest man mentioned in all of the Bible, but he was also one of the weakest. It really doesn't take much to destroy a person. Satan needs only one weakness, one area of compromise, one point in a person's life in which God is not in control, and the rest is history.

When I was in graduate school, a professor asked me a very challenging question. "Mr. Esmond," he asked, "what's wrong with just good old-fashioned lust?" I wasn't sure what he was talking about, so he kept on talking. "You know, lust. Not love, but just lust. What's wrong with lust?"

I gotta admit that he really caught me off guard. I wasn't trying to make a name for myself as KING CHRISTIAN, but I wasn't about to let people just diss me and my faith. So I answered him.

"Well, Dr. Blackmon," I began, "the problem with lust is that it cares only about itself. Lust doesn't focus on what it can do for the other person. It's all about what it can get from the other person." Years later I still think I got that answer right.

Long before the Philistines gouged out Samson's eyes, bound his hands and feet, and forced him to grind grain like an ox, lust had done all those things to him. What else explains the fact that Samson went to another town to visit a prostitute? Trapped in Gaza, Samson simply tore out the city gates and walked off with them. He escaped that time, but a much more dangerous temptation awaited him, and this time his strength would fail him because he had failed God.

Samson met Delilah and fell in love with her. The Bible doesn't say that she loved him. What's more, she belonged to the very people whom God sent him to destroy. But Samson couldn't see the danger. Lust had blinded him, and God had left him.

To be sure, God forgave Samson. When he asked for strength to destroy the Philistines, God gave it to him. But wouldn't it have been better simply to obey God and remain pure? Guard your purity with all the strength you have.

///////// HOT READ /////////

What are you doing to let God know that He is welcome in your life?

——> FUZZY MATH <

In those days Israel had no king; everyone did as he saw fit. Judges 21:25.

From the very beginning the book of Judges paints a horrible picture of what happens when we forget God. After Joshua died, "another generation grew up, who knew neither the Lord nor what he had done for Israel" (Judges 2:10). What happened next was predictable. The Israelites did evil, serving the Baals or false gods. Basically, they subtracted God from their lives, added a ton of fake gods, and expected everything to go well with them. Not! The end of Judges proved just how fuzzy their math had been.

Judges ends with one of the sickest crimes in all of Scripture. (If you haven't read chapters 19-21, you won't understand much of what I'm saying.) Here's a quick recap. A member of a Levite tribe traveled to a far city to reunite with a woman he loved who had left him. As he began his trek back home he grew tired, but was afraid to stop for the night in any city that did not belong to the Israelites. They all could easily be killed.

At last he came to Gibeah, a city owned by the tribe of Benjamin. No one but an old farmer offered him a place to stay. That evening a large gang of men came to the farmer's house and demanded his male guests to have sex with them. (Can you say yuck?). Before the night was over, the woman with the Levite was gang-raped and died.

Distraught by what had happened, the Levite laid her across his donkey and went on home. Then he cut her body into 12 pieces and sent a piece to each of the 12 tribes. When the 11 tribal leaders found out what the men from Benjamin had done, they raised an army to attack the whole tribe. When war finally broke out, God used the other tribes to almost totally destroy the tribe of Benjamin. It lost 25,000 men in the struggle, and that's not counting other men, women, and children who were killed. Only 600 men from the entire tribe remained.

God had been Israel's king—until they got to the Promised Land and didn't want Him anymore. As the final verse in Judges makes clear, Israel claimed to have no king, and they did whatever they thought was right. The results were disastrous.

Judges teaches us to always cherish God, to always keep Him first in our lives.

####### HOT READ #######

Even though the other Israelite tribes helped defeat the Benjamites, how did they feel about the men who remained after the battle? Judges 21:13-17.

> ALL PEOPLE <

Don't urge me to leave you or to turn back from you. Where you go I will go, and where you stay I will stay. Your people will be my people and your God my God.
Ruth 1:16.

I flew to San Diego early one Wednesday evening. The trip from Philadelphia to San Diego included a five-hour layover in Atlanta, Georgia. It was a long day. I headed to the baggage claim area to claim my luggage, and on the way I began talking to a fellow traveler. I found out that she'd lived in San Diego for 20 years, had three grown kids, and was planning to move to Atlanta. There was only one problem. She had no job prospects in Atlanta. *How can she move?* I thought.

Right there in the airport, I asked if she would mind if I prayed about her situation. "Sure," she said. That's all I needed to hear. As we prepared to pray, a youth pastor friend of mine walked up, and together we held her hands and prayed.

You know, there are Christians, followers of Jesus, who rarely talk to people who don't believe as they do. They talk about reaching out to others, but it's all talk. The book of Ruth shows us what it truly means to help people—all people.

Naomi was an Israelite from the tribe of Judah who lived in the heathen country of Moab. Ruth was her Moabite daughter-in-law. The people of Moab were longtime enemies of the Israelites. When Naomi's husband and sons died, she decided to go back home to Judah, and Ruth wanted to go too. She refused to leave Naomi, and even accepted Naomi's God, the true God.

In the Jewish culture of that time, a woman without a husband often had to beg in order to survive. She could own no property—not even the property owned by her husband. Her only hope was that a close male relative would "redeem" her by taking her in as his wife. Sounds weird to us, but this was God's way taking care of those in need.

Ruth went even further. When Naomi begged her to stay in Moab, Ruth chose to stay and care for Naomi. It was Ruth's love and care for Naomi that impressed Boaz and moved him to "redeem" both Ruth and Naomi.

Like Boaz, God has called you to help Him redeem all people.

///////// HOT READ ////////

You won't believe how God honored Ruth (Ruth 4:13-22). Ruth became the great-grandmother of David, and out of David's family came Jesus!

──→ IT RUBS OFF <

And the Lord was gracious to Hannah; she conceived and gave birth to three sons and two daughters. Meanwhile, the boy Samuel grew up in the presence of the Lord.
1 Samuel 2:21.

reatness has a way of rubbing off on everything and everyone it touches. Mohandas Gandhi, the famous Indian champion of nonviolence, was a person who changed the world. The British Empire had ruled and dominated India for more than 200 years, reducing millions of Indian citizens to servitude. But then a quiet, shy, unassuming leader who was unafraid of British guns and who couldn't be bought by British bribes arose.

Through a series of nonviolent demonstrations, and at great loss to himself and his family, Mohandas Gandhi broke the hold of England over India. The British became so frustrated and shamed by the unwillingness of the Gandhi's followers to fight them that they began to act violently against the Indians. Every time the British massacred Indians or passed an unjust law that oppressed them, Gandhi and his followers grew stronger. India won its independence because of a man whose greatness rubbed off on an entire nation.

The greatness of God has a way of rubbing off on everything and everyone it touches. Today you read about a boy, Samuel, who grew up in the presence of true greatness. For many years his mother had longed for a child, and could not have one. At last she came to the tabernacle to pray, promising God that if He gave her a son, she would give that son back to Him. Ever made a desperate deal with God?

"God, if You do this for me, then I'll do . . ." we say to God. But then we forget our promise. Hannah didn't forget. While Samuel was still quite small she brought him to Eli, the high priest, to be raised in the tabernacle. She even made little priestly clothes for him to wear as he grew in God's presence. Hannah didn't know it, but her little boy would grow up to become a prophet and would anoint Israel's first two kings. In fact, Samuel is considered one of the greatest Israelite prophets. He was great because greatness was on him.

Today you are in the presence of God. Let His greatness rub off on you.

///////// HOT READ ///////

What fearful message did God give Samuel for Eli (1 Samuel 3:11-19)?
How would you, a teen, like to give such a message to an adult that you love?

——> FROM BADDER TO WORSER <

When he mentioned the ark of God, Eli fell backward off his chair by the side of the gate. His neck was broken and he died. . . . He had led Israel forty years.
1 Samuel 4:18.

Imagine the worst day of your life. It couldn't be any worse than the day Israel took the ark of God into battle. You remember this story, don't ya? The Philistines had put the smackdown on the Israelites—not like that hadn't happened before—and they were frantic. "What happened?" they screamed at God. "Where were You? A little thing happened out there on the battlefield. YOU DIDN'T SHOW UP!" God must not have been amused, because He didn't answer.

Actually, God never got a chance to speak. The Bible explains that after crying and yelling at God, the leaders of Israel decided to take the ark of the covenant with them into battle. You see, they'd realized the reason that they'd lost: God was not with them.

Hophni and Phinehas, the two wicked sons of Eli, felt sure that God would give Israel victory over the Canaanites, especially if they had the ark with them. So they sent for it, and towed the ark into battle. Boy, were they wrong! The Philistines killed 30,000 Israelite foot soldiers, slew Hophni and Phinehas, and captured the ark.

A messenger from the tribe of Benjamin managed to escape, and ran to tell the town of Shiloh of the Israelite defeat. Hearing the terrible news, the people let out a bloodcurdling scream. Ninety-eight-year-old Eli, who was sitting on a chair in front of the tabernacle, heard it and asked what was wrong. He wept at the news of the death of his sons, but when he learned that the ark of the Lord had been captured, the old priest fell backwards in his chair, broke his neck, and died. And Phinehas' pregnant wife, hearing that her husband was dead and that the ark was lost, went into premature labor. When her son was born, she named him Ichabod, meaning "the glory has departed" from Israel.

The Israelites were God's people. Why did God abandon them? After losing the first battle to the Philistines, they asked God that question. However, they didn't wait to hear His answer. Instead, they tried to solve the problem on their own, and were massacred by the Philistines.

What good is it to ask God a question and not wait for His answer?

####### HOT READ #######

Some spoils of war are not worth keeping. Check out 1 Samuel 6:1-9.

——> TRYOUTS <

Listen to all that the people are saying to you; it is not you they have rejected, but they have rejected me as their king. 1 Samuel 8:7.

hen I was in high school, I tried out for the varsity basketball team. I had a decent game—nothing spectacular. No killer crossover, no crazy hops—but I could lock down my man pretty good on defense, I was fast, and my jump shot was decent. So I thought I had a pretty good shot at making the team.

I wasn't the only guy who dreamed of greatness on the hardwood. Guys who had game tried out, but the majority of those who showed up were just there to get a little exercise. *I'm not one of them*, I said to myself. I was going to play varsity at all costs.

I ran all the drills as hard as I could. Shot the ball the best I could. Played defense as well as I could. I knew I would make it. I made the first cut, and then the second. But then came the day for the final cut. I was almost there. I could taste the satisfaction of knowing I had made it.

When the final list came out, I read every square inch of it, only to discover that my name wasn't there. I didn't make it. Twelve other guys were better than I was! For the first time in my short basketball career I felt the sting of rejection. I felt horrible.

Would you believe that the God of the universe feels rejection? He does. Samuel was troubled when the Israelites came to him and asked for a king. He knew immediately that Israel was asking for trouble, but he had no idea just how much their request would hurt God.

Israel was holding a tryout to find a king, but one player wasn't allowed even to come. Samuel felt insulted that Israel didn't trust his leadership—even though his sons were not leading Israel as they should have been. But God encouraged Samuel by pointing out that Israel had rejected, not him, but God!

Israel didn't know what they were asking for when they asked for a king, but they soon found out. Countless suffered under the rule of ruthless kings before they realized that God's way was truly the best.

/////// HOT READ ///////

God never lets us have what we want without warning us of the consequences. Read 1 Samuel 8:8-21.

——> CHANGED! <

As Saul turned to leave Samuel, God changed Saul's heart, and all these signs were fulfilled that day. 1 Samuel 10:9.

ew people in this world mean more to me than my fifth-grade teacher, Mrs. Hall. Until I got to her class, I did OK in school, but in her class I did even better.

You probably remember teachers who wowed you with exciting videos or knocked you over with fascinating stories. Mrs. Hall didn't do any of that. She had one gift that stood out. She always encouraged us to do our best.

She knew I was pretty good at English and reading, so one day she paired me up with James. He was totally lost when it came to reading, but she believed I could help him. I did my best, and James started to improve. I thought no more of it.

Well, Mrs. Hall thought what I did was very cool. How did I know? Well, when my mother showed up at school for parents' night, Mrs. Hall took my mother over to the side and just raved about me. She took her to the board where she put stars for every kid who was doing something great in class, and showed my mom the stars I'd earned. My head grew so big during that parents' night that I had to sleep in the classroom.

I didn't much believe in myself before I got to Mrs. Hall's class. But when I left it for sixth grade, I was a totally different person. Something inside me had changed.

That's how Saul felt as he turned to leave Samuel. Drops of warm olive oil were still visible on his humble face. With a deep sense of astonishment he must have looked longingly at Samuel, unsure of what the future would hold. Just a few hours earlier he was wandering the countryside looking for his father's lost donkeys. He never would have guessed that this day would change his life forever, that he would become Israel's first king!

As Saul left Samuel, God changed his heart. God gave him a new heart, a new mind, and new opportunities to be the very best he could be. When God comes into our lives and calls us for a big job, He doesn't just douse us with oil and let us go. He changes our hearts and positions us for success. Are you ready to be changed?

//////// HOT READ ////////

What one lesson did you learn from Samuel's farewell speech? See 1 Samuel 12.

——> SAUL'S BIG FALL <

"You acted foolishly," Samuel said. "You have not kept the command the Lord your God gave you; if you had, he would have established your kingdom over Israel for all time. But now your kingdom will not endure." 1 Samuel 13:13, 14.

f you've been reading through the Bible with me this year, and I sure hope you have, you know that God is very—VERY—particular about worship. Several days ago we read about the 70 men of a small town called Beth Shemesh. The Philistines had stolen the ark, but after they began breaking out with huge tumors they decided to put it on a cart and send it away.

The ark arrived in Beth Shemesh—Israelite territory—and everyone was excited. In fact, several of the men decided to take a look inside. Bad idea! The presence of God was so closely connected with the ark that the 70 men who looked inside it died (1 Samuel 6:19). Why? God had specified that only Levite priests were supposed to touch the ark, let alone open it up and examine its contents (Numbers 4).

Fast-forward a few chapters, and Saul, the hero of yesterday's devotional, is about to feel the burn. A mere seven days after Saul became king, Samuel made a sad prediction about his future. He would lose his kingdom because he had sinned.

The Israelites were preparing to fight the Philistines, as God had commanded. Before the battle the Israelites worshipped God by presenting burnt offerings to Him. It was a symbol of their trust that He would give them victory. Typically, the high priest—in this case, Samuel—performed the ceremony. Samuel had told Saul to go to a place called Gilgal, prepare for the ceremony, and wait on him. Saul did everything asked of him, but when Samuel didn't show up on time, Saul made a tragic error. He offered the sacrifices—something he was forbidden to do.

Almost immediately after he became king, Saul committed a big blunder that cost him the throne. That may seem like an awfully hard punishment for a one-time act, but God expects us to obey His commands.

There is a reason for everything God asks of you. Take every opportunity to obey God.

///////// HOT READ /////////

Think you're pretty good at making excuses? Think again. See 1 Samuel 13:11-15.

⟶ THE RIGHT STUFF <

But the Lord said to Samuel, "Do not consider his appearance or his height, for I have rejected him. The Lord does not look at the things man looks at. Man looks at the outward appearance, but the Lord looks at the heart." 1 Samuel 16:7.

ason McElwain always wanted to play varsity basketball for Greece Athena High School in Greece, a suburb of Rochester, New York. He tried out but never made the team. Jason never sulked at not being able to play for Greece Athena. Jason lived out his passion for the game by serving as team manager—that's the guy who makes sure that the team has all its equipment, that the Gatorade coolers are full—all the little things that nobody sees.

Jason did his job so well that in the final game of the season the varsity team coach gave him the opportunity to live his life's dream. Jason entered the game with four minutes to play. His first was a three-pointer, and he airmailed it. It didn't hit anything. His next shot? A layup. Yep, he missed that, too. But Jason was fearless. He kept shooting.

He made his next three-pointer, and his next three-pointer, and his next three-pointer, and yeah, his next-three pointer, and his next-three pointer! And yep, his next three-pointer, too! In four minutes Jason McElwain hit *six* three-pointers in a row. He simply could not miss. He was in the zone.

As great as Jason's feat was, his greatest accomplishment may have been his willingness to play at all. Jason is autistic, but he refused to let anything stop him. No one expected much from Jason, but he surprised them.

The man we know today as King David wasn't much to look at either. When the prophet Samuel went to Jesse's home to find Israel's next king, he took one look at Eliab, David's oldest brother, and thought, *Ah, let me get my oil out. This has gotta be the guy.*

But he was wrong. God rejected, one by one, all of Jesse's sons, except the youngest—David. He was just a shepherd boy, but God knew that David had the right stuff to be king. Samuel looked at David's outward appearance and didn't see a king. God looked at David's heart and saw a king.

What does God see when He looks at your heart?

////// HOT READ //////

What trait of greatness does David display in 1 Samuel 17:34-50?

──→ BEST FRIENDS ‹

But if my father is inclined to harm you, may the Lord deal with me, be it ever so severely, if I do not let you know and send you away safely. 1 Samuel 20:13.

f you're not stoked after today's reading, pinch yourself. Check your pulse. Pour some cold water on your head. First Samuel 19-21 is intense.

God has removed His Spirit from Israel's current king, Saul, and His prophet Samuel has secretly anointed David to be the next king. After slaying Goliath and leading Israel to several stunning victories over the Philistines, David becomes the hottest thing since sliced cheese in all of Israel. This upsets Saul greatly, and he puts out a hit on David. It all reads like a movie script.

But the coolest part of this story is the great friendship that develops between Jonathan, Saul's son, and David, Saul's greatest warrior and the man he desperately wants to kill.

I've got friends. You've got some too, I bet. My friends are very special to me. I've got a friend who calls me every week to check on me and see how I'm doing. He's a really busy guy, but he never forgets to call. I've got other friends I can count on to help me if I need just about anything. But I don't have many with whom I would trust my life.

The Bible doesn't tell us whether David felt this way when he first got to know Jonathan. However, Jonathan quickly proved himself worthy of David's trust. Jonathan knew that his father wanted to kill David, and he refused to play along. He vowed to David, "You are not going to die! Look, my father doesn't do anything, great or small, without confiding in me" (1 Samuel 20:2). Jonathan had volunteered to be David's spy in Saul's house.

Saul suspected that Jonathan was helping David, and one day while eating dinner, he exploded at Jonathan's defense of his friend. Saul grabbed his spear and hurled it at Jonathan, narrowly missing him. But even this didn't stop Jonathan from keeping his oath to warn David of danger. Because of their friendship, David was able to escape from Saul. Jonathan was willing to sacrifice his own life for his friend.

//////// HOT READ ////////

What does today's reading teach you about the dangers of jealousy?

──→ THE VOID <

> *Saul was told that David had gone to Keilah, and he said, "God has handed him over to me, for David has imprisoned himself by entering a town with gates and bars."*
> 1 Samuel 23:7.

hat happens to a person when God's Spirit leaves them? It's a tough question, and I've always wanted to know the answer. Do they feel it? Do they sense a void in their heart? Do they get a pounding headache? I'm guessing that when God leaves a person's life, they have no clue. In fact, they may still believe that they're doing God's will. That seems to be what King Saul thought as he chased after David.

Saul was livid when he heard that David had visited Ahimelech, the priest at a place called Nob. "How could the priest not tell me that David was there?" he stormed. So he summoned Ahimelech, along with his entire family, and had one of his henchmen "off them," *Sopranos* style. Saul slaughtered 85 priests that day, as well as all the citizens of Nob—children and infants included (1 Samuel 22). He even killed their cattle.

You'd think that a guy who killed that many people would know that what he was doing was wrong! Right? Not Saul. He believed that God was on his side. Did you notice what he said to himself when he found out that David and his men were in the city of Keilah? "God has handed him over to me," he said (1 Samuel 23:7). He really believed that God was helping him find David so that he could kill him. But nothing could have been further from the truth.

Some of the worst crimes ever committed were by people who claimed that God told them to do it. But there is an enormous difference between people who claim to have God and those who actually do. Know how you can tell? It's easy.

Don't listen to what people say; watch what they do. Then look at God's Word to see if what they're doing lines up with the Scriptures. As you do, remember that people are human and they will make mistakes. We all do. However, Jesus made it clear that many "God talkers" are not "God walkers" (Matthew 7:21).

How can you welcome God's presence into your life today?

/////// HOT READ ///////

How do we know God was with David? See 1 Samuel 24:1-13.
How do you treat your enemies?

——> TWO HOTHEADS AND ONE COOL SISTA <

David said to Abigail, "Praise be to the Lord, the God of Israel, who has sent you today to meet me." 1 Samuel 25:32.

try to stay calm when I drive. I pray before I get on the road. I take deep breaths. I ignore the bikers dodging in and out of highway traffic. I overlook the old man who is going 45 when the speed limit is 65. I even manage to stay cool when everything grinds to a halt. Philadelphia traffic has taught me well.

I'm not sure what came over me one morning on my way to work. Oops— yes, I do. It was a woman in a small gray car—smoke is billowing from my ears right now. I was in the passing lane just driving along when she cut me off. I slammed on my brakes. *She didn't see me,* I thought initially. My heart skipped a beat at the near miss. I kept repeating in my head, *It's OK. Just relax. Deep breaths.* But it wasn't working. She sped away from me, weaving in and out of different lanes. When the traffic in the fast lane slowed, she moved to the right into a slower lane to pass several cars.

But then the traffic ahead of her slowed, so she jumped back into my lane, cutting me off. Again I barely missed hitting her. *That's the last straw*, I thought angrily, and decided to go Formula One on her. I latched onto her bumper and drove hard, tailgating her for several exits. (I can't tell you what I was yelling at her in my car.)

It was not one of my better moments. After several near crashes, I saw the sign for my exit and flashed across the highway just in time to make it. When I got to work, I was so angry that I had to sit in my car to cool off. Then I had to ask God to forgive me for my attitude on the road that day—and thank Him for saving my life. I once saw two road-raging lunatics kill a young boy and severely injure his brother and sister. There, but for the grace of God, go I!

We can make really big mistakes when we're angry. In today's reading David made a huge mistake when he decided to kill Nabal and the men of his home. Nabal had insulted David, but David seriously overreacted. God used Abigail, a coolheaded woman, to save the lives of Nabal and all the males in his household.

If you're prone to getting hot, take a chill pill. Ask God to help you calm down.

//////// HOT READ ////////

It is the song that never ends. Saul's at it again: 1 Samuel 26.

——> DAVID RISING <

*Then David said to Abiathar the priest, the son of Ahimelech, "Bring me the ephod."
Abiathar brought it to him, and David inquired of the Lord, "Shall I pursue this raiding
party? Will I overtake them?" 1 Samuel 30:7, 8.*

We've come to end of the book of 1 Samuel. What a great ride it's been! The book began with the birth of a boy named Samuel. The little tyke grows up to be one of Israel's greatest prophets, and in the final chapters of the book that bears his name, he dies. Saul also dies at the end of 1 Samuel. He commits suicide rather than be captured by the Philistines. What a sad end to his life.

Sure, there's weeping at the end of 1 Samuel, but there's also a great deal of hope. After years on the run, a fearless shepherd boy was about to become king. David's journey to the throne would have to wait a while, though, because he still faced many fierce enemies.

Chief among David's enemies were the Amalekites, who waited for him and his troops to ride off into battle. Once they were gone, the Amalekites attacked Ziklag, the city in which David and his men lived, destroying much of it and kidnapping all the women and children. When David and his troops returned to Ziklag, the sight of their burnt-out homes and missing loved ones was too much to bear. The men began to weep, then turned on David. It was one of the lowest moments in his life.

Have you ever had one of those moments when all seemed lost? Once when I was in college, I returned to the dormitory washroom and discovered that all my clothes were gone. Someone had stolen everything—even my underwear. ILL!

When things seemed hopeless, David went back to the Source. When you grow up a shepherd with no one but sheep to talk to, you learn to talk to God. David could have flown into a rage and went after the Amalekites—sort of the way he did when Nabal insulted him. Instead, David asked God what he should do.

One of the big secrets to handling tough times is knowing whom to go to. When you're in trouble, ask God what you should do, then look for His answers. If you do that, you will rise!

//////// HOT READ ////////

Did you notice that David was hiding out among the Philistines—sworn enemies of Israel? Perhaps this is why David wrote Psalm 23:5.

——> EPISODE 2: THE SAGA CONTINUES <

Then the men of Judah came to Hebron and there they anointed David king over the house of Judah. 2 Samuel 2:4.

All good movies deserve a sequel, and so do good Bible stories. If you thought 1 Samuel was interesting, wait till you get a load of 2 Samuel. But first, a little update.

If you've been faithfully reading the Bible through up to this point, you can't help concluding that humans are really, really messed up. And if you were bold enough to admit it, you've got some hard questions for God—such as *What's up with all the murder of whole groups of people? I thought you were a God who didn't believe in killing* (Exodus 20:13). It's OK. God is not afraid of your questions, or mine—even the hard ones.

From the fall of Adam and Eve in Genesis to David being anointed king over Judah (2 Samuel 2), and later over all of Israel, the picture that the Bible paints of humans is terrible. By the time David takes the throne, Israel is split into two groups. Saul's hit man, Abner, sets up a shadow kingdom in Israel with Ish-Bosheth, Saul's only heir, as king. Israel and Judah fight each other for supremacy. (Cue the *Family Feud* jingle here.)

I've got three older brothers, and the thought of fighting any of them makes me wince. Not because I'm afraid of them, but because I love them. They are my brothers, and brothers just aren't supposed to fight, let alone kill each other.

As you read 2 Samuel, look for the ways in which we humans behave and how God responds to us when we mess up. The star of this sequel is King David. You're about to get a big dose of him, and it's not all good. You'll watch his power grow, and then you'll see him fall from the dizzying height of his power. You'll meet his kids, and if you think their dad's got issues, just keep on reading. Some of his kids are real freaks.

But most of all you'll see God in 2 Samuel. You'll see a God who tells us when we're wrong, sweeps up our messes, loves us through the rough times, and gives us chance after chance to be what He designed us to be.

This sequel's all about God, and that means it's also all about you!

////////// HOT READ //////////

One of the marks of a great leader is the willingness to forgive. Check out David's reaction to news of Saul's death (2 Samuel 1:17-27). David was a great man!

⎯⎯> KARATE IN CHURCH? <

David and the whole house of Israel were celebrating with all their might before the Lord, with songs and with harps, lyres, tambourines, sistrums and cymbals.
2 Samuel 6:5.

ook. *That's gotta be aerobics. But this is a church. Nah, gotta be karate. What's* wrong *with that guy?* Thoughts flashed through my brain like the fireworks from a meteor shower. I wasn't sure what to make of the man in the aisle of my favorite church in Atlanta, Georgia. But one thing was sure: there was no way you could miss him.

I loved visiting this church—which shall remain nameless to protect the innocent and the guilty—whenever I went to see my family in the ATL. The praise and worship time was known to be spirited, and I loved it all. I loved how the pastor came out to the pulpit to prepare the church for worship. He has one of the most beautiful gospel voices you'll ever hear, and his vocal range seems limitless.

On this Sabbath he signaled the beginning of the worship service with a nice slow song, perhaps a little Fred Hammond and his musical group, Radical for Christ. Then Hammond gave way to something a little more up-tempo—a dash of Kurt Carr's "In the Sanctuary," maybe. By this time everyone was on their feet, worshipping God in song. The sound filled the entire room. The church seemed to be levitating.

That's when a man moved into an aisle and started doing karate kicks, jumping in the air and raising one leg way up, almost to his face. I'd never seen anything like it. I knew some people were upset to see that in their church, but I refused to judge this man. I didn't know what was happening in his heart or what God had done for him. So I focused on God instead.

When King David and the people of Judah celebrated the return of God's ark (2 Samuel 6), the Bible says they did so "with all their might." They played every instrument they had, sang loudly, and lifted up the name of the God who had delivered them from all their enemies. David danced before God, even removing his shirt. I don't recommend you go that far, but don't be afraid to praise God with your whole heart.

///////// HOT READ /////////

How did Michal react to David's worship? See 2 Samuel 6:16-23. How did God punish her for her response to David's act of praise?

> DIDN'T COST A THING <

"Don't be afraid," David said to him, "for I will surely show you kindness for the sake of your father Jonathan. I will restore to you all the land that belonged to your grand-father Saul, and you will always eat at my table." 2 Samuel 9:7.

hen Hurricane Dean hit Mexico's Yucatan Peninsula on August 21, 2007, everyone knew there would be significant damage. Packing winds of more than 160 miles per hour, Dean was a rare category 5 hurricane. Only three have ever come ashore in the United States in more than 100 years. The first happened in 1935. That storm was so powerful that it washed a rescue train off the rails and killed nearly 400 people, according to a CNN report on killer hurricanes. Dean did extensive damage to the glitzy tourist area of Cancun, but the damage it did to small Mexican villages near the coast went unreported.

On October 10, 2007, the Chicago *Sun-Times* carried this report on good Samaritan efforts to help. "When Hurricane Dean hit the small Mexican fishing village of Mahahual, Tim Boesen, 18, of Crete, was there working on a five-week conservation project through Global Vision International. Boesen's efforts quickly shifted to hurricane relief, clearing away rubble and rebuilding houses. He'll re-turn home later this month. But for now, he's in Antigua, Guatemala, learning Spanish and building ovens for the indigenous people."

Most people do good deeds only when they know they'll be seen or rewarded for what they do, but not Tim Boesen and not King David. David understood the power of a good deed and the blessing that comes from reaching out to someone in need when you really don't have to.

David found out that the only remaining connection to his best friend, Jonathan, was Mephibosheth, Jonathan's crippled son. He'd made a vow to Jonathan that when he became king he would take care of his descendants, and he never forgot his promise. David brought Mephibosheth to his home, took care of him and his family, and then gave him all the land his father and grandfather once owned. David was king. He didn't have to do anything for Jonathan's kid, but he did it because he remembered how good God had been to him.

Do something good for someone today. Keep it anonymous.

///////// HOT READ /////////

How could a noble king like David fall so fast? See 2 Samuel 11.

> DON'T GO SIGHTSEEING <

In it he wrote, "Put Uriah in the front line where the fighting is fiercest.
Then withdraw from him so he will be struck down and die." 2 Samuel 11:15.

A few years ago I was asked by a youth director to be the camp meeting speaker for the youth of his conference. I was a bit scared at first—public speaking is the *numero uno* fear of most Americans, and I'm in that group. (It even beats out terrorism.) The first night went well. I got to know many of the teens and kids, and they were really cool. On the fourth night—don't ask me why—I felt impressed to talk about the importance of sexual purity. I even shared the testimony of how I had struggled to overcome pornography—a problem that began when I went sightseeing in some of my friends' dirty magazines. This is the mistake that I regret most in my life, because that decision started something that dogged me for many years.

The day after my message a few guys asked to speak with me. "Dwain," they began somewhat sheepishly, "you know how last night you talked about purity, and about King David's sin, and how you'd messed with watching porn?"

"Yeah," I answered.

"Well, we got the same problem." By now the guys' heads were down. They knew what they were doing was wrong. But then they said something else. "Last night we went off into the woods and destroyed all our porn. We just want you to pray for us, that God will help us to stay pure." I was really touched by what they'd shared with me. When they went sightseeing, they never figured on getting addicted.

Neither did King David. When he stood on his palace roof and watched Bathsheba take a bath, he had no clue that his sightseeing tour would cause so much grief. Not only did he summon Bathsheba to him—he took her to bed, then arranged the murder of her husband. After Uriah's death David made Bathsheba his wife. It was definitely a scandal!

God's judgment was swift and unrelenting. David and Bathsheba's baby died, and God made it clear that because David murdered Uriah with an Ammonite sword, "the sword will never depart from your house" (2 Samuel 12:10).

######### HOT READ #########

Read 2 Samuel 12:13, 14. How do our sins make God look to others?

——> "THE JUMPOFF" <

In the course of time, Amnon son of David fell in love with Tamar, the beautiful sister of Absalom son of David. 2 Samuel 13:1.

esterday we read about David's sin with Bathsheba. Today we'll read about the fallout from that sin. Remember, God told David through the prophet Nathan that "the sword will never depart from your house" (2 Samuel 12:10). Translation? There will be fighting and killing in your family for as long as your descendants walk the earth.

Nathan's fearful prediction didn't take very long to come true. When Amnon, King David's son, "fell in love" with his half sister Tamar, he must've bumped his head. I love my little sister, but the thought of dating her has never crossed my mind. Man, I used to go bananas if other guys tried to hook up with her.

Amnon wanted Tamar so badly that he got sick over the situation. A turning point in his life happened when he listened to Jonadab, his cousin, who told him how he could get Tamar. (Note to self: Be careful whom you listen to!)

"Am, I got the hookup, man," Jonadab whispered. "Act like you're sick, and tell your dad to send her to your room with some food, and hey! She's yours, man." Amnon listened. Then—just as his father did with Bathsheba—he hatched a plot to have her.

When Tamar came to his room with food, Amnon grabbed her and raped her, despite her pleas for him not to do it. Shamed and confused, Tamar told her brother Absalom. He was outraged, and he was not alone. "When King David heard all this, he was furious" (2 Samuel 13:21)—and yet David did nothing about it. Two years passed, and still Amnon's father, the king, had not confronted or punished him. Absalom grew more and more angry. *How can my father do nothing about this?* he raged, and finally he decided to make Amnon pay.

Absalom arranged a feast and invited all of the king's sons. He specifically asked his father to send Amnon, who, by now, had forgotten all about Tamar. At the height of the feast a drunken Amnon was approached by several of Absalom's men. And on Absalom's order, the men slew him. With that, the sword entered David's house, and his home would never be the same again.

####### HOT READ #######

Why did Absalom try to overthrow his father? See 2 Samuel 14:24-33.

⎯⎯> PLEASE BE GENTLE <

The king commanded Joab, Abishai and Ittai, "Be gentle with the young man Absalom for my sake." 2 Samuel 18:5.

A t the time of this writing, Coach Andy Reid of the Philadelphia Eagles is going through a major crisis. The Eagles aren't playing well—they're 2-4—but that's not his biggest problem. His problems are more personal.

On January 30, 2007, in an odd twist of fate, both of his sons, Britt and Garret, had major run-ins with law enforcement. Britt Reid, the younger of the two Reid boys, had words with another motorist during a road-rage incident. Reid threatened the other motorist, then pointed a gun at the man and smiled before driving off. The frightened man called police and gave them Reid's license plate number.

The cops searched for Britt Reid, but didn't find him until later the same day when he arrived at the scene of an accident. His older brother, Garrett, had just run a red light and hit another driver. When the cops checked both vehicles, they found drug paraphernalia. Garrett Reid later admitted that he had shot up with heroin the morning before he got on the road.

In November 2007, the Reid boys were sentenced to jail terms for gun and drug charges. The judge called the Reid home a "drug emporium," as numerous drugs and weapons were found there. Sitting in court that day, Andy and Tammy Reid no doubt hoped that the judge would be merciful. That's how King David felt as he prepared to battle Absalom, his son. He begged Joab, his deadly military general, to "be gentle" with Absalom, to bring him back alive.

But Joab had other plans. Perhaps he remembered that Absalom had burned his field a few years earlier (2 Samuel 14:28-33). When Joab found Absalom caught in an oak tree by his head, he "took three javelins in his hand and plunged them into Absalom's heart" (2 Samuel 18:14), doing exactly what the king had begged him not to do.

Once again, the sword returned to David's house as a result of his sin with Bathsheba.

///////// HOT READ /////////

Do you have a friend like Ittai, someone who would help you in a crisis? Read 2 Samuel 15:19-21.

——> THE SNOWMEN <

The king said to Barzillai, "Cross over with me and stay with me in Jerusalem, and I will provide for you." 2 Samuel 19:33.

It happens right after a major snowstorm in cities and towns all over the northeastern United States. The sane dare not leave their homes, save for the sheer pleasure of skiing through normally busy streets, taking some hills on a snowboard, or engaging in a little mortal combat—snowball-style!

Having an insanely great time is about the only reason to be outside on major snow days, but that's not true for everyone. The "snowmen," as I like to call them, have no time for making angels in the snow or admiring the pristine beauty of a near whiteout. No, for these captains of capitalism, white powder means green cheese.

Even before the snow stops falling, teenage boys trudge their way through thick drifts in search of people who need their walkways, driveways, or sidewalks shoveled. They'd take a stab at your roof if you paid them enough. I know—I used to be one of these abominable snowmen, and there wasn't anything we wouldn't do to make some money.

We'd move mounds of snow, but only for those who would pay. But I did have half a heart back then. I couldn't just walk by a senior citizen struggling to clear their walkway. But many guys could do it without a problem. They wouldn't help a bit until the deal was made.

King David understood the importance of caring for seniors. Barzillai, a man who was not an Israelite, helped the king and his men when they were forced to flee from Absalom. They brought bedding and bowls, wheat and barley, flour and grain, beans and lentils, cheese and milk—a feast for David's hungry band.

Barzillai wanted nothing in return, but King David did not forget the kindness. As he prepared to return to Israel as the rightful king following Absalom's death, he begged Barzillai to come back with him. "Let me take care of you," David pleaded. Barzillai refused the offer. He wanted to die in his own country, close to his home.

There are many things we can to do for senior citizens and not ask anything in return. It's nice to give to others and let God return the favor.

///////// HOT READ ///////

Read 2 Samuel 19:18-23. Do you forgive people who wrong you?

⟶ GIVE IT UP! <

For who is God besides the Lord? And who is the Rock except our God?
2 Samuel 22:32.

ing David is the best musician and songwriter in all of Scripture. Oops! Strike that. God is the best musician and songwriter in the Bible, because He is the one who gives us puny humans the talent. But among humans, David is about as good as they come.

Through many hard struggles David learned that God is the only being worthy of praise. Think David's wrong about that? You won't after you hear the story of Hwang Woo Suk, of South Korea. John C. Maxwell, guru of all things leadership, recounted the story of Hwang in his book *Talent Is Never Enough.*

Maxwell noted that Hwang's place at the top of medical science seemed almost assured. A 2004 issue of *Time* magazine said, "Hwang and his team at Seoul National University became the first to clone human embryos capable of yielding viable stem cells that might one day cure countless diseases." That may not sound like much, but Hwang and his team had managed to pull off something that no other researcher in the world had been able to do. Or did he?

Hwang's fame grew so much that he was named supreme scientist by South Korea's Ministry of Science and Technology. He was da man. But questions started to arise shortly after Hwang's discovery. Some of his coworkers questioned his processes, and later investigations showed that Hwang had lied. He had not cloned human embryos.

Hwang's fall from the top was swift. When asked about why he falsified his findings, this is what he said. "I was blinded by work and my drive for achievement." Hwang had grown up poor and worked hard his entire life to achieve greatness. When he got close to his goal, his desire to be recognized made him compromise his integrity.

God is about the only being who handles praise well. This does not mean that we should not recognize people who do great things. We should, but praise is a like perfume: Wear it lightly, and don't ever drink it.

///////// HOT READ /////////

What do you think King David meant when he sang, "He [God] makes my feet like the feet of a deer" (2 Samuel 22:34)?

——> 'BYE, DAVE—HELLO, SOL! <

Take your lord's servants with you and set Solomon my son on my own mule and take him down to Gihon. There have Zadok the priest and Nathan the prophet anoint him king over Israel. Blow the trumpet and shout, "Long live King Solomon!"
1 Kings 1:33, 34.

t's never easy to say goodbye. In 2 Samuel we met a fearless teen who slew a giant, survived numerous assassination attempts, and became Israel's greatest king. Not bad for a simple shepherd boy, huh? Now the years, though kind, have caught up to him. His successor waits in the wings. God had told King David that Solomon would succeed him, but David failed to tell his other sons, especially Adonijah.

Perhaps David was trying to avoid regurgitating the whole Bathsheba incident—you remember that, don't you? David lusted after Uriah's wife, slept with her, then proceeded to have Uriah killed when he found out that she was pregnant. Adonijah sure didn't get the e-mail about Solomon's imminent reign, so he, along with Joab, David's military genius, started a coup. Adonijah declared himself king, found a priest to anoint him so, and prepared to rule the realm. But it was not to be.

King David, though feeble and at the point of death, acted quickly after hearing what Adonijah had done. He summoned Zadok, the priest; Benaiah, his military enforcer (you'll want to remember this guy); and Nathan, the prophet who had confronted him about his sin with Bathsheba. Together they successfully installed Solomon as Israel's next king.

Adonijah's supporters fled when they heard that God, through David, had declared Solomon king. Solomon could have killed his older brother for his treachery—later he does, because of another evil act (1 Kings 2), but he didn't then. Solomon forgave Adonijah (1 Kings 1:52, 53).

First Kings is Solomon's coming-out party. It is also the book that most powerfully captures the story of Solomon falling away from God and how that changed Israel forever. As you read 1 Kings, once again you'll come face to face with one of the main themes of the Bible: obeying God is not optional; it is essential to success in life.

//////// HOT READ ////////

Please do not fail to read 1 Kings 3. If God promised to give you anything you wanted, what would you ask for? Solomon's answer should be yours!

April 7 • *1 Kings 4-6*

——> WHAT A CRIB! <

> *In the four hundred and eightieth year after the Israelites had come out of Egypt, in the fourth year of Solomon's reign over Israel, in the month of Ziv, the second month, he began to build the temple of the Lord.* 1 Kings 6:1.

s King Solomon set out on the most ambitious, most "awesomest" building project ever tried in the biblical world, he decided that he'd spare no expense and cut no corner. God had tabbed Solomon to be the architect of His house, something that many Israelites—including King David—had yearned to do for more than 400 years.

Not many people build exquisite places for God. Humans usually build great structures for themselves. Take, for instance, the "sick" crib that Bill Gates, Microsoft founder and world's richest man, created for himself in Medina, Washington.

The 50,000-square-foot house sits on just over five acres, and is built into the side of a hill overlooking Lake Washington. Compared to the 2,500 square feet of the average American home, Gates's spot is gargantuan. Does your home sport a pool with an underwater sound system, an exercise facility better than most health clubs, a reception hall, library, offices, gatehouse, boathouse, activities building, or an estuary stocked with salmon and cutthroat trout? I didn't think so. When was the last time homeland security shut down the airspace around your place for a dinner party? Of course, it was a two-day party for the nation's governors. Show-off!

Solomon's house for God took about the same time to complete as Gates's compound—seven years. But unlike the Gateses, Solomon couldn't hire a contractor to bring in heavy equipment to prepare the site. Trucks weren't going to roll into Jerusalem with the wood and stone needed for the Temple. When Solomon wanted cedar wood for the Temple walls, the logs were cut in Lebanon and floated down the river where Solomon's workers hauled them out from the river road. All of this was done via human power (i.e., sweat).

As great as Solomon's Temple for God was, there was something more special about what he did. He built God's house before he built his own. Before he hooked up himself, he took care of God. Have you built a place in your life for God?

////// HOT READ //////

How wise was King Solomon? 1 Kings 4:29-34 says it all.

105

——> INSIDE JOB <

When the priests withdrew from the Holy Place, the cloud filled the temple of the Lord. And the priests could not perform their service because of the cloud, for the glory of the Lord filled his temple. 1 Kings 8:10, 11.

Ever notice that things get better when certain people show up? They don't have to be the best dressed or the most popular. They're known more for what they have on the inside than what they do on the outside. Wesley Autrey is one of those people, and Donald Trump wrote in the 2007 *Time's 100 Most Influential People in the World* about what it was like to meet him.

Wesley Autrey never craved fame or attention, but it found him on January 2, 2007 in, of all places, a subway platform in New York City. Autrey was waiting for a train when nearby a young man had a seizure and fell onto the tracks. Wouldn't you know it! A train was just entering the station. The youth faced certain death.

Autrey, a construction worker, figured that if he could cover the young man and keep him still, there might be enough space for the train to pass over them without killing them. In a heartbeat he jumped onto the tracks and pressed his body atop that of the helpless young man. The train roared into the station, screaming as it went by. As it exited the station, Autrey rose to his feet and helped carry the young man to safety.

The train passed over them so closely that Autrey's cap was covered in train grease. Millionaire businessman Donald Trump was so moved by Autrey's bravery that he wanted to meet him, presenting him with a check for $10,000. Trump noted, "I wanted to meet a real hero." The unassuming hero felt that what he did was simply the right thing to do.

When God's presence filled the temple Solomon built for Him, all Israel stopped to pay attention. Entering their presence was a Being whose selfless love had brought them from Egyptian slavery to peace in the Promised Land. What had been a terrific dedication took on new meaning when the Guest of honor showed up! God's presence was the reason Solomon built the Temple.

////// HOT READ //////

Read carefully Solomon's prayer of dedication over the Temple (1 Kings 8:22-61). Why do you think Solomon was so specific in His requests of God?

———> THE WORLD AT YOUR DOOR <

The whole world sought audience with Solomon to hear the wisdom God had put in his heart. 1 Kings 10:24.

hen God gives people special gifts and talents, He really holds nothing back. As a teen I sat in stunned silence as Michael Jordan dropped a "double nickel" on the New York Knicks on March 28, 1995. Jordan's otherworldly B-ball skills had made him the first global sports icon in history. Kids from Africa to America wanted to "be like Mike."

Who could blame them? He seemed to have it all. Millions in the bank, a gorgeous wife, beautiful kids, a fragrance bearing his name, exotic cars, a mansion in the Chicago suburbs—not to mention an entire city that worshipped his every move. He had it all, but then he lost it all—at least most of it, anyway.

The riches are still there, as are the cars, houses, and some fame. His wife? Well, she's gone. Why? A few years ago she found herself at the center of the nation's attention when one of her husband's extramarital affairs became public. After a brief reconciliation, Michael and Juanita Jordan divorced. God gave Michael Jordan his superior physical ability. This ability drew people to him, but like a long string of failed public figures, Jordan lacked the character needed to manage his gift.

King Solomon also lacked the all-important character needed to manage the gifts of wisdom and riches that he possessed. Solomon's great wisdom made him *the* global icon of the then known world. As you will read today, the queen of Sheba came to ply him with difficult questions. Solomon's greatness left her dazzled (1 Kings 10:6-9).

But Solomon's greatness was corrupted because he "loved many strange women" (1 Kings 11:1, KJV). God knew that love relationships with the wrong people can destroy one's gifts *and* one's relationship with Him. Solomon built temples to the gods of his many wives, causing all of Israel to commit sin. Even wise guys can mess up.

Never let a friendship or relationship take you away from God.

/////// HOT READ ///////

What terrible judgment did God pronounce on Solomon? See 1 Kings 11:11-13. Do you see a bit of God's grace in these verses?

107

——> SPLITSVILLE! <

I tore the kingdom away from the house of David and gave it to you, but you have not been like my servant David, who kept my commands and followed me with all his heart, doing only what was right in my eyes. 1 Kings 14:8.

esterday's Hot Reads scripture is the window to understanding the rest of the book of 1 Kings. Here's a quick Cliff Notes summary of yesterday's main points. Solomon married many foreign women who turned his heart away from God (1 Kings 11:4); as a result, God removed the kingdom of Israel from Solomon's son, Rehoboam, except for the tribes of Judah and Benjamin. He was allowed to rule Judah only because God wanted King David's legacy to live on. (David was from the tribe of Judah.) The other 10 Israelite tribes, referred to as the northern kingdom, would be ruled by Jeroboam, the subject of the Scripture above.

If there ever was a guy in the Bible who had "hookup"—you know, everything going for him—it had to be Jeroboam. When God tore the Israelite kingdom away from Solomon because of his idolatry, He sent the prophet Ahijah to Jeroboam, letting him know that God had selected him to be king over 10 of Israel's 12 tribes (1 Kings 11:34-38). God promised Jeroboam that he would be king over all his heart could ever desire. He promised Jerry a dynasty as great as King David's. But there was one requirement: obedience. God would exalt Jeroboam, but only after Jeroboam exalted God!

That's as good a deal as anyone in the Bible had been offered, next to the gift of salvation God offers to you and me. But Jeroboam didn't want it. He went "Paris Hilton" on God. Heir to a great blessing if he remained obedient, he spent his riches doing what pleased him instead.

When Jeroboam became king, he built two golden calves—does that ring a bell?—for the Israelites to worship. He feared that the people would follow Rehoboam if they traveled each week to worship at Jerusalem in Judah. He didn't stop there. Jeroboam made altars to foreign gods in the hills, and hired his own priests to serve the people. God was so hurt by Jeroboam's actions that He said, "You have . . . thrust me behind your back" (1 Kings 14:9). Why did Jeroboam forget the God who had given him everything?

////////// HOT READ ////////

What made King Asa a special king? See 1 Kings 15:11-14.

> TRIAL BY FIRE <

Elijah went before the people and said, "How long will you waver between two opin-ions? If the Lord is God, follow him; but if Baal is God, follow him." 1 Kings 18:21.

everal months ago I told you the story of Aron Ralston, the mountain climber who amputated his arm after getting it caught between a rock and a hard place. What are the chances that someone else would be forced to do the same thing?

Most recently Sampson Packer, a corn farmer from South Carolina, faced the same daunting choice. He'd been clearing his field using his corn picker when stalks got caught in the machine's rollers. Sampson stuck his right hand in to remove the stalks. Oops!

The more Mr. Packer attempted to free his hand, the worse the situation became. Beginning to panic, he grabbed a metal pole and stuck it into the machine. That briefly stopped it, but soon made things worse. Sparks from the machine ignited the ground, causing a fire. Packer would lose his life if he could not free his hand.

Sampson Packer then took out a small knife that he carried with him and began removing his fingers. He then cut his arm off and pulled away from the corn picker that was by now engulfed in flames. The fire made Packer's decision easier, he said. He wanted to live!

When Elijah called a big showdown on Mount Carmel to see whether King Ahab and Queen Jezebel's god, Baal, was greater than the true God, he did so because God wanted Israel to make a choice. Ahab and Jezebel had led Israel into deep sin, erecting temples to evil gods. No king had done more evil in God's sight than Ahab (1 Kings 16:30).

Before he began, Elijah yelled to the thousands of Israelites assembled, "If Baal is your God, follow him. But if the Lord is God, then follow Him." The Bible goes on to say, "But the people said nothing" (1 Kings 18:21). The nation of Israel faced certain destruction if they continued in sin, yet when given the chance to choose God—to live—they made no choice. It wasn't until after God sent fire down from heaven and consumed Elijah's offering that the people shouted, "The Lord—he is God!" (verse 39).

Have you chosen to follow God today? Why not do it now?

/////// HOT READ ///////

If God sent birds to feed Elijah, why is it so hard for us to trust Him?

——> I HATE HIM <

The king of Israel answered Jehoshaphat, "There is still one man through whom we can inquire of the Lord, but I hate him because he never prophesies anything good about me, but always bad. He is Micaiah son of Imlah." 1 Kings 22:8.

ow's that for a rousing recommendation? "There is a guy who God speaks to, but I hate him," said King Ahab to King Jehoshaphat of Judah. If you're honest—and I know you are—you've been there. You've either disliked certain people for what they say or do, or you've been "dissed" because of what you said or did.

At college I met a young man who was a lot like Micaiah. No, he wasn't a prophet, but he was the son of one. OK, his dad probably doesn't think of himself as a prophet, but he is a pastor, and God speaks through him. But I digress. I met Morris while working as a resident assistant in the freshman dormitory. Morris was from Alabama, and talked with a slow, deliberate Southern drawl. He had a bright smile and he carried a peace about him that most freshmen didn't possess.

Morris had friends, but it was clear from the time he walked on campus that he wasn't going to be the "da man." Guys wouldn't be crowding into his room late at night to hang out. He was just too straight for that. At night he went to bed, unlike those guys we caught sneaking through windows to go who knows where. Morris was a godly presence, a quiet unassuming witness who made many guys uncomfortable. Unlike some, he wouldn't do things to get into to trouble, so many people sorta wrote him off. He was wound way too tight for their liking.

That's exactly how evil King Ahab felt about Micaiah. He hated him because everything Micaiah prophesied seemed to condemn Ahab. When Micaiah told Ahab that he'd die in battle, Ahab responded by throwing him in prison. Ahab should have listened, because Micaiah was right again! It never occurred to Ahab that instead of hating Micaiah, he should try to be like him—obedient to the voice of God.

Don't "diss" people who stand for what's right. Join them.

/////// HOT READ ///////

Ever wonder why more girls aren't named Jezebel? Read 1 Kings 21:1-11. Why was Jezebel able to corrupt Ahab so completely?

——> UP, UP, AND AWAY! <

As they were walking along and talking together, suddenly a chariot of fire and horses of fire appeared and separated the two of them, and Elijah went up to heaven in a whirlwind. 2 Kings 2:11.

don't know about you, but my heart is kinda torn as I begin reading the book of 2 Kings. I don't want to say goodbye to Elijah, do you? Who else would have to the nerve to go up on a mountain to duel with 850 devil-worshipping priests? Who else would dare ask a poor widow for her last meal? Who would lie down on the dead body of a young boy—not once, but three times?

Elijah is one of the true heroes of the Bible, and in many ways he is a "type" of Christ. The miracles he performed in the service of humanity represent the same love and care for people that Jesus showed during His earthly ministry. And Elisha, his protégé, exceeds even Elijah in this way.

As I read today's section, I felt the same vacuum that Elisha must have felt when he knew that his master, Elijah, was going to be taken away by God. If you carefully read 2 Kings 2, you see that Elisha knows that something is about to go down—or rather, up! When Elijah begged him to stay behind as he prepared to go to Bethel, Elisha responded, "As surely as the Lord lives . . . , I will not leave you" (verse 2). Elijah tried to ditch him two more times, but Elisha didn't take the bait. He knew that God was going to take Elijah, and he wanted to be there to see it.

Then one day, as they walked together, the sky suddenly seemed like fire. Toward them, on a roaring whirlwind, raced horse-drawn chariots bathed in fire. Elisha froze, as in an instant Elijah's feet left the ground, pulled heavenward by the powerful wind. Gathered into one of the fiery chariots, he dropped his cloak for Elisha and disappeared in a whirl of fire. "My father! My father!" Elisha cried, and he saw Elijah no more.

God wanted Elijah with Him so badly that He refused to let him die. Isn't that amazing? Though Elisha missed Elijah, he was not left powerless. Before Elijah's ascension, Elisha asked him for a double portion of his spirit (verse 9), and he got it!

///////// HOT READ /////////

Elisha's bold request changed his life forever. Why did God grant his wish?

——> BLESSED ARE THE MERCIFUL! <

When the king of Israel saw them, he asked Elisha, "Shall I kill them, my father? Shall I kill them?" 2 Kings 6:21.

ighty-six years I have served Christ, and He never did me any wrong. How can I blaspheme my King who saved me?" Those are the words of a Christian martyr named Polycarp. Polycarp was a disciple of Christ who learned the gospel from John the revelator, the disciple left on the island of Patmos to die. Like John, Polycarp's faith seemed almost indestructible.

As bishop of Smyrna, Polycarp wrote letters encouraging the believers in the church at Philippi, where the apostle Paul had established congregations. He combated heresies and shared the good news of Jesus' death and resurrection with all who would listen.

This attracted the attention of the Roman authorities, who viewed the tiny sect of Christ followers as a cult that needed to be destroyed. The Romans began to kill Christians everywhere. It wouldn't be long before they would get to old Polycarp.

When his pursuers caught up to him, the old man arranged a meal for the soldiers and fed them until they were full. Then he asked them for one moment to pray before they took him to be judged. They agreed, and Polycarp prayed. Later, given a chance to recant his faith and deny Christ, he said the now-famous words quoted above. Sadly, Polycarp was killed.

If you got the upper hand on your enemy, would you do something good for them? I've often wondered why Polycarp didn't lace the soldiers' meal with poison. After reading 2 Kings 6, I have to ask a similar question about Elisha. Why didn't Elisha let the king of Israel slaughter the garrisons of soldiers sent by the king of Aram to kill him? After all, Elisha had healed Naaman, the commander of the Aramean forces.

Here's what Elisha directed the king to do: "Set food and water before them so that they may eat and drink and then go back to their master" (2 Kings 6:22). The feast was prepared, the soldiers ate all they wanted, and then were sent back home.

What good did this act of kindness bring? Read 2 Kings 6:23. Amen!

////// HOT READ //////

Why did Elisha refuse Naaman's gifts of appreciation (2 Kings 5)? Did you notice how greed destroyed the life of Elisha's servant, Gehazi (verses 19-27)?

112

——> RISKS WORTH TAKING <

Now there were four men with leprosy at the entrance of the city gate.
They said to each other, "Why stay here until we die?" 2 Kings 7:3.

ave you been faithful in reading the Bible through so far? If not, today's Bible passage is a great place to get started again. If you're into swashbuckling battles, there's no shortage of it in the next few chapters we'll read together. Sadly, though, God's people—both Israel and Judah—are reaping the consequences of their many sins.

Yet things are not all gloom and doom. There are light moments in the middle of the chaos, such as the one found in 2 Kings 6 and 7. King Ben-Hadad of Aram, Israel's enemy, surrounded Samaria, the capital city of the Israel—the northern kingdom—and refused to let anything or anyone in or out of Samaria. Soon Israel began to run out of food. With each passing day Ben-Hadad and his troops could hear the wail of hungry children and cries of animals. He could smell the rank, rotting carcasses of Israel's dead.

The Israelites grew so hungry that they began to eat animals they'd never ever dreamt of eating. A donkey's head was a prized item, selling for an expensive price (2 Kings 6:25). Some parents even ate their children! The king of Israel lost it when a woman came to him complaining that she had made a pact with another woman (verses 28, 29). They'd decided that they'd cook their sons and share the meals. Her son was killed and eaten first, but then the second woman refused to let *her* son be killed! (Uh, can you say horror movie? Quick, call Stephen King!)

In desperate times, people sometimes do desperate things—like eating humans—while others take far bigger risks. Four lepers decided that they'd rather go to the camp of the enemy Arameans—where there was plenty of food—than die of starvation in Samaria. "Who knows," they reasoned, "they might take one look at our scrawny, emaciated bodies and pardon us. Either way, it's better than staying here." When they reached the enemy's camp, they found it deserted. Food was everywhere! They ate and ate and ate, and then ate some more. They couldn't believe their good fortune.

Sometimes you just have to take a risk, even when things look hopeless.

//////// HOT READ ////////

Jehu was one of the most fearsome leaders in the Bible, as you will soon find out. Are there times when it is necessary to use violence? See 2 Kings 9:6-10.

——> HIT MAN <

> So Jehu killed everyone in Jezreel who remained of the house of Ahab, as well as all his chief men, his close friends and his priests, leaving him no survivor.
> 2 Kings 10:11.

oes God have hit men? That question kept punching its way through my head as I read today's Bible passage. The answer, I'm afraid to say, is yes. But God's enforcers are quite different from the old pizza-eating monsters of *Soprano* fame. God rarely dispatches His hit men, and He does so only after all other offers of mercy have been rejected.

Jehu was the enforcer that God raised up to destroy Ahab and his descendants. King Ahab, as we learned a few days ago, was perhaps the wickedest king in Israel's history. So wicked were he and Jezebel that God sent Elijah to Ahab with this message: "You have sold yourself to do evil in the eyes of the Lord. 'I am going to bring disaster on you. I will consume your descendants and cut off from Ahab every last male in Israel—slave or free'" (1 Kings 21:20, 21).

Why was God "hatin'" on Ahab? Not only had Ahab and Jezebel led Israel to worship the heathen god Baal—they had built a temple for Baal in the heart of Israel's capital, Samaria, and worshipped there. They had tried to murder all of the true priests who worshipped Israel's God. If Obadiah had not hidden some of them, all would have been killed (1 Kings 18:3-5). Add to that the fact that even after Elijah called down fire from heaven on Mount Carmel, leading Israel back to God, Ahab and Jezebel led Israel back into Baal worship again. All of Ahab's descendants were evil. His gene pool was tainted.

When Jezebel engineered the murder of Naboth because he refused to give up his land to King Ahab (1 Kings 21), God prepared to unleash Jehu on the house of Ahab. Jehu stamped out Ahab, Jezebel, all their descendants—including Ahaziah, king of Judah whose mother was Athaliah, Ahab's daughter. He disposed of the priests who served Baal and turned the temple of Baal into a public toilet.

At times God raises a strong, decisive—some might say cold-blooded—leader to execute his judgments on the earth. Jehu was one of these men.

///////// HOT READ /////////

Some people claim that God has sent them to "punish" sinners. How can we be sure that God sent them? Do you think the Israelites believed that God sent Jehu?

——> NO CHANGE <

Then Jehoahaz sought the Lord's favor, and the Lord listened to him, for he saw how severely the king of Aram was oppressing Israel. . . . But they did not turn away from the sins of the house of Jeroboam, which he had caused Israel to commit.
2 Kings 13:4-6.

ld habits die hard," the old saying goes, and that's no more true for anyone than it is for Amy Stultz's father. I came across her story on scrapjazz.com, a site for people who love to do scrapbooking. I'm not one of those people, but I'm glad I found Amy's story. Here's what she wrote about her dad's unbreakable habit of taking two showers a day:

"My father has to take two showers every single day of his life. It does not even matter if he has not left the house or not gotten dirty over the course of the day; he must take two showers. The first of these showers is taken immediately after waking up, and the second is taken prior to going to bed. After exiting the shower he must brush his hair with the same brush he has owned all 29 years of my life and let it air-dry before he can do anything else. . . . Once we challenged him to go to bed without showering. . . . [But] in the middle of the night we caught him taking a shower and fixing his hair with that same old yellow hairbrush."

Sound like anyone you know? One of our biggest blessings as humans is our ability to form habits. Unfortunately, that's also one of our biggest curses, especially when negative habits get in the way of positive changes.

Ancient Israel, the northern kingdom, faced this problem. Jeroboam set up a counterfeit system of worship in Israel (1 Kings 12:25-33) that remained in place until Israel was finally captured by the mighty Assyrians. In Judah, five generations of kings—Asa, Joash, Amaziah, Azariah, and Jotham—all failed to destroy idol worship.

When Israel's evil king Jehoahaz cried out to God for help against the Arameans who had occupied huge swaths of Israelite land, God heard his cry and promised to raise up a deliverer to free Israel (2 Kings 13). And so He did. You'd think that after being freed by God they would put away their other gods and worship the true God. NOT! They kept on sinning as they had before!

Do we sometimes return to old sins even after God has offered us grace?

//////// HOT READ ////////

What violent pattern do you see in 2 Kings 15? What's the lesson here?

——> THE BULLY, PART 1 <

This is what the king says: Do not let Hezekiah deceive you. He cannot deliver you from my hand. 2 Kings 18:29.

ullies come in all shapes and sizes. Some are short. Others are tall. Some of the hottest guys and girls in school who get all the attention bully other students. Some kids become bullies to get attention. Whatever the reason for bullying, one thing's for sure. No one likes to be bullied. Not even bullies like to be bullied.

The kingdom of Assyria is one of the Bible's biggest bullies. While Israel and Judah were growing weaker because of their sins, Assyria was getting stronger. The Assyrians were the kind of bullies who pummeled you and then told the world about it. If you tried to become friendly with them to avoid their wrath, you became their slave. That's what happened to King Ahaz of Judah when he asked Tiglath-Pileser—I call him Tiggy—for help against King Rezin of Aram, and Pekah, king of Israel (2 Kings 16:7-9). Why the king of Israel was helping an enemy nation destroy their brothers and sisters in Judah, I'll never know. Nothing screws up a family like the hate caused by sin, huh?

After bribing Tiggy with gold and silver stripped from the Lord's Temple and his own palace, Ahaz bought the bully's support. Tiggy delivered a massive victory against Aram and Israel. He killed Rezin, and forced Pekah and Israel to pay huge sums of money to him to prevent total destruction. Ahaz was ecstatic!

"Now what you got to say, Israel?" I hear him yell. "Who's da man now?" Ahaz traveled to Damascus, the capital of Assyria, to meet with his powerful friend, Tiggy the Bully. He made drawings of its temples to heathen gods and recreated them in Judah. He even changed Judah's worship service to please the Tigster (verse 16:18).

All people who try to make nice with bullies soon find out that bullies are never, ever satisfied. After Tiggy, Shalmaneser rose to power in Egypt. What Tiggy began, Shalmaneser finished. When Hoshea, Israel's new king, stopped paying tribute to Assyria, Shalmaneser totally destroyed the kingdom of Israel and deported all its people to Assyria. Ahaz's deal with the bully got rid of Israel, but bullies are never satisfied.

///////// HOT READ ////////

Ever wonder why God would leave someone? Second Kings 17:7-23 will answer that question for you. God is forgiving, but even His grace has an end.

——> THE BULLY, PART 2 <

Then Isaiah son of Amoz sent a message to Hezekiah: "This is what the Lord, the God of Israel, says: I have heard your prayer concerning Sennacherib king of Assyria." 2 Kings 19:20.

o bully is really worth his or her salt if he or she can't talk a good game. I once heard a bully say to someone, "Say one more thing and I'm gonna come over there and punch you, dead in your eye!" I knew he meant what he said, because his words just stunk up the whole joint. There was major halitosis in that fulmination—if you know what I mean.

No Bible bully—this side of Satan, of course—could talk more game than Sennacherib, the king of Assyria who followed Shalmaneser. Here's what he wrote to Hezekiah king of Judah (and yes, that's the same Judah whose King Ahaz made a deal years earlier with Assyria to destroy Israel and Aram): "On what are you basing this confidence of yours? You say you have strategy and military strength—but you speak only empty words. On whom are you depending, that you rebel against me?" (2 Kings 18:19, 20). Translation? "Are you sure you want a piece of me?"

Sennacherib said a bunch of other threatening stuff, then he called out a Who's Who list of nations he'd defeated, all of whom thought their gods could protect them from him. Old Senn talked more trash than Muhammad Ali, the "mouthiest" cat ever! Ah, but Sennacherib made one big error. He underestimated Hezekiah.

Hezekiah was no bully basher, but he knew Someone who was! The Bible says that Hezekiah spread out Sennacherib's letter before God and prayed. Here's what he said. "O Lord, God of Israel . . . , you alone are God over all the kingdoms of the earth. You have made heaven and earth. Give ear, O Lord, and hear; open your eyes, O Lord, and see; listen to the words Sennacherib has sent to insult the living God" (2 Kings 19:15, 16). Now, *that's* a prayer. Hezekiah called God out!

Hezekiah also sought the help of someone who knew God—the prophet Isaiah. Isaiah told the worried king that God had heard his prayer. In one night God's angel killed 185,000 Assyrian troops. Assyria's reign of terror came to a bloody end.

///////// **HOT READ** ////////

Why did God hear Hezekiah's prayer? Read 2 Kings 18:1-8. Does God respond only to the prayers of the righteous?

——> PHAT JOE <

He did what was right in the eyes of the Lord and walked in all the ways of his father David, not turning aside to the right or to the left. 2 Kings 22:2.

efore I get to PHAT Joe, mind if I backtrack a bit? Did you see God give Hezekiah 15 extra years to live when he was at the point of death (2 Kings 20:2-6)? Sweet! And I know you didn't skip over Hezzy's big mistake (verses 12-21).

But back to Joe—and no, today's title doesn't refer to Fat Joe. I'm talking about PHAT Joe, the kid in the Bible whose "rep" blew up because of his faithfulness to God. Let's kick it for a minute. Suppose you were a prince, say like Princes William and Harry in England. How would it make you feel to know that one day you could be king over the entire land? Wouldn't that be something?

Well, imagine becoming king at the ripe old age of 8. You heard me—8. As if that wasn't complicated enough, Joe was anointed king after his dad was assassinated by some of his own officials. His dad lasted a mere two years on the throne and was one of the most evil kings in Judah's history. Oooh, but wait, there's more. His grandfather, Manasseh, was the real black sheep of the family. The Bible says, "Manasseh . . . shed so much innocent blood that he filled Jerusalem from end to end—besides the sin that he had caused Judah to commit, so that they did evil in eyes of the Lord" (2 Kings 21:16).

Josiah's genes were all screwed up, but that didn't stop him from making a positive difference. He listened to wise older counselors, and learned well how to be king. But something life-changing happened when he was in his early 20s: someone found the book of the Law. It was a record of all the laws that God had given Moses, the one that Israel was supposed to treasure. You read where it was found, right? Yep, in the Temple. How does one lose the Bible in church?

When Josiah realized what had been found, he tore his clothes and wept. He then led the nation into ceremony of repentance, begging God's forgiveness for having broken the laws in the sacred Book. Josiah's faithfulness transformed Judah, and he started it all while he was a teenager (2 Chronicles 34:3).

//////// HOT READ ////////

Even after Josiah's reformation, Judah returned to its sins. What was Judah's end? Read 2 Kings 25:1-13.

——> "NOTHING TO SEE HERE, FOLKS!" <

Adam, Seth, Enosh, Kenan, Mahalalel, Jared, Enoch, Methuselah, Lamech, Noah.
1 Chronicles 1:1-3.

et me be honest. Your eyes will probably glaze over the moment you begin reading the book of 1 Chronicles. After the mega adventures of 2 Kings, reading a bunch of names—most of which we can barely pronounce—is not exactly fun.

You're probably wondering why all this genealogy is necessary since we already know Adam, Enoch, Methuselah, and Noah. Why get caught in the weeds with folks like Havilah, Nebaioth, Jetur, and Zaavan? *If they had done something significant, wouldn't more have been said about them?* I reason to myself. As I begin 1 Chronicles, I hear the voice of a cop, waving onlookers by.

"Move along, folks!" His left hand is raised as he motions them on with his right. "Nothing to see here." But of course, there's a whole lot more to see, if you look past the cop and beyond the yellow tape. That's how the first part of 1 Chronicles is. To get a glimpse of what's really going on, you have to peer past the cop in your head telling you to skip these chapters.

For instance, it was cool to see that Father Abraham was a descendant of Shem, one of Noah's boys (1 Chronicles 1:17-27). King David is a direct descendant of Abraham (1 Chronicles 2:1-15). If you read until we get to the New Testament, you'll discover that a certain guy whose name begins with J is a direct link to this mighty line of people.

A chronicle is a record or narrative of past events. First Chronicles takes us back to the life of King David and fills in some of the holes left open by 1 and 2 Samuel. This book replaces key stories of David's life, such as the slaying of Goliath, his struggles with Saul, Absalom's rebellion, the recovery of the ark of the covenant, the building of the Temple, and Israel's worship services. What's the message here? God forgives sin, and He's willing to restore anyone who worships him with all their heart. As you read, underline passages that show David's close connection with God.

As you begin this awesome book, ask God for a deeper, closer walk with Him.

///////// HOT READ /////////

In the middle of all the names mentioned, Jabez is singled out. Why?
See 1 Chronicles 4:9, 10.

──> THE GATEKEEPERS <

*In earlier times Phinehas son of Eleazar was in charge of the gatekeepers,
and the Lord was with him.* 1 Chronicles 9:20.

First Chronicles 9 signals the end of the genealogies. Couldn't have happened at a better time, right? While you're shouting for joy, remember this: the first nine chapters trace Israel's history from creation (Adam) to Judah's return from exile in Babylon (2 Kings 23-25). Beginning with chapter 10, 1 Chronicles then goes backward to tell the story of Saul's death and David's rise to power. So, chapters 1-9 bring us up to speed on where the nation stands. Chapters 10-29 are one giant David flashback window into David's godly reign, many, many years before Israel and Judah were taken captive by Assyria and Babylon. Got it? (No, you don't!)

After I understood the genealogy and flashback thing, 1 Chronicles 9 stopped me cold. Why did the writer of 1 Chronicles spend so much time talking about gatekeepers after writing the genealogies (chapters 1-8) in such a matter-of-fact way? What's up with that? When Bible writers spend time on a subject, it's important.

Gatekeepers, or doorkeepers, in ancient Israel were special people, priests who guarded the Temple at all times, day or night. Under Phinehas' leadership, they opened and closed the Temple gates at appointed times, and they made sure that no one who was unclean entered the sacred Temple. The gatekeepers also took special care of all of the vessels used by the priests in worship, counting them each day to be sure that none were missing. God was "with" Phinehas as he led out in this seeming simple task.

The job of today's doormen is largely boring. Doormen open doors, greet people, answer questions, hail taxis, etc., but that's not how it was in ancient Israel. I believe that the gatekeepers could see the visible presence of God shining through openings in the tabernacle. They watched Moses enter the tent of meeting to talk face to face with God. The writer of 1 Chronicles was excited at the sight of these gatekeepers because their presence meant that the worship of the true God would once again begin. The gatekeepers were a symbol of God's forgiveness and restoration of Israel.

How do you treat the ushers at your church? How do you handle God's "stuff"?

//////// HOT READ ////////

What did King David say about doormen? Psalm 84:10.

⟶ THE MAGNET <

Day after day men came to help David, until he had a great army,
like the army of God. 1 Chronicles 12:22.

Posses are a dime a dozen. Seems like everybody's got one, especially the "stars." When Margaret R. Ray stole David Letterman's Porsche, she reported told police that she was his wife. She stalked David Letterman for years, repeatedly breaking into his home.

Not to be outdone, a Wyoming man once threatened the life of comedian Jerry Lewis, breaking into his home and holding him at gunpoint. Gary Benson, who had terrorized Lewis for years, wrote the following to Lewis after being released from prison: "Dear Jerry. Your [sic] Dead. Your friend, Gary Benson."

Everybody needs a "good" posse, even if they don't tote guns or sport bulging biceps. (I better be careful here, since most of the posses we read about in the news are horrible—for example, Michael Vick's "canine crew.") But King David needed one to help him deal with Saul. In fact, he needed a whole army to protect him from Saul's treachery.

The Bible says that fighters from the 12 tribes of Israel began defecting to David's side in an endless stream. That was no small thing, since Saul was king. To fight for David meant death if caught. No ifs, ands, or buts about it!

Some of the meanest hombres around showed up. There were ambidextrous soldiers on his team who could drop you with either hand. The Gadite fighters had faces like lions and could run like gazelles. The men of Zebulon showed up 50,000 strong with every type of weapon imaginable back then. Then there were the "three"—Josheb-Basshebeth; Eleazar, son of Dodai; and Shammah, son of Agee (2 Samuel 23). These three mighty warriors headlined a team of awesome fighters who would do anything for David.

These great fighters were attracted by David's mighty victory over Goliath many years earlier, and the victories he achieved while still commander of Saul's forces. But the main reason David was a magnet to these great men was that "the Lord Almighty was with him" (1 Chronicles 11:9). God was the magnet in David's life.

No matter what you face, know that you are stuck to God, and He to you!

///////// HOT READ /////////

What do you think did the writer meant when he wrote that the "men of Issachar . . . understood the times and knew what Israel should do" (1 Chronicles 12:32)?

———> FAMILY AFFAIR <

He said to them, "You are the heads of the Levitical families; you and your fellow Levites are to consecrate yourselves and bring up the ark of the Lord, the God of Israel, to the place I have prepared for it." 1 Chronicles 15:12.

oday I'm "vibing" on the family thing going on in 1 Chronicles 13-15. It reminds me of the times my family worshipped together.

I still struggle sometimes to understand why my mother and father felt it necessary to wake up my four siblings and me at 5:00 a.m. for morning devotions. What in the world is awake at 5:00 a.m? Dogs are still napping, squirrels are getting the last bit of beauty sleep, even cats ain't up!

I used to feel that my mom and dad were punishing us for some wrong that we'd done. Whether we stayed up late watching sports or not, a 5:00 a.m. wake-up call came all too soon. As I've grown older, I have mellowed a bit. I see worship moments with my family very differently.

My family is scattered now. I and my second-oldest brother live on opposite ends of the state with the highest property taxes in the nation—New Jersey. (No New Jersey jokes, please. Thank you.) The rest of the family is holed up in the ATL, Atlanta, Georgia—although my brother who is right before me lives on the road 24/7. He's a truck driver, so you can't really say that he lives anyplace but in his truck.

Though we hated it at the time, worshipping together was the glue that held us together growing up. Going to church together was so cool. Watching my dad share God's Word was something I took for granted. Now I cherish those moments.

When King David decided to restart Israel's worship of the true God, he began by asking the heads of the Levite families to lead out. Notice, though, that David called the Levites and their families to serve, return the ark, *and* lead out in the worship services. Families in Israel worshipped together. Worshipping God was the foundation of every Israelite family, not just the families of the priests.

What can you do to strengthen the family worship in your home?

///////// HOT READ ////////

Ever want to do something for God but forget to ask His guidance? David did, and he learned a difficult lesson. Read 1 Chronicles 15:11-15.

——→ MUSIC MINISTRY <

Heman and Jeduthun were responsible for the sounding of the trumpets and cymbals and for the playing of the other instruments for sacred song.
1 Chronicles 16:42.

ou can't read today's Bible passage without noticing how serious and particular King David is about the worship of God.

Anyone can do the prayer. What's the big deal about who collects the offering? we sometimes think. *All the deacons do is walk down the aisles, pass the offering buckets down each pew, and so on.* Maybe you don't think that way, but as a teenager I surely did.

I was always willing to do "stuff" in church, if asked. I would get really scared, but after watching my dad offer prayers, preach sermons, and do baby blessings, I wasn't afraid to give anything a try. But in spite of my willingness to do things for God, I still didn't quite get how sacred each task was—whether I was cleaning bathrooms or speaking for youth day. It all was sacred and holy, but all of that was lost on me.

I get it now, though, especially after reading 1 Chronicles 16. When the ark finally returned to Israel, King David organized a great dedication ceremony. Every Israelite attended. The king and the priests were dressed in the finest linen clothes they could find. The ark was cleaned and shined up by Aaron's descendants, who alone could do this work.

Special musicians were chosen to "sing joyful songs, accompanied by musical instruments: lyres, harps and cymbals" (1 Chronicles 15:16). They did so "regularly" before the ark of the covenant of God (1 Chronicles 16:6). King David even wrote a special song for the occasion and gave it to Asaph, one of Israel's best musicians.

David's care for God's worship moved me deeply, especially the minor detail recorded in 1 Chronicles 16:42. Heman and Jeduthun were put in charge of tuning the instruments. They made sure that every instrument had the right pitch and sound. For King David, every detail of worship had to be right, because the God was his audience.

How would the worship in your church change if you knew that the president of the United States would be attending next Sabbath?

//////// HOT READ ////////

What did King David do with all the wealth that he got from his military conquests? See 1 Chronicles 18:9-11. Shouldn't we dedicate the blessings we get to God?

——> THE CENSUS BUREAU <

Satan rose up against Israel and incited David to take a census of Israel.
1 Chronicles 21:1.

wain, I really don't want to fill this thing out," said Sherelle, a friend of mine. "I hate these things. Why do they need so much information, anyway?" she yelled.

"Let me look at that," I retorted, reaching for it. Turns out that Sherelle's home had been chosen to complete a survey for the U.S. Census Bureau. If you don't know who they are, that's too bad, because they know who you are!

The Census Bureau does an estimated count of the nation's population every 10 years. The census keeps track of how many homes are built from year to year and who occupies them. The government wants to know the age, sex, race, and ethnic makeup of each geographical area. This general information makes up the short form, which most people get; but the government also has a long form. Sherelle got that one.

The long form asks for detailed information, such as the value of the property owned, the number of rooms, its plumbing and kitchen facilities, marital status of the owners, place of birth, place of work, household income—and that's just the beginning.

It's a grip of info for sure, but the government "says" it uses it to determine, for instance, if a community needs a new road or not. Sherelle wasn't buying it.

King David, like the government, thought it a good idea to do a census of Israel's fighting men. Actually, he got the idea from Satan. David felt proud after dispatching numerous enemies, so he wanted to get a count of his forces. He ordered the count of his forces to demonstrate just how powerful he was. God was *so* not impressed.

"This command was . . . evil in the sight of God; so he punished Israel" (1 Chronicles 21:7). Read the rest of 1 Chronicles 21 to learn what those punishments were. Here's what God was saying to David: "You and the armies of Israel didn't win any battles. I did. Therefore, don't go strutting around as if you did something."

King David learned the hard way that victories in life come from God.

///////// HOT READ ///////

Where do you see God's mercy in 1 Chronicles 21? What does this tell you about God?

> FATHERS AND SONS <

David said, "My son Solomon is young and inexperienced, and the house to be built for the Lord should be of great magnificence and fame and splendor in the sight of all the nations. Therefore I will make preparations for it." 1 Chronicles 22:5.

A few years ago I saw a *60 Minutes* interview with Will Smith—a.k.a The Fresh Prince, Hollywood movie star. The old school rapper turn actor is doing quite well. He lives in a mega-mansion on the outskirts of Los Angeles, has a beautiful wife and kids, and makes around $20 million per movie. Not bad, huh?

Will Smith's life wasn't always that way. In fact, his father was quite hard on him and his brother. They grew up in Philadelphia, where Smith's father owned a store. "One day he tore down the front wall of the store," as Smith put it, "and said to me and my brother, 'The two of you are going to build this wall back, brick by brick.' " They were stunned.

"We can't do this," they told their father. His response: "Yes, you can. Let's get started." Smith's father taught them how to mix mortar, dress the stones, and place them. One year later the three of them stood in front of a completed wall.

Smith's dad then said, "Don't you ever tell me what you can't do!" Will Smith credits that experience, among others, for teaching him a strong work ethic.

The story of Will Smith and his dad bears some resemblance to story of Solomon and his dad found at the end of 1 Chronicles. This building project was the most ambitious ever attempted in Israel—to build God a Temple for worship. As you read several days ago, King David wanted to build it, but God said no. David's son, Solomon, a man of peace, would have the honor. But God didn't prohibit David from making preparations.

David did everything within his power to assemble everything Solomon would need for building the Temple. All the materials were there (read about them in 1 Chronicles 22 and 29), and men to oversee the work were chosen. David's long-range goal was to see built a "house" worthy of his God. So he did all within his power to make sure that Solomon would succeed at the task—sort of how Will Smith's dad helped prepare him for his success.

As you read today, think deeply about how much King David loved God.

///////// HOT READ ////////

King David had a gift for organization (1 Chronicles 24). Why is important to be organized in any task you undertake?

——> MY SACRIFICE <

Besides, in my devotion to the temple of my God I now give my personal treasures of gold and silver for temple of my God, over and above everything I have provided for this holy temple. 1 Chronicles 29:3.

here is a reason King David is considered the greatest biblical king who ever lived. When you read today's Bible selection, you'll know why.

David was a great leader and military strategist. He knew how to organize a task, break it up in to bite-sized chunks, and give those chunks to the right people. He was generous, and he never forgot anyone who showed him kindness.

Many of us would give our big toe for some of David's qualities, but there was something else that set King David apart from the other great kings in the Bible. He made personal sacrifices for the cause of God. First Chronicles 26-29 is a case in point.

King David could have wiled away the final years of his life taking long leisurely vacations. Instead he sacrificed a life of ease to plan for the building of God's Temple, a very difficult task even for a young man—and David had grown old. But David gave more than that. He gave away his personal fortune for the building of the Lord's house.

Recently I came across the story of 83-year-old Hal Taussig. Mr. Taussig would be a millionaire—if he didn't keep giving his money away.   •

Taussig and his wife live in a little house that they've owned since 1986. His wife drives their 12-year-old Toyota Corolla to work. He rides a bike. Taussig and his wife do not draw salaries from the travel company they founded. They give away 100 percent of the company's profits to a foundation that offers very low-interest loans to poor people, groups, and organizations who do not qualify for help from most financial institutions.

Hal Taussig and his wife, Norma, are working to build a society in which all people are cared for and have the chance to make it in life. They don't just mouth it. They put their money behind it.

King David didn't just talk about building God a magnificent Temple. He put his money behind it. He put his treasure where his heart was!

/////// HOT READ ///////

Read 1 Chronicles 29:10-20. How was King David able to keep his vast wealth and honor in the right perspective?

April 29 • *2 Chronicles 1-3*

———> WHAT A WITNESS! <

Praise be to the Lord, the God of Israel, who made heaven and earth! He has given King David a wise son, endowed with intelligence and discernment, who will build a temple for the Lord and a palace for himself. 2 Chronicles 2:12.

on't look now, but you're almost a third of the way through the Bible. Keep going! You're doing great!

Today we begin a new exciting book of the Bible. Second Chronicles is a continuation of 1 Chronicles. Get it? OK, just kidding, so calm down. Just as in 1 Chronicles, worship is at the heart of 2 Chronicles. The question lurking just below its pages is "Whom will you worship?" Or better yet: "Can a person live a full life without making God a priority?"

This terrific book begins where 1 Chronicles leaves off. King Solomon assumes the throne and promptly asks God for help. He didn't ask God for long life, or great wealth, or the heads of Israel's enemies. He asked for wisdom and knowledge to know how to rule God's people, and he got it—and then some (2 Chronicles 1:11, 12).

Armed with God's wisdom, Solomon set about the task that his father, King David, dreamed of: building the Temple. Though David had provided most of the materials, Solomon also needed special cedar logs available only from King Hiram of Tyre *and* a skilled tradesman to do the beautiful carving he dreamed up for the Lord's house. King Hiram's response to Solomon was, well, spiritual.

"Sure, Solomon," he says in essence, "I'll hook you up. God surely gave your father a wise son, and He picked the right guy to rule His people. Solomon, you are one smart young man!" Such godly praise from a heathen king? What gives?

Truth is, Hiram respected Israel's power, and that partially explains his warm greeting. King Hiram had cunningly made himself an ally of King David, but over time the two developed a genuine friendship. King Hiram helped Solomon because of the friendship and positive witness of David, Solomon's now-deceased father.

A godly life lives on, long after the owner is gone.

///////// HOT READ ///////

Is it important to learn a skill, even if you plan on going to college?
See 2 Chronicles 2:13-16.

127

──> A DAY IN THE LIFE <

"He is good; his love endures forever." Then the temple of the Lord was filled with a cloud. 2 Chronicles 5:13.

As I write this morning's devotional (in December 2007) people all across North America are mourning the death of Sean Taylor, a hard-hitting safety for the Washington Redskins. Taylor, his girlfriend, and their new baby were in his Miami, Florida, home when several gunmen broke into the property during an attempted robbery. Surprised to see Taylor, they shot him. He later died from his injuries. His funeral was very sad.

Let's be honest: countless people whose names we'll never know died on the same day that Taylor did. Yet something about Taylor's death struck a chord with people. From time to time he'd been in trouble with the law, but the birth of his baby seemed to change all that. He took to fatherhood as best he could, and worked to be a better person.

On the same day that Sean Taylor was buried, a man who'd been missing in northeast England was found alive. After the shattered remains of John Darwin's canoe were found in March 2002, an all-out search by the Royal Navy of England produced nothing. Five years later Darwin turned up at a local police station. Unfortunately for him, the cops discovered that he'd faked his death.

When we hear about the sad death of someone like Sean Taylor, we can't help wondering why God permitted him to die, and not a bozo like John Darwin, who faked his death so that he and his wife could cash in his life insurance policy.

At the dedication of the God's Temple the priests and the people sang these words: He is good. His love endures forever. They weren't saying that bad things don't happen, or that God never allows us to feel pain. They were saying, "No matter what we face, God is working all things out for our best good, because His love for us is unchanging and never-ending."

God weeps at the loss of every Sean Taylor. He weeps at the loss of your friend or family member. But one day soon God is going to prove just how good He is. He will wipe away every tear from our eyes and create a world without sorrow or pain (Revelation 21:4).

///////// HOT READ ///////

Read 2 Chronicles 6:26, 27. King Solomon asked God for more than His forgiveness. What else did he want God to do?

——> PLACES <

Solomon brought Pharaoh's daughter up from the City of David to the palace he had built for her, for he said, "My wife must not live in the palace of David king of Israel, because the places the ark of the Lord has entered are holy." 2 Chronicles 8:11.

I've been to lots of places, but I'll never forget the time I spent in Punta Cana, Dominican Republic. Punta Cana's known as a tourist destination. Couples go there to get married, honeymoon, and celebrate anniversaries. (Why am I telling you all of this when you're waist-deep in high school drama, right? Stick with me. There's a reason.)

I went to Punta Cana with my wife to celebrate our tenth wedding anniversary. After putting up with me for 10 years, she needed a break.

But—isn't there always a *but* somewhere—to get from the airport to our plush resort, we had to drive through many small towns and villages. That ride was an eye-opening, unsettling experience. Our driver was an expert at weaving through cars, vans, motorcycles, potholes, and meandering pedestrians. It was a fun ride.

The unsettling part came when I saw how some of the local people lived. I'm sure that they didn't consider themselves poor, but many of the homes were little more than shacks with thatched roofs. To be sure, all of the Dominican Republic wasn't this way, but I saw enough to make me feel guilty about staying at a five-star resort when so many people were in need. The resort itself was far from where the poor lived. The poor stayed in their place, and we stayed in ours. We each had our compartments.

We humans have a special talent for compartmentalizing our lives. What do I mean? Well, for instance, we say we love God, but some of us watch TV shows that He'd never watch. Right now, MTV's bisexual dating show, *A Shot at Love With Tila Tequila*, is the number one show on cable. And many Christians are among its regular viewers.

Compartmentalization is nothing new. King David did it, and so did Solomon! God had told Israel never to intermarry with foreign nations, but neither of them got the memo. Solomon knew it was wrong, because he refused to let his new bride go into any place the ark of the covenant had been. So he made a place for her in his life far away from the place that he made for God. Bad move. His pagan wives destroyed Solomon's walk with God.

/////// HOT READ ///////
What kind of witness does your life give to others? Read 2 Chronicles 9:3, 4.

──>PRIDE KILLS! <

> *After Rehoboam's position as king was established and he had become strong, he and all Israel with him abandoned the law of the Lord.* 2 Chronicles 12:1.

It sure didn't take long for the glory days of King Solomon's reign to come crashing down to a sorry end. You probably remember reading how the kingdom of Israel was divided between Rehoboam, one of Solomon's boys, and Jeroboam, son of Nebat (in 1 Kings 11-14). First Kings laid it out pretty good, but 2 Chronicles 10-13 gives us some tantalizing details that 1 Kings does not.

For instance, I didn't know that after Jeroboam began to rule the 10 tribes that made up the northern kingdom of Israel, all the priests and Levites fled to Judah, the southern kingdom, where Rehoboam reigned. Why? They weren't down with the calf worship Jeroboam had set up for the people of Israel (2 Chronicles 11:13-17).

Then there's the little tidbit found in 2 Chronicles 12:1. For starters, Rehoboam began his reign by angering all of Israel so that the nation split into two. When he attempted to win the people back by forcing them into slavery (like *that* was going to make them happy!), they stoned his enforcer and almost killed him. Rehoboam became so arrogant that God had to humble him.

Author and pastor Craig Brian Larson told the following story about the dangers of pride and arrogance. "Pali, this bull has killed me," said Jose Cubero, one of Spain's most brilliant matadors, before he lost consciousness and died.

"Only 21 years old, Cubero had enjoyed a spectacular career. However, in this . . . bullfight, Jose made a tragic mistake. He thrust his sword a final time into a bleeding, delirious bull, which then collapsed. Considering the struggle finished, Jose turned to the crowd to acknowledge the applause. The bull, however, was not dead. It rose and lunged at the unsuspecting matador, its horn piercing his back and puncturing his heart."

Arrogance and pride caused Jose Cubero his life, and it almost did the same to Rehoboam. It wasn't until Rehoboam humbled himself that God called off King Shishak (2 Chronicles 12:7, 8).

///////// HOT READ ///////

Why did Rehoboam do what was evil in God's sight? See 2 Chronicles 12:14. Have you set your heart on seeking the Lord?

---> WANT TO KNOW? <

> *We are observing the requirements of the Lord our God. But you have forsaken him. God is with us; he is our leader.* 2 Chronicles 13:11, 12.

ne of the most challenging questions in life is "How do I know that God is with me?" I once met a teenager during a Week of Prayer who struggled with this question.

John was one of the nicest guys you'd ever want to meet. He was into computers and electronics big-time. While still a teen he started his own computer repair business and was making money. He was one of the smartest kids I'd ever met, but there was something missing in his life, so he pulled me aside after one of the services so we could chat.

"Pastor Dwain," he began, "I hear what you've been saying this week and everything, but I don't really feel God in my life." I perked up as John continued.

"I don't get into trouble or anything like that," he said. "I try to do what's right all the time, but I still don't have that connection with God. Know what I mean?"

"Yeah, I think so," I replied. I wasn't sure what to say next. I too had experienced a time like John's when I wasn't sure if I "felt" God or whether God was "feeling" me. I later found out that John basically had no family. He had some relatives, but he wasn't close to any of them. Somehow he ended up going to church with some friends, and joining the local youth group.

I told John that Jesus understood what it felt like to be cut off from a connection with God—His Father. I told him not to trust his feelings, because feelings can mislead us when it comes to our walk with God. God is nearest during our most challenging times (Psalm 34:17-22), even though we might not "feel" Him there. We can know for sure that God is with us when we obey His Word. If we seek Him, we will find him (Jeremiah 29:13).

In today's reading you'll meet King Abijah, the good king of Judah who fought against evil King Jeroboam of the northern kingdom of Israel. Abijah knew that God was with Him in the battle, even though his forces were outnumbered two to one. Why? Because he had been obedient to God's Word. You too can have the assurance that God is with you. Simply seek God through prayer, Bible study, and service. Then obey God!

////// HOT READ //////
Want God's presence? 2 Chronicles 15:1, 2 tells you how to get it.

131

——> MAD AT GOD <

In the thirty-ninth year of his reign Asa was afflicted with a disease in his feet. Though his disease was severe, even in his illness he did not seek help from the Lord, but only from the physicians. 2 Chronicles 16:12.

he year was 1982—yep, long before you were born. Your parents were probably my age back then. I was a major Philadelphia 76er fanatic. In 1982 my team needed a miracle, and I was praying hard for one. The Sixers were led by the legendary Dr. J, Julius Erving. He was Jordan before Jordan, Kobe before Kobe. He could fly!

My beloved Sixers faced the evil Los Angeles Lakers. I just knew we'd win in four games, but I was horribly, sadly, maddeningly WRONG. The Sixers lost the first game, won the second, then lost the third and fourth. They came back to win game 5, but still they stood on the brink of elimination—they needed to win the next two games to become the champions. All my hopes and dreams of Sixer glory, all the trash talk I'd been planning for Laker fans I knew—was on the line.

As game 6 arrived, I went to the only Source who could turn the series around—God! *God had to be a Sixer fan*, I thought. If He was a fan of King David, then he had to be a Sixer fan. After all, King David defeated Goliath with God's help. The Lakers were led by Magic Johnson and Kareem Abdul-Jabbar. They were the Goliaths of the NBA! (Forgive me, but my mind was a little warped back then.)

I prayed for help in game 6, but no help came. God, to my surprise, was not a Sixer fan. We lost, and it was all God's fault. Well, not really, but at that time I was very angry at the Sixers, but more so at God. He could have changed the outcome.

Have you ever gotten totally mad at God? I mean mad enough never to speak to Him again? King Asa of Judah did. King Asa made a treaty with the heathen king Ben Hadad, to buy his support against Jeroboam of Israel. God was not pleased.

Why was God so, uh, nonplussed? Years earlier God had helped Asa defeat a vast Cushite army (2 Chronicles 14), but somehow Asa had forgotten that. When God sent a prophet to tell him about his sin, he threw the prophet in jail and never spoke to God again. Even when Asa contracted a disease in his feet, he refused to ask God for help. King Asa's anger toward God at the end of his life took the shine off of his great kingship.

/////// HOT READ ///////

What was King Jehoshapaht's passion? Read 2 Chronicles 17:6.

──> STAND STILL AND SEE! <

You will not have to fight this battle. Take up your positions; stand firm and see the deliverance the Lord will give you, O Judah and Jerusalem. 2 Chronicles 20:17.

marvel at people who've experienced miracles. They're sick, so they go to a doctor, who finds a malignant tumor in their brain. They pray to God for a miraculous healing and—wouldn't you know it—the thing disappears. The doctor is left baffled.

I love to hear those kinds of testimonies. I've never had one of those otherworldly healing experiences, but I'm not typical of most people. I tend to see God's fingerprints in every scrape or cut that heals. Blood coagulating, a scab forming, a wound turning back to skin—all of these are mind-boggling to me. I see miracles in life's little cuts.

I saw God work a miracle to help Joe,★ a close friend of mine, and He used me to do it. For some time Joe had been praying for a new job. He liked his current job, but his heart was really in youth ministry. Joe loves youth!

One day I received a call from the secretary of a conference who wanted me to consider taking a position as a youth director. I wasn't sure about it, but I agreed to consider it. My wife and I visited the conference, but decided that it wasn't quite the right time for us to move.

I thought about the job for a few days after my visit and continued to pray about it. That's when God told me, quite distinctly, that I should call Joe and ask him if he'd be interested. Here's where things got really interesting. As I told Joe about the job opening, he grew silent on the phone. I thought that maybe he wasn't interested. Boy, was I wrong.

It turns out that the day before I called, Joe and his wife had prayed that God would open a door for him to change jobs. The next day I called with God's answer. Joe had found the position that he'd been looking for, and God allowed me to play a small part in that miracle. Isn't God awesome?

Today you'll read about a miraculous military victory. King Jehoshaphat and all of Judah prayed for deliverance, and boy, did they ever get it—and they never had to raise a single weapon. God is working miracles every day. Ask Him for yours!

───────

★ not his name

/////// HOT READ ///////

How powerful is your praise? See 2 Chronicles 20:21-24.

——> THAT'S MY MOMMA! <

He too walked in the ways of the house of Ahab, for his mother encouraged him in doing wrong. He did evil in the eyes of the Lord, as the house of Ahab had done, for after his father's death they became his advisers, to his undoing. 2 Chronicles 22:3, 4.

veryone has a "crazy" family member or relative. It's a fact of life. If you don't have any, then say a special prayer of thanks. You and your family are rare. Either that, or your parents don't think you're quite ready to handle all the hidden family secrets.

We know that family members can make huge mistakes, but how do you explain this bit of family drama? Daniel P. Twomey, 52, of Toms River, New Jersey, was arrested and jailed for—get this—employing a juvenile to commit a crime. *Happens all the time*, I thought as I read the story. But there were other details that I didn't expect.

Twomey was caught on a TV surveillance camera videotape pushing a young girl, later identified as his granddaughter, under a security door at Lucky Leo's Arcade on the boardwalk in Seaside Heights, New Jersey. Why? To steal an employee's purse. Twomey also was with his 8-year-old grandson at the time. What a role model.

You might expect a brother, a sister, a friend, to encourage a kid to do wrong—but a grandfather? But as sick as Daniel Twomey's crime, the Bible does him one better. For King Ahaziah, his momma was the problem.

He did evil in the sight of God (2 Chronicles 22:4), as had several kings before him, but the reason for his evil behavior was even more striking. His momma led him into sin. That's even worse than what Daniel Twomey did to his grandchildren, don't you think? Young Ahaziah was cursed from birth, because not only was his father evil (2 Chronicles 21:12-15), but his mother's father was one of the most evil men who ever lived. Her descendants controlled young Ahaziah and taught him how to sin.

But think of this: Athaliah, the young king's mother, may have taught him to sin, but she did not force him to sin. He had examples of godly rulers, such as Jehoshaphat, whom he could have emulated. If you have that terrible situation, take a stand against family members who are sinning and encouraging you to do the same.

//////// HOT READ ////////

What group of people led the rebellion that overthrew Athaliah (2 Chronicles 23:1-10)?

——> "IT AIN'T PRETTY" <

But after Uzziah became powerful, his pride led to his downfall. 2 Chronicles 26:16.

f you have fallen off on your Bible reading lately, please, please don't miss today's passage, 2 Chronicles 25-27. These chapters are a must-read.

I'm not sure if you've picked it up yet, but there is a sickening consistency found in the behavior of most of the kings who ruled Israel and Judah. The pattern goes something like this. Gets anointed king at a relatively young age, remains faithful to God for a while, gets a big head and totally forsakes God—and finally meets destruction. This pattern plays itself out in the lives of King Amaziah and his son, Uzziah.

Amaziah listened attentively to God's prophet when he needed God's help to defeat the Edomites (2 Chronicles 25:7-10). But after he conquered them, he "brought back the gods of the people of Seir. He set them up as his own gods, bowed down to them and burned sacrifices to them" (verse 14). The next verse says, "The anger of the Lord burned against Amaziah." (Ummm, just for the record: God. Burning anger. Bad.)

God sent a prophet to Amaziah who asked, "Why do you consult this people's gods, which could not save their own people from your hand?" (verse 15). I'll let you read what happens next, but trust me. It ain't pretty.

Amaziah's pride passed down to his son in the same way, sort of, that alcoholics may pass down alcoholism to their children. Uzziah followed his father, Amaziah, and became king of Judah at age 16, ruling faithfully for most of his 52 years. He was one of the most brilliant military minds seen in all the Bible. He built cannonlike machines that could hurl arrows and huge boulders at the enemy with frightening velocity, and stationed them around Judah's cities. In an instant he could call up his force of 307,500 men.

But something changed when King Uzziah reached the zenith of power. Pride took over his life. He looked at his wealth, at his fearsome army and adoring citizens, and it all went to his head—just as it did his father's. Hopped-up on delusions of grandeur, he decided to enter the Temple of the Lord and burn incense to God, something that only priests were permitted to do. Big mistake, dude!

I won't tell you what happens next, but trust me. It ain't pretty.

///////// HOT READ ///////

Read 2 Chronicles 26:17-21. Ask God to remove your pride today.

——> YOU TOO MESSED UP <

But aren't you also guilty of sins against the Lord your God? 2 Chronicles 28:10.

ell if that's not the pot calling the kettle black, then I don't know what is." *Say what?* you must be thinking after reading that strange sentence. Try it on your parents or some adult to see if they know what it means. (Go do it now if you can.)

How'd the adults do? Most adults, especially senior citizens, have heard and probably used this phrase before. I've heard my mom use it, and I've added it to my list of homespun proverbs. It is used to expose someone who is acting like a hypocrite.

Today's reading begins by describing the actions of Ahaz, another evil king. After Amaziah and Uzziah, Jotham—Uzziah's kid—learned the lessons that his father and grandfather had failed to learn. He "grew powerful because he walked steadfastly before the Lord his God," and didn't let it go to his head (2 Chronicles 27:6). But something happened to his son, Ahaz. He burned sacrifices to foreign gods, and even sacrificed some of his children on their altars. Ahaz was one sick puppy.

When God had had enough of Ahaz's evil, He allowed not one but two nations to defeat Judah. First the Arameans soundly defeated them, then later Pekah, king of Israel, finished them off, killing 120,000 Judean soldiers in a single day (2 Chronicles 28:6). Pekah's troops didn't stop there, however—guess they forgot that Judah was part of their family. They took more than 200 women and children captive from the cities of Judah.

God had sent Israel to humble Judah, but the people of Israel went a little overboard. They had hoped to enslave their brothers and sisters from Judah. But God wouldn't have any of it. He said to Israel, "You have slaughtered them in a rage that reaches to heaven. And now you intend to make the men and women of Judah and Jerusalem your slaves." Now here's the kicker. "But aren't you also guilty of sins against the Lord your God?" (verses 9, 10). Israel was acting as if they hadn't sinned, when they had. It was the pot (Israel) calling the kettle (Judah) black. Both of them had been burned by same sins; both were guilty of the same wrongs against God. Both nations had committed sin.

Before pointing the finger at others, we should first check ourselves.

///////// HOT READ ////////

How did Israel show mercy to the prisoners of Judah? See 2 Chronicles 28:12-15.

⟶ ONE WAY WE WORSHIP <

Since the people began to bring their contributions to the temple of the Lord, we have had enough to eat and plenty to spare, because the Lord has blessed his people, and this great amount is left over. 2 Chronicles 31:10.

oday's Bible passage highlights the life of one of the Bible's greatest leaders— King Hezekiah. He was the son of Ahaz, a king who sacrificed—burned—some of Hezekiah's brothers and sisters on altars to foreign gods. Yet when Hezekiah became king, he did what was right in God's eyes, removing all of Judah's idols, rebuilding the Temple of the Lord, and restoring the worship of the true God. He was an awesome leader who gave God his all.

I found something very interesting in today's passage. Did you notice it? When the worship of God was restarted, there were not enough priests to perform services, partially because many of them had engaged in idol worship. But the ranks of the godly priests were also thin because they had little support from people, since during Ahaz' rule almost everyone worshipped heathen gods.

God had ordained that the priests and Levites who worked in the Temple be supported by the tithes and offerings brought to the Lord's house (2 Chronicles 4-8). However, at that time the people didn't bring money the way we do today. Instead they brought a tenth of all their produce, grains, livestock, and so on. The priests and Levites were supported this way.

King Hezekiah "ordered the people living in Jerusalem to give the portion due to the priests and Levites." Why? "So they could devote themselves to the Law of the Lord" (2 Chronicles 31:4). The people obeyed, bringing their tithes to the Temple of the Lord, so much so that the priests and Levites had more than they needed. They had to gather the remaining tithes and offerings into huge heaps.

God didn't want His workers worrying about where their next meal would come from. He wanted them focused on their spiritual leadership of Israel. When you and I bring our tithes and offerings each Sabbath, we help care for the needs of those who serve God as pastors, teachers, and others in spiritual leadership. Giving is essential to worship.

///////// HOT READ ////////

King Hezekiah did have his faults (2 Chronicles 32:24-26). How did he correct them?

——> MY JUDAH <

In his twelfth year he began to purge Judah and Jerusalem of high places, Asherah poles, carved idols and cast images. 2 Chronicles 34:3.

hether you're into video games or not, you've probably heard about the Sims, the "needy, relationship-hungry party animals that players of *The Sims* franchise love to manage." That's how Jinny Gudmundsen, editor of *Computing With Kids* magazine, described earlier versions of *The Sims* franchise by Electronic Arts for Nintendo Wii and Nintendo DS. But Gudmundsen was impressed by *MySims,* a game EA developed for kids.

Gudmundsen wrote in her CyberSpeak column for *USA Today*, "In both versions, you arrive at a town that has fallen on hard times and has lost a lot of its residents. Through your actions, you help improve the town until it earns a five-star rating." Players are given tasks by the city's mayor to help make the town a better place, such as charming tourists or planting trees, Gudmundsen explains. As each task is done, the town brightens up. Residents come back, businesses open, and people are happier.

The game designers have probably never read the story of King Josiah found in 2 Chronicles 34 and 35. Though the game's premise seems modeled after this story, I doubt that's the case. When Josiah became king of Judah at the ripe old age of 8, Judah was a wreck, but not for long.

Manasseh, Josiah's grandfather, was so evil that God permitted the king of Assyria to conquer Judah, capture him, put a hook in his nose, bind him with bronze shackles, and take him to Babylon (see 2 Chronicles 33:11). OUCH!

This humbled Manasseh and he repented, but Amon (his son and Joe's dad) didn't learn that lesson. Amon did evil in the Lord's sight, without any remorse. Josiah inherited a broken nation, but through seeking God during his teen years, he caught a vision of a better Judah and wasted no time creating it. At age 20 he began to remove all idol worship from the nation. When he was 26, something really big happened that changed his life forever and further fueled his reforms. I'll let you read what happened next.

With God's help Josiah created his vision of a transformed Judah. Josiah could've called the place *My Judah*, but the new Judah was God's Judah, and it was beautiful.

//////// HOT READ ////////

God's Judah didn't last. Don't miss reading 2 Chronicles 36. How sad!

——> LET'S TRY AGAIN <

The Lord, the God of heaven, has given me all the kingdoms of the earth and he has appointed me to build a temple for him at Jerusalem in Judah. Ezra 1:2.

urray! Now we're getting somewhere. Don't stop reading now, friend. Things are about to get interesting.

The end of the book of 2 Chronicles captured the final chapter in Judah's destruction. King Nebuchadnezzar—the one who threw the three Hebrew boys into the fiery furnace—had taken the nation of Judah into exile. The book of Jeremiah should be read alongside the end of 2 Chronicles, since Jeremiah prophesied during Judah's final days, telling the people that they would go into exile for 70 years. The book of Daniel discusses some of what occurred during that period of time. But we'll get to all of that later. For now, it's important to note that much of the rest of the Old Testament flashes back to what you read from Genesis to 2 Chronicles.

If the ending of 2 Chronicles made you as sad as it did me, then we're both in for a pick-me-up. The book of Ezra is a breath of fresh air because it shows us that God doesn't just throw away people who mess up. He may punish them. He may even allow others to rule over them, but one thing is for sure. He never, ever forgets His people.

After the 70-year period was up, King Cyrus of Persia swept into Babylon—as directed by God—and blew the Babylonians away. King Cyrus and the Persians were much more merciful to their prisoners than the evil Babylonians. Cyrus freed the remnants of many conquered nations, including the Jews from Israel.

Not only did he free them, but Cyrus—a heathen king—obeyed God by giving the freed Israelites a chance to rebuild the Temple of the Lord. Remember, the Temple built by Solomon was burned to the ground by the Babylonians. The book of Ezra tells the story of how the small remnant of people who survived the Babylonian exile rebuilt their lives by reconnecting with God.

The first group to come back was led by Zerubbabel, a descendant of King David. Ezra led the second group of returnees back to Jerusalem. The major theme of Ezra centers on the rebuilding of Israel's broken connection with God through worship.

/////// HOT READ ///////
What did Zerubbabel and the exiles begin rebuilding first? See Ezra 3. Why?

——> THE PRICE OF WORSHIP <

Despite their fear of the peoples around them, they built the altar on its foundation and sacrificed burnt offerings on it to the Lord, both the morning and evening sacrifices. Ezra 3:3.

erving God always costs us something. This is something that Pastor Richard Wurmbrand and his wife, Sabina, experienced firsthand in Romania.

Pastor Wurmbrand had the misfortune—or fortune—of leading a band of believers in Romania when Communists captured the country in 1945 at the end of World War II. The Communist leaders attempted to control the churches and to use them to control the people. Pastor Wurmbrand opposed them with all the fight he could muster.

Wurmbrand built an underground movement of believers worshipping faithfully, until he was arrested in 1948 for his activities. For the next 14 years Wurmbrand was brutally tortured. He spent the first three years in solitary confinement, seeing no one but his captors. Communist secret police dressed as former prisoners told his wife that he was dead and that they'd attended his burial. But she refused to believe them. She heard a still small voice deep inside telling her that her husband was not dead.

In 1964 Richard Wurmbrand was released with many others prisoners during a national amnesty, but many feared that he would be imprisoned again and killed. Christians from Norway negotiated with the Communists to get him released from Romania, and they succeeded, after paying $10,000. The going price for a prisoner then was $1,900.

Wurmbrand later traveled to the United States to testify about his imprisonment. Before the Senate Internal Security Subcommittee, Pastor Wurmbrand stripped to his waist, revealing 18 deep torture wounds. The room was silent at the sight of this man who had been tortured for his faith yet continued to trust in God.

As the returning Israelites began to worship God again, ferocious enemies plotted to destroy them. But, as today's key text notes, they continued to worship God.

///////// HOT READ ////////

What two prophets helped the exiles to stay strong? Ezra 5:1. Remember them. We'll meet them later. Today, encourage someone to stand strong for God.

——> HOOKING UP <

When I heard this, I tore my tunic and cloak, pulled hair from my head and beard and sat down appalled. Ezra 9:3.

ey, Ez, calm down. It's not the end of the world, man," I felt like saying after reading the first few verses of Ezra 9. But Ezra shouted back, "Dwain, you don't get it. We really made a big mistake here. This is serious."

I know that Ezra has been dead for centuries, but when I read how hot Ezra got when he found out that the Israelite exiles had hooked up with women from the heathen nations, I started looking closer at what they had done.

Before Israel got settled in the Promised Land, the dust from their wilderness sojourn still clinging to their clothes, God said, "Do not intermarry with them. Do not give your daughters to their sons or take their daughters for your sons" (Deuteronomy 7:3).

The practice of marrying women from surrounding heathen nations began in earnest under King Solomon, who "loved many strange women"—Ammonites, Edomites, Sidonians, Hittites (1 Kings 11:1-3, KJV). This was one of the main reasons that God allowed Israel and Judah to be conquered. Being unequally yoked had turned their hearts away from serving the true God to serving the gods of the "spiritual aliens" whom they loved. If two people can't agree on the God they serve, should they really be together?

Ezra was upset because the same sin that led God to break Israel into two nations and led to both kingdoms going into captivity was back again. "How could we dis God like this, after all the pain we've already been through?" Ezra seems to say. "How can we do the same old sins again, after He forgave us, and returned us to the land of our fathers?" Ezra was so distraught that he tore his clothes, pulled out clumps of hair from his head and face, refused to eat, and then fell down before God in prayer. Whew!

Do you get angry at sin? Does it bother you when family friends are doing wrong, or do you just conclude that it's their problem? For Ezra, Israel's sin was his problem, and he worked to bring the people he loved back to the God he adored.

/////// HOT READ ///////

Three times in Ezra 7 the Bible mentions that Ezra was a "teacher" of the Law of Moses and the God of heaven. Did this have anything to do with Ezra's reaction to Israel's sin? Ezra didn't just teach the law; he lived it.

——> BOLD MOVE <

When I heard these things, I sat down and wept. For some days I mourned and fasted and prayed before the God of heaven. Nehemiah 1:4.

The book of Ezra ends with a spiritual reformation. The book of Nehemiah begins with the makings of a physical transformation. The two have one thing in common.

But before we get to that, some background is essential. Nehemiah, like Ezra, was an exile under King Artaxerxes of Persia. He held one of the important positions in the king's court, as you'll read today. Before Jerome, Latin translator of the English Bible, gave the name Ezra to his book and Nehemiah to the one that bears his name, these two books were considered one. Others have used the titles 1 and 2 Ezra. Ezra and Nehemiah knew each other, though their callings were different.

Ezra focused on building up Israel's broken spiritual life. Nehemiah felt called to build back the walls around Jerusalem, which had been broken down and burnt by Nebuchadnezzar and the Babylonians when they took Judah into exile.

When Nehemiah heard that the Jewish remnant were in great distress because Jerusalem's wall lay broken and its gates in tatters, he sat down and cried. Again, I wasn't ready for all the emotion. I'm not a weepy guy, so the fact that Nehemiah bawled when he heard that Jerusalem was "wall-less" didn't grab me. But then I did a little checking on the importance of walls back in that time.

Walls were very important in Nehemiah's day. Hey, they still are today! Without a wall, the people were sitting ducks—anyone could get in and steal, harm, or kill them. For the 50,000 returning exiles, the broken wall was a symbol of their humiliating defeat by the Babylonians. Imagine America without a military to protect its citizens. That's how Nehemiah saw the Jewish remnant in Jerusalem. So he did what Ezra did when confronted with a big challenge. He prayed. Nehemiah wanted God's guidance!

If you want to know what it means to be a godly leader during difficult times, if you want to do something huge for God, then this is your book. Nehemiah is your G!

/////// HOT READ ///////

Nehemiah's prayer is important for several reasons. What does Nehemiah 1:8, 9 tell us about the importance of claiming God's promises when we pray?

---> UNSTOPPABLE! <

Tobiah the Ammonite, who was at his side, said, "What they are building—if even a fox climbed up on it, he would break down their wall of stones!" Nehemiah 4:3.

bstacles cannot crush me. Every obstacle yields to stern resolve. He who is fixed to a star does not change his mind."—Leonardo da Vinci.

Da Vinci's words best describes the work of another master painter and sculptor—Michelangelo. In 1508 Pope Julius II summoned him to paint the ceiling of the Sistine Chapel in Rome. The chapel was built to the exact dimensions of Solomon's Temple built in Jerusalem—40 feet wide and 130 feet long. Pope Julius II envisioned a painting of the 12 Christian apostles, but at first Michelangelo refused the job because he wanted to paint scenes from the Bible too. Eventually the pope compromised.

The project posed some major challenges, not to mention the problems that Michelangelo overcame. The ceiling is some 68 feet above the ground. Michelangelo had to build a platform from which to work; then he began painting. When mold set in on his masterpiece, he had to start over. For four years he painted. The task was so demanding that it almost permanently altered his eating patterns. And unable to do other paying jobs, he and his family almost came to poverty.

But on November 1, 1512, Michelangelo's masterpiece debuted in Rome. Instead of 12 Christian apostles, he had painted numerous biblical scenes with more than 300 figures. Michelangelo refused to let anything stop him from completing his masterpiece.

Nehemiah possessed the same grit that made Michelangelo great. Nothing could stop him from building back the walls of Jerusalem. Tobiah and Sanballat, two enemies of God's people, taunted and jeered Nehemiah, saying that the wall they were building would fall down if a fox walked on it. What a dis, huh? They threatened to kill Nehemiah and the people working on the walls. Nehemiah responded by posting guards around the building site. Those who carried supplies held them in one hand and a weapon in the other. The secret to Nehemiah's staying power was prayer. He took everything to God.

////// HOT READ //////

When you don't give up, amazing things happen. Read Nehemiah 6:15, 16.

143

——> NO TIME TO CRY! <

Then Nehemiah the governor, Ezra the priest and scribe, and the Levites who were instructing the people said to them all, "This day is sacred to the Lord your God. Do not mourn or weep." For all the people had been weeping as they listened to the words of the Law. Nehemiah 8:9.

pastor told the story of a young man he met after preaching one day. I'll call him Phil, because that's not his name. For weeks the evangelist had given appeals for people to give their lives to God, but Phil "hid" backstage as he listened to the powerful messages. One night after yet another appeal for people to give their hearts to Christ, the evangelist left the platform and found Phil crumpled behind one of the backstage curtains. Phil had wept so much that his tears had stained the floor.

The pastor threw his arms around Phil as he prayed and encouraged him. After a while Phil explained why he was hiding. In the past he'd responded to appeals several times, but afterward he'd go back to his old ways. Some of the congregation knew about his sins, and they never let him forget them. And when he stepped forward at appeals, they acted as though he didn't exist. Finally he stopped responding, and stopped attending church.

That's a true story, and it's repeated in churches all over the world. Sometimes it's really tough to forget the mistakes you've made, especially when others keep reminding you of them. In Nehemiah 8 Ezra the priest reads the Book of the Law of Moses to the Jewish returnees to Jerusalem. Standing on a raised platform, Ezra began to notice something as he read. The people were crying. He could see their bowed heads, their tears hitting the dust at their feet. Nehemiah noticed it too.

The Book of the Law recounted all of the commands that God had given Israel before entering the Promised Land, the ones they'd broken. Nehemiah and Ezra urged the people not to cry, because they had a bright future with God. This day was going to mark a brand-new beginning for them. Nehemiah added, "The joy of the Lord is your strength" (verse 10). God didn't want His people to be locked in their past failures. He wanted them to repent and embrace the joy of a new life in Him. The joy that comes when your life is right with God is very powerful. If you've messed up, make it right with God—now.

///////// HOT READ /////////

Why was it so important that exiles confess their sins? Nehemiah 9:2.

——> NEHEMIAH'S LAST STAND <

Remember me with favor, O my God. Nehemiah 13:31.

ude, I hate to say goodbye to Nehemiah. I have learned so much about leadership from listening and watching him in action that I feel like anything's possible with God's help.

Nehemiah saw a vision of a strong, vibrant, holy Jewish remnant, and he never allowed anything to block his view. Why? He knew that his vision was God's vision. God wanted a people who lived and looked like His children, and so did Nehemiah.

The final four chapters of the book covers Israel's repentance for their past sins, their pledge to obey all that God asked of them, the amazing dedication ceremony for the newly rebuilt wall, and Nehemiah's departure.

After the job was done, Nehemiah returned to King Artaxerxes in Persia, who'd allowed him to go back and rebuild the walls of Jerusalem. Some time later Nehemiah asked the king's permission to go back to Jerusalem, and what he found almost made him pop a blood vessel.

The people who had pledged not to intermarry with the other heathen nations were hooking up everywhere with them. Nehemiah got so upset that he beat some of them and pulled out their hair (Nehemiah 13:25). People had also stopped bringing their tithes and offerings to the Temple, forcing the Levites and priests to go to their homes to work, instead of serving God at the Temple. They even did business on the Sabbath. This really incensed Nehemiah.

Nehemiah wasn't about to let this stand. He removed those priests and Levites who'd been sinning against God. He restarted the Temple worship, and stopped the practice of doing business on the Sabbath by locking the city gates so that no merchants could come in or go out during Sabbath hours.

Why did Nehemiah go to all this trouble again when he'd endured so much rebuilding the wall? Nehemiah wanted to please God. He wanted God to remember what he had done to bring glory to His name. Nehemiah wouldn't quit until he pleased God!

////// HOT READ //////

What two lessons have you taken away from reading the book of Nehemiah? Also, read Nehemiah 12:27-31. What is the true purpose of music?

⟶ YOU GO, GIRL!

But when the attendants delivered the king's command, Queen Vashti refused to come. Then the king became furious and burned with anger. Esther 1:12.

We're into the book of Esther. I love this book for several reasons, one of which is the fact that while God is not mentioned in this book, He's there behind what's seen.

As we learned in Ezra and Nehemiah, a remnant—a small group—of Israelites left Persia to go rebuild Jerusalem after King Cyrus of Persia freed them (Ezra 1:1-4). However, many Israelites remained in Persia and dispersed into other territories. Esther tells the story of one of the trials they went through.

Xerxes was the king of Persia in Esther's time. He was the son of Darius the Great, but unlike his father, he was undisciplined and had a thing for listening to the wrong people. He was a party animal, and he wasn't afraid to flaunt it. Esther opens up with King Xerxes throwing one of the biggest parties in all of Scripture. "For a full 180 days he displayed the vast wealth of his kingdom and the splendor and glory of his majesty" (Esther 1:4). Know anyone today who is rich enough to throw a party for 180 days straight?

Liquor flowed like water. The guests got drunk, slept, woke up, and partied some more. Everyone patted Xerxes on the back. They talked about the "Rollies" in his garage, the "ice" in his ears, and the platinum around his neck. Xerxes was "flossin'" big time.

When he had gotten himself totally drunk, he had a not-so-bright idea. "These guys haven't yet seen the best of my possessions," he said to himself. "Wait till they see Queen V!" He gave orders to bring in Vashti, his trophy wife, "in order to display her beauty to the people and the nobles, for she was lovely to look at" (Esther 1:11). Xerxes loved to march her around like a prize poodle!

But V was much more than gorgeous. She was a woman of principle. How do we know that? She stood up to a king who, at the time, ruled just about the whole world. "No," said Vashti, "I'm not going in there. He's drunk, and the men in there are drunk. Who knows what else they're doing in there with all those other women. I refuse to be treated like a piece of meat." That's not all in the Bible, but I know that's how she felt.

Vashti respected herself, even if it meant that she could no longer be queen.

////////// HOT READ ////////
How does alcohol and other substances mess up one's judgment?

——> "HATEORADE" <

When Haman saw that Mordecai would not kneel down or pay him honor, he was enraged. Esther 3:5.

e took huge gulps of the stuff, so that it ran down his beard and dripped onto his Armani suit. "Hateorade" was his drink of choice, and if there was a commercial for the stuff, he would've been in it.

The guy drinking the hate-o-rade in the book of Esther is one of the Bible's major haters. It wasn't enough that King Xerxes had elevated him to Persia's second in command. It wasn't enough that everyone knew his name. The nice rides, the big homes, the women—none of it was enough to please him. His drug of choice was fear. Haman didn't just want to be respected; he wanted to be feared!

Mordecai respected Haman, but he never feared him. Everyone else bowed low when Haman came by, but Mordecai didn't bow. Know anybody who likes to flaunt their titles, their jobs, how much money they have, the cool clothes they wear? They might just have a little Haman in them.

Haman's solution to Mordecai's "dis" was to destroy all the Jews in Persia. Think he might be overreacting just a little? Yeah! Haman got so enraged at Mordecai that he cooked up a story about a group of the king's subjects who served a weird God (so he said) and didn't follow the customs of Persia, and he asked the king for power to destroy them. Get this. King Xerxes—that idiot— never asked Haman who the people where! "Have at it," Xerxes said.

When Mordecai heard of the plot, he "tore his clothes, put on sackcloth and ashes, and went out into the city, wailing loudly and bitterly" (Esther 4:1). Haman's trap was set. He had an unbreakable law from the king—for once passed, laws of the Medes and Persians could never be revoked. So the Jews faced certain destruction. Even those who'd left to go rebuild the Temple of the Lord in Jerusalem would be annihilated. Haman the hater was about to have his revenge, but God was watching over His people.

///////// HOT READ /////////

Read Esther 6. God is not mentioned in the book of Esther, but where do you see His fingerprints in Esther 6?

——> WHAT A BEAUTY? <

This girl, who was also known as Esther, was lovely in form and features, and Mordecai had taken her as his own daughter when her father and mother died. Esther 2:7.

According to a study by behavioral scientists at the University of California published in August 2007, "attractive people make more money than middle attractive people, who in turn make more money than unattractive people." That's not all. Attractive people are judged to be more cooperative than unattractive people, and they tend to get better jobs and better pay as a result. (So that's my problem!)

You need only look around your school—or even your church—to notice that some kids are just plain more popular, more cool, more in demand, than others. At my high school was a cat named Brice who was the chillest dude I'd ever met. Well, actually, I never met him. He was just way outta my league, too "smoove" for the ugly people. He was the star running back on the varsity football team. Brice was "nice."

Beautiful people like Brice seem to have it all, but you know, beauty is much more than what's on the outside. True and lasting beauty is all about what you've got on the inside. The Bible tells us that Queen Esther was "lovely in form and features" (Esther 2:7). She was so stunning that she won the favor of everyone who looked at her (verse 15). But there was more to this beauty than beauty.

Esther's inner courage was not something people could see from the outside, but it was surely revealed in a time of crisis. Mordecai told Esther of Haman's plot and said that she had to tell the king. But Esther was scared to death of going to King Xerxes without being summoned. To do so could mean instant death. But after fasting and praying earnestly to God—hint, hint—Esther courageously put her life on the line for her people. She exposed Haman's plot, then got the king to issue a new law that saved the Jewish nation. How hot is that!

Queen Esther's beauty opened doors for her, but it's what she did when she got past those doors that made her truly special. No matter how we look, God can use us to be a blessing to someone else. Now, *that's* a beautiful thing!

///////// HOT READ ////////

Mordecai went from a death sentence to the king's palace (Esther 10). What would you like for God to do for you? Trust Him to do it!

148

——> BLOWN AWAY <

In the land of Uz there lived a man whose name was Job. This man was blameless and upright; he feared God and shunned evil. Job 1:1.

We just read the book of Esther together. Throughout Esther, God is never mentioned by name, but the spectacular way in which Haman's plot to destroy the Jews blew up had to be God's doing. When you get to the book of Job, however, you see that God—the one who works behind the scenes to save lives—has seemingly left the building.

Daniel Nickels, 21, a student who volunteered as an EMT in the aftermath of Hurricane Katrina, tells the story of a man he met in Gulfport, Mississippi: a man sitting on a porch with no house around it. His house had been blown away. You need to hear Daniel Nickels tell it. His story was published in *The Channels Online*, a news Web site published by Santa Barbara City College, the school Nickels attends.

"He said he'd found his neighbor's two little twin girls underneath a door, holding hands, dead. His other neighbor had tied himself to a tree and tried to ride out the storm, and 'all of his skin was ripped from his body.' Nickels helped get the man from his porch to a hospital. 'He'd lost his family too,' Nickels added. The man died the next day." Of course, that's just one of the horror stories from Katrina. People in New Orleans tell equally tragic, gruesome tales of loss.

When bad things happen to people, we scratch our heads and ask, "Where was God?" The book of Job deals with this question. The first verse of the book tells us that Job was "blameless" and "upright." He loved God, and he stayed far away from evil. Yet God allowed Satan to whip up a personal Katrina in Job's life. In fact, Satan doesn't raise the name of Job when he meets with God. God "dropped a dime" on Job (Job 1:8). In a single day Job lost everything—his home, his possessions, and all his children. Only he and his wife survived, and his wife was highly upset. Can we blame her?

"In all this, Job did not sin by charging God with wrongdoing" (Job 1:22). What did he do? He worshipped God (Job 1:20, 21).

The book of Job is going to challenge everything you believe about God and His goodness. You will learn that life "ain't fair, but God is faithful."

////////// HOT READ //////////

Read Job 2:4-6. What does this tell you about God's power over Satan?

——> WHO NEEDS FRIENDS? <

Consider now: Who, being innocent, has ever perished? Where were the upright ever destroyed? Job 4:7.

ne of the first reactions people have when you're going through a tough trial is sympathy. But not everyone tries to feel your pain.

Yesterday I talked a bit about the mighty Hurricane Katrina that destroyed much of New Orleans and the gulf coast of Mississippi. Perhaps you saw the pictures of the people wading in chest-high water, dead bodies floating around, and people sitting on housetops waiting for help to arrive. It was something out of a disaster movie, except it was real.

While some people expressed sympathy for the victims, others blamed them. In fact, Michael Brown, the director of the Federal Emergency Management Agency—that's the government organization that helps people when natural disasters strike—was one of the chief persons who blamed the victims. When told that the death toll from the hurricane could reach into the thousands, Brown told CNN, "Unfortunately, that's going to be attributable a lot to people who did not heed the advance warnings."

Some residents did decide to ride out the storm, but most of the people who stayed in New Orleans and suffered the most damage were the poor who had nowhere to go and no way to get there. Brown was saying, in effect, that they had it coming. They should have left the city.

That's old news, right? Why rehash the past? Well, we can learn a lot from the past, like what not to say to people who have lost everything—whether they brought it on themselves or not. Of the three who came to "comfort" Job, his friend Eliphaz was the first to speak. Eliphaz believed that Job must have committed some hidden sin that caused God to punish him. If you were covered from head to toe with burning, oozing sores, would you want a friend to say that to you?

"Would I lie to your face?" Job replied. "Relent, do not be unjust; reconsider, for my integrity is at stake" (Job 6:28, 29).

Eliphaz shows us what *not* to say to a friend who is struggling.

//////// HOT READ ////////

What else did Job say about friendship? Read Job 6:14-17. What point was Job making about true friends and fake friends? Was he right?

150

——> PLEASE, NOT MY KIDS! <

When your children sinned against him, he gave them over to the penalty of their sin. But if you will look to God and plead with the Almighty, if you are pure and upright, even now he will rouse himself on your behalf. Job 8:4-6.

T elling a man whose children just died that they died because they had sinned against God has got to be the cruelest thing in the world. Yet, that's exactly what Bildad said to Job.

Yesterday you read what Eliphaz said to Job. He basically pulled out a knife and stabbed Job with it—blaming him for the calamity that struck him and his family. As painful as it was for Job to refute Eliphaz's personal attack, at least Eliphaz didn't hate on Job's kids. Your parents will tell you that as tough as it is to deal with people who attack their personal integrity, there's nothing more distressing than having to deal with someone who attacks their children. And that's exactly what Bildad did.

"Job," he begins, his forehead crinkling with righteous indignation, "are you saying that God is not fair? That God just attacks people for no reason?" Bildad was referring to what Job had said in response to Eliphaz. Job didn't know why his life had been turned into a living nightmare, so he said some hard things to God. Can you blame him? Here's a bit of what Job said to God.

"Will you never look away from me, or let me alone for an instant?" Job cried. "If I have sinned, what have I done to you, O Watcher of men? Why have you made me your target?" (Job 7:19, 20). If destruction was stalking you at every turn, wouldn't you plead with God to find some answers? Maybe people who don't know God don't struggle when bad stuff happens, but those who serve God know to go to the Source for answers. Our rants will not scare God off. He wants to hear from us.

Agitated, Bildad continued. "Stop playing yourself, dude. Your kids died because they sinned against God!" He closes his little "pick-me-up" with this gem: "Surely God does not reject a blameless man or strengthen the hands of evildoers" (Job 8:20).

If Bildad wanted to encourage Job, why didn't he say something like "Job, I know you're hurting right now, and you don't know why. Mind if I pray with you?"

######### HOT READ #######

How does Job respond to Bildad? Job 9:12-15. Is Job right about God? What does Job say about himself?

151

──> YOU'RE DUMBER THAN I THOUGHT! <

Surely he recognizes deceitful men; and when he sees evil, does he not take note? But a witless man can no more become wise than a wild donkey's colt can be born a man. Job 11:11, 12.

I t's hard to read Job 10 and not feel Job's pain. Check out this expression of grief: "Why then did you bring me out of the womb? I wish I had died before any eye saw me. If only I had never come into being, or had been carried straight from the womb to the grave! Are not my few days almost over? Turn away from me so I can have a moment's joy" (Job 10:18-20). Can you say—PAIN?

You're know you're hurting pretty bad when you find yourself wishing that you had died before you were born. A year ago *Insight*, the teen magazine I work for, printed the personal testimony of teen named Joe.★ His life seemed to be cursed.

One of Joe's sisters died during birth; another sister died of a drug overdose; his father, a gang member, was shot by a rival gang; and his mother contracted HIV. It was by far one of the saddest stories I'd ever read. If there was someone who was dealt a bad hand, Joe was that someone. On top of all of that, one of his mother's boyfriends swindled her out of all the insurance money she received from the death of Joe's father. Since his mother was an illegal alien living in the U.S., she could not file any charges against the perpetrator.

This series of unfortunate events made Joe give up on God, but God never gave up on Joe. An Adventist guy invited Joe to church, and he visited a few times, then a few times more. The church took him in and offered to pay for him to go to an Adventist academy. When he wrote the story for *Insight*, he was in his senior year.

While Joe had friends who took an interest in him, Job did not. Eliphaz "dissed" him, Bildad "dissed" his kids, and Zophar called him "witless." "You won't silence me, with your idle talk," Zophar retorts. "You have lost your senses. A donkey has a better chance of giving birth to a man than you have getting back your senses."

Zophar's attack on Job was the worst of his three friends.

───────
★ not his name

──> I WON'T LET GO! <

Keep silent and let me speak; then let come to me what may. Why do I put myself in jeopardy and take my life in my hands? Job 13:13, 14.

ophar's words pushed Job to the limit of his patience. As Job scraped the pus-filled boils that dotted the landscape of his body, he grew tired of the constant attacks from the men who'd come to comfort him.

"What you know, I also know," he shouts at Zophar. "I am not inferior to you" (Job 13:2). Job takes offense to the suggestion that he has lost his mind simply because he dared to question God about his pain.

Haven't you questioned God a time or two before? When my cousin was gunned down on the streets of New York, I questioned God. I wanted to know why He didn't save Owen's life. If he could program the stars to shoot through the night sky, couldn't he "unprogram" that shooting? I still don't have the answers to my questions.

"But I desire to speak to the Almighty and to argue my case with God," Job continued (verse 3). He wanted to talk to God directly. Job wanted a little one-on-one face time with God to get some answers. His friends were basically saying that he had no right to question God this way. "You have sinned and your kids have sinned, and that's the reason for the punishment. Just 'fess up,' and God will give you your stuff back." WRONG!

Job's answer: "I haven't done anything wrong! I know I haven't. God has targeted me, and I want to know why." If you read Job 1, Job was right about this. He was blameless, and God had singled him out for Satan's wrath (verse 7-12).

But there was another reason, a very important reason, that Job felt comfortable questioning God. The reason is found in Job 13:15, and I just have to quote this power text: "Though he slay me, yet will I hope in him; I will surely defend my ways to his face" (Job 13:15).

Did you get that? Job refused to stop pleading his case to God because none of God's responses would make him leave God. Job was saying, "It doesn't matter what God allows to happen to me. I won't stop trusting Him, so I'm not afraid to talk to Him."

//////// HOT READ ////////

What powerful note of hope did Job mention in Job 13:16? That's faith!

——> I WOULD ENCOURAGE YOU <

I also could speak like you, if you were in my place; I could make fine speeches against you and shake my head at you. But my mouth would encourage you; comfort from my lips would bring you relief. Job 16:4, 5.

dward Steichen, a famous photographer, painter, and art gallery and museum curator, died in 1973, but the world almost didn't get a chance to see his unique gifts and talents. *Bits & Pieces,* a magazine that publishes motivational stories, included the following story in its February 4, 1993, issue. (Yes, there *wa*s life before you were born!)

"Edward Steichen, who eventually became one of the world's most renowned photographers, almost gave up on the day he shot his first pictures. At 16 young Steichen bought a camera and took 50 photos. Only one turned out— a portrait of his sister at the piano.

"Edward's father thought that was a poor showing. But his mother insisted that the photograph of his sister was so beautiful that it more than compensated for 49 failures. Her encouragement convinced the youngster to stick with his new hobby. He stayed with it for the rest of his life, but it had been a close call."

Before the age of the digital camera, film had to be developed in a dark room. It was not a process that a novice could do very easily, yet young Edward Steichen gave it a try. Forty-nine of his photos failed. His father focused on the 49 that failed, but his mother focused on the one that came out, and she *encouraged* him about that one. Imagine that. The world was almost robbed of a great artist because a father couldn't see past his son's failure.

Like Steichen's father, Job's friends couldn't see past his supposed "failures." They could point to no sin that he'd committed but that didn't stop them from hurling accusations. In Job 15 Eliphaz calls him a liar: "Your own mouth condemns you" (verse 6). Job responds, telling him that "it's easy for you to stand there and throw bombs at me while I'm all messed up. If the tables were turned, I wouldn't do that you. I would encourage you!" What an awesome testimony.

/////// HOT READ ///////

Read Job 17:10-16. How might your lack of encouragement hurt your friends?

——> TRUTH AND ERROR <

The lamp of the wicked is snuffed out; the flame of his fire stops burning. Job 18:5.

efore Job responds to Bildad for the second time, he has to endure this insult: "When will you end these speeches? Be sensible, and then we can talk" (Job 18:2). Guess Job's plea for a little understanding from his friends is not working.

Bildad's second response to Job can be summed up this way: "Job, no one who is innocent experiences the kind of trouble that you have." That's about the sum of it. In Job 20 Zophar takes this theme to new heights.

It is true that many wicked people suffer for their wrongs. Nicolae Ceauşescu (pronounced chow-ches-kew) died when mobs of Romanian citizens caught him and his wife as they attempted to flee the country following the fall of Communism. Ceauşescu had brutally ruled his nation, starving and killing thousands of its people.

But for every Ceauşescu, there's a General Augusto Pinochet. He was brought to power in Chile by a CIA-engineered coup in 1973. The U.S. spent more than $11 million to fund the coup that toppled Chile's democratically elected president. Pinochet went on to torture and kill thousands of his own citizens. After the rainy season, poor peasants in the Chilean countryside would see headless bodies with their arms tied behind their backs in the nation's rivers. Unlike Ceauşescu, Pinochet lived a long, comfortable life. He died on December 10, 2006, at the age of 91, never having to answer for his crimes.

Bildad's argument that only the evil suffer the hardship that Job was facing was only partially true. Many, like Augusto Pinochet, won't answer for their crimes until Jesus comes. Job was very hurt by Bildad's comments. "If it is true that I have gone astray, my error remains my concern alone," he retorted (Job 19:4). Job knew he had done nothing to warrant this kind of punishment from God, and even if he did, it was none of his friends' business. They were supposed to encourage him in a time of great need.

As human beings we like to draw bright lines between those who commit sin and those who do not. While we can know people by their "fruits" (Matthew 7:16, KJV), we don't know everything. Since God does, we'd better leave the judging to Him.

//////// HOT READ ////////

Read Job 19:25, 26. This is the earliest known Bible reference pointing to Christ's resurrection from the dead as redeemer of the world.

155

——> MAKE IT UP <

Is not your wickedness great? Are not your sins endless? Job 22:5.

f you can't catch someone committing a crime, well, just accuse them of something. Make it up out of thin air. In fact, throw as many charges at them as you can muster. One is bound to stick.

That's the way some police forces around the world operate. Aung San Suu Kyi, a Nobel Peace Prize winner and the elected prime minister of a small country called Myanmar, has spent most of the past 10 years under house arrest. And you think being grounded is for a day or two after school is tough?

Her crime? Getting elected. Myanmar's military dictators allowed elections in 1990, believing that they would easily win. They were wrong. Suu Kyi's party won a majority of the votes, and she stood to become the country's first female head of state. But she has never been allowed to serve. The military dictators have repeatedly extended her house detention, refusing to let her travel anywhere in the country. The have nothing to charge her with, so they just make up charges and extend her stay at home. Crazy, don't you think? Better be glad you live in the United States. At least North American governments are not that nutty.

When Eliphaz, Job's friend, couldn't point to a sin in Job's life that led to his sufferings, he started making stuff up. See if you can guess what he accused him of when he said this: "You demanded security from your brothers for no reason; you stripped men of their clothing, leaving them naked" (Job 22:6). Any ideas?

This one's a bit easier: "You gave no water to the wary and you withheld food from the hungry, though you were a powerful man owning land—an honored man, living on it" (verses 7, 8). What a strong charge, huh?

Eliphaz was basically accusing Job of being greedy, manipulative, and heartless. He charged Job with demanding payment from "brothers" who couldn't pay, leaving them with nothing.

Job's deeply moving response is summed up in Job 23:11: "My feet have closely followed his steps; I have kept to his way without turning aside." Job knew that he had been faithful to God, and Eliphaz's words could not shake his innocence.

//////// HOT READ ////////
How do you respond when people accuse you falsely? See Job 23:10.

156

——> GOING TOO FAR <

I will never admit you are in the right; till I die, I will not deny my integrity. I will maintain my righteousness and never let go of it; my conscience will not reproach me as long as I live. Job 27:5, 6.

When you are going through a really devastating crisis that you don't fully understand, it's easy to blame God. In the next few chapters Job crosses the line with God.

To be sure, Job didn't willingly push the envelope with God. Eliphaz, Bildad, and Zophar drove Job crazy with their sickening reasons for his suffering. Job had gotten tired of telling them that he had done nothing wrong. He had searched his life with a magnifying glass, combing through his boyhood, his teenage years, his young adulthood, his adulthood—nothing! He couldn't point to a single thing that he had done and not gotten God's forgiveness for. He was blameless, upright in all his ways. In fact, that's what God said about him.

I have a friend whose father died in a car accident. He woke up one morning and found out his dad had been killed. The pain was unbearable. He stopped talking to God. *Why didn't God protect my dad?* he wondered. *My dad was a police officer. He protected people. Why did God let him die?*

After a while he accepted his father's death, though he still didn't understand it. But getting to where he and God could talk again wasn't easy, and at times he still struggles with it, as any teen would.

In today's reading, Job is where my friend was when he first heard that his father had died. He's having a very difficult time understanding what God is doing in his life. Job feels that all he has left is his integrity, his "rightness" before God. So he vows that no one will take that from him. Not Eliphaz, Bildad, or Zophar—not even God.

That is when Job went too far. When he began to demand answers from God because of his "rightness," he crossed the line.

//////// HOT READ ////////

Have you ever "crossed the line" in your attacks on God? Job 27:2.

——> BRING BACK THE DAYS! <

Oh, for the days when I was in my prime, when God's intimate friendship blessed my house, when the Almighty was still with me and my children were around me. Job 29:4, 5.

oth of my grandfathers have been dead for several years, but memories of them are still fresh in my mind.

My grandpa Joseph, my father's father, was unlike just about any man I've ever met. He came to live with us after he'd had a stroke. What I cherished most about Grandpa Jo was the fact that he always had time for us. It really didn't matter what time of day or night it was, if you showed up at his room he would perk up.

When he first came to us, he had a pretty strong smoking problem. I've written about how I used to sneak up behind him, waiting for the moment he would toss his cigarette butt to the side. I'd wait until he was gone, pick it up, and take a puff. It was wrong, but I just had to try it. He looked so cool that I just had to be like him. A few heavy puffs and a whole lot of choking later, I decided to quit before I ever got started. Later my grandfather also quit when he accepted Jesus as his Savior.

If only I could turn back the clock and see both my grandfathers again.

Grandpa Jo played games with me and my four siblings, gave us all nicknames, and shared whatever he had with us. Because of how much he cared about us, how willing he was to give up his time for us, how unselfish he was with his stuff, we had nothing but respect for him. I surely did, but even now I can't remember anyone ever saying or doing something to disrespect Grandfather. He had earned that respect, and everyone gave it to him—including my parents.

One of the things that Job hated most about losing his children, his posses-sions, and his health was the way that it changed how people saw him. "The young men saw and stepped aside and the old men rose to their feet," Job sighed (Job 29:8). "But now they mock me, men younger than I, whose fathers I would have disdained to put with my sheep dogs" (Job 30:1). Job got no respect from the young or the old.

But the thing he missed more than the respect of others was his friendship with God. Job missed God's presence is his life, and he was going crazy thinking about it.

/////// HOT READ ///////
What does Job 31:1 tell us about how to stay pure and holy?

——> LET ME TALK! <

Now Elihu had waited before speaking to Job because they were older than he. But when he saw that the three men had nothing more to say, his anger was aroused.
Job 32:4, 5.

eens will try just about anything. Don't believe me? You know I'm telling the truth.

Perhaps Michael Sessions ran for mayor of Hillsdale, Michigan, as a prank, but you'd never know it. The 18-year-old high school senior ran a tough campaign, managing to unseat the current mayor by a whopping two votes. With a campaign budget of $700, Sessions ran a strong campaign. At the time he ran, he had not yet turned 18 and was unable to vote in his own election.

Think that guy's got guts? How about a teen who became famous back in 2007? Vífill Atlason, a 16-year-old high school student from Iceland, decided to call the White House for a chat with President Bush. (Don't they "Guantanamo" people for that?)

According to ABC News, Atlason found what he believed to be President George W. Bush's allegedly secret telephone number and phoned, introducing himself as Ólafur Ragnar Grímsson, the actual president of Iceland, requesting a private meeting with him. "I just wanted to talk to him, have a chat, invite him to Iceland and see what he'd say," said Atlason.

The White House folks took the bait and gave Vífill Atlason President Bush's private secret number, a number requiring the highest security clearance. Shortly after speaking with the president's secretary, police arrived at Atlason's home and took him to the police station for questioning.

There's not much that youth won't do or say, and young adults are not far behind them in this. Today you will read the speech of the last of Job's friends who happened by. You heard from Eliphas, Bildad, and Zophar, but Elihu trumps them all. He is a young, fiery guy who sat listening to the attacks of the older friends, and Job's responses. He's not impressed by the arguments of either. So he takes God's side. Elihu's defense of God goes on for the next six chapters. It's worth the read, and unlike the others, he is right!

//////// HOT READ ////////

How does Elihu respond to Job's main charge that God does not speak?
Job 33:12-18.

——> NOW HEAR THIS <

Hear my words, you wise men; listen to me, you men of learning. Job 34:2.

lihu had grown tired of listening to the "graybeards" sound off on what was happening to Job. When they ran out of words, he began to speak, and he wasn't bashful.

Maybe he feared that once he stopped he'd never get a chance to say anything else. Something like in some churches when teens are asked to join the church's elder board. The teen gets one shot, if that, to weigh in on the heavy matters of the church. Then the adults pat themselves on the back for including kids in the church's work. Yeah, right! If Elihu had been in one of those churches, he would've never made it to the "big show."

Elihu had listened carefully as Eliphaz, Bildad, and Zophar made the case that Job's suffering was the result of sin in his life. Though they could produce no proof, they beat Job all about the head with their baseless charges. Then Elihu paid closed attention to Job's defense. He'd heard Job say all the things that he'd done right, how he knew he'd done nothing to offend God in any way. Elihu had heard Job say he was ready to "sign now my defense—let the Almighty answer me" (Job 31:35). In fact, he probably took special offense to Job's demanding an answer from God.

"Far be it from God to do evil," began Elihu, "from the Almighty to do wrong. . . . It is unthinkable that God would do wrong, that the Almighty would pervert justice" (Job 34:10-12). Elihu is saying, "Job, it's one thing to claim that you are innocent of all sin, but accusing God of doing you dirty? That's going too far!"

Elihu doesn't stop there. He adds: "Those who suffer he delivers in their suffering; he speaks to them in their affliction. [God] is wooing you from the jaws of distress to a spacious place free from restriction, to the comfort of your table laden with choice food" (Job 36:15, 16). That image was probably hard for Job to conjure through all his pain, but Elihu was trying to say—be it a bit harshly—that God is just and in time He will work things out for you, Job. He wasn't just talking to Job.

/////// HOT READ ///////

Notice the poetry in Elihu's description of God's creative power (Job 36:22-33).

——> QUESTIONS, QUESTIONS <

Who is this that darkens my counsel with words without knowledge? Brace yourself like a man; I will question you, and you shall answer me. Job 38:2, 3.

t took a mere 37 chapters in the book of Job before God spoke up for Himself. It was time to clear the air. From the very start of Job 38, God's target is not Eliphaz, Bildad, Zophar—and definitely not Elihu. Job is the guy with the bull's-eye on his forehead.

The world is filled with people who are unsure about God. Some, like Lance Armstrong, seven-time winner of bicycling's Tour de France, go even further.

"I asked myself what I believed. I had never prayed a lot. I hoped hard, I wished hard, but I didn't pray. I had developed a certain distrust of organized religion growing up, but I felt I had the capacity to be a spiritual person, and to hold some fervent beliefs. Quite simply, I believed I had a responsibility to be a good person, and that meant fair, honest, hardworking, and honorable. . . . At the end of the day, if there was indeed some Body or presence standing there to judge me, I hoped I would be judged on whether I had lived a true life, not on whether I believed in a certain book, or whether I'd been baptized. If there was indeed a God at the end of my days, I hoped he didn't say, 'But you were never a Christian, so you're going the other way from heaven.' If so, I was going to reply, 'You know what? You're right. Fine' " (*My Journey Back to Life,* pp. 116, 117).

Lance Armstrong is an atheist. He doesn't believe in God. You'd expect him to sideswipe God in a crisis. But Job was a believer. He knew God. He just didn't believe that God was dealing fairly with him. He questioned God's justice.

God responded by asking Job a series of very difficult questions. "Where were you when I made the earth?" God begins. "Did you see the blueprints, Job?" Things go pretty much downhill from there. What's more, God wasn't just talking to hear Himself talk. He wanted answers from Job.

God welcomes the questions of atheists and believers alike. We are free to question, but He is also free to answer, sometimes—as He did for job—in ways that blow us away.

///////// HOT READ ///////

Why did God use the wonders of nature to question Job? Job 38; 39. Does nature better testify to the existence of God than human beings?

June 3 • *Job 40-42*

——> GOD'S FINAL QUESTION <

After Job had prayed for his friends, the Lord made him prosperous again and gave him twice as much as he had before. Job 42:10.

oday we close the book of Job, one of the most awesome pieces of literature ever written. We met a man who, in a single day, suffered more loss than most people ever will suffer in a lifetime. But the story's not done yet. One of its hidden gems is found in Job 42:10, which you read above.

It's so easy to focus our attention on God's questions to Job and his humble responses. I was moved deeply when Job said to God: "Surely I spoke of things I did not understand, things too wonderful for me to know. . . . My ears have heard you, but now my eyes have seen you" (Job 42:4, 5). God never told Job why he was suffering, yet Job feels better just knowing that God had not abandoned Him.

Job's reconnection with God was sweet to see, but there was still the little issue of all the stuff he'd lost—his family, his health, his wealth. What was God going to do about that? Well, it appears that God hadn't forgotten about Job's losses, but if he wanted things to be restored, he had to answer one final question from God: Would he forgive his friends?

God rebuked Eliphaz, Bildad, and Zophar, and told them to go to Job with burnt offerings for themselves. God instructed Job to pray for them. God was testing Job here. If he had refused to pray for them because of his anger, I believe God that would not have restored Job. Job had to choose to forgive his friends. In so doing, God forgave them and restored him.

Speaking of forgiveness, Archbishop Desmond Tutu, a great freedom fighter and world leader, once noted, "If you can find it in yourself to forgive, then you are no longer chained to the perpetrator. You can move on, and you can even help the perpetrator to become a better person too." That's exactly what Job did by forgiving his friends, and God blessed him for it. God blesses those who forgive others.

/////// HOT READ ///////

Read Job 42:11-16. What do you think it would have been like to listen to Job talk about this rough spot in his life? Job's story reminds us that trials don't last forever.

162

——> THE SONG BOOK <

Blessed is the man who does not walk in the counsel of the wicked or stand in the way of sinners or sit in the seat of mockers. But his delight is in the law of the Lord, and on his law he meditates day and night. Psalm 1:1, 2.

Is there a more famous book in the Bible than Psalms? I doubt it. And it's probably the most quoted of any in book in the Bible too. Why? That's easy. No other book contains the range of human emotions that Psalms does. Angry, sad, happy, serene—whatever your mood, there's a psalm that will speak to you.

The book of Psalms is really a grouping of songs that were sung in worship to God. The Levites would sing a psalm for each day of the week, and on Sabbaths and special festival days, instrumental music accompanied their singing. But not all the psalms were written for this purpose. King David wrote many for private use.

Most people believe that King David wrote the book of Psalms, but in truth, he wrote only 73 of them. Among his many talents, David was a musician and composer. Songwriting was his hobby, his way of telling God exactly how he felt at the time. Asaph, a well-respected worshipper and musician in David's time, penned 12 psalms; the sons of Kora wrote 10; King Solomon contributed two; Moses did one; Heman, one; Ethan, one; and 50 psalms are anonymous. Many of them are thematic. For instance, Psalms 1 through 41 are songs of worship, 42 through 89 are concern Israel, and 90 through 150 are psalms of praise.

Despite its different authors, many chapters, and varied subject matter, the book of Psalms teaches us how to worship God with our lives. Psalm 1 says it all. We are encouraged not to walk where sinners hang out. Why? If you walk there long enough, you just may pause to see what they do. If you keep standing where sinners stand, there's a good chance that you'll become comfortable and sit down with them. The language is symbolic, but the message is clear: If you want to be happy, stay away from evil, think deeply about what God has said, and obey Him. This is the secret to a full life. Psalms is all about living a life that honors God at all times!

///////// HOT READ ////////

Psalm 3 was written while David was on the run from his son Absalom. What words did David use to describe the emotions he was feeling?

——> WATCH THE REP! <

O Lord my God, if I have done this and there is guilt on my hands—if I have done evil to him who is at peace with me or without cause have robbed my foe—then let my enemy pursue and overtake me. Psalm 7:3-5.

No one likes to be talked about. I've never met anyone who was tickled at the thought that someone was spreading lies about them. Have you?

Yet our society thrives on lies. There are magazines and Web sites that make gobs of money, purely based on lies. When one Web site claimed that basketball player Tony Parker—you know, the guy who married Eva Longoria, one of the stars of ABC's *Desperate Housewives*—had broken his marital vows with another woman, he sued the tabloid site for $40 million in an effort to clear his name. Did that stop the Web site from smearing other "stars"? Absolutely not!

People who care about their reputations don't take it lightly when someone tarnishes the good name they worked hard to build up. I found this out the hard way when a guy approached me after hearing something I'd said about him. He was trying to be cool about the whole thing, but he was definitely "swolled up" about it. I learned my lesson that day for sure.

King David wrote Psalm 7 in response to lies that Cush, a member of the tribe of Benjamin, had circulated about him. Many scholars believe that the Cush who was running off his mouth about David was actually King Saul, whose father's name was Kish, from the tribe of Benjamin. That would make a ton of sense, because Saul grew so jealous of David's military successes that he spread lies about David, claiming that David wanted his throne (1 Samuel 20:30, 31). Can you say "insecurity"?

David didn't confront his accuser, as many of us would have immediately done. David pleaded his case to God. He was willing to live without the protection of God if it could be proved that he'd done what Cush accused him of. Of course, David had done nothing wrong, so he had nothing to fear. Yet the thought of someone destroying his "rep" hurt him deeply.

How do you respond when someone lies about you?

//////// HOT READ ////////

Psalm 8 is one you should memorize. Check out verses 3 and 5. Sweet!

164

──> PURE <

And the words of the Lord are flawless, like silver refined in a furnace of clay, purified seven times. Psalm 12:6.

The batch of psalms that you'll read today are some of the most powerful readings in all the Bible. In Psalm 11 you'll read David's question "When the foundations are being destroyed, what can the righteous do?" (verse 3). This simple verse gets at the heart of one of the recurring themes in King David's writing: why the wicked appear to prosper while the righteous suffer. If your friends have been "dissing" you because you won't wear revealing clothes, listen to provocative music, or get involved in sexual practices, don't get upset. The righteous have always been hated for following God. Consider it a badge of honor to suffer as Jesus did for doing what was right.

King David knew how it felt to have the whole world against you. Even when you know God is with you, it's still tough to watch the wicked do their thing against you and get away with it. In Psalm 12 David's rage bubbled over and flowed out to God. "Help, Lord," he sang, "for the godly are no more; the faithful have vanished from among men. Everyone lies to his neighbor; their flattering lips speak with deception" (Psalm 12:1, 2). While the wicked lied, David prized the words of God because they were "flawless," like silver refined seven times.

In David's day refining silver was no easy task. Dug out from the ground, it carried several impurities. To free the pure silver from all the dirty stuff that was on it and in it, the silver ore was "burned" several times. To remove certain impurities, the fire didn't need to be very hot. However, to burn away others, the fire had to be scorching. So the silversmith did several controlled burns to get rid of all the impurities, until what was left was "pure" silver. Pure silver was extremely expensive back then—just as it is today!

David believed that God's words were very precious. Why? Because the flattering words of the powerful were nothing but a bunch of lies, and those lies were everywhere. He longed for God to shut their mouths with His words of truth.

God's words are precious. Value them highly.

/////// HOT READ ////////

Wanna know what kind of people God hangs out with? Read Psalm 15.

——> LOOKING AROUND! <

The heavens declare the glory of God; the skies proclaim the work of his hands.
Day after day they pour forth speech; night after night they display knowledge.
Psalm 19:1, 2.

ude, I'm out of words today. There's just way too much to write about in Psalms 16-20. I was reading through Psalm 16, you know, just merrily going my way when, BAM! Verse 8 punched me in the eye: *I have set the Lord always before me. Because he is at my right hand I will not be shaken.* After reading that, I asked myself, "Dwain, have *you* put God before everything else in your life?" (Sorry, gotta go pray now!)

I got back into the groove, then the praise party in Psalm 18 overwhelmed me. After God had delivered Dave from all his enemies—including Saul—he penned this awesome song. Have you ever thought about sitting down and writing a song to God for delivering you from finals week? That's sort of what David did when he wrote Psalm 18.

I worshipped hard with Dave in Psalm 18, but then he kicked it up a notch in Psalm 19. Just for the record, Psalm 19 is one of those pieces of Scripture that you should memorize. Yep, the whole thing. If you apply yourself, learning two verses a week, you'll have the whole thing down in seven weeks. Trust me, it's worth it.

There are two parts to Psalm 19. In the first part—verses 1-6—King David wants us to get this message: God speaks to us through His creation. If you look at the heavens, you'll hear God's voice. A few years ago NASA's Hubble Telescope discovered something scientists call "dark matter" or "dark energy" in the outer recesses of the universe. What is it? They don't really know, but whatever it is, scientists believe it's speeding up the growth of the universe. Scientists who believe in the big bang had concluded that our universe came into being 14 billion years ago and hadn't changed much since. Oops. They are now rethinking that conclusion! Could God be behind the "dark matter"?

King David urges us to look up and around at God's visual book. Keep looking, and you'll come to the same conclusion that he came to. There is a God, and He is speaking!

/////// HOT READ ///////

What place did David pray that God would send us help from? Psalm 20:2.
Based on what you've read so far, what is the significance of that place?

——> PASS IT DOWN <

In you our fathers put their trust; they trusted and you delivered them. Psalm 22:4.

wo years ago I took a bus tour of Manhattan, New York. I'd been to New York several times before—to shop, see shows, and visit Ground Zero. Of course, nothing in New York moved me more than the site where so many people lost their lives on September 11, 2001.

The bus tour was great because I got to learn some of the history of how Manhattan came to be Manhattan. For instance, who knew that Wall Street was once home to a large auction block—for slaves? I surely didn't. Our tour guide spouted lots of startling trivia like that, but the trip got really interesting when we drove through the Upper East Side of Manhattan, the place the rich and famous call home.

Awesome old mansions dot Manhattan's 70th Street overlooking Central Park. The rich and famous built their 20- and 30-room mansions close to nature. Of course, they were the only ones who could afford the view. The mansions were owned by a Who's Who list of wealthy elites—the Rothschilds, the Rockefellers, the Fricks, the Carnegies, etc. (You might still be able to snag the Rothschild mansion for a cool $35 million.)

Manhattan's earlier elites built homes that were monuments to their power and status. (Today most of the mansions have been converted into very expensive townhouses and apartments, owned by a host of "stars." What will they be remembered for besides rich luxurious mansions? Not much.)

Whether we know it or not, we all are in the process of leaving a legacy, something that we hand down to the next generation. Many people pass on money or property to their children and grandchildren, but whether they know it or not, they are passing much more than that.

King David understood the power of a godly legacy. During his struggles he remembered that his ancestors trusted in God, and He delivered them from Egyptian slavery, took them through the wilderness, and gave them the Promised Land. David drew strength from this legacy of trust that had been passed down to him.

Don't have a godly legacy in your family? Start creating one of your own.

///////// HOT READ ////////

Read Psalm 25:1-7. What is David longing for from God?

———> ONE THING <

One thing I ask of the Lord, this is what I seek: that I may dwell in the house of the Lord all the days of my life, to gaze upon the beauty of the Lord and to seek him in his temple. Psalm 27:4.

I came across the following anonymous rant by a fed-up pastor.

"Football in the fall. Basketball in the winter. Baseball in the spring and summer. This pastor has been an avid sports fan all his life. But I've had it! I quit this sports business once and for all. You can't get me near one of those places again. Want to know why?

"Every time I went, they asked me for money.

The people with whom I had to sit didn't seem very friendly.

The seats were too hard and not at all comfortable.

I went to many games, but the coach never came to call on me.

The referee made a decision with which I could not agree.

I suspected that I was sitting with some hypocrites—they came to see their friends and what others were wearing rather than to see the game.

Some games went into overtime, and I was late getting home.

The band played some numbers that I had never heard before.

It seems that the games are scheduled when I want to do other things.

I was taken to too many games by my parents when I was growing up.

I don't want to take my children to any games, because I want them to choose for themselves what sport they like best."

Care to guess what place this pastor is referring to? You got it—church!

Have you ever gotten tired of going to church? When I was a teen, there were times when I could do without "da saints," if you know what I mean. As I got older I realized that going to church actually isn't about all the other stuff that goes on at church. It's about being in God's presence, gazing on His beauty, pouring out my love to Him from the depths of my heart. Church is all about God. That's David's message in Psalm 27. Read it and be blessed!

——> THE WEIGHT-LOSS PLAN <

Blessed is he whose transgressions are forgiven, whose sins are covered. Blessed is the man whose sin the Lord does not count against him and in whose spirit is no deceit. Psalm 32:1, 2.

riter and author Harry Osbourne hates to visit the doctor. "It seems as though there is something wrong when you pay a guy $50 to tell you that you're too fat!" he once commented. "Even though it is the truth, it seems to me that I should not have to pay $50 to hear a doctor tell me what I could have told him by looking in the mirror."

Osbourne tells about a recent visit when the nurse kindly broke the news that he was overweight. She expressed it in a way that made him consider the problem from a different angle. As he tells it, the nurse looked very surprised as she adjusted the scale weights upward, then said, "You hide your weight well."

"I'd never heard that before, nor do I believe she looked very closely, or she would have discovered where I was hiding it," Osbourne said. But it did make him think about something.

What if we could "hide the weight" from other people? Would it change the weight total? Would it change the effects of our added weight? Of course not. The effect on our bodies is the same whether our weight is hidden or obvious. Hiding the problem makes no difference. Whether the nurse, the doctor, or the patient thinks the burden is hidden, it still exists, and the effects remain.

Considering this neat little story, I remembered times I was sick and tried to play doctor. Once I developed a bad case of strep throat and decided to ride it out by gargling with salt water. Bad idea. I avoided the doctor, but I couldn't avoid the pain.

King David knew the devastating effects of unforgiven sin. He stole a man's wife and then had the man killed. He knew from experience that the weight of sin crushes those who try to carry it themselves. Sometimes we need God's weight-loss plan.

And what is that? It's that we must take our sin to God, confess it, and accept His forgiveness.

You'll see how great you look without the weight!

/////// HOT READ ///////

Worried about something? Aim Psalm 34 right at your fears and watch them disappear.

——> THINGS TO DO <

Show me, O Lord, my life's end and the number of my days; let me know how fleeting is my life. Psalm 39:4.

There's too much power in today's Bible passage—Psalms 36-40—for one day. Reading through the Bible is like going on an African safari. There is so much to see that you sort of get overwhelmed. That's how I have felt while reading through the Psalms. I am highlighting scriptures that I want I to revisit for future study. I hope you are too.

One of the scriptures that I underlined and highlighted is Psalm 39:4. When I first read this verse, it sounded kind of morbid. Who is crazy enough to ask God, "Would You tell me how much time I've got left? When am I going to kick the bucket?" David—that's who!

I started to dismiss David's plea to know "his end," but then I started thinking about it. Why would someone want to know how many days they have left on earth? Probably because they want to do something big, chase a dream, or live more purposefully. Let's face it. Who wouldn't live differently if the doctor found an inoperable malignant tumor in their brain?

King David didn't wait for some life-threatening diagnosis. I believe that he asked God to show him how fleeting his life was so that he wouldn't waste time on meaningless stuff. He wanted his life to matter, to count for God.

On December 26, 2007—the day after Christmas—MSNBC.com published the story of 17-year-old Rachel Rosenfeld of New York. Here's an excerpt: "Hundreds of Cambodian villagers welcomed the arrival of a new school Wednesday, a gift from an American teenager who raised $52,000 after reading about the hardships of growing up in Cambodia. Rachel Rosenfeld . . . made her first visit to the Southeast Asian country for the opening of the R. S. Rosenfeld School, which brings five computers and Internet access to 300 primary school students in a small village of Siem Reap province, a poverty-stricken area that is home to the country's famed Angkor Wat temple complex. . . . 'It makes me feel great to know that I was able to help so many people,'" said Rosenfeld.

Think about your own life. Make every moment of every day count for God!

//////// HOT READ ////////

Do you really want to please God? Psalm 40:8 will show you how!

---> PANTING DEER <

> *As the deer pants for streams of water, so my soul pants for you, O God. My soul thirsts for God, for the living God. When can I go and meet with God?* Psalm 42:1, 2.

Psalm 42 begins what is called Book II of the Psalms, and covers Psalms 42-72. As you read them, you'll notice that many focus on Israel's trials and triumphs, prayers and petitions. They begin with one of the most quoted scriptures in the Bible, Psalm 42:1.

The authors of this beautiful song were the sons of Korah. You remember Korah, don't you? He was the foolish man who helped lead an unsuccessful rebellion against Moses and Aaron. He met a spectacular end when God opened up the earth and swallowed him up, along with all his coconspirators. The sons of Korah were not his actual children, but they were descended from him.

The sons of Korah likened their desire for God to a spent, exhausted deer looking for water. Why a deer? Well, in a society in which agriculture was the basis of the economy, deer were used for food and their hides for warmth. The sons of Korah knew the eating habits of deer. They knew how fast they could run. (White-tailed deer have been clocked at 36 miles per hour.) They also knew that after all that running they would have to find water—fast!

Studies show that deer can survive close to a month without food, but they won't make it that long without water. If a deer goes three days without water, it will stop feeding almost entirely. The deer will stop foraging for food and go in search of water—any water, anywhere! By contrast, human beings can survive up to a week without water, provided that they're not in, say, a desert.

The sons of Korah painted a vivid picture of how much they longed to be in the presence of God. We human beings, like deer, do a lot of running at school, at work, on the Internet. Also like deer, we sometimes get winded, spent, and empty. God is our source of life, and must do everything within our power to remain connected to Him.

Feeling thirsty? Go to the Source of life and drink deeply.

///////// HOT READ /////////

What do you think the sons of Korah mean by "Deep calls to deep" (Psalm 42:7)? Not sure? Talk it over with an adult you trust.

——> MONEY FOR LIFE <

No man can redeem the life of another or give to God a ransom for him—
the ransom for a life is costly, no payment is ever enough." Psalm 49:7, 8.

was reading through Psalm 49 when verses 7-9 got me thinking about an interview I'd heard in the news recently. The man being interviewed was Dr. Jawad, an Iraqi doctor who had lost his wife and son during a violent attack by armed security contractors.

Dr. Jawad was waiting for his wife, Mahasin, and his eldest son, Ahmed—a medical student. They were supposed to pick him up from work, but they never arrived. Members of the U.S.-based Blackwater private security force opened fire on the car carrying Ahmed and Mahasin Jawad, killing them both. The FBI has since concluded that there appeared to be no justification for the attack.

A few days later, still mourning the loss of his wife and son, Dr. Jawad was invited to the Green Zone, the heavily fortified headquarters of the U.S. command in Iraq, to meet with State Department officials. He was unable to attend the meeting, but later learned from others who had also lost loved ones and attended the meeting what had happened.

Speaking through an interpreter, Dr. Jawad said, "Some people, about seven or eight people, went to that meeting in the embassy. And they told me that they were given $10,000 each for their loss, for the lives of their family. . . . I was disgusted when I heard this news."

Dr. Jawad was disgusted by the thought that someone would offer money to compensate for the death of their loved ones. No amount of money would bring back his wife and son. The State Department officials understood that, but offering money was their way of apologizing for the wrongs done. However, money is a poor substitute for a life.

Human beings are precious to God! Peter captured it best when he wrote, "For you know that it was not with perishable things such as silver or gold that you were redeemed from the empty way of life handed down to you from your forefathers, but with the precious blood of Christ, a lamb without blemish or defect" (1 Peter 1:18, 19).

/////// HOT READ ///////

Where do you go when you are afraid? The sons of Korah wrote a song about their place of refuge. Read about it in Psalm 46, one of the greatest psalms.

——> GET SOME, GIVE SOME <

Then I will teach transgressors your ways, and sinners will turn back to you.
Psalm 51:13.

f you've ever been caught in a boatload of trouble, then Psalms 51-55 are just for you. We can experience trouble because of something we've done. We mess up, and we suffer because of it. But sometimes trouble finds us when we haven't done anything wrong. In Psalm 51 David painfully admits his sin with Bathsheba after the prophet Nathan called him out. Psalms 52-55 capture David's struggle to handle challenges that came his way because of no fault of his own. So, whether you brought it on yourself or not, God's got a word for encouragement for you today!

You can't read Psalm 51 and not feel King David's pain. After Nathan left David's presence, the seriousness of his sin began to sink in. *How could I be so close to God and commit adultery with the wife of one of my most courageous soldiers?* he must've thought. *What kind of man am I that I could I kill an innocent man to cover up my sin?* (I might have to ask David about that when we get to heaven.)

David's breakdown happened when the road of his life got smooth. His battles with Saul were over. God had established him on the throne of Israel, and his enemies had been virtually wiped out. Without a crisis to pray about, David stopped praying as much. He stopped talking to God regularly, and soon his relationship with God was broken. That's usually how most of people fall into sin. They stop communicating with God. When the vertical relationship ends, their horizontal relationships are affected.

In his prayer David understood that his sin was not just against Bathsheba and her husband, Uriah; he had sinned against God (Psalm 51:4). He pleaded with God to clean him up, to give him a new heart, to restore his joy, and then David promised to do one more thing. He promised to teach transgressors the ways of God.

King David knew that his repentance would not be complete until he helped up others who had fallen into sin, as God had helped him. He decided to use his very public failure to lead others to God.

That's how grace is supposed to work. When you get some, give some!

/////// HOT READ ///////

What did the law say should have been done to David and Bathsheba? Leviticus 20:10.

——> "HEY, MORNING! GET UP!" <

Awake, my soul! Awake, harp and lyre! I will awaken the dawn. Psalm 57:8.

irds. I love birds. It doesn't much matter whether I know what kind they are or not. I love birds—all birds. Even pigeons, which are almost universally hated for their lack of hygiene. The thing I love most about birds, however, is not their gorgeous colors, aerial acrobatics, or their weird rituals. I love to listen to birds sing. Their unique calls always catch my attention, especially in the early morning right before the sun comes up.

Several years ago I moved to Hagerstown, Maryland. My wife and I settled into a beautiful little home a few months into our marriage. Those were some of the sweetest days of my life, though I didn't know it at the time. The house was a gift from God, and he included an extra-special blessing just for me—birds that woke me up every morning.

The birds would begin singing around 5:30 a.m. or so. I would lie in bed letting stanza after stanza of their intricate songs wash over me. They sang so loudly that they seemed to wake up the morning. There was no "shame in their game," no half-throated praise. When I heard them I knew that God had smiled on the world again. Morning had come, and soon the sun would drench the earth with warmth. The little morning ambassadors from God had done their job again.

Birds are not the only creatures that bring the morning to life. In Psalm 57 King David declares, "I will awaken the dawn" (verse 8). How does he plan to do that? "I will praise you, O Lord, among the nations; I will sing of you among the peoples" (verse 9).

This was a strange thing for David to do, given his circumstances. David wrote the song found in Psalm 57 after he had been forced to flee to a cave to avoid being killed by King Saul. David knew that his life could be taken at any moment, but he refused to dwell on his negative circumstances. He decided to sing, instead, and not just some tired old song. He wrote God a fresh song, a fresh morning praise. In fact, he promised to sing so loudly that that he—not the birds—would awaken the morning!

Don't let the birds outpraise you. Rise early and wake up the morning!

/////// HOT READ ///////

Ever wished God would destroy your enemies? You're not alone. Read Psalms 58 and 59. Do you share those feeling with God, as King David did?

---> THE ONE-TWO! <

One thing God has spoken, two things have I heard. Psalm 62:11.

ou're talking out of both sides of your mouth." Ever had someone tell you that? I have. When someone says that about you, it often means that you say different things to different people about the same subject. When someone says it about you, they're not throwing you a compliment. It's a pretty offensive put-down.

Many people accuse God of speaking out of "both sides of His mouth," and when they do so, they're not being kind to God, either. They claim that He says one thing in once place and something different about the same subject in another place. Here's a question: Is it possible that God could say something and different people interpret it differently, or hear different things? Psalm 62:11 seems to suggest that that is the case.

King David opens the psalm by stating that he finds rest in God and God alone. That's a big theme in the songs written by David. No Sealy Posturepedic, no Serta Perfect Sleeper, no Sleep Number bed needed. King David knew that the best kind of Z's are those you get when you put your total faith in God, no matter what.

David sums up his song with a powerful message. "God said one thing to me, but I heard two." What did he hear?

"I heard that God is strong," he says to you and me, "but wait there's more. God is also loving." I don't know about you, but strong and loving is hard to find, especially among humans. I once had a coworker named Ken who was extremely strong. He worked in the press room at the publishing company. Sometimes he and the guys played a game of football. If you tried to rush the quarterback and happened to run into Ken you discovered that hitting Ken was like running into a brick wall. He wasn't going to move.

Ken was strong, but what made him truly special was his loving spirit. He was very soft-spoken, and he'd give you whatever he had if you needed it. He was a gentle giant. Ken died tragically in an automobile accident several years ago, but his love for God and kindness to everyone lives on today.

Strength that is controlled by the love of God is an awesome blessing.

///////// HOT READ /////////

List the times and places David remembered God (Psalm 63).

——> MY VOWS <

*I will come to your temple with burnt offerings and fulfill my vows to you—
vows my lips promised and my mouth spoke when I was in trouble.* Psalm 66:13, 14.

hese two verses are speaking to me today, guys. They reminded me of several beatings that I've received at the hands of my dad. Some of you probably object to the word "beatings," but I don't know how you can call what my father
did to us anything but that. Today it's considered child abuse, but my dad didn't
much care about what the police might do to him. He was more concerned about
what they might do to us if he and my mother didn't discipline us. (OK, he didn't
try to kill us, but he sure could wear out some buttocks!)

I would yell and scream, plead for mercy, promised never ever to steal what
wasn't mine, hit my sister, come home late, talk in church—whatever. In any
given week he would have a cornucopia of stuff that he could whip me for. I had
issues, OK? I'm not afraid to admit that I had a little hell in me, and my father
tried his best to beat it out of me. (I think Dad got just about all of it out. Jesus is
working on what's left, and I definitely prefer Jesus' way to his.)

The things I promised to do when trying to slow down the rapid fire coming from my father's belt were not soon forgotten. When I was tempted to mess
up again, I'd remember the severe discomfort I'd experienced, and that was usually enough to help me keep my promises. But then there were the other times—
when I'd forget my promises, and Dad would remind me of them again. With his
belt, of course!

King David got caught up in several dangerous situations during his lifetime.
As you've read through the Psalms you've probably noticed his deep prayers to
God for help—such as the one found in Psalm 69. He also made promises to
praise, trust, and honor God during the tough times and after they had subsided.
King David was keen to keep his promises. He went to the Temple with his offerings and sacrifices to let God know that he hadn't forgotten how good God had
been to him. He kept his vows.

Don't forget the promises you make to God when you're in a pickle. Keep
them.

///////// HOT READ ///////

**Dude, how beautiful is the picture painted in Psalm 68:24-30. Do you get
excited about going to church? Why or why not?**

——> THE GREAT ESCAPE <

Deliver me, O my God, from the hand of the wicked, from the grasp of evil and cruel men. Psalm 71:4.

irl, 7, chews away tape to escape captors. That was the title of a Chicago *Sun-Times* story about a daring escape engineered by a kidnapped 7-year-old and two other children playing nearby where she was being held.

Erica Pratt, of Philadelphia, Pennsylvania, had been playing in front of her home with her little sister when two men pulled up, called her by name, and pulled her kicking and screaming into their car. They then wrapped her arms and legs in duct tape and took her to a safe house, and left her in the basement on a mattress. (Dumb criminals!)

Erica chewed through the duct tape, smashed a nearby window, and called out for help to the children playing nearby. The kids ran over to where Erica was and pulled her through the window. Then they ran to safety. Pretty brave kids, huh?

Drastic situations sometime require drastic measures. Erica Pratt was being held for ransom by her captors, but at age 7, she most likely didn't understand that waiting for the ransom to be paid was probably her safest bet. The only thing that crossed her little mind was getting to freedom.

King David knew what it felt like to be surrounded by the enemy. Once, while running from King Saul, he was forced to go live among the Philistines—sworn enemies of the people of God. David and his forces had killed many of them when he'd served as Saul's military general. It was a strange thing to do, but it was the only place that he could go where Saul couldn't get his paws on him. Can you imagine the looks that David and his men got as they rode into Philistine territory!

David often pleaded with God to deliver him from the hand of the wicked, from the grasp of evil men. Make no mistake about it, friends—the wicked have hands that grasp very tightly. That's one reason we should be careful whom we hang with. Evil people seem to have more fun, more money, more girls, more guys—more of everything. But it's all a lie. If something evil is holding you, ask God to break it, so you can be free.

///////// HOT READ ///////)

How did Asaph feel when he looked at the prosperity of the wicked? Psalm 73:1-4. What made Asaph change his perspective? Verses 16, 17.

──→ REMEMBER WHEN ‹

I will remember the deeds of the Lord; yes, I will remember your miracles of long ago. Psalm 77:11.

'm feeling Psalm 77 today. Why? I just love Asaph's appreciation for history. I love learning about history, especially the history of nations and the rulers who shaped them. How can you not get totally stoked about Abe Lincoln, who overcame severe depression, lost elections, and endured personal tragedies to lead America through its greatest challenge—the Civil War?

Want to read about someone with crazy courage? Read about Queen Ann Nzingha of Angola. In 2003 Minister Dlamini Zuma of South Africa told her story at a gathering on democracy. "Queen Ann Nzingha . . . led the struggle against the armed forces of the Portuguese invasion, rallying the people of the region to fight against Portuguese penetration. She died fighting for freedom at the age of 81." Now, that's hot!

As great as it is to study the exploits of history's great men and women, there's an even better reason to look backward. History tells the story of God's movings. For instance, I believe that God played an active role in deciding the Civil War in favor of the North. I believe He wanted the slaves to be free, and this battle began that process.

The psalms of Asaph—which you'll read today—focus on how God related to Israel. If you want a shorthand version of God's love for the Israelites and how "trifling" they were in response to that love, Psalm 78 is a must-read.

Psalm 77 begins with Asaph in deep distress, unable to sleep, crying out to God for help. When he heard nothing from God, he cried, "Will the Lord reject forever? Will he never show his favor again?" (verse 7). Asaph thought deeply about the situation and decided to try something new. He focused on how God had led Israel in the past. "I will remember the deeds of the Lord," he said. "Yes, I will remember your miracles of long ago" (verse 11).

Read the rest of Psalm 77, then compare how Asaph's attitude at the beginning and his attitude at the end. Remembering how God blessed us in the past is the secret to beating sadness, because it gives you hope for the future.

////// **HOT READ** //////

Want to be a great godly leader? Study David's secret in Psalm 78:72.

——> IT'S THEIR WORLD! <

They know nothing, they understand nothing. They walk about in darkness; all the foundations of the earth are shaken. Psalm 82:5.

When writing about the shift in income between the rich and the poor in America, David R. Francis (a contributor to a terrific international newspaper called the *Christian Science Monitor*), told of a sight that shocked a visitor to Antigua. "[He] saw one consequence of this income shift: a row of 80-foot American-owned yachts lined up at a wharf. One of a dozen crew members on one ship said the owner only came aboard for about two weeks in the winter and again in summer—when the yacht is docked in southern France." Ahh, the toys you get to play with when you're rich.

This devotional is going to sound like a rant against the rich, but it's not. I don't hate the wealthy, and it's not a sin to be rich. However, what people choose to do with their wealth can be sinful—such as purchasing custom-designed yachts that you rarely use, the cost of which could cure diseases in small countries. For instance, children in many poor countries suffer from worms that consume as much as 20 percent of the nutrients the kids eat. A thousand dollars can help de-worm at least 50,000 children, according to Planting Peace, an organization working to remove this scourge from the world. Knowing this, is it OK to spend $40 million on a yacht? You judge.

The richest 20 percent (of the people) in North America own more than 80 percent of the wealth. Did you get that? A fraction of the population owns just about everything, and most people don't know it. That might not bother you, but it does affect you. Many of the extremely wealthy are able to "buy" politicians, who then make laws that favor them and increase their wealth. They use wealth to corrupt the people who are supposed to judge fairly, and justly represent the best interest of all the people!

God has got nothing against wealth or wealthy people. He's wealthy! But God has a serious problem with people who oppress the poor, who "know nothing" and "understand nothing." In Psalm 82 God shouts a special warning to those who sit as judges, people who have the power to care for the poor and the oppressed but instead use their positions to protect the wicked and the unjust. God does not regard injustice lightly!

///////// HOT READ ///////

How much is one day with God worth to you? Psalm 84:10.

——> SEARCHING FOR MEANING <

May the favor of the Lord our God rest upon us; establish the work of our hands for us—yes, establish the work of our hands. Psalm 90:17.

salm 90. Psalm 90! **Psalm 90!** Psalm 90 is one of my favorite psalms. I memorized the first few verses when I was a kid, and they have stuck with me. After reading the last verse, I wish I had kept on going. When Moses wrote that verse, he couldn't possibly have known how connected it is to good health.

According to a 2003 study published in the *Annals of Behavioral Medicine*, finding meaning in life just may beef up one's immune system. Here's what sciencedaily.com, a Web site that covers the latest news in research, had to say about the study: "Pursuing goals related to living a meaningful life may boost the activity of certain cells in the immune system, according to a small study of women who lost a relative to breast cancer.

"Women who placed more importance on these goals at the beginning of the study had higher levels of activity among their 'natural killer' immune cells. In addition, women who elevated the importance of these goals over a one-month period showed increases in natural killer cell activity, compared to women who said that the importance of these goals had decreased for them."

I know what you're thinking: *What does Moses have to do with breast cancer, dude?* A whole lot, I think. Remember, Moses was the guy who wandered aimlessly through the desert for 40 years without a hotel room or air-conditioning. Throw in about a million "whiners," and you've got a recipe for a really meaningless life.

At the end of Psalm 90 when Moses begged God to establish the work of his hands, he was really asking God to make his life meaningful. All the years spent leading the Israelites and then never making it to the Promised Land had to take a toll on Moses. He needed to know that his life was not lived in vain—that something he did would live on.

As the breast cancer study showed, pursuing goals that add meaning to our lives not only makes us feel good. It just might save our lives.

///////// HOT READ /////////

Heaven will be a place where all will be welcome (Psalm 87). What's significant about the people and places mentioned in this psalm?

180

——> RAISING A TIGER <

Blessed is the man you discipline, O Lord, the man you teach from your law.
Psalm 94:12.

He was the youngest ever to win 50 tournaments; the youngest ever to win all four majors, and the youngest ever to win 13 majors championships. He has spent the most consecutive weeks at number one in the history of the sport, and he is considered the best to have ever played the game. Oh, and by the way, he rakes in more than $100 million a year. Who is he? Eldrick "Tiger" Woods.

By now you've probably heard the stories of how little Eldrick grew into a tiger on the golf course. His father, Earl, loved golf and played every chance he got. When Tiger was little more than an infant, his father rigged up the family garage into a modified driving range, complete with a net to catch the balls.

Young Tiger watched his dad hit the ball time and again, and soon he wanted to try. His father sawed off a golf club so his young boy could take cuts at the ball. Tiger Woods was not yet a year old.

When he was 4, his father got him a coach. It was he who taught Tiger the game. To help him concentrate, Tiger's dad would stand like a tree in front of him and challenge him to hit the ball over his head. (I'm sure he had a few welts for his efforts.) He would make loud sounds when Tiger putted, and roll golf balls in his line of sight. It all worked to help his game, and today Woods is known for his unshakable concentration when playing.

As a teenager young Eldrick began to beat seasoned golfers. He went on to dominate the amateur golfing ranks, and blew away the field at the Masters tournament in his first year as a pro. But none of Tiger's success on the golf course would have happened without the discipline instilled in him by his father.

Earl Woods, now deceased, took great pains to prepare his son both physically and mentally for the spotlight that would come with his unique athletic gift. Think for a minute. Have you ever heard of a scandal involving Tiger Woods?

God wants us to be the best that we can be. To get there, we must submit to the discipline of His Word. We must obey God's laws, and trust God's plan for our lives.

///////// HOT READ ///////

What does it mean to be covered with God's feathers? Psalm 91:4.

——> BRIGHT LIGHTS! <

Light is shed upon the righteous and joy on the upright in heart. Psalm 97:11.

hristian author Philip Yancey told a story of one of Sir Isaac Newton's experiments. You do know who Sir Isaac Newton was, right? Mathematician, physicist, and one of the brightest people ever to walk the earth! Newton demonstrated that the movement of objects on earth and in the sky are governed by natural laws. Yeah!

Yancey wrote, "Once, as an experiment, the great scientist Isaac Newton stared at the image of the sun reflected in a mirror. The brightness burned into his retina, and he suffered temporary blindness. Even after he hid for three days behind closed shutters, still the bright spot would not fade from his vision. 'I used all means to divert my imagination from the sun,' he writes, 'but if I thought upon him I presently saw his picture though I was in the dark.' If he had stared a few minutes longer, Newton might have permanently lost all vision. The chemical receptors that govern eyesight cannot withstand the full force of unfiltered sunlight.

"There is a parable in Isaac Newton's experiment, and it helps illustrate what the Israelites ultimately learned from their wilderness wanderings. They had attempted to live with the Lord of the universe visibly present in their midst; but, in the end, out of all the thousands who had so gladly fled Egypt, only two survived God's Presence. If you can barely endure candlelight, how can you gaze at the sun?"

Philip Yancey's question is a tough one. In the psalms we'll read today, we are urged to praise God with all we've got, to worship Him with "gladness" and to "come before him with joyful songs" (Psalm 100:2). The writers also place great emphasis on the awesome "holiness" of God. But if God is sinless (holy) and we are sinful, is it safe to enter His presence? Won't we end up like Newton, nearly blinded by God brightness?

The answer may be found in Psalm 97:11. God shines His light upon the righteous and gives joy to those who are doing what is right. The presence of God transforms us. That's why it's a good idea to start and end your day with worship, for instance. See yourself in God's presence at all times. When we live in the light of heaven, we become accustomed to it. We begin to reflect it in our lives, and others see it!

///// HOT READ /////

Psalm 100 is really short. Why not commit it to memory?

——> GRACE NOTES <

He will not always accuse, nor will he harbor his anger forever; he does not treat us as our sins deserve or repay us according to our iniquities. Psalm 103:9, 10.

t all happened after a long trip home from work. I was pretty tired, and that usually makes my right foot pretty heavy, but not this time. I wasn't speeding at all—probably because it was rush hour and there were cars all around me. There was no way that I could get around the awful traffic. So I just drove like a snail until I turned onto the road that led to my home.

I didn't get far.

Up from behind came an SUV that looked like a spaceship, complete with flashing lights. With a siren that could wake the dead, the vehicle dipped in and out of a line of cars behind me. *Surely this has nothing to do with me,* I innocently thought. But cars spilled out of the lane behind me as the police truck burrowed its way to my car. I've had people call me a criminal from time to time, but I had no idea it was true. I sure felt like one.

As the cop pulled up behind me, I did what all the other cars had done. I spilled over to the shoulder to let him go, but he didn't—uh, go. He decided to stay—right behind me. Having had other run-ins with cops, I knew to be very still, to keep my hands on the steering wheel in plain sight. (You might have to be Black to understand my fear of cops. I've had some interesting experiences with the police.)

To make a long story short, the cop somehow had noticed that the registration sticker on my windshield had expired. I told him that I was planning to have it renewed, but he didn't buy my story. Maybe because it had been expired for about six months! OK, I deserved the ticket he gave me. I'd earned it. But it would've been so much cooler for him to let me go with a warning. Don't you think?

When I thought about that ticket some more, I realized something else: the six months that I had to get my registration renewed was my time of warning, my "grace" period. I believe God had given me grace then, but I had squandered it. God's goodness—as described in Psalm 103—is designed to lead us to do what is right. That's the message I got from Psalm 103 today.

///////// HOT READ ////////

Check out Psalm 104. What do God's creations tell you about God?

──→ SAY SO <

Give thanks to the Lord, for he is good; his love endures forever. Let the redeemed of the Lord say this—those he redeemed from the hand of the foe. Psalm 107:1, 2.

Have you picked up the unmistakable theme of today's Bible reading? It stars with a p and rhymes with raise. Psalm 106 commands it by reminding us of why God had punished Israel for joining itself to lifeless gods. The point of this psalm? Remember God's goodness to you. Build a life of obedience on His blessings. Unfortunately, we use God's blessings to please ourselves.

Let's look at one example. God gives us a special gift called sex, but He puts it in a lockbox called marriage. He asks us to wait until we're married before opening this explosive gift. But what do we often do? We come as close to it as possible without actually "doing it." We peel away the wrapping paper for a closer look. Then . . . we actually do it, trading future happiness for present pleasure and pain. Not cool.

I've heard countless young adults express how much they wished they'd obeyed God and waited before indulging. They had messed up, but God had forgiven them, and now they were willing to use their testimony to help others.

Once while cruising around YouTube I came across some teens who'd made a serious commitment to no sex before marriage during a True Love Waits ceremony. "I plan to wait because I want me, my children, and my children's father to all have the same last name," said one teen. I had to laugh when she said that. She didn't want to end up on *Maury!*

She didn't stop there. Somewhat nervously she continued: "Marriage is very special, and I don't want to do anything to mess it up. I want us both to be pure when we get married." As one of God's children, she had decided to keep her life pure, and she wasn't afraid to say so to the entire world.

Whether you've messed up or never plan on messing up, as a redeemed child of God you owe the world a testimony. Let the world know that you're standing for the God who saved you!

////// HOT READ //////

Read Psalm 108:12, 13. How do you know that you're depending on God for help, as opposed to those whom God sends to help you?

——> THE GOOD <

Good will come to him who is generous and lends freely, who conducts his affairs with justice. Psalm 112:5.

World War I general Peyton Conway March once said: "There is a wonderful mythical law of nature that the three things we crave most in life—happiness, freedom, and peace of mind—are always attained by giving them to someone else." But who needs happiness, freedom, or peace of mind? Most teens would settle for an iPod mini, don't you think? Isn't that the way to find happiness, freedom, and peace of mind—all set to a soundtrack?

Peyton March was right about the blessing that comes from giving. I was reminded of that again when I read this: "For nearly seven years Melina Salazar did her best to put on a smile and tend to the every need of her most loyal and cantankerous customer.

"She made sure his food was as hot as he wanted, even if it meant he burned his mouth. And she smiled through his demands and curses. The 89-year-old Walter 'Buck' Swords obviously appreciated it, leaving the waitress $50,000 and a 2000 Buick when he died."

Are you kidding me?! A mean old World War II vet left a server $50,000 and a car? What am I doing wrong? I've got to be nicer to people, dude!

Now, let's be clear. Unlike me, Melina Salazar didn't show kindness to Buck because she wanted a buck. Sure, she expected a tip for her service, but 50 grand is a bit beyond the average tip. She didn't peer into his bank account before deciding to be kind to the cantankerous old dude. She was kind to him because she was a kind person, and he never forgot it. She gave what she could, so he gave her what he could!

Melina Salazar is the kind of person that the Bible describes in Psalm 112, one of the psalms that I just added to my favorites. Verse 5 promises that good will come to the person who is generous and fair. Will it always come in the form of a $50,000 check? Probably not, but kindness shown to others will be repaid—by God!

///////// HOT READ /////////

Read Psalm 115:1-8. What idols do you need to give up?

185

——> FOREVER FAITHFUL <

Praise the Lord, all you nations; extol him, all you peoples. For great is his love toward us, and the faithfulness of the Lord endures forever. Praise the Lord.
Psalm 117.

Now, if you can't memorize Psalm 117, then I'm going to have you sent to the funny farm. It's the Bible's shortest. (Psalm 119 is the longest. Notice the emphasis on God's words and commands!) All nations and people should praise God, writes this psalmist. Why? God's love for us is great, and his faithfulness? Forever.

What is faithfulness? *Merriam-Webster* has several definitions. The first is "full of faith," but that one is no longer in use. I wonder why? The second definition is "steadfast in affection or allegiance." The third? "Firm in adherence to promises or in observance of duty." Number 4 is "given with strong assurance"; and the fifth and final definition is "true to the facts, to a standard, or to an original."

Can you think of a better word to describe God than *faithful?* God is steadfast in His affection and loyal to a fault. God is firm in keeping His promises to us. He never goes back on His word. His promises are given with strong assurance. Why else would He send His Son to die for sins He didn't commit? Why? Because He had promised to send us a Savior, and hinted at it in Genesis 3:15. Finally, God is faithful to a standard that is literally out of this world. While we break our promises, He cannot, because He always does what He says. The whole universe depends on God keeping His word.

In *Beyond Hunger* Art Beals told of a senator who visited Mother Teresa, the woman who lived her life helping the poor of Calcutta, India. "Mark Hatfield tells of . . . visiting the . . . 'House of Dying,' where sick children are cared for in their last days, and the dispensary, where the poor line up by the hundreds to receive medical attention. Watching Mother Teresa minister to these people, feeding and nursing those left by others to die, Hatfield was overwhelmed by the sheer magnitude of the suffering she and her coworkers face daily. 'How can you bear the load without being crushed by it?' he asked. Mother Teresa replied, 'My dear senator, I am not called to be successful, I am called to be faithful.'"

God was at work in Mother Teresa. She was faithful. Are you?

####### HOT READ #######

Did you know that Psalm 117 is the center of the entire Bible? Many people consider Psalm 118:8, 9 the center verses of the Bible. Read what they say!

──> I LIFT UP MY EYES . . . <

> *I lift up my eyes to the hills—where does my help come from? My help comes from the Lord, the Maker of heaven and earth.* Psalm 121:1, 2.

ow would you like to have your college tuition paid in full—before you got there? No, not through loans, like most college students are forced to get to pay the high cost of a higher education. This payment is a gift from someone who simply believed in you.

"Ain't gonna happen," you say? "Did happen," I say. Let me tell the story.

It happened to 59 Black and Hispanic grammar school kids, way back in 1981. Eugene Lang, a successful businessman and graduate of the same public elementary in East Harlem, New York, had been invited to speak to the 1981 graduating class. Lang looked at the poor underprivileged kids and all the family members gathered in the small auditorium, and he wondered what to say.

Lang had prepared a speech, but as anyone who has ever talked to kids will tell you, it's a tough crowd. He scrapped his notes and spoke from the heart. He talked about the importance of working hard and of staying in school. When he got on the importance of getting an education, he felt moved by the great need he saw. He looked at the kids and said, "If you want to go to college, you can go, because I promise you that if you do, I will give you the necessary scholarship support." For a moment everyone in the auditorium sat in stunned silence—then the place erupted. Parents applauded and leaned over to congratulate each other. Of course, the graduating class wasn't quite sure what had just happened.

How did it all work out? About half of the sixth graders graduated from high school, and two thirds of them were headed to college. Not a bad success rate considering that 75 percent of high school kids in 1980's East Harlem dropped out of school, and virtually none went to college. What made the difference for the sixth graders in that school? In a word—HOPE!

Without hope, there is little that humans can do. Psalms 121 and 123 both begin with the words "I lift up my eyes . . ." Why? The writers of those psalms needed help that only God could give, so they looked up to God! Whatever the challenge, God offers you hope.

HOT READ

Got a friend who is heartbroken? Share Psalm 126:5, 6 with them.

——> "FOGETTABOUTIT" <

Unless the Lord builds the house, its builders labor in vain. Unless the Lord watches over the city, the watchmen stand guard in vain. Psalm 127:1.

ach of the psalms we'll read today has something powerful to teach us. Psalm 126 reminds us that even though God may allow us to face the consequences of our sins, He does not throw us away forever. He restores us again, and gives us stuff to laugh about again. You may not have noticed, but it's very tough to un-cork a good gut-bustin' laugh when things aren't going well. And if you do man-age to get one out, it is soon replaced by sadness. God wants us to laugh. (And that's just Psalm 126!)

You'll have to pause at Psalm 127. I surely did. For starters, it's almost impos-sible to get by the first verse. If God doesn't build the house, the builder might as well drop the hammer, return the nails to Home Depot, and send the work crew home. Furthermore, the psalmist warns, setting out an army of watchmen to guard a city may make the residents feel safe, but if God doesn't have His eye on the city, "fogettaboutit!"

One of the saddest tragedies in history occurred on April 14, 1912. The great-est ship in the White Star cruise line set sail from Southhampton, England, on its first voyage—to New York. Its 2, 223 passengers were pampered by the best lux-uries offered on any ship during that time. Flyers boasted about its revolutionary safety mechanisms. In *The Shipyard*, a well-known shipping magazine of the time, someone wrote that the doors were designed so that "the captain can, by simply moving an electric switch, instantly close the doors throughout and make the ves-sel practically unsinkable." Unfortunately, the writer of that line was mistaken.

On April 14, 1912, the *Titanic* hit an iceberg and sank, taking with it 1,500 passengers. The builders believed the ship to be so unsinkable that its lifeboats were designed to save a little more than half of its passengers.

Human beings are great builders. From skyscrapers to automobiles, we amaze ourselves with our ingenuity. But no matter how great we think we are at build-ing things, we can never outbuild God. That should keep us humble, don't you think?

Only what God builds lasts forever! Only what God guards is safe!

///////// HOT READ ////////

What does the writer of Psalm 130 love most about God? Why?

188

——> LET IT POUR <

How good and pleasant it is when brothers live together in unity! Psalm 133:1.

ing David wrote that verse, and I can't help wondering what he was think-ing about when he wrote it. He had seven brothers, all of them older than he. He got into a few scrapes with them, such as when they wimped out against Goliath and the Philistines.

David arrived on the scene just in time to watch Goliath punk the Israelites. When Eliab, his oldest brother, heard him talking with the other soldiers about Goliath, he barked, "Why have you come down here? And with whom did you leave those few sheep in the desert? I know how conceited you are and how wicked your heart is; you came down only to watch the battle" (1 Samuel 17:28). Actually, it was Eliab who came to watch the battle. David came to fight.

Did you feel the hate? Eliab yelled at David for being there, dissed his shep-herding skills, and called him wicked. Bro, dem's fightin' words!

If you've got brothers and sisters, there will be times you disagree. Hey, there'll be a few knock-down, drag-outs. King David knew how sweet it was to get along with his siblings, because he rarely did. Of course, David wasn't only writing about family unity. Since all people are brothers and sisters—because we have one Father, God—David believed we should love each other. David also wrote that when people live together in harmony, "it is like precious oil poured on the head, running down on the beard" (Psalm 133:2). What a weird metaphor, right? But there's a reason for this metaphor.

During David's time there was nothing more sacred than having someone pour oil on your head. It had nothing to do with having a dry scalp or control-ling dandruff. Oil poured on the head was a symbol of God's Spirit being poured out on someone. It meant that that person was set aside for a special, holy pur-pose. David knew how it felt to receive the awesome blessing of being anointed for God's holy use (1 Samuel 16:11-13).

When brothers and sisters live together in unity, the blessing of God rests upon them. If you're having drama with anyone in your family, squash it, and you'll be blessed!

/////// HOT READ ///////

People who serve God should have an attitude! What kind of attitude should they have? Psalm 134.

——> MUSIC THERAPY <

How can we sing the songs of the Lord while in a foreign land? Psalm 137:4.

o you like to sing? I do. You should hear me in full voice. Of course, you'd have to be in the bathroom where my shower is to appreciate my unique musical gifts fully. Yep, the shower is my concert hall. There the fountains of water applaud me, and clouds of soap bubbles sing my praises! (My friends, I think I hear the shower calling!)

I'm crazy about singing, and for good reason. As it turns out, "getting your song on" just might save your life, notes Patricia Preston-Roberts, a board-certified music therapist from New York. In an article entitled "How Singing Improves Your Health (Even if Other People Shouldn't Hear You Sing)," published on sixwise.com, a health and wellness site, she noted that singing can help reduce your heart rate, blood pressure, and stress level.

Tell that to your parents when they're about to pop a blood vessel over the dent you put in the car. If that doesn't work, just break out in song and have them join you on the chorus. It's worth a try, don't you think? You might even live to tell about it.

Singing is a good thing for us, but who wants to sing when times are tough? Certainly the Israelites didn't. Psalm 137 recounts how depressed they had become after being taken captive to Babylon by King Nebuchadnezzar. They would gather on the riverbanks of Babylon to remember Zion, their homeland. They would sing the songs of Zion to remember where they'd come from, but sadness would quiet their song. As they thought about all that they'd lost, they would hang their harps in the branches of the nearby poplar trees and cry.

As if this weren't painful enough, their Babylonian masters would force them to sing the "joyful" songs of Zion as a way of humiliating them. How sad is that? The Israelites responded, "How can you ask us to sing our sings in a strange land?" But perhaps they should've obliged and sung their songs. Studies show that singing seems to block the pathways that pain travels through, and they were in pain.

Feeling down? Sing a song!

//////// **HOT READ** ////////

If you ever doubt whether God cares for you, Psalm 139 is so for you!

——> TEACH ME <

Teach me to do your will, for you are my God; may your good Spirit lead me on level ground. Psalm 143:10.

t's a weird place to end up. Most of us would only dream of walking into the frozen wilderness of Alaska. But most of us are not Chris McCandless. Ever heard of him? He was the subject of the a best-selling book called *Into the Wild*, and film-maker Sean Penn made a movie about him based on the book.

Chris McCandless was a star athlete, an honors graduate of Emory University, and the son of wealthy parents who gave him more than $20,000 after he left col-lege. Why he decided to give all his $20,000-plus trust fund to charity and cut off all contact with his family is anyone's guess, but that's exactly what Chris did. Living as a homeless man for two years, he prided himself on his survival skills. He nicknamed himself Alexander Supertramp, and traveled across the country with little more than rice and beans. He'd take odd jobs here and there, sleep wher-ever, and hitchhike to nowhere.

After doing this for a while, Chris headed for the adventure of a lifetime—surviving the Alaskan wilderness. He got to Alaska and headed north of Mount McKinley, eventually setting up shop in an abandoned bus on the Stampede Trail. (Uh, can you say "middle of nowhere"?)

Unfortunately, Chris never found his way out of the Alaskan wilderness. On September 6, 1992, a group of moose hunters found his body along with a note that read, "S.O.S. I need your help. I am injured, near death, and too weak to hike out of here. I am all alone, this is no joke. In the name of God, please remain to save me. I am out collecting berries close by and shall return this evening. Thank you, Chris McCandless. August?"

Chris McCandless had just about everything going for him, except for one personal weakness: he was not teachable. He had been warned about trying to sur-vive in Alaska without the proper gear and supplies, but he wouldn't listen. His noble determination became his downfall, because he did not let himself be taught.

Psalm 143:10 reminds us that God is ready to teach us—if we are willing.

///////// HOT READ ////////

Read Psalm 141:3, 4. What do you want God to help you overcome?

—> GET YOUR PRAISE ON! <

Praise the Lord. Psalm 146:1; Psalm 147:1; Psalm 148:1; Psalm 149:1; Psalm 150:1.

hen the same phrase is used five times in a row at the beginning of five successive psalms, you can bet that phrase is pretty important. The psalmist almost yells at us to stop everything and "praise God!"

No psalm captures the spirit of praise more than Psalm 150. Read it closely, and you'll notice that God is the total focus of this psalm. We are to praise Him. That might not seem like a big deal, but have you noticed that most people praise God only when He's done something for them for them? Maybe you don't do that, but I tend to.

I remember when my boy Tim called me up and told me what a difficult time he was having trying to sell his home and move to another state. Actually, he had already moved, but his wife was still living in their home, waiting for a buyer to snap it up. Tim missed his wife, and she was getting more frustrated by the day.

I listened to Tim, and then we prayed together. In my prayer I felt impressed to ask God to sell the house within the next week. I don't usually give God timetables, since He kind of works on His own schedule, but this time I did. You're not going to believe this, but Tim called me up the next day and said, "Dwain, the house has been sold!"

The very next day.

I got so excited that I yelled "Praaaiiissssseeee Goooooddddddddd!" I shouted my praise several times—I wanted God to know how much I appreciated what He had just done. My voice was so loud that everyone on my floor at work heard me. Oh, well!

I praised God because I had just watched Him do the impossible. He did in less than a day what I hoped He'd do in a week. That's God! The question is Do I praise Him with all my heart when He doesn't do what I want, when He doesn't answer my prayers on time? Am I willing to praise Him with all I've got simply because He's God? That is the question at the heart of Psalm 150.

If you love God just for being God—then follow the directions in Psalm 150 and get your praise on!

////// **HOT READ** //////

As you read today's psalms, choose one reason to praise God from each and then pray a prayer of thanksgiving for all God's blessings!

⟶ HERO ⟨

The proverbs of Solomon son of David, king of Israel: for attaining wisdom and discipline; for understanding words of insight. Proverbs 1:1, 2.

The assassination attempt was totally unexpected. After all, President Maumoon Gayoom had ruled 1,192 small islands in the Indian Ocean known as the Maldives since 1978. But things had begun to change. Opposition groups wanted a say in the affairs of this tropical paradise with its sandy beaches and powder-blue waters.

While President Maumoon was giving a speech in Bali, Indonesia, in 2008, a would-be attacker pulled a knife and lunged out of the crowd toward him. The man could have killed him, had it not been for a quick-thinking teenager. A 15-year-old Boy Scout named Jaisham Ibrahim stopped the attack.

When the teen saw the attacker lunge toward the president, he reacted without thinking. As the assassin lifted his arm to stab President Gayoom, Jaisham grabbed the blade of his knife. The man resisted, but Jaisham clung to the knife. In a few seconds security guards wrestled the attacker to the ground and rushed young Jaisham to a hospital, where he was treated for his injuries. After the incident President Gayoom noticed bloodstains on his shirt, but the blood was not his own. It was the blood of a Boy Scout who had made a split-second decision that had saved the president's life.

Why did Jaisham instinctively decide to grab the attacker's knife? Was he born with something that each of us does not possess? I don't think so.

Truth is, every good decision requires wisdom and courage. Jaisham loved his president, so he did what he could to protect him, but I believe there was more to his act than love and respect for his leader. I believe he was accustomed to making good decisions, to doing what was right. And when the moment came, Jaisham did right without thinking.

The book of Proverbs teaches us how to make wise decisions. Doing what's right—righteousness—requires wisdom and courage. Wanna be a hero? Then Proverbs is for you.

/////// HOT READ ///////

Meditate on Proverbs 3:17. What two special gifts does wisdom bring to life? Do you want your path in life to be peaceful? If so, ask God for wisdom!

——> DON'T LOSE YOUR HEAD <

Above all else, guard your heart, for it is the wellspring of life. Proverbs 4:23.

roverbs 4 begins with a father talking to his son. And there is one thing that the father in Proverbs 4 wants his son to have more than any other—wisdom. Not a successful career. Not his name in lights. Not a truckload of friends. Not a Ferrari or a Bentley. Just wisdom.

The father likened wisdom to a beautiful girl. "She will protect you," he said to his bright young son. "Love her, and she will watch over you" (Proverbs 4:6). It's almost as if this father had stumbled onto his son's Facebook page and seen all the pictures of him surrounded by hot girls.

"Saw some nice girls on your page, Sol," David might've said if this conversation had transpired in our time. "But I want you to meet a beauty who is more stunning than them all!"

"Well!" Sol might have replied. "Let's see her! What's her name?"

"Wisdom," whispered King David.

But Solomon's dad didn't just introduce him to wisdom. He gave his boy a warning that was even more important than falling in love with wisdom.

"Solomon," he began quietly, penetratingly, "I've told you about wisdom, but above all else, guard your heart. Your life springs from what you put in your heart."

David knew that getting wisdom was directly linked to guarding the heart. He wasn't telling his son to be sure to get yearly checkups on his "ticker." He was warning Solomon to be extremely careful about what he fed the heart in his head—his mind.

What David was saying was "Solomon, don't just watch anything that comes on the TV! Don't hang out with people who aren't into God, or into doing what's right! Don't troll the Web aimlessly, checking out sites you know are sinful. Don't flip through just any book or magazine. Go for the stuff that pleases God."

Friend, keep your mind pure by feeding it the right stuff. As the old saying goes: garbage in, garbage out. To exercise wisdom in life, you must keep your mind pure.

/////// HOT READ ///////

Why does Solomon tell us to check out the ants? Proverbs 6:6. Also, don't miss the seven sins that God hates found in Proverbs 6:17-19. Whew! Deep!

194

──> IT'S MINE! <

I love those who love me, and those who seek me find me. With me are riches and honor, enduring wealth and prosperity. Proverbs 8:17, 18.

A few years ago I traveled to New York City. After doing some sightseeing, I stopped at Junior's for lunch—and, of course, some of their world-famous cheesecake. If you're not from the East Coast, then Junior's probably means nothing to you. But if you're from anywhere close to New York, or, better yet, if you've tried some of their sinfully sumptuous cheesecake, then you know how excited I was to get there.

After dinner I went outside to catch some air and ran into "Clay" when he reached out a cup to me for some spare change. I checked around to be sure that I wasn't being set up before opening my wallet to give him a dollar. That's all I had on me at the time. (I have a bad habit of never carrying cash.)

The air was cold, the sky was a ghostly gray, and a soft rain fell was falling—not enough to make you run for cover, but just enough to make you wonder how anyone could survive on the streets in such miserable weather.

I didn't want to just give him a couple of coins and pass on my way. Maybe God sent him my way for more than that, so we started talking. "You from New York originally?" I asked.

"Yeah," he answered, warmly welcoming the conversation. "I grew uphere, but then I got into trouble. I had a good job and everything, but I got a serious gambling problem." (Now I wanted my dollar back!)

"I lost my apartment and everything. I just gambled my life away," he continued. I wasn't sure what to do for him, but I promised that I'd pray for him. He was caught in the grip of a serious addiction that he now wanted to break, but he couldn't do it without help. He was honest about it.

Clay's story reminded me that having money means nothing without the wisdom to know how to use it. Wisdom helps you manage the resources that God gives you.

///////// HOT READ ///////

What is the "fear of the Lord" spoken of in Proverbs 9:10? Are we supposed to afraid of God? Why is this considered the "beginning of wisdom"?

---> 'NOUGH SAID <

Reckless words pierce like a sword, but the tongue of the wise brings healing.
Proverbs 12:18.

had heard that Dave★ and his mom were fighting all the time. He was 16 going on 25, and she was getting tired of his taking the car without her permission, hanging out late with his friends, and just generally doing whatever he pleased. As a single parent, she was concerned for the safety of her only son. She wanted nothing but the best for him, but somehow her love and concern for Dave never quite made it into her words.

"Dwain, she doesn't have anything good to say about me! Never!" said Dave as anger creased his face. "That's why you're talking to me right now. Because she told somebody about me, who told you. She's always riding me about everything." Scarcely taking a breath, the words tumbled out like a river. "I can't do nothin' right, Dwain," he finished.

Whether that was true or not, my friend had been deeply hurt by what he felt was a constant barrage of negative comments from his mom. Ever been there?

"When was the last time that she complimented you?" I asked, prepared for more anger. What I got instead was silence. He looked at me, then slowly dropped his head. Tears started to run down his face and drip onto the floor as he tried to hold in the pain.

He knew he wasn't perfect. He had made mistakes in how he had treated his mom, but her words weren't helping the situation, at least from his point of view.

Many times teens get accused of using harsh, disrespectful language, but they don't have a monopoly on cutting lingo. Adults can wield the word-swords with the best of them. That's not an excuse to stoop to their level, mind you. As a teenager you are still supposed to respect your parents and other adults, even when they don't seem to respect themselves. That's was part of what I told Dave.

If the adults around you don't measure their words carefully, then you show them how it's done. Be respectful and choose your words wisely. Why bother? Ellen White summed it up best when she wrote, "The voice and tongue are gifts from God, and if rightly used, they are a power for God" (*Sons and Daughters of God*, p. 180). 'Nough said!

★ not his name

196

⟶ A MATTER OF PERSPECTIVE ‹

He who walks with the wise grows wise, but a companion of fools suffers harm.
Proverbs 13:20.

ulia posted this on her blog:
"If you're wondering about the title, that's because I always feel like such a wannabe-rich person when I got to the mall I went to today. I shopped at Guess, and Bloomingdale's, trying on tons of clothes by brands such as Juicy Couture, Lucky Brand Jeans, Guess, and Free People. I'm not rich . . . my whole closet doesn't consist of these brands, but I like to punctuate my wardrobe with nice pieces. When I'm trying on/buying these nice pieces, however, I feel so phony because I have this thing where I can't go shopping in an outfit I hate or I'll buy everything in sight. So I wear my nice clothes to go shopping, and thus project the image of a rich fashionista. Therefore, the salespeople often treat me very well, which is nice, but it makes me feel like a liar."

Now, I gotta admit that I have no clue who Julia is. For all I know she could be a he, with the Adam's apple, goatee, tatts, and all that. But I doubt it after reading her blog. It seems that people everywhere are trying hard to look like what they're not. One Sunday I went to the mall with my wife. We did some window shopping before going to get her a new pair of glasses. (She couldn't fully appreciate my good looks!)

As we walked and talked we laughed at all the people who were "profilin'" in their hot gear. Did we miss the mall and end up in the middle of Fashion Week in New York? I got a little self-conscious about my Sears jeans and grubby old boots. But that all changed when I thought about these startling statistics. According to the Council of Economic Advisers—whoever they are—in 1982 Americans saved an average of 10.9 percent to their income per year. By 2001, the percentage had dropped to 2.3 percent. In 2005 the percentage went to **negative 0.5** percent. That means that the average American doesn't save at all. Most of those people going berserk in the mall were probably broke.

Why are we so obsessed with looking rich when we're not?

⫻⫻⫻⫻ HOT READ ⫻⫻⫻⫻
Read Proverbs 14:8. Why is it important to think carefully about your ways?

——> GOT CHARACTER? <

A wise servant will rule over a disgraceful son, and will share the inheritance as one of the brothers. Proverbs 17:2.

ilton Academy is one of those schools that your parents dream about sending you to. This 209-year-old private academy just south of Boston, Massachusetts, is home to some of our nation's future politicians and leaders. If your parents wanted you to schmooze among the 680 or so fortunate kids who are given entrance, it would set them back a mere $38,275—and that's just the cost of tuition and boarding.

The academy is by no means the most exclusive in North America, but it is well respected for the high-quality instruction kids get from great faculty and staff who love them. (Hey, I could learn to love those kids too, if their parents could afford a school like that.) But for all of its high standards and strong ethical codes, there's no stopping a highly motivated teen with no scruples. In this case, several unscrupulous "young'ns."

Four teenagers hacked into the school's computer system, changed grades, altered attendance records, and got access to a test before it was given. Pretty bold, huh? (OK, don't get any ideas. This story ain't over yet.)

According to the outgoing headmaster of the school, whose letter of resignation was cited in the story that ran in the Boston *Globe,* "a male student from the upper school obtained access to e-mail and network passwords in October. Over recent weeks, . . . the boy downloaded to a personal computer others' passwords and changed his attendance record, several of his grades, and the grades" of other classmates. This student then shared his tricks with three friends.

Milton Academy is by no means unique. Teens everywhere do dumb stuff. Even kids at Seventh-day Adventist academies make mistakes. Can you believe that? Proverbs 17:2 reminds us that those who will achieve success in life don't necessarily come from a great family or have a great name. It's the person who does what's right when no one's watching. Whether that person is a rich daughter or a poor homeless kid, good character is an elevator that will always take one up.

####### HOT READ #######

If there's one chapter of Proverbs you must read, it's chapter 16. Notice verse 3. What is this verse saying to you? Don't miss verse 25! Drink in Proverbs 16!

——> TOO MUCH ZEAL <

It is not good to have zeal without knowledge, nor to be hasty and miss the way.
Proverbs 19:2.

There are many scriptures in Proverbs 19 to 21 that will make you scratch your head and say, "Yeah, I gotta admit. Solomon was right!" The first verse that socked me in the mouth was Proverbs 19:2: "It is not good to have zeal without knowledge, nor to be hasty and miss the way." Wish I'd read that one before my trip to nowhere. A year ago I traveled to Stamford, Connecticut—a pretty small city close to New York. I stayed at the Westin Hotel and conference center. My room was really nice, and the staff was ready to help with anything I needed. I had a great time there, except for the night I decided to go out for food someplace nearby. Bad idea!

If you ever drive on the East Coast you discover that the streets of most cities are not perfectly laid out on a grid, like say, Los Angeles. Some streets run straight, then meander around a bend, end, and continue four blocks later. I figured, "How difficult can it be to get around a small town? If I get lost, I'll just look up at the small skyline of the city. There's no way that I could miss the sign for the Westin Hotel in the night sky." Boy was I ever wrong.

I drove and drove, and then drove some more, and I seemed to get nowhere. I saw a few restaurants here and there, but there was never parking nearby, so I had to drive on by. After close to an hour my stomach began to yell things at me that I cannot mention. My head took a cue from my stomach and started to let me have it too.

"You dummy!" it began. "When have you ever been able to go anywhere without directions? If you get lost while holding MapQuest directions in your hand, what makes you think that you could get around Stamford on your own? Cuz, let's face it, you have no sense of direction, so get your butt back to the Hotel and get some!" My head was right!

After being lost for more than an hour, I found the hotel again, asked the concierge for directions, and found an eating spot less than 10 minutes away. Yep. Solomon was right after all. "It's not good to have zeal without knowledge."

####### HOT READ #######

What important practice do wise people undertake before they begin working toward a goal? Proverbs 20:18. Do you do this?

——> STATS AND FACTS <

Wine is a mocker and beer a brawler; whoever is led astray by them is not wise.
Proverbs 20:1.

uick, which of the following leads to the death of the most people in North America each year? A. Guns. B. Drugs. C. Alcohol. D. Suicid., E. Heart attacks. How'd you do? If you guessed E, you would be right. According to the Centers for Disease Control, there are roughly 1.5 million heart attacks each year, and of those, more than 500,000 people die. How sad is that!

Gun-related homicides claim more than 32,000 people each year. If you compare that number to the less than 100 gun-related deaths yearly in Great Britain, you start to wonder if there isn't something genetically wrong with us here in America. Besides that, each year approximately 30,000 people end their lives through suicide, and alcohol plays a role in the deaths of more than 100,000 people.

That last statistic—the average number of people who die from an alcohol-related death each year—is most striking to me. If you watch the news, you'd believe that gun homicides are number one. Every night we're treated to a "per walk" of someone who gunned down someone else. A few days before writing this devotional entry, the "Killadelphia" (that's Philadelphia for you who need an interpreter) evening news told the story of some "hoods" who broke into a man's home, tied up his family, and tortured him. Then they killed him. But get this. The crooks actually went to the wrong house. The person they were intending to injure lived a few houses down, so they terrorized and murdered an innocent man.

As sick as that episode, the number of people who die from gun-related crimes pales in comparison to alcohol-related injuries and fatalities. Ever wonder why cigarette commercials are banned and beer commercials are not? You should!

King Solomon makes it clear that those who drink are not wise, but the original Hebrew text of Proverbs 20:1 goes even further. It says that alcohol "deceives" or reels in the user and causes him or her to go astray. How true is that, dude? If you're thinking about taking a sip, better think again. If you already have, it's time to quit.

////////// HOT READ /////////

Read Solomon's personal advice to you found in Proverbs 23:20, 21.

──> STRUNG OUT <

Like a city whose walls are broken down is a man who lacks self-control.
Proverbs 25:28.

wo years ago I interviewed a teen named Brandon for a story that ran in *Insight* magazine. He lived close to the place where I work, and we quickly struck up a friendship. He'd come by and hang out at the magazine. It was nice having a real live teenager around—since *Insight* is written for teens. Duh, it was a no-brainer.

Today Brandon is a cool college guy, but even back in high school he had it going on. But Brandon had one problem, one really big blind spot in his life that all the cool in the world couldn't hide. He was a serious video game addict. His game? *World of Warcraft*, a massive multiplayer online video game that millions of people play. Brandon was one of the best at it. His avatar was so strong that it was worth more than $1,000.

How addicted was he? So addicted that one summer he once played the game for three days straight. *That's not that bad*, you're probably thinking. There's more. Brandon would wait until his grandmother was sound asleep. Then he'd sneak down the hallway from his room to her room, carefully avoiding every creaky spot in the floor. (He had memorized the floor plan, along with each creaky spot.) Once he got to her room, he'd turn on the wireless router—which he was forbidden to touch—and go back to playing.

"But who hasn't done that?" you ask. Well, there's more. The little addict would barely pause for the Sabbath. Since his mind was on *World of Warcraft* anyway during the Sabbath hours, Brandon decided to go all-out and play the game! When you can't stop what you love to do to spend time with God, you've got a big problem.

Brandon knew he was out of control when his grades started to go south—as in totally down. He was just about to flunk out of school when God woke him up, and he decided that this part of his life had to change. We prayed about his addiction, and with some determined effort Brandon began to change. He became more self-controlled.

Those who lack self-control are like a city with broken walls. You know what happens to cities that are left unprotected, don't you? They get captured!

─────────────────────────────────
////// HOT READ //////
What metaphors does Solomon use to describe lazy people? Proverbs 26:13-16.
─────────────────────────────────

——> LIVE STRONG! <

The wicked man flees though no one pursues, but the righteous are as bold as a lion. Proverbs 28:1.

ime and space just won't let me do justice to these final chapters of Proverbs. There is so much great wisdom here that it would be a shame for you to skip reading them. Please—I'm reduced to begging you now—read these verses carefully and prayerfully. What you learn here will save you a whole lot of pain. Guess how I know!

Here's one example: Proverbs 28:20 says, "A faithful man will be richly blessed, but one eager to get rich will not go unpunished." People everywhere are "dying" to get rich. They destroy their health, their peace of mind, their family, and their friends just to run with the big dogs. But God has a better way. Be faithful to Him, and He will bless you with what you need. My young friend, God knows what He's doing when He warns us to avoid certain things. Life is so much better when you trust God to supply your needs.

But I digress. Now back to "Live Strong"—and I ain't talkin' 'bout Lance Armstrong or yellow wristbands. The wicked man runs, says Solomon, when no one is chasing him. There is a law buried deep in the DNA of every human being, and it goes something like this: Sin makes one anxious, nervous, and troubled.

Here's what I mean. Police in Portsmouth, Rhode Island, had no intention of arresting Gregory Rosa, but when he did the 100-yard dash at seeing their cruiser, they decided to pick him up. Now, let's be clear. He was doing nothing wrong at the time. He was just standing close to a public vending machine. It's more of a crime to eat the stuff inside the machine than it is to stand there.

But turns out they were right to nab him. They charged him with a string of vending machine robberies, a charge he probably could've beaten had he not tried to post bail with $400 worth of coins. (Homie, you can't make this stuff up!)

Sin makes us uneasy, because we were created to serve God in righteousness and truth. Those who obey God can live strongly, boldly—fearing nothing. Live strong!

////////// HOT READ ////////

Read Proverbs 31:10-31. Would the woman described in these verses be respected and sought after today? What makes her priceless?

⟶ GET READY TO BE SCHOOLED! <

"Meaningless! Meaningless!" says the Teacher. "Utterly meaningless!"
Ecclesiastes 1:2.

It's not the way I'd start a book, that is, beginning with the ending and then working backwards. But then again, you don't see any of my writings in the Bible, and last I checked, there's not a new Bible coming out any time soon. Yet "the Teacher," the guy spitting knowledge in this book, puts his conclusion in the opening verse of his work. That ought to give you some idea of just how important he regards that conclusion.

This teacher is no poor person who chased after life's goodies only to come up empty. He is rich, he is respected, and he is free to do whatever he wants, how he wants, and when he wants. And, friend, he tries just about everything "under the sun."

The teacher reminds me of an urban cowboy in San Francisco who believed in living on the open range. I saw this cowboy—actually, he was an inner-city runaway living homelessly in San Francisco with his runaway girlfriend—on a documentary about kids who head out into the unknown in search of greener pastures. The cowboy—whom I'll call Jeremy, because his name escapes me now—said something really deep when a reporter asked him why he stays on the street instead of trying to get out.

"I wanna suck everything out of life," he said with a weathered smile, his hair matted from the rain that had begun to fall. "I don't ever want to be tied down. Life is meant to be experienced, and I want to soak it all in, everything. I gotta try it all."

Even though I thought he was crazy, I had to admire his philosophy. He was determined to find what it was like to experience everything life had to give. If Jeremy could fast-forward his life, he just might come to same conclusion that the teacher did: "Everything is meaningless." *What did he mean by that?* I hear you say. Let's read through Ecclesiastes and find out. I think you'll feel where he's coming from if you let him explain himself.

The name Ecclesiastes comes from the Hebrew term *Qoheleth,* which means "Teacher" or "Preacher." *Ecclesiastes* means "one who assembles people." You and I are now assembled. Let's get ready to be schooled.

/////// HOT READ ///////

Read Ecclesiastes 3:1-14. Then read verse 15. Do you agree with him that *"whatever is has already been"?*

⟶ A GIFT FROM GOD <

Moreover, when God gives any man wealth and possessions, and enables him to enjoy them, to accept his lot and be happy in his work—this is a gift of God.
Ecclesiastes 5:19.

id you catch the message at the end of Ecclesiastes 5? If God gives a person wealth, and he or she is able to enjoy it, that wealth is a special gift from God. Not only is the gift special—it is also rare.

The teacher contends that rich people who are truly happy and content are not the norm. Surely doesn't seem that way when you look at the rich and famous. I once saw—saw on TV, of course—P Diddy roll up to a club in a Maybach. If you don't know what that is, don't sweat it. Let's just say it's a very expensive automobile. I'm not sure that he owned the ride, but since he's worth a gazillion dollars, it's not so far-fetched to think that the Maybach was his. He sure looked pretty happy getting out of it. The teacher would beg to differ with me on that proposition.

Why so? The teacher spells it out in chapter 5 and verse 12: "The abundance of a rich man permits him no sleep." The rich have a sleeping problem, he says, because they're constantly worried about losing it all. What's more, he notes, "whoever loves money never has money enough; whoever loves wealth is never satisfied" (verse 10).

The teacher was right about that, and something Sean Combs, the aforementioned P Diddy, said proved his point. Two years ago I caught an episode of Diddy's much-hyped show *Making the Band*, which aired on MTV. Diddy did a talent search to find five guys to start a hot soul group. After he'd whittled the group down to 16, Diddy flipped the script and brought in eight new guys to push the old cats.

One day while the group of 16 was sleeping, Diddy marched the eight new singers up to their apartment and into their rooms. Groggy and tired, they awoke to this message from the Right Reverend Combs of the Greater Church of Hip-Hop and R&B: "These new guys right here came to take your spot. While you sleepin', there's somebody workin' to take your spot. I didn't get to where I am by sleepin'."

This teacher knows what he's talking about. Wealth isn't all its cracked up to be.

///////// HOT READ ////////
What is the answer to the questions found in Ecclesiastes 6:12?

——> A PIG'S A PIG <

Lo, this only have I found, that God hath made man upright; but they have sought out many inventions. Ecclesiastes 7:29, KJV.

Ever been to a county fair—you know, one of those where chickens win medals, cows get ribbons, and pigs race? I haven't been to one of those as yet, but a friend of mine who moved from the asphalt jungle of New York down to semirural North Carolina did, and told me what he saw.

The pig races fascinated him the most. *Why are pigs racing?* I wondered as he described the whole sordid, muddy tale in detail. *What are they going to do next? Fly?* It all sounded a bit hokey to me, but I'm a city boy, so what do I know?

As I listened, I was struck by the connection between two sets of pigs at the fair. There were pigs that looked as though they'd never seen mud in their lives. These were show pigs, bred and fed to win ribbons for their size, weight, and overall good looks—if a pig can ever look good. The racing pigs? Well, they were glorified mudrats destined to win a race or end up on someone's table. Their future didn't look bright.

Believe it or not, there "ain't" a lick of difference between the show pigs and the regular pigs. If given a chance, the show pigs would feel quite at home rolling around in the muck and mire of the pigsty. Don't get it twisted, young'un. A pig's a pig!

The same is true of human beings. Human beings are pigs. Well, not exactly, but let me explain. When God made Adam and Eve, as the teacher notes, He made them upright, or righteous. But when they chose to sin, something changed in their DNA. They began to seek out ways—inventions—to please themselves instead of God. The more they hid their sins, the more they changed. Like show pigs, they looked good on the outside, but they were still pigs on the inside.

No matter how much we dress ourselves up, without God working in us to change us we will return to the dirt. This is why we ought to really thank God for Jesus. Because Jesus' life, death, and resurrection shows us that through Him we can live a pure life.

If you're stuck in the mud, ask Jesus to come in and clean you up. He will!

/////// HOT READ ///////

Read Ecclesiastes 7:13, 14. Is Solomon right when he says that "man cannot discover anything about his future"?

——> IN CONCLUSION <

Now all has been heard; here is the conclusion of the matter: Fear God and keep his commandments, for this is the whole duty of man. Ecclesiastes 12:13.

The teacher who has been schooling us for the past four days is none other than King Solomon. Who else had the riches and power to explore all that life has to offer?

King Solomon threw himself into his work as king, building grand palaces and ruling much of the then-known world—yet he found all this meaningless. He gave himself over to sexual immorality with countless foreign women, but this too couldn't satisfy him.

He married hundreds of wives and concubines, and so made alliances with many other countries, but that didn't satisfy him. (And just think of trying to keep even half of all those women happy!) He amassed more wealth than any other king before him, but his heart remained empty.

Ecclesiastes is Solomon's confession, but he didn't sing about it as Usher did a few years ago. Rather, he detailed his regrets for future generations to learn from. In chapter 12 he aims a zinger right a you, my young friend: "Remember your Creator in the days of your youth, before the days of trouble come and the years approach when you will say, 'I find no pleasure in them'" (verse 1).

When is the time to give God your heart? Right now, while you're young, because in a short time you will be old, and you just might regret not doing so earlier.

Solomon then describes what it's like to be facing death, with no way to undo all the wrongs he'd done. He describes going blind by saying, "The sun and the light and the moon and the stars grow dark" (Ecclesiastes 12:2). He says that "the grinders cease because they are few" (verse 3). That's a poetic way of saying that my teeth are falling out and I can't even chew my food.

The unmistakable conclusion of King Solomon's confession is not "everything is meaningless," as stated in Ecclesiastes 1:2. That's just part one of it. The summary of what he learned is found in the final two verses of his book.

When Solomon finished tallying up the score of his life, he came to the realization that the best way to live is to "fear [respect] God and keep his commandments" (Ecclesiastes 12:13). This, he says, is the "whole duty of man" (verse 13). And truly, this is all that God requires of you and me. When we live this way, we have no regrets.

//////// HOT READ ////////

Why is it important to live for God? Ecclesiastes 12:13.

⟶> WHEN A MAN LOVES A WOMAN <

My beloved is mine, and I am his. Song of Songs 2:16, KJV.

The Song of Songs is one of the most misunderstood books in the Bible. Some people hate it because they consider it too sexually explicit. Others comb its chapters and verses in search of God, and find only expressions of love. God can't be in a book like that, right? Consider this powerful quotation by Ellen White:

"Like every other one of God's good gifts entrusted to the keeping of humanity, marriage has been perverted by sin; but it is the purpose of the gospel to restore its purity and beauty. In both the Old and the New Testament the marriage relation is employed to represent the tender and sacred union that exists between Christ and His people, the redeemed ones whom He has purchased at the cost of Calvary. 'Fear not,' He says; 'thy Maker is thine husband; the Lord of hosts is his name; and thy Redeemer the Holy One of Israel.' 'Turn, O backsliding children, saith the Lord; for I am married unto you.' Isaiah 54:4, 5; Jeremiah 3:14. In the 'Song of Songs' we hear the bride's voice saying, 'My beloved is mine and I am his.' And He who is to her 'the chiefest among ten thousand' speaks to His chosen one, 'Thou art all fair, my love; there is no spot in thee.' Song of Solomon 2:16; 5:10; 4:7" *(Thoughts From the Mount of Blessing, p. 64).*

God is really into relationships, and the type of relationship that He chooses to best explain the kind of connection He wants with us is the relationship between a husband and a wife. No other book captures the joys of marital love like Song of Songs.

The husband in the Song of Songs is not afraid to tell his wife just how much he loves her, her body, her mind, her everything. She's not bashful either. She praises the beauty she sees in him. But they are not alone in this love. Their friends surround them to help them strengthen their love. As you read this book, ask yourself: Do I love God with my whole heart, as these two people love each other?

In today's world, the kind of love you'll read about in Song of Songs is rare. Premarital sex and other early dating experiences ruin the joy that God intended for us to experience only in marriage. Don't even think about dating until you've given your love life to God!

///////// HOT READ ////////

Why shouldn't you "awaken" love too soon? Song of Songs 2:7.

——> PICKUP LINES <

Your temples behind your veil are like the halves of a pomegranate.
Song of Songs 6:7.

t's hard to read Song of Solomon and not notice King Solomon's pickup lines. I figured that since I'm married, and Song of Songs celebrates the love between two newlyweds, I'd turn back the clock and see if some of Solomon's lines would work on my wife.

Sitting in the living room one Sunday morning, I dropped the voice a few octaves and started firing.

"Babe," I called out to her as she buried her head in her laptop, "your hair is like a flock of goats descending from Gilead." All morning she'd been doing work projects, but something happened when I said that line to her. I'm not sure if it was the goats descending from Gilead, but she looked up and smiled at me. Chalk one up for Solomon! (She probably couldn't believe that I had just compared her hair to a flock of goats. Her smile said, "Do you have any idea what goats smell like?")

But who has time to worry about that? I kept on going.

"Your temples behind your veil are like the halves of a pomegranate," I swooned. That one didn't go over too well. She looked at me as if to say, *Even you have better lines than that, Dwain. And you know you're line-challenged.*

Taking a note from her visual cue, I asked, "Do you remember any lines I said to you back when we started dating?"

"Yeah, actually I do," said Kemba, a wry smile creasing her face. "We were in the campus skating rink when you said to me, 'I love love.'"

The words were scarcely off her lips before I broke out in laughter. I can't believe I said that cheese-ball line. Must've worked, though, because I'm married to the girl I said it to more than 17 years ago. (Now, that's what you call SKILLZ!)

Seriously, guys, it's hard to read Song of Songs and not see that the love between a husband and wife is most beautiful when God ordains it, and when both parties wait until they are married before they explore it in all its fullness—and cheesiness.

////// HOT READ //////

Song of Songs 7 is pretty open sexually. Ask a pastor or Bible teacher why this book is included in the Bible!

———> REMEMBER WHEN? <

The vision concerning Judah and Jerusalem that Isaiah son of Amoz saw during the reigns of Uzziah, Jotham, Ahaz and Hezekiah, kings of Judah. Isaiah 1:1.

Friend, welcome to one of the greatest pieces of literature ever written. The book of Isaiah is awesome for many reasons. For one, you really can't understand all the mess that Israel and Judah got into without the eyewitness testimony of Isaiah found in the book we're about to read. You've read 1 and 2 Kings and the two books of Chronicles—both of which mention Isaiah, by the way—but it's not until you get to this book that you begin to understand just how far God's people had strayed from Him.

After speaking at a youth event one day, a young man named Mike★ pulled me to the side. He looked to be in his early 20s, clean-cut and mellow. However, the way he looked on the outside masked what he was feeling on the inside.

"I'm not sure where to be begin," he said, "but have you ever felt as though there was a time you really heard God in your life?"

I nodded my approval as he continued: "Well, I remember a time like that years ago, but I don't hear that voice anymore." He shook his head. "I don't even know if I want God."

I wasn't sure what to say to Mike, so I prayed that God would tell me how to calm his heart. The Lord showed me then that what Mike was feeling was the emptiness of separation from God. God reminded me that that Mike was created to be tight with God, so I shared with him that it didn't much matter how he *felt*. What mattered was what God has said in His Word. God wanted to be a part of his life again, I said, and then I shared several scriptures with him.

The story of Israel and Judah is a lot like Mike's story. Both had broken their covenant with God, the one that many years earlier they had sworn to keep (Deuteronomy 30:11-20). They'd become separated from God and weren't sure how to get back to Him. God gave Isaiah the task of warning both nations of His impending judgment.

However, Isaiah doesn't stop at God's judgment. He points to the day Jesus would come to save the world from sin. It is this latter point that makes Isaiah's book great!

★ not his name

HOT READ

Read Isaiah 2:20-22. What is Isaiah's central message to the people?

——> CHANGED BY HIS PRESENCE <

"Woe to me!" I cried. "I am ruined! For I am a man of unclean lips, and I live among a people of unclean lips, and my eyes have seen the King, the Lord Almighty."
Isaiah 6:5.

There are some sights that change the way you see the world forever. For years I'd seen commercials of guys and girls frolicking on powdery beaches flanked by sky-blue oceans with water so clear you could see the fish swimming below. It looked quite spectacular in the commercials, but then my wife and I actually went to one of those places on vacation.

And there's more! In addition to doing our own frolicking on the beach, my wife and I went snorkeling close to a beautiful reef. (Imagine that. Me, as "city" as you can get, snorkeling in the middle of the ocean! Do Black people snorkel?) I can't say that the snorkeling experience was a great success. Truth is I was so scared of drowning that I didn't see much. (Yes, I was wearing a life vest. Quit laughing!) But fear squeezed all the air out of my lungs. Gasping, I decided to make like a fish and breathe. Bad idea! I almost drank up the whole ocean.

But for a few fleeting moments I saw beauty that I'll never forget. One of our guides swam up under me and dropped a big dab of fish food right there. (He truly wanted to make my trip enjoyable, and I gave him a huge tip. He saved my day!) In an instant fish of all different colors and sizes danced and knifed through the water just below me. The gorgeous frenzy lasted but a few moments, but to me it seemed like hours. Back on land I told everyone the beauty and excitement I'd seen—minus the drama.

If you took that day's sightseeing extravaganza and multiplied it a billion times, it still wouldn't compare to the sight Isaiah described in Isaiah 6. At a sad moment in his life—the year that King Uzziah died—Isaiah was carried away in vision to the temple in heaven, the place God goes to church! There he saw God, and God's glory was so luminescent that it filled the entire building. Angels veiled their faces and bodies, crying "Holy, holy, holy!" The sight unnerved Isaiah—and changed him forever.

From that moment on, Isaiah impressed upon Israel and Judah just how holy God is.

///////// HOT READ /////////

Have you seen examples of what is talked about in Isaiah 5:20? Share one.

——> HELP IS ON THE WAY <

> *Therefore the Lord himself will give you a sign: The virgin will be with child and will give birth to a son, and will call him Immanuel.* Isaiah 7:14.

ing Ahaz and Judah were between a rock called Israel and a hard place, Syria. Isaiah 7:1 sort of sets the scene: "When Ahaz son of Jotham, the son of Uzziah, was king of Judah, King Rezin of Aram and Pekah son of Remaliah king of Israel marched up to fight against Jerusalem."

I don't know if you have siblings, but you're in for a fight when your brother or sister gets with your worst enemy and they both gang up against you. That may sound a bit far-fetched, but it wasn't for Judah. Their brothers and sisters in Israel had sold them out to the Syrians.

King Ahaz of Judah was scared to death of this deadly alliance. God knew it and sent word to His servant Isaiah.

"Go out, you and your son Shear-Jashub, to meet Ahaz," God told Isaiah (verse 3). "Say to him, 'Be careful, keep calm and don't be afraid. Do not lose heart because of these two smoldering stubs of firewood'" (verse 4). Through Isaiah God assured Ahaz that the plans of Syria and Israel would not succeed.

Then God urged Ahaz to stand firm. "If you do not stand firm in your faith," warned Isaiah, "you will not stand at all" (verse 9). That nugget of wisdom is as true today as it was back then. Ahaz should have believed it, but he was still unconvinced.

Finally God said to Ahaz, "Ask the Lord your God for a sign, whether in the deepest depths or in the highest heights" (verse 11). God literally asked Ahaz, "What will it take for you to believe that I'll protect you?" But Ahab refused to, as he said, "put the Lord to the test" (verse 12).

So to calm Ahaz's heart further, God sent him a message that echoed for the next 700 years. "The virgin will be with child and will give birth to a son, and will call him Immanuel" (verse 14). *Immanuel* means "God with us." There was probably no message Ahaz needed to hear more than that God would be with him. He did not know that Isaiah was speaking of Jesus, the Messiah, but God told him the good news anyway.

///////// HOT READ ///////

Read Isaiah 8:19, 20. Do you think this counsel applies to, say, reading your horoscope?

——> SOME TREES DON'T DIE <

A shoot will come up from the stump of Jesse; from his roots a Branch will bear fruit. Isaiah 11:1.

ne of the best things about God is that even though He sometimes has to punish us, He never leaves us hopeless. This was also true of Israel and Judah. God used the nation of Assyria to humble the 10 breakaway tribes that made up Israel. But God refused to destroy His people completely. He promised that a remnant of them would remain, even in Assyrian bondage.

Then God, through Isaiah, went further. Here's what God said, as only *The Message* can put it:

"A green Shoot will sprout from Jesse's stump, from his roots a budding Branch.

The life-giving Spirit of God will hover over him, the Spirit that brings wisdom and understanding, the Spirit that gives direction and builds strength, the Spirit that instills knowledge and Fear-of-God.

Fear-of-God will be all his joy and delight.

He won't judge by appearances, won't decide on the basis of hearsay.

He'll judge the needy by what is right, render decisions on earth's poor with justice.

His words will bring everyone to awed attention.

A mere breath from his lips will topple the wicked.

Each morning he'll pull on sturdy work clothes and boots, and build righteousness and faithfulness in the land" (Isaiah 11:1-5, Message).

Care to guess whom that passage is referring to? Isaiah is writing about Jesus—His birth and His life, and he penned the words nearly 700 years before Jesus was born. Through Isaiah, God sent the message that from the very people He was now punishing the Savior of the world would come. The Savior would be a descendant of Jesse's "branch," or son—David.

No matter how bad things get in your life, God offers you the same hope He offered Israel and Judah during tough times.

Jesus.

//////// HOT READ ////////

How did Isaiah say Israel would one day respond to God's punishment? Isaiah 12.

---> I WILL BE . . . <

How you have fallen from heaven, O morning star, son of the dawn! You have been cast down to the earth, you who once laid low the nations! Isaiah 14:12.

t was a spectacular collapse, one of the biggest comedowns in political history. All the news reports led with some version of "New York Governor Caught in Sex Scandal."

Like most people I was caught up in the buzz surrounding this news. It had all the juicy tidbits—a high-powered political star, adultery, a career left in ruins. But the more I watched that sad moment in the life of Eliot Spitzer, the disgraced governor of New York caught in the firestorm, the more I felt sorry for him, and especially for his wife and children.

Many powerful New York businesspeople took great pride is watching Spitzer crash back to earth. While he was attorney general of New York he had investigated and convicted some of them. Spitzer had made his career on being a straight arrow, a Boy Scout who refused to be corrupted by money or power. He had even spoken openly of someday becoming president of the United States. But unfortunately, he couldn't tame his own inner drives. Truth is, none of us can. Not me. Not you.

Isaiah 14 introduces us to another "guy" who couldn't tame his own inner drives. He was one of the most beautiful creatures in heaven. He was even given a special name—*Lucifer*—which means "son of the morning." Yet this was not enough for Lucifer. He wanted more.

"I will ascend to heaven," he said in his heart, though he was already there. "I will raise my throne above the stars of God; I will sit enthroned on the mount of assembly, on the utmost heights of the sacred mountain" (Isaiah 14:13). Lucifer decided in his heart to overthrow God, but as you'll read in the rest of Isaiah 14, Lucifer failed.

But he's no quitter.

In fact, it was Lucifer and his evil angels who seduced, tempted, and finally brought down the career of Eliot Spitzer. And here's a news flash for you and me: he's trying to do the same thing to us (1 Peter 5:8).

///////// HOT READ ///////

Why did God give Isaiah these insights into Lucifer's motivations?

——> LOVE POWER <

In love a throne will be established; in faithfulness a man will sit on it—one from the house of David—one who in judging seeks justice and speeds the cause of righteousness. Isaiah 16:5.

ove is not quite the word that comes to mind when I think of national leaders. Sure, they dress in dark-blue suits, perfectly starched white shirts, and red ties, and they'll be happy to tell you how much they love the good ole U.S.A. They'll fall all over themselves telling anyone who'll listen how much they hate OBL (Osama bin Laden), how they'll hunt him down until he's found and brought to justice—or justice is brought to him. Most of them would be telling you the truth, but hating OBL isn't the test of whether or not you love your nation. Who doesn't hate OBL? (OK, so God doesn't. But that's another story.)

Isaiah 16:5 establishes a different standard by which we can judge leaders: do they love their people? You can apply the same standard to any candidate, whether they're running for prime minister of Canada, president of the United States, or president of the Student Association. If they don't have the love, they're not qualified to lead, for their government will not stand on a solid foundation.

But what kind of love do they need? According to Isaiah 16:5, every leader demonstrates their love by being faithful, just, and fair, and very, very concerned about righteousness. God gave this special leadership principle to Isaiah smack in the middle of a fearful prophecy about the destruction of Moab.

The Moabites were born of incest between Lot and one of his daughters (Genesis 19:37), and through the centuries they'd been a constant thorn in the side of the Israelites. God, through Isaiah, prophesied their coming destruction. What did Moab do that was so wrong? You'll have to read Isaiah 16:6-12 to find out. God wanted to draw a direct contrast between the evil leadership in Moab and the godly leadership that would one day rule the earth.

A true leader expresses love for their followers by being faithful to their tasks, seeking justice, and extending the cause of righteousness or rightdoing.

HOT READ

What do you think Isaiah meant when he wrote that God's leader would "speed the cause of righteousness"? Should today's national leaders be righteous?

⟶ IN THAT DAY <

The Lord Almighty will bless them, saying, "Blessed be Egypt my people, Assyria my handiwork, and Israel my inheritance." Isaiah 19:25.

Some of the great things to look for in the book of Isaiah are hints of Jesus' first coming. Though His presence is hidden, Jesus is sprinkled throughout this great book of the Bible, and one example is found in Isaiah 19.

In the past several chapters we read pronouncements of God's punishment on different nations, including Israel, Ethiopia, and Egypt. In chapter 19 God focuses His ire on Egypt. The Egyptians of old were cruel enemies of Israel. Because of their idolatry and oppression, God vowed to come into Egypt with a force so strong that "the idols of Egypt will totter at His presence" (Isaiah 19:1, NKJV). Now, that's scary, dude!

God vowed to turn the Egyptians against each other, neighbor against neighbor, and city against city (verse 2). The Egyptians would seek help from witches and warlocks, but none would come. In fact, they would be given into the hands of a cruel master. Many scholars believe this cruel leader to be the Ethiopian ruler Shabaka.

According to the *Encyclopaedia Britannica*, Shabaka ruled from 718 or 719 B.C. to 703 B.C. Then it notes this about Shabaka: "Succeeding his brother Piankhi, in Cush (in the modern Sudan), Shabaka moved north, captured Bocchoris, the second king of the 24th dynasty, and, according to tradition, burned him alive." Shabaka surely does fit the description of the ruler spoken of in Isaiah 19:4.

But while Isaiah 19 begins with the prophecy of Egypt's destruction, the chapter ends in a very different way. God went out of His way to let all people, including the Egyptians, know that although Egypt would be punished, God would not forget them.

Not only would God remember Egypt, the people who had oppressed the chosen nation of Israel, but one day the Egyptians, the Ethiopians, and the Israelites would be joined together as one. All the hate that existed among them during the time of Isaiah would give way to peace.

What day was God referring to? The day that Jesus returns to earth the second time. In that day all hate will cease.

/////// HOT READ ///////

Read Isaiah 20. Whom do you rely on for help during tough times?

——> THE BEAT GOES ON <

The Lord Almighty planned it, to bring low the pride of all glory and to humble all who are renowned on the earth. Isaiah 23:9.

y now you've noticed the trend in this portion of Isaiah's book. What is that trend? you ask. In a word—judgment. We've read about God's judgment against Egypt, Assyria, Ethiopia, and even Israel. God ends His judgment theme on foreign nations by focusing on Tyre. Why Tyre? A little history is needed here.

During Isaiah's time, Tyre was one of the world's most powerful seaports. It had an advanced civilization and is credited with developing the first alphabet. The empire was also quite large, extending to North Africa and some say even to Spain.

Tyre's first ruler, a guy named Hiram—remember him?—was a friend of King David's. In fact, he was the one who supplied skilled tradesmen and supplies to help Solomon build the Jewish Temple. But Hiram's friendship with David didn't mean that Tyre followed the true God. In fact, Tyre's citizens worshipped several pagan gods, including Baal and Ashtoreth, the gods imported to Israel by Jezebel, who was from—you guessed it—Tyre. These were the gods that Elijah humiliated on Mount Carmel (1 Kings 18).

When we put false gods before the true God, He is not pleased. In a few weeks we'll get to the book of Ezekiel, where all of Ezekiel 28 is dedicated to Tyre. Here's a preview of just how God felt about Tyre and its evil leadership:

"God's Message came to me, 'Son of man, tell the prince of Tyre, "This is what God, the Master, says: Your heart is proud, going around saying, 'I'm a god. I sit on God's divine throne, ruling the sea'—You, a mere mortal, not even close to being a god, a mere mortal trying to be a god.

""Look, you think you're smarter than Daniel. No enigmas can stump you. Your sharp intelligence made you world-wealthy. You piled up gold and silver in your banks. You used your head well, worked good deals, made a lot of money. But the money has gone to your head, swelled your head—what a big head!"'" (Ezekiel 28:1-5, Message).

Sounds like God is getting a bit personal, doesn't it? He gets that way when humans try to replace Him. There's only one God. Why not put Him first in *your* life?

///////// HOT READ /////////

To what event is Isaiah 24:20 is referring?

——> WHAT'S ON YOUR MIND? <

You will keep him in perfect peace, whose mind is stayed on You, because he trusts in You. Isaiah 26:3, NKJV.

ollin down the street, smokin indo, sippin on gin and juice, Laid back with my mind on my money and my money on my mind."

Hopefully you haven't heard that line before, or the song from which it comes. Ever since rapper Snoop Dogg dropped it in one of his hits years ago, it has been repeated many times in many different hip-hop songs, as well as on TV. As crude as his line was, Snoop was prophetic about one thing: Most people have their mind on their money, and their money on their mind.

Amanda Congdon, the former host of the popular Rocketboom blog, traveled across the U.S.A. trying to find out what one thing most citizens have in common. She was later interviewed by author and columnist Guy Kawaski on his blog. Here's what Congdon said:

"Americans are obsessed with money. I know it's common sense, but driving across the country and actually, literally—seeing all these different Americans living such radically different lives—it was fascinating that they all seemed to be concerned about the same things: where their money was going, how it was being spent, how much they were saving, and on and on. It was quite eye opening. Whether they were rich or poor—or somewhere in between—everyone seemed to have money on the brain."

Now, you and I both know plenty of people who aren't thinking about money all day. Or do we? How many of those whom we think are not obsessed with money would want to go without it for a significant period of time? Not many.

We obsess over money because to us money equals security. As the apostle Paul wrote to a teen named Timothy: "Some people, eager for money, have wandered from the faith and pierced themselves with many griefs" (1 Timothy 6:10). Paul was right.

God has something so much better for us to think about—Him. He promises that when our minds are on Him He will bring us peace—and that's worth all the money in the world.

HOT READ
What does the rest of Isaiah 26 tell us about God's forgiveness?

——> DEEP SLEEP <

The Lord has brought over you a deep sleep: He has sealed your eyes (the prophets); he has covered your heads (the seers). Isaiah 29:10.

id you know that during an average night of sleep a person goes through five separate stages of rest? Each stage lasts about 90 to 100 minutes. In the first two stages, one can be easily awakened. The heart rate slows down, eye movements slow and eventually stop, and breathing slows down.

The third and fourth stages offer much deeper sleep. This is where you get that deep sleep your body craves after nights spent cramming for midterms or updating your Facebook page. You're not really sleeping until you get into these stages. It's during this time that your body begins to repair itself and to prepare you to face a new day. If you burst into the room while your roommate is in the third or fourth stage, you're liable to hear some things you might not understand. Who hasn't been there?

The fifth stage is REM, or rapid eye movement, sleep. That's right, your eyes start dancing and, typically, your limbs don't move. This is the stage in which you dream that you're head of the United Nations and people from all over the world are asking you what you plan to do about the world's next big crisis. REM sleep— if you ever get to it—is the icing on a good night of rest. Can't remember any of your dreams? You might not be getting enough sleep.

When God, through Isaiah, spoke of putting the nation of Judah into a deep sleep (Isaiah 29:10), He was probably talking about the third or fourth sleep stage. Now, God didn't mean that all the people would be passed out in the middle of the street catching some z's. No, Judah would grope around incoherently because of the absence of prophets. These prophets were Judah's spiritual eyes, enabling them to see and comprehend the times and the warnings of God.

Even though the nation would be awakened by impending destruction—and they were, after the mighty Assyrian king Sennacherib invaded Judah in 701 B.C. (Isaiah 37)—the nation would be caught groggy and unprepared.

What does this tell us about listening to and obeying God's warnings?

---> WHO YA GONNA CALL? <

Woe to those who go down to Egypt for help, and rely on horses, who trust in chariots because they are many, and in horsemen because they are very strong, but who do not look to the Holy One of Israel, nor seek the Lord! Isaiah 31:1, NKJV.

ne of the great messages we can take away from today's Bible reading is that God is ready and waiting to help us fight any battle in life. But that doesn't mean a thing unless we're willing to call on Him for help.

We've all heard sad stories of teens who have been bullied by other teens. Bullying is nothing new. I remember when I first got to middle school. I'm not a big guy now, but I sure was a runt back then. I was scared of my shadow!

I remember when one of older guys started messing with me—you know, hitting me, making jokes about my grocery store tennis shoes and my out-of-date clothes. Middle school was a big step up in the game of life, and I was having a tough time as it was just fitting in. This dude was not making it easy.

So I did what anybody who had three older brothers would do. I kindly reminded the guy that I would sic one of my older brothers on him if he didn't cease and desist. He was "soooo" not impressed with that statement. And now I can understand why.

You see, in East Orange, New Jersey, where I grew up, guys would beat you up right on the spot if you threaten to get backup. I guess they figured, "Hey, if he's gonna get his big brother on me, why not kick his butt now?" The logic seemed a bit off to me at the time, but I sure understand it now—this side of a little butt-kicking.

When Israel faced a fearsome enemy in Assyria, they, too, went for help, but they didn't go to God. They looked to Egypt with its mighty soldiers and awesome weaponry. They thought that if they could ally themselves with Egypt, they could face Assyria. They had no idea how wrong they were.

There was no way that they could face Assyria without God's help. God had been their help in ages past, and God was anxious to stand up for them again. But they had grown so dependent on looking out for themselves that they never consulted God. That's exactly what I did when I faced my bullies. I never ever thought of talking to God. Oops!

HOT READ

What did God promise to do for Judah? Isaiah 31:4-9.

——> IS GOD A HATER? <

The desert and the parched land will be glad; the wilderness will rejoice and blossom. Isaiah 35:1.

f you stopped reading Isaiah after the first 34 chapters, you'd be left with one dangerously incomplete picture of God. For in the first 34 chapters Isaiah is delivering a message of God's judgment against all the nations of the earth. God seems to be at the end of His rope, ready to smash everything in sight, and He comes off as a big cosmic "hater." (Don't tell me you've never felt that way about God. I know I have sometimes.)

The focus of Isaiah's first 34 chapters is no accident. The message is simply this: God hates sin. And those who continue to commit known, willful sin after being given many chances and warnings to change—and the power to change— will be punished. To be sure, we see glimpses of the relief and restoration God promised to His remnant people, but Isaiah's primary message was one of wrath and fury.

Often God's punishment comes in the form of the natural consequences of our sins. At other times He simply removes his hedge of protection from us and lets us feel what it's like to live without Him around. But either way, the effects are life-changing.

But punishment for sin is not all there is to God, and Isaiah 35 proves it. God told Isaiah to encourage the faithful by letting them know that one day the broken desert places of their lives would become lush and fertile again. One day the glory that once crowned Israel's cities would return. The blind would see, the lame walk, the deaf hear, and the mute talk. These words were to "strengthen the feeble hands, [and] steady the knees that give way" (Isaiah 35:3).

The rest of chapter 35 describes the restoration that God's people would experience someday. However, the Israelites who heard the message never got a chance to experience the fulfillment of those promises, for Isaiah 35 points forward to the day when God will create a new heaven and a new earth for those who remain faithful to Him to the end (Revelation 21; 22).

Maybe God has allowed some tough times to come your way lately. Don't judge God by these moments alone. Focus instead on His goodness. God is not out to get you. He's out to save you!

///////// HOT READ ////////

What did Sennacherib say that made God upset? Isaiah 36:18.

——> TRAPPED <

It is true, O Lord, that the Assyrian kings have laid waste all these peoples and their lands. Isaiah 37:18.

or 33 years she was on the run. She'd escaped five separate times from the Georgia Women's Correctional Institution in Baldwin County, Georgia. Each time she was caught and returned to serve out her sentence for armed robbery. The sixth time was the charm. This time Deborah Gavin vanished for good. The year was 1974.

She changed her name, donning several aliases before marrying Richard Murphey and settling down in Frankston, Texas. She had two children, got a job at which she worked for several years before health problems made her quit. Hey, she even started her own business.

You can imagine her surprise when federal marshals surrounded her home to arrest her—33 years after her final escape from prison. One of the arresting officers on the fugitive task force was asked if she had anything to say. "She just said she knew this day was going to come," the officer noted. "But she hadn't prepared for it yet."

Deborah Gavin's date with destiny was a foregone conclusion. It was coming, whether she was prepared or not. In today's Bible reading, King Hezekiah faced a similar date with destiny. OK, he was no fugitive, but I'm sure he thought about running to avoid a head-on collision with King Sennacherib of Assyria.

The Assyrian strongman sent King Hezekiah a letter detailing all the nations who thought their gods could protect them from his deadly forces. "Your god ain't no different, Hez," he calmly asserted. "I'm gonna kill you and him!"

When Hezekiah got the message, the Bible says that he went directly to the Temple, spread the letter out before God, and prayed. (Now, that's stress relief!) Hezekiah said, "Lord, have you seen this letter? This dude is insulting You, the Living God" (Isaiah 37:17). Hezekiah knew which buttons to push to get God's attention. God does not take kindly to folks who diss His people or His rep.

Hezekiah didn't know it at the time, but God had already begun to work this situation out for him. Before Hezekiah prayed, the answer was on the way.

/////// HOT READ ///////

What did God eventually do to Assyria? Isaiah 37:30-38.

——> VERBAL FIRST AID <

Comfort, comfort my people, says your God. Speak tenderly to Jerusalem, and proclaim to her that her hard service has been completed, that her sin has been paid for, that she has received from the Lord's hand double for all her sins. Isaiah 40:1, 2.

At the time Isaiah spoke those words to God's people, they still faced hard times. The people of Jerusalem faced more than 100 years of trouble, which would end in the destruction of their city. After being conquered, they then would be in exile for 70 years.

The people of Jerusalem had been listening to Isaiah and the other prophets, though many didn't want to believe that their dire predictions would ever come true. It was a scary time in Jerusalem, so God told Isaiah to speak words of comfort to Jerusalem.

"Don't yell words of destruction at them," God seems to say to His spokesperson. "Right now they need hope."

Sometimes when a situation is bad and will only get worse, comforting words are a kind of verbal first aid to those who are hurting. Many doctors and behavioral therapists have studied the effect of words on the mind. For instance, studies have shown that if two patients with identical symptoms are given the same medicine, the outcome of their treatment can be greatly affected by what their doctors tell them. In studies in which one person is given the real medication and the other is given a placebo or fake pill, the person taking the placebo will sometimes develop side-effect symptoms—especially if the doctor mentioned those side effects to them before treatment. Words really do matter.

Just as doctors are careful about what they say to their patients, God is careful about what He says to us. He knows what we need to hear at just the right time.

Through Isaiah God promised: "Every valley shall be raised up, every mountain and hill made low; the rough ground shall become level, the rugged places a plain. And the glory of the Lord will be revealed, and all mankind together will see it" (Isaiah 40:4, 5).

The citizens of Jerusalem needed to hear their God say, "Better days are coming."

//////// HOT READ ////////

Need a "muscle" text to encourage you? Here it is. Isaiah 41:10.

——> THE SMELL TEST <

Who says of Cyrus, "He is my shepherd and will accomplish all that I please; he will say of Jerusalem, 'Let it be rebuilt,' and of the temple, 'Let its foundations be laid.'" Isaiah 44:28.

t's tough to predict anything on earth with certainty, besides death and taxes. If you and I keep living eventually we're going to kick the bucket. (I'm definitely hoping that God whisks me away to heaven before I get going on my "bucket list.") As for taxes—you better believe some genius accountant is in a dark room figuring out how to make you and I pay from the grave.

Some people can predict other things with near certainty, though. For instance, Dr. Sydney Spiesel, a Yale graduate and frequent medical contributor to National Public Radio, has a special gift for predicting specific illnesses with—get this—his nose. I bet you didn't know that someone with, say, diabetes has a faint sweet smell. Dr. Spiesel would know almost instantly. Wouldn't you like to invite him to sniff some of your friends? There might be more to their aroma than a few missed showers.

As great as Dr. Sydney Spiesel is, he's not perfect—at least not as perfect as the new medical marvel that will make his nose obsolete. The device, which was still being tested at the time of this writing, can literally sniff out illness with near certainty based on the molecules from the BO of the person being analyzed. Pretty good, huh?

As great at that machine is, God has to be the all-time greatest predictor of the future. Here's one example. In today's reading Isaiah continues to deliver God's message of warning and redemption to Israel. God's people are urged to put away their idols and serve Him faithfully. (God could give the same message today, don't ya think?) God promised that one day, Jerusalem would be rebuilt, including the Jewish Temple. In Isaiah 44:28, the prophet actually told the name of the king who would allow it to happen.

Isaiah spoke those words almost 150 years before a king named Cyrus became ruler of the Persian Empire. King Cyrus later fulfilled Isaiah's prophecy to the letter (Ezra 1:2-4). After the Babylonian exile, King Cyrus allowed Ezra, Nehemiah, and the remnant to begin rebuilding Jerusalem.

///////// HOT READ /////////

What was the nation of Israel supposed to be on earth? Isaiah 43:10, 11.

——> BABYLON <

Sit in silence, go into darkness, Daughter of the Babylonians; no more will you be called queen of kingdoms. Isaiah 47:5.

abylon. It's a name that you hear mostly in churches. But there once was a time that Babylon was more than just a word spoken by preachers.

According to historical records, the ancient Babylonian empire was located between the Tigris and Euphrates rivers, about 60 miles southwest of modern-day Baghdad, Iraq. If you got to the site today you'd be hard-pressed to find any hint of that once-great city.

The name Babylon is derived from a word in the language of the day that meant confusion. The site of ancient Babylon is also believed to be the spot on which the Tower of Babel was erected, and we all know what God did to the language of the people who were building the tower, don't we? (See Genesis 11.)

The Bible refers to the city of Babylon as a woman, a virgin to be exact. It's called a virgin because it had never been conquered by another nation. It was a title that made the nation proud. When we get to the book of Revelation, Babylon will be called by a very different name.

God used Babylon as a tool to conquer the Jewish nation because of their sins. Here's how God put it: "I was angry with my people and desecrated my inheritance; I gave them into your hand, and you showed them no mercy. Even on the aged you laid a very heavy yoke. You said, 'I will continue forever—the eternal queen!' But you did not consider these things or reflect on what might happen" (Isaiah 47:6, 7). Babylon did the job, but then it went too far. The Babylonians cruelly oppressed their slaves. And King Nebuchadnezzar was willing to burn to death anyone who did not worship him.

God orchestrated the destruction of mighty Babylon by the Medes and Persians, but the term *Babylon* lives on. In the Bible the term has come to mean everything evil about the kingdoms and nations of the world. Remember Babylon. You'll see it again.

/////// HOT READ ///////

Read Isaiah 48:18, 19. Did God really want His people to suffer in Babylon?

———> A MOTHER'S LOVE <

Can a mother forget the baby at her breast and have no compassion on the child she has borne? Though she may forget, I will not forget you! Isaiah 49:15.

oes your mother love you? What a dumb question, right? Of course your mother loves you! But not all people can say that about their mothers.

I remember a story that a teen sent to *Insight* a few years ago. It was unlike any other story we'd ever received. This teen's mother stole her identity and wrote several fake checks in her name. The cops arrested the teen for crimes committed by her mother! When her mom came to pick her up from the detention center, she didn't even bother to apologize.

Not all mothers are loving. If yours is, be very, very thankful!

The love of a truly dedicated mother comes closest to the love God has for His children. That's why in Isaiah 49:15 God makes it clear that just as a mother can never forget the baby who depends on her for food, He cannot forget His children. The children of Israel needed to hear this message, especially when it seemed like their years of exile in Babylon would never end.

In his book *Illustrations Unlimited* author James S. Hewett tells the story of a mother who made an unusual—and supreme—sacrifice to save her son.

Years ago a young mother was making her way across the hills of south Wales, carrying her tiny baby in her arms, when she was overtaken by a blinding blizzard. She died there, in the storm. When the blizzard subsided, searchers found her body beneath a mound of snow. They also discovered that she'd taken off her outer clothing and wrapped it about her baby. To their surprise and joy, the baby was alive and well. She had mounded her body over his and given her life for her child, proving the depths of her mother love. Years later that child, David Lloyd George, became prime minister of Great Britain—without a doubt, one of England's greatest statesman.

Now, that's love! And God's love for us is even greater than that!

///// HOT READ /////

What else did God say to Israel to prove that He would never forget them? Isaiah 45:17. How did Jesus fulfill this promise?

⟶ GODS DON'T DIE ‹

He was oppressed and afflicted, yet he did not open his mouth; he was led like a lamb to the slaughter, and as sheep before her shearers is silent, so he did not open his mouth. Isaiah 53:7.

ods don't die, and certainly not by choice. Quick, name a god worshipped by people around the world who voluntarily chose to die for the world. Is there one besides Jesus?

Jesus is unique in many ways, but one of the most special things about Him—one of things that sets Him apart from all other gods—is that Jesus willingly surrendered His life to atone for the sins of every human being. He even died for the ones who hated Him. And more than 700 years before Jesus died on the cross, God gave Isaiah a vision of what our Savior would be like. There is no other chapter quite like Isaiah 53, so allow me to quote a bit of it from *The Message.*

"There was nothing attractive about him, nothing to cause us to take a second look. He was looked down on and passed over, a man who suffered, who knew pain firsthand.

"One look at him and people turned away. We looked down on him, thought he was scum. But the fact is, it was *our* pains he carried—*our* disfigurements, all the things wrong with *us*. We thought he brought it on himself, that God was punishing him for his own failures. But it was our sins that did that to him, that ripped and tore and crushed him—*our sins!*

"He took the punishment, and that made us whole. Through his bruises we get healed. We're all like sheep who've wandered off and gotten lost. We've all done our own thing, gone our own way. And God has piled all our sins, everything we've done wrong on him, on him" (Isaiah 53.2-6, Message).

Jesus is the defining character in the story of our planet. There is no other God like Him. He alone deserves our worship.

//////// HOT READ ////////

Read Isaiah 52:13-15. The Servant of the Lord described in these verses is Jesus, the Messiah. How did God say the world would react to Him?

——> DESERT SHIPS <

Come, all you who are thirsty, come to the waters. Isaiah 55:1.

id you know that there ships in the desert? Not every desert, for sure, but they sail around the Gobi Desert in Mongolia. They are the only way to get around remote stretches of Afghanistan, Turkey, the Soviet Union, Iran, and China.

I know what you're thinking. *Who in the world would put a ship in the desert?* God would, that's who! But God's desert ships don't have a mast and sails, engines or sailors. These ships have two weird humps on their backs, cushioned feet that allow them to glide through desert sands, tough skin, and two rows of eyelashes that enable them to withstand the fiercest sandstorm. God's desert ships are called camels.

If anyone doubts that God is creator of all life, the camel will make you think again. There are few animals as amazing as camels. According to an article featured on the science and Scripture Web site Discoverymagazine.com, camels store water inside small flasks that line their stomach. (No, they do not store water in the humps on their back.) Their powerful digestive systems can suck water from plants and shrubs that would make other animals gag. They rarely ever sweat, so they don't lose water the way you and I do. And when they breathe, "their nostrils remove moisture from their breath and recirculate it through their bodies."

But even though camels are extraordinarily adapted to desert life—able to walk in the heat for up to 18 hours at a time while carrying very heavy loads—they too need water. When they get thirsty, they get *thirsty*. The average camel can drink as much as 25 gallons of water in less than 10 minutes.

Believe it or not, you and I are a lot like camels—only better looking. No, we can't survive without physical water for very long, but we do think that we can survive without the Water of Life—God. We often get up and go about our day without even thanking God for waking us up. We make plans and ask God to bless them. Before long we get spiritually hungry and thirsty.

Here's the good news. God has what we need, but we must take our thirst to Him.

////// HOT READ //////

Muscle text alert! Isaiah 55:6-11 is one of the most powerful of passages in the Bible. You should memorize these verses, my friend!

——> THE REAL FAST <

Is not this the kind of fasting I have chosen: to loose the chains of injustice and untie the cords of the yoke, to set the oppressed free and break every yoke? Isaiah 58:6.

The way that Judah worshipped God during the time of Isaiah was a constant source of pain for God. The praised God with their lips, but their hearts were far from Him. They brought their sacrifices to the Temple, but there was no change in the way that they lived—especially in the way that they treated the poor. They would fast—go without food—in hopes of convincing God to answer their prayers, but even that was just a show.

"For day after day they seek me out," God said sadly. "They seem eager to know my ways, as if they were a nation that does what is right and has not forsaken the commands of its God" (Isaiah 58:2). God didn't stop there. He continued, "They ask me for just decisions and seem eager for God to come near them. 'Why have we fasted,' they say, 'and you have not seen it? Why have we humbled ourselves, and you have not noticed?' Yet on the day of your fasting, you do as you please and exploit all your workers" (verses 2, 3).

Did you get that? The people of Judah were hypocrites. They wanted God to help them, while at the same time they were mistreating those who worked for them. That's why God called them out and showed them their sins. But He didn't stop there. God told them the kind of fasting that He accepts—the type of acts that please Him.

"Is not this the kind of fasting I have chosen: to loose the chains of injustice and untie the cords of the yoke, to set the oppressed free and break every yoke? Is it not to share your food with the hungry and to provide the poor wanderer with shelter—when you see the naked, to clothe him, and not to turn away from your own flesh and blood?" (verses 6, 7).

When Judah started living the truth, God promised them a special blessing. "Then your light will break forth like the dawn, and your healing will quickly appear; then your righteousness will go before you, and the glory of the Lord will be your rear guard" (verse 8).

When you live the truth every day, you will be blessed!

//////// HOT READ ////////

What does Isaiah 59:1, 2 tell you about the things that can separate us from God? Is anything separating you from God?

——> BORN TO GRAPPLE <

The Spirit of the Sovereign Lord is on me, because the Lord has anointed me to preach good news to the poor. He has sent me to bind up the brokenhearted, to proclaim freedom for the captives and release from darkness for the prisoners.
Isaiah 61:1.

ou don't know who Marcelo Garcia is. You've probably never even heard his name. He's not wealthy. He's not a president or prime minister of a country. He's not tall or overly handsome. Like you and me, he's not great at most things in his life, but there is one thing that he does very, very well.

At age 26, Marcelo Garcia is considered the best jiu jitsu grappler in the world. For those of you who don't know anything about martial arts—and that includes me—jiu jitsu, or the art of softness, was practiced by the Japanese Samurais. The ancient Samurai warriors mastered a series of specialized wrestling techniques to overcome an armed opponent in close quarters without a weapon of their own. Marcelo Garcia is the acknowledged master of this ancient art. It doesn't matter how big or strong the opponent is, Garcia's masterful technique, strength, and amazing flexibility makes him almost unbeatable.

Marcelo Garcia was born to grapple, it seems. So was Jesus. Isaiah 61:1-3 paints us a picture of a Savior ready to go to the mat for those who hurt. But Jesus wasn't just born to grapple with sin and its consequences; Jesus was anointed to do it.

The word "anointed" used by Isaiah to describe Jesus in Isaiah 61:1 and is the Hebrew word *mashach*. *Mashach* means to anoint, to rub with oil, especially in order to consecrate someone or something. This is the word used to describe what Moses did to Aaron and the rest of the priests serving in the Temple.

From *mashach* we get the word *mashiyach,* which means Messiah or anointed one. This is why Jesus is called Jesus the Messiah and Jesus the Anointed One. When *Messiah* was translated into Greek—the primary language of the New Testament—the word the Grecians used was *Christos.* From Christos we get Jesus Christ.

But no matter how the language changes, Jesus was anointed to win our lost world back to God. Isaiah 61:1-3 captures the focus of Jesus' mission on earth.

///////// HOT READ ///////

Do you pray for your friends the way Isaiah prayed for the salvation of his country in Isaiah 62:1-7? Which one of your friends needs your prayers right now?

August 10 • *Isaiah 64-66*

——> HAPPY ENDING <

*"As the new heavens and the new earth that I make will endure before me,"
declares the Lord, "so will your name and descendants endure."* Isaiah 66:22.

The prophet Isaiah closes his book with a vision of the end of time. He addresses several strong warnings to the wicked, such as this: "But as for you who forsake the Lord and forget my holy mountain, who spread a table for Fortune and fill bowls of mixed wine for Destiny, I will destine you for the sword, and you will all bend down for slaughter; for I called but you did not answer, I spoke but you did not listen" (Isaiah 65:11, 12).

Ouch.

Thank God that Isaiah doesn't stop at warnings like the one above. He also wrote this special message to those who remain faithful obedient followers of God to the end: "Behold, I will create new heavens and a new earth. The former things will not be remembered, nor will they come to mind. But be glad and rejoice forever in what I will create, for I will create Jerusalem to be a delight and its people a joy. . . . The sound of weeping and of crying will be heard in it no more" (verses 17-19).

Yes!

As you read the final chapters of Isaiah's awesome book you'll see a great urgency to his writing. He is saying to the people of his time—and us today— "Choose to follow God now, while you have the chance. God is preparing a special place for all who love Him, and you just cannot afford to miss it."

Two years ago I traveled to Australia to speak for a special youth rally. It was the greatest spiritual experience I've ever had ministering for God. The youth there were terrific, and I'll never forget my last day there. Several teens said goodbye to me. Others wished me a safe trip home. But the teens I remember most were those who promised to meet me in heaven if we never met again on earth. I was so stoked that they were focused on going to heaven! I have to get there, because we have a "meet-up" planned for heaven.

If you're serious about going to heaven, then follow Isaiah's counsel and surrender your life to God right now. Heaven is the happy ending God planned for you.

///////// HOT READ /////////

What will heaven be like? Check out Isaiah 65:25; 66:22, 23.

———> THREATENED <

> *Before I formed you in the womb I knew you, before you were born I set you apart; I appointed you as a prophet to the nations.* Jeremiah 1:5.

obody likes to be threatened, especially when they're trying to do what is right. A few years ago I attended a youth conference at which a young woman I'll call Pamela shared a testimony that I'll never forget. While walking on her college campus Pamela noticed a girl who seemed to be having a really bad day. She looked like she'd been crying, so Pamela went up to her and asked her what was wrong.

At first the girl hesitated to answer. But after some coaxing, she opened up and told Pamela the whole story. Her parents were devil worshippers, and she lived in their home. Not only did they worship the devil, but they had occult symbols hanging all around the house, and they forbid the girl to worship anyone else. She knew devil worship was wrong, but she couldn't say anything about it.

Pamela was stunned, but the young woman shared her story with such sincerity and honesty that Pamela felt she couldn't be making it up. The girl told her that she'd sneaked a Bible into the house and was, of course, reading it. But her mother had found the hidden Bible and burned it. Then she threatened to kick her daughter out of the house if she ever brought another Bible into their home. Pretty sick, huh? (In life we sometimes encounter horrible situations. If you are trapped in one of those, get help.)

Serving God is not always a walk in the park. Sometimes it causes us to be ridiculed, laughed at, threatened, or worse. Perhaps no other biblical book captures the challenges of serving God faithfully than Jeremiah. He was still a teenager when God called him to deliver a message of warning to the nation of Judah. It was a message no one wanted to hear—especially from a teen!

For nearly five decades Jeremiah passionately tried to get God's own people to repent of their sins and turn back to Him, only to be ridiculed and attacked. Can you imagine making appeals for 50 years straight and getting almost no response? How would you feel? Would you keep on going?

Jeremiah took courage in one important fact: God called him, and God would always be with Him.

///////// HOT READ ////////

Why is God so angry with Israel? Jeremiah 2.

──> FEELING HER PAIN <

Oh, my anguish, my anguish! I writhe in pain. Oh, the agony of my heart! My heart pounds within me, I cannot keep silent. Jeremiah 4:19.

I don't know of anyone who loves to get shots—you know, get stuck with needles—but of all the needle-phobic people in world, my wife has got to be the worst of them all. I'll never forget the time I went to the doctor with her for a minor checkup. After poking and prodding her here and there, he said the words that she didn't want to hear: "Kemba, I think we're going to have to have some bloodwork done."

At that Kemba whirled toward me as if to say, "Did he just say what I *thought* he said?" I gave her a smile, and before the doctor could say another word, Kemba gave a monster sigh. I knew that getting blood out of my wife was like getting gold out of Fort Knox. 'Taint gonna happen, dude!

When the nurse came in to draw the blood, Kemba squirmed on the examination table. Trying to calm her, I reached for her hand, but it was no use. *Get your hands off me*, her angry expression said.

"Mrs. Esmond, would you extend your left arm, please?" the nurse asked. But the arm remained securely tucked by her side. (The nurse shouldn't have asked a question. The answer was NO.) Then nurse reached for the hidden arm and tried to pull it out. NOT.

Once the nurse got her arm extended, it took several fits and starts before Kemba relaxed enough for the needle to enter a vein. When it did, you would've sworn that someone was sawing her head off.

As I watched my baby squirm in fear and pain I wished that I could give the blood for her. She and I are one, so I knew how she was feeling. (OK, I didn't really, but I wanted to. OK, I really didn't want to!)

One of the unique gifts God gave Jeremiah was the ability to feel His pain, to feel how God felt when Israel sinned. Jeremiah could feel God's pain much better than I could feel my wife's. Jeremiah hurt when God hurt. He cried when God cried.

──→ KEEP YOUR STUFF! <

The Lord . . . , the God of Israel says, Away with your offerings and sacrifices!
It wasn't offerings and sacrifices I wanted from your fathers when I led them out
of Egypt. That was not the point of my command. Jeremiah 7:21, 22, TLB.

hile surfing the Internet one day I came across Roger Staubach's story. Now, I knew Roger Staubach. He was the quarterback of my favorite football team, the Dallas Cowboys. (Don't hate!)

I believe I was destined from birth to be a Cowboys fan. The Cowboys won the Super Bowl the same year that I was born, and several times more after that. You get my drift. Roger Staubach was unquestionably one of the greatest quarterbacks playing at that time, but he was different from the others in one huge way: he never called his own plays.

Any quarterback will tell you that you're not really "da man" until you can call your own plays. As great a player as Staubach was, Tom Landry, the legendary coach of the Cowboys, called every play. It was a tough pill to swallow for a future Hall of Famer. "I faced up to the issue of obedience," Roger Staubach later said. "Once I learned to obey, there was harmony, fulfillment, and victory." Staubach understood that if he was willing to be led by his coach, if he was willing to sacrifice being "da man" for the good of the team, the Cowboys would be winners. The coach didn't need his play-calling skills. The coach needed his obedience for the good of the team.

One of the (many) problems God had with Israel was their unwillingness to obey Him. They were determined to play the game however they wanted—they'd apologize to the Coach later. Confused? Let me explain. The people of Israel purposefully disobeyed God, then brought their offerings and sacrifices to the Temple to ask forgiveness. God saw through their charade. He didn't want their sacrifices. God wanted their obedience! Obedience was the path to life, while their way led to death.

Jeremiah captured God's anger: "I gave them this command: Obey me, and I will be your God and you will be my people" (Jeremiah 7:23).

God will forgive us when we mess up, but what He really wants is our obedience.

HOT READ

Why was it so hard for Israel to obey God? Jeremiah 8:7.

——> KILL THE MESSENGER <

I had been like a gentle lamb led to the slaughter; I did not realize that they had plotted against me, saying, "Let us destroy the tree and its fruit; let us cut him off from the land of the living, that his name be remembered no more."
Jeremiah 11:19.

eremiah 11 to 13 captures a conversation between Jeremiah and God. We learn several things about "Jerry" from these verses, such as the plot to murder him.

The men of Anathoth, a city given to the priestly sons of Aaron when Israel conquered Caanan (Joshua 21:13, 18; 1 Chronicles 6:54-60), didn't like Jeremiah's message. In fact, everywhere that Jerry went, people wanted him dead.

The Anathoth mafia decided to put out a hit on young Jerry. They did the math. "If we subtract him from the earth," they reasoned, "that would also remove his gloom-and-doom message." It was the perfect solution. Or was it?

The men of Anathoth left one important factor out of their equation—God. God revealed the plot to Jeremiah before it happened, and He promised to prepare a special punishment for those who dared to silence His prophet: "I will punish them. Their young men will die by the sword, their sons and daughters by famine. Not even a remnant will be left to them, because I will bring disaster on the men of Anathoth in the year of their punishment" (Jeremiah 11:22, 23). (Dude, God is no joke!)

The words God spoke against Anathoth were no idle threat. When the Assyrian forces of Sennacherib—you read about him a few days ago when he threatened to destroy King Hezekiah—swept through the city of Anathoth as he tried to lay siege to Jerusalem, they destroyed just about everything in sight. And what Sennacherib didn't destroy, Nebuchadnezzar and Babylon did. Only 128 exiles from Anathoth survived the Babylonian captivity (Nehemiah. 7:27).

The men of Anathoth didn't realize that trying to kill God's messenger wouldn't change God's message. All it would do is what it did: upset God. Don't hate those who try to correct you. It's better to accept what they have to say and learn from it.

///////// HOT READ ////////

Examine Jeremiah 12:1-6. Jeremiah was no superhuman servant of God. He had some very down times. How did God respond to his complaints? Verses 5, 6.

⟶ WATCH YOUR MOUTH <

Why is my pain unending and my wound grievous and incurable? Will you be to me like a deceptive brook, like a spring that fails? Jeremiah 15:18.

Is this the same guy who we read about yesterday—you know, the one whom God told about the murder plot on his life? Yep, it's Jerry, but this time he's a bit upset.

For the past few chapters God has been breathing fire against the people of Judah. How upset was God? When was the last time you saw God say this to someone in the Bible: "Do not pray for the well-being of this people. Although they fast, I will not listen to their cry; though they offer burnt offerings and grain offerings, I will not accept them" (Jeremiah 14:11, 12).

Did you get that? God told Jeremiah to stop praying for Jerusalem. You know you're in deep when God tells people to stop praying for you. Translation? Why waste good prayers on people who will not change?

Jeremiah understood that God was angry at His people, but he worried that he too would get swept up in a perfect storm of God's judgment.

"Jerry, I got you! Boo!" God seemed to say, although those weren't His exact words. "Surely I will deliver you for a good purpose," God comforted him. "I will make your enemies plead with you in times of disaster and times of distress" (Jeremiah 15:11).

Jerry didn't listen. Instead he got real with God.

"I never chilled at the club. I didn't party. In fact, I spend most of my time alone, yet You leave me in pain," Jeremiah told Him (verse 17). Tough words, huh? It gets worse. "God, You are deceptive brook, a spring that fails." That one had to hurt.

Jeremiah was saying that God was like a beautiful babbling brook beckoning the thirsty to come drink. The water looked great from afar, but as they got closer, they discovered that the brook was just a mirage. It never existed!

Few people in Scripture have ever spoken tougher words to God than Jeremiah. Sometimes in our pain and distress we can say very harsh things to God or about God. Yet God doesn't give up on us, and He didn't give up on Jeremiah, either.

/////// HOT READ ///////

God got very upset with Jeremiah's charges. How did God respond to him? Jeremiah 15:19.

——> YOU CAN RUN . . . <

For I am closely watching you and I see every sin. You cannot hope to hide from me.
Jeremiah 16:17, TLB.

he following story was told in the April 1, 1993, issue of *Bits and Pieces* magazine. A telemarketer called a home one day, and a small voice whispered, "Hello?"

"Hello! What's your name?"

Still whispering, the voice said, "Jimmy."

"How old are you, Jimmy?"

"I'm 4."

"Good. Is your mother home?"

"Yes, but she's busy."

"OK, is your father home?"

"He's busy too."

"I see; who else is there?"

"The police."

"The police? May I speak with one of them?"

"They're busy."

"Any other grown-ups there?"

"The firemen."

"May I speak with a fireman, please?"

"They're all busy."

"Jimmy, all those people in your house, and I can't talk with any of them? What are they doing?"

"Looking for me," whispered Jimmy.

Some people just know how to hide, don't they? We humans can hide things from each other, but we cannot hide anything from God. The Israelites thought that they could hide their sins from God. They thought that because God didn't immediately punish them, they'd gotten away with it. But God doesn't miss anything that we do, so why not do what is right?

//////// HOT READ ////////

What does Jeremiah 17:5-10 promise those who trust in God?

———> PASHUR'S PUNISHMENT <

When the priest Pashhur son of Immer, the chief officer in the temple of the Lord, heard Jeremiah prophesying these things, he had Jeremiah the prophet beaten and put in the stocks at the Upper Gate of Benjamin at the Lord's temple.
Jeremiah 20:1, 2.

wo days ago we read how Jeremiah got upset with God and called Him a deceptive brook, a spring that fails. That was before he was arrested, beaten, locked up, and put on display in the public square, where everyone could see him. I, for one, couldn't wait to see what Jeremiah would say to God after this travesty.

Pashur, the chief enforcer at the Jewish Temple, felt insulted by young Jeremiah. Could you blame him? Jerry came to Jerusalem from a place called Topheth, where God had sent him to prophesy. He didn't stop at a hotel for a shower and a shave. He walked directly to the court of the Temple, where a large crowd had gathered, and said, "This is what the Lord Almighty, the God of Israel, says: 'Listen! I am going to bring on this city and the villages round it every disaster I pronounced against them, because they were stiff-necked and would not listen to my words'" (Jeremiah 19:15).

Jeremiah's words were like a dark cloud racing in on a perfectly sunny day. Many of the people in the crowd had heard about the young man with the big mouth who always had something negative to say. But now they were hearing him for the first time, and they didn't like it.

Whenever I read Jeremiah 20, I always wonder, "Why did Pashur get so upset about the ravings of a nobody?" Jeremiah wasn't famous. His parents weren't "running things" in Jerusalem. Why did Jeremiah's words have such a powerful effect on all who heard them?

Jeremiah's words were effective because they were the truth. Whenever truth is lived and spoken openly, those who want to continue doing wrong are going to get very angry. And God's Holy Spirit rested on every word Jeremiah spoke.

If Pashur thought that his rough treatment of Jeremiah would break his will, boy, was he wrong. Read Jeremiah 20:4 to learn what Jeremiah said to Pashur the following day.

/////// HOT READ ///////

What did King Zedekiah beg Jeremiah to do? Jeremiah 21:2. How did Jeremiah respond to the king? Was Zedekiah's desire for forgiveness sincere?

——> THIEVES AT THE TOP <

The prophets follow an evil course and use their power unjustly. Jeremiah 23:10.

ower tends to corrupt, and absolute power corrupts absolutely. Great men are almost always bad men." Those prescient words were written by English historian and moralist, John Emerich Edward Dalberg-Acton—Baron Acton, for short.

I once came across a list of the 10 most corrupt world leaders published by Transparency International Global Corruption Report in 2004. The list was made up of former political leaders who have been accused of embezzling the most funds from their countries over the past two decades. The list may have changed a bit since 2004, but I doubt that any recent former leaders could knock these guys off the list. Topping the list is Mohamed Suharto, former president of Indonesia, who is believed to have stolen $15 to $35 *billion* of the people's money. He is followed by Ferdinand Marcos, of the Philippines. His take: $5-10 billion. The former president of Zaire is next, having pilfered a cool $5 billion, and then there's President Sani Abacha, of Nigeria, who packed away $2-5 billion during his presidency. You get the drift. These powerful men enriched themselves while most of their citizens suffered.

What is especially troubling about this list of presidential thieves is that no amount of money was enough for them. After President Suharto got his first $5 billion safely hidden in a Swiss bank, what could have led him to amass another possible $30 billion! When power corrupts, it knows no end.

Corruption may be tolerated and even expected in political leaders, but there's nothing worse than religious leaders who unjustly use their power to benefit themselves. I recently learned of a husband-and-wife team who pastor a megachurch. The husband tools around in a Bentley convertible, and they live in a million-dollar waterfront home—all funded by the tithes and offerings of poor members. This kind of exploitation is even worse than that of politicians, because spiritual leaders are expected to do what's right. They answer to a higher authority—God.

Yet, as you'll read today, corruption among religious leaders was a big reason God sent Israel and Judah into exile. Religious leaders led the people into sin.

//////// HOT READ ////////
What were the false prophets telling the people? Jeremiah 23:16-18.

> THE MEANING OF SACRIFICE! <

But Ahikam (son of Shaphan), the royal secretary, stood with Jeremiah and per-suaded the court not to turn him over to the mob to kill him. Jeremiah 26:24, TLB.

acrifice. It's a word that coaches love. They tell players to sacrifice personal goals for the sake of the team. Give up so that all of us together can go up! This kind of sacrifice strikes a chord with us because it involves giving up a part of one's self for the good of others.

Soldiers know the meaning of sacrifice. Two years ago *Insight* told the story of Sergeant Jonathan Cadavero, a soldier from New York who was killed by a roadside bomb in Iraq. Jonathan was one of the most fun-loving guys you'd ever want to meet. After his death the members of his platoon wept as they remembered the guy who kept them "up" when they felt down.

An Army medic, Jonathan pulled double duty on a team that hunted and defused IEDs (improvised explosive devices). The work was dangerous, and he knew it. After long sweaty days peering at every bump in road, abandoned car, and suspicious looking person, Jonathan would crack a joke to get everyone laughing. Just two days before his death he wrote in the *Army Times*, "With IEDs, either we find them or they find us." Two days later, on February 27, 2007, an IED found him. The work Jonathan did saved the lives of countless soldiers, but it took his.

The Bible is filled with people who know the meaning of sacrifice. You can't even say the word without thinking of Jesus, and you'd be right to do so. But also recorded there are the forgotten heroes such as Ahikam, son of Shaphan, the king's secretary, who acted bravely to save Jeremiah's life.

The first message Jeremiah preached at the temple got him beaten and publicly humiliated (Jeremiah 20). When he returned again to deliver God's fearful warning (Jeremiah 26:2-6), several leaders captured him tried to put him to death. Were it not for some wise older men who spoke up for Jeremiah, and one amazing speech by a young man named Ahikam, Jeremiah would have perished. Ahikam put his life on the line to save him. That is the true meaning of sacrifice.

/////// HOT READ ///////

What did the false prophets tell the people? Jeremiah 27:9-11.

——> BIG TALKERS <

> *Then the prophet Jeremiah said to Hananiah the prophet, "Listen, Hananiah! The Lord has not sent you, yet you have persuaded this nation to trust in lies."*
> Jeremiah 28:15.

arry Bird, the great clutch shooter who played for the Boston Celtics, was a great talker. "I'm gonna hit the shot to win this game," he'd say with a glare at some helpless opponent. "Better not let me get the ball. If I get it, this game is over." More often than not, "Larry Legend" was money in the bank. Bird was a talker, but Bird was also a walker.

On the same team as the famed Celtic great was another player with a monster mouth—M. L. Carr. I know you barely know who Larry Bird is, and now I'm throwing M. L. Carr at you, right? Trust me, you know an M. L. Carr—you just don't know the one who played with Bird.

Carr could outtalk any basketball player on the court, but he didn't have a game to match. So he did most of his talking from the bench. He "rode the pine," as the old guys used to say. If you're going to talk a good game, at least have some game.

Enter Hananiah, one of the M. L. Carrs of the Bible. Hananiah had the misfortune of being a prophet at the same time that Jeremiah was a practicing prophet. Prophet on prophet violence is not something we see much in the Bible, but these two big talkers almost came to blows one day in King Zedekiah's court.

Hananiah told the people that in two years King Nebuchadnezzar would return all the costly articles he took from Lord's Temple and break the hold that Babylon had over Judah. How did he know this? God had told him—so he said. The message sounded good, and the people were stoked by the good news, but there was one problem. It was totally and completely wrong. God had not said a word to this false prophet.

Jeremiah knew that a dose of truth serum would cure Hananiah and the people of Judah of their delusions. There was no way that Israel was going to escape the 70 years of captivity that God had decreed. No amount of lies would change that. Jeremiah told Hananiah that because of his lies, he would die that very year. Seven months later Hananiah dropped dead.

Jeremiah walked and talked with God. Hananiah just talked.

HOT READ

Notice how God comforts His people even when he's correcting them.
Jeremiah 29:4-10.

──> I AM THE LORD <

I am the Lord, the God of all mankind. Is anything too hard for me? Jeremiah 32:27.

s I read chapter 32 today it started me thinking about *The Antiques Road Show.* You know, the TV program that airs on many PBS stations. "What's that?" you say. Allow me to explain.

Back in the Stone Age, the time before humanity got tangled up in the World Wide Web, people used to watch something called a television. There were these things called family shows—you know, programs without crime, sex, and violence. They're obsolete now, but trust me, they did exist. *The Antiques Road Show* was one of these.

Here's how it worked. The show traveled from city to city. At each place people brought in their antiques (uh, JUNK!) to the show's site for an appraisal. People would haul in old furniture, their grandma's favorite purse, apple peelers, paintings—you name, they brought it.

But occasionally something of real value showed up. One man was about to throw out some trash he found in a house he'd bought when he decided to keep a picture just because he thought it was cool. Good thing he did. The picture was a rare print worth many thousands of dollars. It looked worthless, but it was quite valuable.

Jeremiah had one of those "aha" moments while locked in a dungeon. God decided to be Jeremiah's real estate agent, since he was in no shape to help himself.

"Jerry," said God, "tomorrow your cousin Hanamel is going to come here and ask you to buy his land in Anathoth. Buy it and hold on to the deed."

I'm sure Jeremiah wanted to say, "But Lord, I'm a bit tied up at the moment," but he didn't. The next day Hanamel came as God had said he would. Jeremiah signed the deed, gave instructions for its safekeeping, and waited.

Now, you've got to understand something. God had told Jeremiah that Nebuchadnezzar would burn down Jerusalem and destroy everything in sight, but he was not to worry about that. Jeremiah's holding on to the deed to this land was a living object lesson that God would one day bring him back to that very land. That God was going to restore the land and bring health and healing to His people.

/////// HOT READ ///////

Whom is Jeremiah 33:14-16 referring to? Why was this important?

——> A LEARNING LESSON <

"Will you not learn a lesson and obey my words?" declares the Lord. "Jonadab son of Recab ordered his sons not to drink wine and this command has been kept."
Jeremiah 35:13, 14.

ometimes you can learn a lot from the discipline of people who don't believe in God. God seems to think so.

Today you'll read in Jeremiah 34 how the Israelites angered God by enslaving their relatives, something that God forbade them to do. Every seventh year
slaves who had sold themselves to their owners were to be let go (verse 14). But
once God turned away, the Israelites captured their former slaves and forced them
into bondage again.

To try to get His people to obey Him, God sent Jeremiah to the Recabites,
a group of aliens living in Jerusalem, descendants of a man named Jonadab, who
had warned them never to drink wine. For effect, Jeremiah offered them some
wine to test them, and to a person, all of them refused to drink. If the Recabites
could obey a dead human being, God wondered, why didn't the Israelites obey
Him?

I confess, I've learned some things from people who don't claim any special
relationship with God. Sean "P. Diddy" Combs is one of them. I caught an
episode of MTV's *Making the Band*, the Combs reality vehicle, and I got a lesson.

Before you put me in hell, hear me out. I've learned that there's nothing that
people won't do to be famous. I kind of suspected that, but now I know it's true.
During an old episode, one of the contestants trying to make the guys' band found
out that the baby his pregnant fiancé was carrying would be born with a significant disability. Instead of dropping the show to be with her, he stayed in the show
to pursue his dream.

I also learned that Diddy is dedicated to making hits for the devil. If Christian
musicians were half as committed to honoring God as Diddy is to honoring Satan,
many lives would be changed by their music. Time and again Combs would send
the groups back to the recording studio to redo songs that they had painstakingly
"perfected." He can't sing a lick, but he knows a hit when he hears it.

If he can go all-out for Satan, I can go all-out for God.

///////// HOT READ ////////

What did King Jehoiakim do with Jeremiah's scroll (Jeremiah 36)? Why?

——> THAT SINKING FEELING <

So they took Jeremiah and put him into the cistern of Malkijah, the king's son, which was in the courtyard of the guard. They lowered Jeremiah by ropes into the cistern; it had no water in it, only mud, and Jeremiah sank down into the mud.
Jeremiah 38:6.

ing Nebuchadnezzar and his storm troopers had left the siege of Judah to go handle a little beef they had with Pharoah and the Egyptians. The people of Judah read this turn of events as a sign that—despite what Jeremiah had been screaming for years—Babylon would not conquer Judah. But they were sadly mistaken. No matter what they did to Jeremiah, his message remained the same: "Whoever stays in this city will die by the sword, famine or plague, but whoever goes over to the Babylonians will live" (Jeremiah 38:2).

The response of the king's courtiers was swift and decisive. "This man should be put to death. He is discouraging the soldiers who are left in this city, as well as all the people, by the things he is saying to them" (verse 4).

So King Zedekiah's evil henchmen lowered Jeremiah into a deep well, and he sank down—until he hit the bottom of the mud. There was little hope he would be saved. The Babylonians had already destroyed most of the Israelite towns and cities. Only Judah with its towering walls was left standing, and the forces of Babylon had surrounded it.

There in the dark pit Jeremiah must have thought, *OK, I've had a good run. I've been cursed, disrespected, beaten, and now thrown into the bottom of a well. This is the end of the line.* Sure, he was no stranger to harsh treatment. He'd been on Judah's Most Wanted since he was a teen, but this time was different.

This had to be the lowest moment in Jeremiah's life. He was deep below the ground, there was no one in sight, and he'd been left to die.

/////// HOT READ ///////

Have you ever been there? Ever felt abandoned by God? Read Jeremiah 38:7-12. What do these verses tell you about God's care for His servants? Why did God allow Jeremiah to be put in the well since obviously He could have prevented it?

———> NO MATTER WHAT <

Whether it is favorable or unfavorable, we will obey the Lord our God, to whom we are sending you, so that it will go well with us, for we will obey the Lord our God.
Jeremiah 42:6.

t was my first real job after college. I was happy to be getting a paycheck—any paycheck! After four years exhausting just about all the money both my parents and I had, I was ready to earn some real cash.

Like most college students, I never really had any money. Now and then my brothers would send me $10 or $15. And when that money arrived, you couldn't tell me anything. Dude—I was rich! At that time Taco Bell had a promotion going called 59, 79, 99. You could get a bean burrito for 59 cents. Since I didn't eat meat, there was no need to examine the beef burritos that cost 79 and 99 cents. I could OD on the bean burritos. I would deal with any latent flatulence by staying close to the men's dormitory. (Guys tend not to worry about flatulence.)

The hardships of living on dimes gave way to a job that paid about $300 every two weeks. I worked as an editorial intern on a magazine. It was a cool gig. The job was great, the money wasn't bad either, but there was one problem: tithes and offerings.

In truth there is no problem with tithes and offerings, but there is when you don't want to return them. Every week when it was time for me to be faithful to God, I made up excuses. I was renting a small one-room apartment, and rent seemed to be due every week. Of course I had to buy food, and that's not even counting the long-distance phone bill I ran up talking to my girl in LA. It was ugly, man! I'd return a faithful tithe and offering when my pockets were overflowing, but when they were not? Well . . .

In all my excuses there was one unmistakable truth. I didn't trust God to take care of my needs, so I stole what was His to look out for myself. I lacked the kind of obedience that Jeremiah spoke about in Jeremiah 42:6. Since that time I've learned that it pays to obey God completely.

////// HOT READ //////

Read Jeremiah 40:2, 3. Was this Babylonian captain a believer in God? Is it possible for unbelievers to see the moving of God in certain situations?

—→ TOUGH STUFF <

Now this is what the Lord God Almighty, the God of Israel, says: Why bring such great disaster on yourselves by cutting off from Judah the men and women, the children and infants, and so leave yourselves without a remnant? Jeremiah 44:7.

ow! I'm sorry, but I'm a bit speechless right now. I've been reading through the Bible with you for more than 236 days straight. In that time we've read some very difficult verses, verses that made us stop and take a second look at God. But this one stopped me cold. Why? God's anger is not aimed at some heathen nation bent on destroying His chosen people, but on the very people God had chosen to represent Him on earth.

It's difficult to understand or explain why God was willing to kill children and infants (who did no wrong) because of the misdeeds of their parents. If God could do all things, why didn't He take out the parents and provide a group of loving caretakers for the kids? I don't have the answer to the question, but I do plan to ask God about it when I see Him.

That being said, the parents of these kids got "some splainin' to do." Jeremiah wore out his vocal cords warning them that there was no way to escape Babylon's conquest of Judah and the slavery that would follow. But instead of listening to him, the small remnant left in Judah headed for the safety of Egypt. (Bad idea!)

"O remnant of Judah, the Lord has told you, 'Do not go to Egypt,'" Jeremiah cried. "Be sure of this: I warn you today that you made a fatal mistake when you sent me to the Lord your God and said, 'Pray to the Lord our God for us; tell us everything he says and we will do it'" (Jeremiah 42:19, 20). The citizens had asked Jeremiah to find out from God what He wanted them to do, and then they promised to do it.

When Jeremiah returned with God's message—go willingly into Babylonian captivity, and I will save you—they refused to honor their word. They even forced Jeremiah to go with them to Egypt. Even worse than that, they began worshipping Egyptian gods—a total slap in the face of God.

We often charge God with being harsh and cruel. But if we're honest with ourselves, we'd have to admit that we bring most of our troubles on ourselves.

/////// HOT READ ///////

Just how stiff-necked were the wayward Israelites? Read Jeremiah 44:24-27.

——> THE RECKONING <

Do not fear, O Jacob my servant; do not be dismayed, O Israel. I will surely save you out of a distant place, your descendants from the land of their exile. Jacob will again have peace and security, and no one will make him afraid. Jeremiah 46:27.

eremiah 46:27 and 28 reminded me of why I love God so much. These verses also remind me of something that happened many years ago in a country called South Africa.

For many years the government of South Africa practiced a form of institutional racism called apartheid. Apartheid laws were enacted to protect and extend the power the nation's White minority over the larger Black native population. Blacks were huddled together in dilapidated areas called shanty towns on independent "homelands." They were not considered citizens.

Anyone who protested these unjust laws risked imprisonment and death. One infamous event occurred in 1960 when a large group of Blacks refused to use the passes required for travel from their "homeland" areas. The government declared a state of emergency which allowed authorities to brutally repress the demonstrators. By the end of the "state of emergency," which lasted for 156 days, 69 people were dead and 187 were wounded. These gruesome scenes were repeated for another 30 years before apartheid ended.

When Nelson Mandela, the nation's first Black president, was elected in the nation's first open multiracial election, he faced a dilemma. He could hunt down those who had imprisoned him for 28 years on false charges; he could seek revenge on the racists who had killed scores of people; or he could do something to heal his nation. Mandela chose to work for the healing of South Africa.

Nelson Mandela helped develop a Truth and Reconciliation Commission, the rules of which were very simple. Those who had done wrong would be forgiven if they came forward and told the truth about what they had done. This allowed Black South Africans to find out the truth about lost loved ones, and it allowed many White South Africans to remove the guilt of their past crimes. No other nation had ever done anything like it—and it worked. It helped to heal South Africa. Nelson Mandela showed that even those most guilty need to be restored.

Humans are very good at punishment and terrible at healing. God does both perfectly!

///////// HOT READ ////////

Jeremiah 48:46. What gods are distracting you from worshipping God?

——> THIS IS YOUR MOMENT <

"Why do you boast of your valleys, boast of your valleys so fruitful? O unfaithful daughter, you trust in your riches and say, 'Who will attack me?'" Jeremiah 49:4.

We have come to the end of the book of Jeremiah. A few days ago we met a shy teen who was called by God to deliver a message that would make him the most hated person in all of Judah. Through it all Jeremiah remained faithful. He never bit his tongue in the face of sin. He did what God asked him to do—and then some.

The book closes sort of how it began, with God uttering judgments on the nations that thumbed their noses at Him. In Jeremiah 48:14 God asked the Moabites, "How can you say, 'We are warriors, men valiant in battle'?" The Moabites were fierce warriors who took pride in their ability to the put the beat-down on any group that dared mess with them. The Moabites trusted in their awesome military power to deliver them from all comers. (But they underestimated God.)

Know any nations that trust greatly in their military might?

In Jeremiah 49:4 God focused like a laser on at the Ammonites, who loved to admire their wealth. If they were around today, they'd take you for a ride in their yacht on the French Riviera, wine you and dine you in the finest restaurants, and fly you back home in their private jets. Rocked to sleep by a false sense of security, the Ammonites faced sudden destruction for their sins, yet they refused to change.

The Edomites too faced destruction because of their immense pride. They were a people who lived high in the caves of mountains. It would be an exercise in suicide to attack them from below, but God wasn't impressed. "Though you build your nest as high as the eagle's, from there I will bring you down," God warned (Jeremiah 49:17).

The book of Jeremiah holds many lessons, but none more important than this: when God gives us time and opportunity to repent and turn from sin, we must do so. If we cling to pride, possessions, or human power, we will suffer. God really does know what's best for us!

/////// HOT READ ///////

What did King Nebuchadnezzar and his Babylonian soldiers do to Jerusalem? Just think. All the pain and anguish that Israel endured could have been prevented had the nation simply obeyed God.

──> TAKE MY LIFE, PLEASE <

How deserted lies the city, once so full of people! How like a widow is she, who once was great among the nations! She who was queen among the provinces has now become a slave. Lamentations 1:1.

ver wanted to sell you life? On March 18, 2007, the world met a person who wanted to do just that. Here's how the *Inquirer,* the respected British newspaper, reported the story.

"A 45-year-old Australian man from Perth [Australia] is selling his entire life as a package deal on eBay after his wife left him. Ian Usher, originally from England, decided that he needed a clean break and a 'new life' after his eight-year marriage to his wife, Laura, ended abruptly.

"His Web site gives potential buyers the who, what, how, where, and when of it all, with the home page reading: 'Hi there, my name is Ian Usher, and I have had enough of my life! I don't want it anymore! You can have it if you like!'"

I don't know who Laura is, but she must be quite a woman.

Ian Usher was so heartbroken at losing the woman he loved that he auctioned off everything that he owned, including his friends and his job. He made a deal with his employer in Australia, who agreed to allow a two-month on-the-job trial for the person who purchased Mr. Usher's life.

Tragedy can profoundly affect us. In the book of Lamentations we peer into one man's deeply personal nightmare. For more than 40 years Jeremiah preached about the coming destruction of Jerusalem by the Babylonians, but nothing prepared him for the horror of the actual event. He watched the city burned to the ground, the Temple looted and burned, and Judah's citizens killed, tortured, and carried away as captives. Jeremiah wept.

As you read Jeremiah's lament for Jerusalem, remember the opportunity that you have to get tight with God right now. Make the most of every opportunity to love God with your whole heart!

//////// HOT READ ////////
Jeremiah found a reason to hope in the midst of his pain. Lamentations 3:21-26.

——> BACK IN THE DAY <

Restore us to yourself, O Lord, that we may return; renew our days as of old.
Lamentations 5:21.

hen I was a kid back in the early eighties—yes, two decades ago—there were several TV shows that I would not miss. When I got home from school in the afternoon, *He-Man* and *Voltron*—don't even get me going about Transformers—were my shows. Optimus Prime was my dawg! (TV ruined my life, as you can tell!)

In the evening I'd catch an episode of *The Cosby Show*, which usually came on around 8:00. And I'd pull every trick in the book to get my parents to let me watch my favorite show—*The Greatest American Hero*. (Never heard of it? YouTube! YouTube!)

The Greatest American Hero was built around the crime-fighting adventures of a cat named Ralph Hinkley, who happened to be given a special suit by aliens. The suit gave Ralph superhuman powers, but Ralph had one problem. He had lost the manual that came with the suit, so he didn't know how to use it. Trust me, you've never seen a superhero like this guy. He didn't know how to fly—or, more frighteningly, how to land. Dude, it was hilarious!

Recently I decided to check YouTube to see if there were any clips from my old show. I almost fell out of my chair. There were hundreds of 'em. I sang the "Believe It or Not" theme song. I watched Ralph flying and crashing. I was a kid all over again.

I was back in the little apartment my parents rented above the dental clinic. I could smell my mother's bread baking, the sound of cars rushing by our busy street, the yells coming from the neighbors downstairs whom we'd never see. It was all good—OK, maybe not all of it!

I've gone back home to my old "hood" a time or two, and it's totally different now. Drugs basically destroyed the life of the community. The people I saw looked like shell-shocked refugees from another country. After seeing how things had changed, I decided to cherish my memories.

Jeremiah knew the pain of losing his entire childhood. The memories were good, but he wanted more. He wanted God to restore his nation to prominence again. I can feel his pain.

HOT READ

Lamentations 5:1-10. What challenges do you want God to remember?

──⟶ READY TO RIDE? <

In the thirtieth year, in the fourth month on the fifth day, while I was among the ex-
iles by the Kebar River, the heavens were opened and I saw visions of God.
Ezekiel 1:1.

f the Bible hasn't challenged you yet, better buckle your seat belt, friend, because you're about to take a ride with a guy whose name means "God strengthens." That's the first clue to the meaning of this awesome book.

Ezekiel was trained as a priest during the reign of King Jehoiakim. When the
people of Jerusalem were deported to Babylon by King Nebuchadnezzar (597
B.C.), Ezekiel was among that group. He was called to minister to the exiles in
captivity, while Jeremiah—now at the end of his ministry—continued to share
God's messages with the small remnant left in Jerusalem.

Perhaps you haven't noticed as yet, but Ezekiel is one "different" homeboy.
God relates to him in a very mystical and symbolic way. The visions and messages
God gave Ezekiel rival the ones He gave to Daniel—but we'll get to Daniel later.

No matter how weird certain parts of the Bible may seem, there's always a
method to God's "madness." For instance, chapter 1 records Ezekiel's first vision—of beings that look like men, each with four faces and four wings (verse 6).
That wasn't just for effect. God's special effects communicated with Ezekiel in a
way that captured his mind and the mind of a people who had been demoralized,
destroyed, and depressed.

And what was the message God wanted Ezekiel to pass along to them? I'm
glad you asked. *Every individual is responsible to God for what he or she does.* No one
can hide behind anyone else. If the exiles were willing to join their lives to God
personally, He would transform them. It is one of the most beautiful offers in all
the Bible.

Through Ezekiel God gives three important explanations. In chapters 4
through 24, God explains why He judged Judah so harshly; in chapters 25 through
32, God explains His judgment of the heathen nations; and the book closes with
God's promise to bless all who serve Him faithfully (chapters 33 through 48).

May God strengthen you as you read the book of Ezekiel.

//////// HOT READ ////////

Read Ezekiel I and 2. Are we all called by God to give a special message
to the world?

——> THE ARTIST <

Now, son of man, take a clay tablet, put it in front of you and draw the city of Jerusalem on it. Ezekiel 4:1.

Brain scientists who have studied short- and long-term memory have discovered that short-term memory or working memory is about 30 seconds long. This is the memory you use when you put your car keys on the front seat of your car while you run back inside the house to grab your cell phone. Of course, it's also the memory you're most likely to hate when you come back outside and see your car rolling down the road without you.

Many years ago I saw a movie about a guy who suffered from short-term memory loss. (On the list of things you might want to thank God for: short-term memory.) For this man, new memories and experiences were forgotten within minutes. To compensate for this problem, he got important information tattooed to his body (ouch), took Polaroid photographs of himself, and then wrote notes about each photograph.

After reading Ezekiel 4-6, I am convinced that the Israelites had not only short-term but long-term memory loss. Why else would God go to such extremes make His point about how unfaithful they'd been? And just how did God try to jog their memory and get their attention? He made Ezekiel do some very strange things.

In the first part of Ezekiel 4 God calls on Ezekiel's drawing skills to show the exiles in Babylon just how He engineered their capture. If you think God is still harboring a little rage from Israel's repeated sins, you'd be right. Even in captivity God continued to try to get the descendants of the 10 tribes of Israel and the two tribes of Judah to see how deep their sins were.

In Ezekiel 5:1 God tells the prophet to get a haircut, but this was not a barbershop special. Instead of a barber's razor, God told him to use a sharp sword to cut off all the hair on his head and his beard. What was the point of this exercise? You gotta read it for yourself (Ezekiel 5:1-5).

Friend, God will do whatever it takes to get our attention. He'll speak to us through people who love us and those who hate us. He'll use a situation to remind us that He is God. Open your heart and your mind to God each day, because He is speaking to you.

///////// HOT READ ///////

What was hidden in the mountains and valleys of Israel? Ezekiel 6:1-4.

⎯⎯> OPEN HOUSE <

And he said to me, "Son of man, do you see what they are doing—the utterly de-
testable things the house of Israel is doing here, things that will drive me far from
my sanctuary? But you will see things that are even more detestable." Ezekiel 8:6.

oday you will read one of the most important chapters in the Bible—Ezekiel
8. It reminds us that the sins we cuddle and hide eventually take over our lives.
The following verses are excerpted from *The Message*. Read them and think deeply
about your life.

"I entered and looked. I couldn't believe my eyes: Painted all over the walls
were pictures of reptiles and animals and monsters—the whole pantheon of
Egyptian gods and goddesses—being worshiped by Israel. In the middle of the
room were seventy of the leaders of Israel, with Jaazaniah son of Shaphan standing in the middle. Each held his censer with the incense rising in a fragrant cloud.

"He said, 'Son of man, do you see what the elders are doing here in the dark,
each one before his favorite god-picture? They tell themselves, 'God doesn't see
us. God has forsaken the country.'

"Then he said, 'You're going to see worse yet.'

"He took me to the entrance at the north gate of the Temple of God. I saw
women sitting there, weeping for Tammuz, the Babylonian fertility god. He said,
'Have you gotten an eyeful, son of man? You're going to see worse yet.'

"Finally, he took me to the inside court of the Temple of God. There between the porch and the altar were about twenty-five men. Their backs were to
God's Temple. They were facing east, bowing in worship to the sun.

"He said, 'Have you seen enough, son of man? Isn't it bad enough that Judah
engages in these outrageous obscenities? They fill the country with violence and
now provoke me even further with their obscene gestures. That's it. They have
an angry God on their hands! From now on, no mercy. They can shout all they
want, but I'm not listening'" (Ezekiel 8:10-18, Message).

////// HOT READ //////

What did the people of Judah say while committing sin? Ezekiel 9:9, 10.

⟶ SAFEHOUSE <

Therefore say: "This is what the Sovereign Lord says: Although I sent them far away among the nations and scattered them among the countries, yet for a little while I have been a sanctuary for them in the countries where they have gone."
Ezekiel 11:16.

uring Babylon's brutal conquest of Jerusalem some of Judah's citizens died, some were taken into captivity, and some were scattered among heathen nations. The citizens who took up refuge in strange lands faced many trials. To be honest, it's never easy to be an alien in a foreign land.

I know what it feels like to be an alien. I was born in a small country at the very top of South America called Guyana. There's a good chance that you have never heard of my country. I left there with my family when I was 10 years old and came to America—land of the free, home of the brave.

There wasn't much that I didn't like about my new country. I remember how amazed I was by grocery stores with aisles and aisles of food. We never lacked food in Guyana, but open-air markets ruled the day there. But here I didn't need an amusement park! I had the grocery store. Just take me there, and all was well with the world.

But some things about my new country weren't so nice. Such as the time a bunch of guys jumped one of my brothers simply because he didn't talk and dress the way they did. I still remember how painful it was to hear that someone had tried to hurt him.

My family went through many changes trying to begin a new life in a strange place, but one thing that remained constant: God's undying love and protection. No matter how tough things got on the streets, God watched over us and protected us.

God promised the scattered Israelites living in foreign lands that He would be their sanctuary, their safety in a strange land. We may never live in another country, or walk unknown streets, but there are times in our lives that we feel lost, like aliens an unfamiliar place. God offers us the same promise: "I will be your sanctuary."

///////// **HOT READ** ////////
What did the Israelites learn from heathen nations? Ezekiel 11:12.

——> HIGHLY RECOMMENDED <

Their visions are false and their divinations a lie. They say, "The Lord declares,"
when the Lord has not sent them; yet they expect their words to be fulfilled.
Ezekiel 13:6.

e came highly recommended by a real estate agent in Philadelphia. My wife and I were just moving to Pennsylvania from Maryland, a place that we grudgingly left in search of new horizons. My wife got a job working for the city of Philadelphia. It was a cool gig—for her. The politics made us both sick—but I digress.

The "he" above is none other than a contractor named Moe. We met Moe at an apartment that he and his workers were rehabbing. The first inkling that I was about to get in over my head was all over the walls of that little apartment, but I couldn't see it at the time. (If you get old enough to hire a contractor, do not hire anyone who paints everything pink.) We bought an old house—major work—and Moe came highly recommended. Who needs references?

"It should only take me three weeks, Mr. Esmond. I have several different crews that'll come and get it done. You guys will be in there in no time." The words spilled out so fast that if you close your eyes you would've swore that you were listening to the Twista—the rapper with a machine gun for a tongue.

Since the work would be done in three weeks, we decided to live in one of the rooms while he worked around the house. (OK, I feel like cussing right now just thinking about this.) Nine months later we were still cooking in a hot pot, a thin coat of dust was on everything—including both of us, and PINK WAS EVERYWHERE! Moe had relieved us a cool $24,000, and was asking for more. Now you understand why bad words started to come to my mind a moment ago. (I'm so glad we have a God to whom we can give our troubles. No need to cuss.)

There are people you should never listen to. There is a real estate agent in Philadelphia whose name I cannot mention here. That agent was a false prophet, at least when it came to recommending Moe.

God warned of prophets who lull people into a false sense of security by saying what they want to hear. If you run into any of them, run away. Fast!

///////// HOT READ ////////
To what did God compare the people of Jerusalem (Ezekiel 15)? Why?

──> SURPRISE, SURPRISE! <

Now this was the sin of your sister Sodom: She and her daughters were arrogant, overfed and unconcerned; they did not help the poor and needy. Ezekiel 16:49.

ometimes the Bible will surprise you. I certainly was when I read Ezekiel 16. This powerful chapter of the Bible is startling in many ways. For instance, God says this:

"Therefore, you prostitute, hear the word of the Lord! This is what the Sovereign Lord says: Because you poured out your wealth and exposed your nakedness in your promiscuity with your lovers, and because of all your detestable idols, and because you gave them your children's blood, therefore I am going to gather all your lovers, with whom you found pleasure, those you loved as well as those you hated. I will gather them against you from all around and will strip you in front of them, and they will see all your nakedness" (verses 35-37).

Is God really comparing the people of Jerusalem to a "woman of the night"? The answer is yes. God likened Israel to a woman who sleeps around for money— but with one twist. Instead of accepting payment for her services, she instead pays her lovers. There is no way to avoid the depth of anger in this metaphor. Judah had prostituted herself with powerless gods.

What God says about Sodom is even more startling than when He compared Jerusalem's citizens to a prostitute. You remember Sodom, don't you (Genesis 19)? You remember the two strangers who came to Sodom and ran into a mob of rabid perverts?

Whenever Sodom is mentioned in conversation, the story of the men who came to Lot's house is the story that gets told. But that's not the one that God tells in Ezekiel 16:49. The sin for which God destroyed Sodom is not its sexual immorality (though that was a contributing factor) but its pride, laziness, gluttony, and lack of care for the poor.

When it comes to sin, we humans tend to pay attention to certain kinds of sin. Sexual sins are at the top of our list, closely followed by any sin that has to do with money. After reading Ezekiel 16:49, we might want to rethink our focus. Read Ezekiel 16:49 and think deeply about your life. Are you living for God or for yourself?

/////// HOT READ ///////

Notice how God judges each person individually for his or her sins? Ezekiel 18:14-18.

——> HISTORY LESSON <

In the seventh year, in the fifth month on the tenth day, some of the elders of Israel came to inquire of the Lord, and they sat down in front of me. Ezekiel 20:1.

re you worn out yet? Still reading through the Bible, right? I know some parts of the Bible can be tough to understand and digest, but trust me, it's worth the effort. When we extend our energies to understand God's Word, it strengthens the mind.

The book of Ezekiel is difficult to read because the picture of God we see there is not the one we learned about in Sabbath or Sunday school. In Ezekiel God's anger is out in the open where everyone can see it, and the view ain't pretty.

In Ezekiel 20 God took a moment—actually, several moments—to outline the reasons He was so upset with His people. You could almost see the tears as God spoke.

"On the day I chose Israel," God intoned, "I swore with uplifted hand to the descendants of the house of Jacob and revealed myself to them in Egypt. With uplifted hand I said to them, 'I am the Lord your God.' On that day I swore to them that I would bring them out of Egypt into a land I had searched out for them, a land flowing with milk and honey, the most beautiful of all lands. And I said to them, 'Each of you, get rid of the vile images you have set your eyes on, and do not defile yourselves with the idols of Egypt. I am the Lord your God'" (verses 5-7).

People who get out of jail after many years of being wrongfully imprisoned don't forget those who freed them. A few years ago CNN reported the release of Willie Earl Green after 25 years. Green was fingered, by a witness who lied to police, for a murder he did not commit. It didn't matter that there was absolutely no evidence connecting him to the crime. Police arrested him, prosecutors convicted him, and 25 years nearly broke him. But now he is a free man, thanks to a judge who finally set him free.

What would you think if you later saw Mr. Green spit in the face of the judge who had freed him? Crazy, isn't it? Yet that is what Israel did to God after He set them free after serving 400 years in an Egyptian jail. They insulted God in every way imaginable, until God was forced to punish them.

////// HOT READ //////

Are you trying to serve two masters? It never works. **Ezekiel 20:39.**

September 6 • *Ezekiel 22-24*

——> LOSING IT! <

On the very day they sacrificed their children to their idols, they entered my sanctuary and desecrated it. That is what they did in my house. Ezekiel 23:39.

I've seen lots of strange people darken the doors of the church, but I can't say that I've ever seen one who arrived after just sacrificing their child to another god. In the long list of sins committed by Israel, the sacrificing of their own children to foreign idols has to be the worst of all.

On March 8, 2008, Dallas newspapers reported a frightening incident. A 27-year-old mother and her two sons, ages 6 and 8, were driving with her father when he stopped for gas near an overpass. While her father filled the tank, Khandi Busby slipped out of the car with her two sons and headed for a nearby freeway overpass.

When she got to the overpass—cars speeding by below—Ms. Busby grabbed one of her sons and threw him over the edge of the overpass into the traffic below. She then did the same with her other son, before jumping from the overpass herself. In what could only be described as a miracle, all three of them survived, though they were in critical condition.

It's obvious that Khandi Busby has mental problems. People in their right minds don't generally throw their children into oncoming traffic 22 feet below. Persons in their right minds also don't sacrifice their children in cultish rituals, then show up to church as if nothing happened. Because of their repeated sins, the people of Israel had drifted so far from God that they didn't think twice about entering His Temple with the blood of their children on their hands.

If we indulge in sin long enough, we will begin to lose our grip on reality. Once we do, there's no telling what we will do.

If there is sin in your life, confess it to God and ask Him to forgive you. Then walk away from it. Resist Satan's temptations and get close to God through prayer, Bible study, and witnessing. God can turn your life around if you let Him.

HOT READ

Read Ezekiel 24:9-13. What is the main point that God is making in these verses? What is the problem with the pot?

⎯⎯> A H A ! <

For this is what the Sovereign Lord says: Because you have clapped your hands and stamped your feet, rejoicing with all the malice of your heart against the land of Israel. Ezekiel 25:6.

o you get a kick out of watching your enemies go down, bite the dust, fall from grace, break a leg? Be honest. God is listening for your answer. I'll admit I do. There are some people on Planet Earth who should do us all a favor by disappearing. Almost everybody feels that way at one time or another—even those of us who should know better.

A reporter was interviewing an old man on his 100th birthday. "What are you most proud of?" he asked.

"Well," said the man, "I don't have an enemy in the world."

"What a beautiful thought. How inspirational," said the reporter.

"Yep," added the centenarian. "Outlived every last one of them."

Before we call a MySpace party to celebrate the demise of our nemesis, we'd better think long and hard about it. God was not pleased when the Ammonites celebrated the fall of Jerusalem. Even though God was the one who caused the destruction of Judah, He still loved them and didn't want anyone popping champagne bottles over their graves.

"I will lay my hand heavily upon you, delivering you to many nations for devastation," warned God. "I will cut you off from being a nation any more" (Ezekiel 25:7, TLB). This was the culmination of a long feud between the Israelites and Ammonites. The conflict started way back during the time of the judges with Jephthah (Judges 10:6-11:33) and continued during the reigns of Saul (1 Samuel 11:1-11), David (1 Chronicles 19:1-20:3), and Jehoshaphat (2 Chronicles 20:1-23).

When King Nebuchadnezzar attacked Judah instead of Ammon, the Ammonites gloated and yelled "Aha," which in the Hebrew is cry of joy over someone else's misfortune. It is for this cry that God decided to punish the Ammonites.

Never celebrate the downfall of another human being. You might be next.

////////// HOT READ //////////

Read Ezekiel 26:12 and 14. This prophecy was fulfilled by Alexander the Great, who so completely destroyed the island of Tyre that to this very day it has never been fully restored.

──> A SONG FOR SATAN <

You were blameless in your ways from the day you were created till wickedness was found in you. Ezekiel 28:15.

The twenty-eighth chapter of Ezekiel is a prophecy against the prince of Tyre. Most scholars believe that he was a ruler named Ittobaal II. I know you were thinking of naming your first son Ittobaal, but you'll have to try again. Ittobaal's momma beat you to it.

God humbled Ittobaal II because "in the pride of your heart you say, 'I am a god; I sit on the throne of a god in the heart of the seas.' But you are a man and not a god, though you think you are as wise as a god" (Ezekiel 28:2). I guess God told him, huh?

The city of Tyre was originally built on an island right off the coast of Lebanon, and this provided the nation with a powerful natural defense against attackers. You can't exactly sneak up on an island that is heavily protected—not even at night. Prince Ittobaal II, like many rulers before him, did not believe that anything or anyone could conquer Tyre. But even while he was yet living, God told Ezekiel to write a funeral dirge for him. Understand this: It's never a good thing when folks begin to write songs about your death while you're still alive. Please don't write about me in the past tense. That ain't cool, chief!

While God was describing Ittobaal's fall, He began to describe the fall of another guy who thought he was "the Don." The description begins at verse 13 of chapter 28 and doesn't end until verse 17. Here's a sampling: "You were anointed as a guardian cherub, for so I ordained you. You were on the holy mount of God; you walked among the fiery stones" (verse 14).

Ittobaal II was never a cherub, and he was never on the holy mount of God. So if these verses do not refer to him, whom can God be talking about? The next verse gives us a clue. "You were blameless in your ways from the day you were created till wickedness was found in you" (verse 15). There is only one being who was an angel in heaven, walked in God's holy presence, and somehow developed a bad case of wickedness. His name is Satan.

Satan is alive and well, but God wrote a song about him, and he's not going to like the ending.

//////// HOT READ ////////

If you ever wonder who rules the rulers of this world, read Ezekiel 30:20-26

⟶ THIS IS A WARNING <

When I say to the wicked, "O wicked man, you will surely die," and you do not speak out to dissuade him from his ways, that wicked man will die for his sin, and I will hold you accountable for his blood. Ezekiel 33:8.

"WARNING! WARNING!"

"YOU ARE ENTERING A RESTRICTED AREA. PLEASE MOVE AWAY IMMEDIATELY. POLICE HAVE BEEN NOTIFIED."

Imagine the loudest, most earsplitting sound you've ever heard in your life, and it wouldn't come close to this one. I heard it every Saturday night for three months straight, but I'll never forget the first time.

Every January my church goes out to feed the homeless people living on the streets of Philadelphia. Philly winters are no pushover, so it takes a special person to sleep behind a building on a night when wind-chill temperatures are below zero. Yet every night that we went out you could find sleeping people everywhere.

During my first trip out with the homeless ministry team, we drove down a deserted alley between two buildings. You wouldn't want to be caught dead in this alley! I privately hoped that we weren't going to stop, but we did. I looked around for a homeless person to help, but saw no one. So I decided to open my door and step outside—carefully!

When I did, I saw the man we were looking for. I'd started over to where he lay hidden below mounds of old blankets when the booming warning nearly knocked me off my feet. The homeless man just smiled and beckoned me closer. The warning that nearly knocked me off my feet came from the building where he lay, but meant nothing to him. He'd grown accustomed to it. It was more bark than bite. No one ever responded to it.

Like Ezekiel, God's people are supposed to warn the world—in love—of the consequences of sin. Whether the world chooses to listen or not is not our concern. Our job is to give God's warning.

/////// HOT READ ///////

How did the people of Jerusalem respond Ezekiel's message? Ezekiel 33:30-32. How did God describe Ezekiel's messages?

──> WHAT'S IN A NAME? <

I had concern for my holy name, which the house of Israel profaned among the nations where they had gone. Ezekiel 36:21.

Two years ago I sat listening to a sermon by my pastor. He was home alone for the weekend. His wife was out of town, his daughter was at college, and his son was preparing to go on tour with his high school choir. Before his son left the house, Pastor D gave him some advice.

"Son," he began, "You're a Doggette! You are wearing my name. Come home with it intact!"

I've been on a few choir trips in my time, and I guess Pastor D had too, because he knew that "things" happen on choir trips that can ruin a great reputation. My pastor wanted his son to know that the name he'd been given was special. His behavior on the choir trip would either build up his good name or tear it down.

Lots of people care deeply about their name, but no one cares as much as God does. God is so serious about His name—His reputation—that the third commandment says, "You shall not misuse the name of the Lord your God, for the Lord will not hold anyone guiltless who misuses his name" (Exodus 20:7).

Israel never fully understood how connected their behavior was to God's reputation. Everyone knew that they belonged to the "true God." The heathen nations that lived around Israel saw how their God had fought for them and had given them a beautiful land. What do you think those same nations thought when Nebuchadnezzar burned down Jerusalem because of Israel's sins? Imagine what they thought about God.

Remember, Israel was chosen by God to be an example to the world, to help God bring the world back to Him. Not only did Jerusalem's sins destroy God's reputation, it also made it harder for God to save the world. (BTW, when we mess up the same thing happens.)

Did you notice the adjective that God used to describe His name? If God is holy and His name is holy, shouldn't His people also be holy?

//////// HOT READ ////////

Read Ezekiel 34:1-3. What did God call the leaders of Jerusalem? What was God's main charge against these leaders? What kind of leader are you?

——> BONES <

He asked me, "Son of man, can these bones live?" Ezekiel 37:3.

A number of years ago researchers performed an experiment to see the effect that hope has on those undergoing hardship. (This was before animal cruelty guidelines were in place.) Two sets of laboratory rats were placed in separate tubs of water and left to sink or swim. Within an hour all the rats in one of the tubs had drowned. The rats in the other tub were lifted out of the water, then returned. The rats in this tub swam for more than 24 hours. Why? Not because they were given a rest, but because—in their little rat brains—they had hope of being rescued again.

Those animals somehow hoped that if they could stay afloat just a little longer, someone would again reach down and rescue them. If hope holds such power for unthinking rodents, how much greater should its effect be on our lives (adapted from *Today in the Word*, May 1990).

Ten years into their stay in Babylon, hope was in short supply for Jerusalem's exiles. Their days were filled with backbreaking work. At night they cried themselves to sleep. God, through Jeremiah, had ordered up 70 years of exile for the nation of Judah, so the exiles still had a long way to go before they'd see freedom again. Like the first group of rats mentioned above, some of them stopped swimming. (BTW, I don't like rats, but even I'm against putting the poor critters in water and making them swim until they die. Rats!)

God wanted Ezekiel to give his people a shot of hope, so God whisked him away to a valley filled with dry rusty, dusty bones. Then God asked His humble servant, "Do you believe these bones can live?"

"Only You know," Ezekiel answered as he struggled to understand the meaning of God's question.

"Prophesy to these bones and say to them, 'Dry bones, hear the word of the Lord!'" said God (Ezekiel 37:4). As Ezekiel spoke to the bones, they began to rattle and come together. The bones then grew flesh and, with a little more prophesying, became a strong army.

Why did God go to such an elaborate "show and tell" for Ezekiel? In a word—hope! The Jerusalem exiles needed to know that God would one day restore them back to life.

//////// HOT READ ////////

What else did God use to send a message of healing to His people? Ezekiel 37:15-19.

——> THE ROAR OF GLORY <

Then the man brought me to the gate facing east, and I saw the glory of the God of Israel coming from the east. Ezekiel 43:1, 2.

n the twenty-fifth year of our exile, at the beginning of the year on the tenth of the month—it was the fourteenth year after the city fell—God touched me and brought me here. He brought me in divine vision to the land of Israel and set me down on a high mountain. To the south there were buildings that looked like a city. He took me there and I met a man deeply tanned, like bronze. He stood at the entrance holding a linen cord and a measuring stick.

"The man said to me, 'Son of man, look and listen carefully. Pay close attention to everything I'm going to show you. That's why you've been brought here. And then tell Israel everything you see'" (Ezekiel 40:1-4, Message).

With those words God showed Ezekiel a temple, but this temple Ezekiel saw was not one that would be built on earth. God was pointing forward to a time His people would worship Him perfectly—unhindered by sin. Ezekiel's angel guide showed him the entire physical layout of the temple in perfect detail. As you read Ezekiel 41-44 you will be impressed by how careful God is about His house of worship.

The dimensions of the building tell us just how careful God is, but Ezekiel 43:1, 2 should give you goose bumps.

"The man brought me to the east gate. Oh! The bright Glory of the God of Israel rivered out of the east sounding like the roar of floodwaters, and the earth itself glowed with the bright Glory. It looked just like what I had seen when he came to destroy the city, exactly like what I had seen earlier at the Kebar River. And again I fell, face to the ground" (Message).

Aren't you jealous that Ezekiel got to see such an amazing sight? Wouldn't you like to worship in a place in which the glory of God cannot only be seen but heard? I know I would. I'd probably fall out cold like Ezekiel did. Oh, well!

///////// HOT READ ///////

What did God tell Ezekiel to do after he saw God's glory fill the Temple? Ezekiel 43:10.

——> KNOW YOUR ROLE <

And my princes will no longer oppress my people but will allow the house of Israel to possess the land according to their tribes. Ezekiel 45:8.

id you know that dogs are pack animals? Pack animals are those that travel in a highly ordered pack. It's hard to believe that dogs fit this description, since most of them live alone with their human families. But travel through the Australian outback, and you'll see dogs in wild predator packs. Australia's dingoes are so ferocious that large predators avoid them.

In every pack there is an alpha leader. The alpha leader is the enforcer of the pecking order in the pack. Try to be top dog, and you'll meet the TOP DOG. If a dog survives this encounter, it'll return to the pack and assume its place in the pecking order. The alpha leader enforces pack rules to maintain order. Dogs instinctively order themselves this way, because it is essential to their survival. Even though we have domesticated them and made them our pets, they still have "pack" needs. Dog trainers will tell you that when you bring a dog home, you'd better assume the rule of alpha leader—or the dog will. Ever seen *The Dog Whisperer*?

People are dogs. OK, that's a bit harsh. We're not dogs, but we too need order in our human packs. God made us that way. God is the leader of our pack, but He also ordained certain people to help lead His pack here on earth. God's leaders have a very important function: They serve for the good of the community. They must create an environment that doesn't just allow the pack to survive, but thrive.

In Ezekiel 45:7-12 God describes the leaders of His ideal kingdom. In God's kingdom the leaders do not steal the people's land and take it for their own. Think for a moment. What would the United States look like today if early settlers of our nation had lived by this principle? Would our Native American brothers and sisters be left with tiny tracts of the worst of the land that they and their ancestors once owned? In Native American culture land cannot be owned. They believe that the Great Spirit in the sky owns all the land. The settlers and those who followed them used this understanding to cheat Native American tribes out of much of their land. What they couldn't cheat them out of, they took by force.

In God's kingdom the strong care for the needs of weak. Aren't you ready for a change?

HOT READ

What is name of the God's model city? Ezekiel 48:35. What does this tell you?

──> BEST OF THE BEST <

But Daniel resolved not to defile himself with the royal food and wine, and he asked the chief official for permission not to defile himself this way. Daniel 1:8.

Are you still reading? Don't quit now, friend; God is just getting warmed up! You're about to enter a book that outlines the future of world history until the second coming of Jesus. Wanna know the future? Then Daniel is the book for you.

God used the prophet Ezekiel to explain the reasons that He allowed Judah to go into Babylonian captivity and that He punished many of the heathen nations. But God went even further. He showed Ezekiel a vision of the day that the now broken people of Israel would be restored. (Remember the valley of dry bones?)

While Ezekiel's message focused on why Judah went into exile, the purpose of the book of Daniel is to give a historical account of the faithful Jews who lived in captivity and to show us that God is in control of heaven and earth.

Like Ezekiel, Daniel was swept up in the group of Jewish exiles who were taken to Babylon. King Nebuchadnezzar wasted no time in trying to change the culture and lifestyle of his new prisoners. He directed Ashpenaz, human resources director of the palace, to find the best and the brightest of the young Hebrew men to serve in the king's court. Tall, handsome, and free of any physical defect, Daniel, Hananiah, Mishael, and Azariah made the cut.

Then the transformation started. First, Ashpenaz gave them all new Babylonian names. Must've been tough to be called by one name your entire life and then suddenly have to get used to a new one, don't you think? Ashpenaz didn't just stop at their names; he tried to change their diet, but Daniel "resolved not to defile himself with the royal food and wine, and he asked the chief official for permission not to defile himself this way" (Daniel 1:8). With that stand, Daniel and the young Hebrews drew a line in the sand for King Nebuchadnezzar. There were things that they would not do under any circumstances.

Do you know where your boundaries are? Have you decided to stand for God?

////// HOT READ //////

Why didn't Daniel take credit for solving the king's problem? Daniel 2:24-28. Why didn't the three Hebrew boys simply bow and then explain it all to God later? Daniel 3:12.

——> A PARTY TO REMEMBER <

King Belshazzar gave a great banquet for a thousand of his nobles and drank wine with them. Daniel 5:1.

The joint was jumpin'. Iced-out homies were everywhere. Cute girls walked around in stylish near nothing. The perfect makeup and wanton eyes said it all. For those lucky enough to score a ticket to the party of the century, this would be a night to remember.

King Belshazzar should have known better. He'd been told how God had humbled his grandfather Nebuchadnezzar when his head got too big for his body. For seven years Grandpa Neb lived like an animal, running around naked and eating grass with the cattle. Grandpa Neb testified, "At the end of that time, I, Nebuchadnezzar, raised my eyes toward heaven, and my sanity was restored. Then I praised the Most High; I honored and glorified him who lives forever" (Daniel 4:34). How's that for a change of heart?

Somehow in his quest for greatness Belshazzar forgot that amazing story. And as the wine flowed freely, Belshazzar's legs got wobbly, and his thinking slowed. That's when he made his last mistake.

"While Belshazzar was drinking his wine, he gave orders to bring in the gold and silver goblets that Nebuchadnezzar his father had taken from the temple in Jerusalem, so that the king and his nobles, his wives and his concubines might drink from them" (Daniel 5:2).

Friend, God loves to party—especially when sinners decide to follow Him (Luke 15:10). But God's wasn't invited to Belshazzar's little shindig. It wasn't His kind of party anyway. But when Belshazzar decided to drink wine out of goblets used in the Temple service, he didn't know it but he'd just sent God an invitation. And wouldn't you know it, God showed up.

"Suddenly the fingers of a human hand appeared and wrote on the plaster of the wall, near the lampstand in the royal palace. . . . [The king's] face turned pale and he was so frightened that his knees knocked together and his legs gave way" (Daniel 5:5).

When no one could interpret the message, Daniel was called in—again. He delivered the bad news to Belshazzar. God had numbered the days of the king's reign and brought it to an end—right there in the middle of his party. That very night Babylon was conquered by the Persians (verses 30, 31).

/////// HOT READ ///////

What kinds of things does jealousy lead some people to do? Daniel 6:4, 5.

⟶ CONFUSED YET? <

As he came near the place where I was standing, I was terrified and fell prostrate. "Son of man," he said to me, "understand that the vision concerns the time of the end." Daniel 8:17.

The meaning of Daniel 7-9 has perplexed theologians and other Bible scholars for centuries. These chapters represent a dream God gave to Daniel in the first year of Belshazzar's reign as king of Babylon. As we found out yesterday, Belshazzar's reign ended abruptly with God's writing on the wall.

Belshazzar was slain that night when Darius the Mede conquered Babylon. It was under the rule of the Medes and the Persians that Jewish exiles were allowed to go back and rebuild Jerusalem. That's what Ezra and Nehemiah were commissioned by God to do.

Daniel and the other exiles knew the prophecy, that after 70 years of captivity they would be free. When Belshazzar took power, the 70 years was almost up. Daniel wanted to know what was going to happen to God's people. You too might want to know the future if you had been given a 70-year prison sentence and freedom was moments away.

God tried to calm Daniel by telling him the future, but not just of Israel's freedom. God gave Daniel a view to the very end of time. The strange beasts described in Daniel 7 and 8 represent kingdoms that have risen and fallen at God's command. God was saying, "Daniel, I'm the guy who runs the future. Trust *me!*"

As Daniel watched in awe, God continued to unfold the future. "As I looked, thrones were set in place, and the Ancient of Days took his seat. His clothing was as white as snow; the hair of his head was white like wool. His throne was flaming with fire, and its wheels were all ablaze.

"A river of fire was flowing, coming out from before him. Thousands upon thousands attended him; ten thousand times ten thousand stood before him. The court was seated, and the books were opened" (Daniel 7:9, 10).

Daniel saw God taking His judgment seat, even as the kingdoms of world continued to boast of their power. As you might imagine, these scenes disturbed Daniel even more.

//////// HOT READ ////////

What was the meaning of the dream in Daniel 8? Verses 18-26. Want to guess whom Daniel 9:26 is referring to? The angel told Daniel about Jesus.

——> HELP FROM HEAVEN <

But the prince of the Persian kingdom resisted me twenty-one days. Then Michael, one of the chief princes, came to help me, because I was detained there with the king of Persia. Daniel 10:13.

ave you ever needed a little help from heaven? Lorrie Anderson surely did. Here's her story.

Lorrie Anderson was a missionary to the head-shrinking Candoshi-Shapra Indians of Peru. One morning she went to the edge of the river to have a quiet place for her daily time of Bible reading and prayer. After reading the Bible, she took up her prayer list.

"Eyes closed, she did not see the deadly anaconda weaving through the water until it struck, burying its fangs into her flesh. It withdrew to strike, hitting her arm again and again as it held her, screaming, in its coils. It reared up for the death blows. Then suddenly the giant snake, never known to release its prey, relaxed its grip and slithered off through the water.

"While Lorrie was being treated, a witch doctor from a nearby village burst into the hut and stared at her. She couldn't believe Lorrie had survived. She said her son-in-law, also a witch doctor, had chanted to the spirit of the anaconda that morning and sent it to kill the young missionary. 'I'm certain,' Lorrie said, 'that except for the protection of God, it would have worked'" (*Our Daily Bread*, Aug. 13, 1990).

You may never be "hugged" by an anaconda, but there is another snake trying to squeeze you to death. God sent an angel to tell Daniel when the Jews would leave Medo-Persia—the thing Daniel wanted to know more than anything else in the world. However, a powerful evil force called the prince of Persia held up God's angel messenger for 21 straight days.

God wasn't about to let Satan (the prince of Persia) stop this important message, so he sent Michael, one of the heavenly enforcers, to deal with him. Michael did, and the angel gave Daniel the message.

If Satan is preventing you from hearing God's special message for your life, just ask God to send you a little help from heaven. Ask for Michael!

//////// HOT READ ////////

Read Daniel 12:1-4. There's that Michael again. Wanna guess who He is?

268

---> MARRY *WHO*? <

> *When the Lord began to speak through Hosea, the Lord said to him, "Go, take to yourself an adulterous wife and children of unfaithfulness, because the land is guilty of the vilest adultery in departing from the Lord." Hosea 1:2.*

ay what? Did I just read that God sent a prophet, one of His prophets, to go find a wife who is a prostitute? The answer is yes, and so begins one of the most interesting books of the Bible.

The lead character in the soap opera we're about to read today is a guy named Hosea. Hosea began his ministry during the decline of the northern kingdom of Israel. God had predicted that both Israel and Judah (the southern kingdom) would be conquered and sent into exile. Israel was invaded in 743 B.C. by one mean hombre named Tiglath-pileser. (Check his name on Google when you get a chance.) Judah's destruction came at the hands of Nebuchadnezzar and Babylon in 586 B.C. Notice that Jerusalem fell much later than Israel. (Note: We are counting down [B.C.] to the birth of Jesus.)

A few books ago we read how Isaiah preached a message of warning and repentance to try to get Judah to change its ways. Jeremiah also did the same thing, overlapping a bit with Isaiah. Then Ezekiel was sent to speak to the people of Judah who had been taken into exile. Things change in Daniel. Instead of focusing on prophets and their messages, we get to see how difficult life was for Judah's exiles—especially three named Shadrach, Meshach, and Abednego.

But now we've come to Hosea, a book that is hard to categorize. It's a love story—but one with an ugly twist. Every guy dreams of marrying the girl of his dreams, one who hasn't "been" with other guys. Can you imagine how Hosea felt when God told him whom he was going to marry? I know how I would've felt. I once dated a girl who I thought was into me, until I found out she was into another guy. Dude, my little heart was crushed!

Before we start hating on God, though, we better read Hosea. Hosea's relationship with his promiscuous wife was an example of the relationship that existed between God and Israel. God went to great lengths to make the point that He and Israel were no longer in love.

///////// HOT READ /////////

What did God promise to do for Israel (Hosea 2:14-19)?

269

——> GOING TOO FAR <

Their deeds do not permit them to return to their God. A spirit of prostitution is in their heart; they do not acknowledge the Lord. Hosea 5:4.

There is a powerful Spanish proverb that says, "Habits are first cobwebs, then cables." Whoever came up with that little bit of wisdom had to be divinely inspired. Perhaps this story makes the point more clearly.

An elderly teacher took a walk through a forest with one of his students. Suddenly the teacher stopped and pointed to four plants growing nearby. The first was just beginning to peep above the ground, the second had rooted itself pretty well into the earth, the third was a small shrub, while the fourth was a full-sized tree. The teacher said to his young pupil, "Pull up this little plant." The boy did. It was easy.

"Now pull up the second," the teacher said. It took a few tugs, but the boy did it.

"Now the third," the teacher said with a smile. It took all his strength, but the boy finally uprooted that one too.

"Now," said the instructor, "try your hand with the fourth." The boy put his arms around the trunk of the tall tree and couldn't even shake its leaves.

"This, my son, is just what happens with our bad habits," the teacher told him. "When they are young, we can easily remove them. But when they are old, it's very difficult, even though we struggle and pray."

The Israelites had become so hardened by their repeated sins that it was impossible for them to return to God. "There is no faithfulness," said God, "no love, no acknowlededment of God in the land. There is only cursing, lying and murder, stealing and adultery; they break all bounds, and bloodshed follows bloodshed" (Hosea 4:1, 2). That's about as strong a comment from God as you'll ever read in the Bible.

Repeated sins don't change God; they change us. God still loves us, and He longs to save us, but repeated sins can push us so far from God that we don't want to return to Him.

///////// **HOT READ** ///////

Why was God angry with Israel's leaders? Hosea 5:10. What point was God making about these leaders?

——> DYING FROM A BROKEN HEART <

When I found Israel, it was like finding grapes in the desert; when I saw your fathers, it was like seeing the early fruit on the fig tree. But when they came to Baal Peor, they consecrated themselves to that shameful idol and became as vile as the thing they loved. Hosea 9:10.

They must have loved each other at some time. Most people marry for love, with nary a thought of divorce. But something went wrong, desperately wrong, in their relationship. Why else would a 20-year-old mother of two commit suicide?

"I love you, darling," Anne Mary Aruldas wrote to her husband, who'd been out of work for some time. Police had found her body hanging from a window grille, a piece of cloth wrapped tightly around her neck. With it was her handwritten note.

Aruldas wrote about how much she adored her husband and the two young sons who were the center of their lives. Were it not for one telltale line, the note could have been a love letter to her husband. But this was no love letter.

Just before she said her final goodbye to the man she loved, Anne Mary wrote: "Now you can hang out until early in the morning and no one will stop you." In that one brief line she told everything that was in her heart—the frustrations of a young wife whose husband had begun to wander.

In Hosea 9:10 God recalls a time He and the nation of Israel first laid eyes on each other. He said that finding Israel—the nation He had saved from centuries of Egyptian slavery—was like coming upon a cluster of succulent grapes in the desert. If you ever have a chance to visit the Mojave Desert in southern California or the Sahara in northern Africa, grapes will probably be the furthest thing on your mind. You'd be lucky to see anything green there.

God's close relationship with Israel didn't last. Just before entering the Promised Land, Israel joined itself to Baal, the god of the Midianites, at a place called Peor. More than 700 years later, as Israel faced captivity, this incident was still fresh in God's mind. Israel had not repented, and God's heart was broken.

####### HOT READ ///////

Notice that as Israel's prosperity increased, their relationship with God decreased. Hosea 10:1. Did this have to happen?

271

———> IT'S ALL IN ME <

Who is wise? He will realize these things. Who is discerning? He will understand them. The ways of the Lord are right; the righteous walk in them, but the rebellious stumble in them. Hosea 14:9.

on't ever accuse God of giving up on you. God may be upset, but He never stops reaching out for you and me. Hosea 14, one of God's last love letters to Israel, is a beautiful example of this:

"O Israel, come back! Return to your God! You're down but you're not out. Prepare your confession and come back to God. Pray to him, 'Take away our sin, accept our confession. Receive as restitution our repentant prayers.'

"'Assyria won't save us; horses won't get us where we want to go. We'll never again say "our god" to something we've made or made up. You're our last hope. Is it not true that in you the orphan finds mercy?'

"'I will heal their waywardness. I will love them lavishly. My anger is played out. I will make a fresh start with Israel. He'll burst into bloom like a crocus in the spring. He'll put down deep oak tree roots, he'll become a forest of oaks! He'll become splendid—like a giant sequoia, his fragrance like a grove of cedars!

"'Those who live near him will be blessed by him, be blessed and prosper like golden grain. Everyone will be talking about them, spreading their fame as the vintage children of God. Ephraim is finished with gods that are no-gods. From now on I'm the one who answers and satisfies him.

"'I am like a luxuriant fruit tree. Everything you need is to be found in me'" (verses 1-8, Message).

You've read Hosea. You know all about Israel's mess-ups. It's easy to point fingers at Israel for being stupid enough to leave a God who loved them so much, but don't we do the same thing today?

Isn't time you made up with God?

HOT READ

What did the citizens of Israel boast about? Hosea 12.8

——> JUDGMENT DAY <

Blow the trumpet in Zion, declare a holy fast, call a sacred assembly. Joel 2:15.

The daily devotional for October 1, 1991, in *Today in the Word* told the story of a forgotten Revolutionary War hero. I have to admit that I hadn't heard the name Israel Bissel before coming across his story.

We all know about Paul Revere's midnight ride from Boston to Lexington, Massachusetts, warning citizens all along the way, "The British are coming, the British are coming." Israel Bissel is less well known, but his heroic ride from Boston to New York makes Paul Revere's ride look like an afternoon stroll.

"After the Battle of Lexington and Concord on April 19, 1775, Bissel was ordered to raise the alarm in New Haven, Connecticut. He reached Worcester, Massachusetts, normally a day's ride, in two hours. There, according to tradition, his horse promptly dropped dead. Pausing only to get another mount, Bissel pressed on and by April 22 was in New Haven—but he didn't stop there! He rode on to New York, arriving April 24, and then stayed in the saddle until he reached Philadelphia the next day. Bissel's 126-hour, 345-mile ride signaled American militia units throughout the Northeast to mobilize for war."

When you've got a life-or-death message to give, you go to great lengths. That's exactly what Joel did in his message to the nation of Judah. He was sent by God to let Judah know that the day of God's judgment was soon to come. This was the time to get reconnected to God by confessing, repenting, and forsaking all sin.

"Call a holy gathering," we can hear Joel yell. "Stop everything! Don't even let grooms marry their brides. Stop everything and let the priests weep and pray for God's forgiveness." Joel's message touched many lives and hearts, but most of Jerusalem's Jews remained unfazed.

There is urgency in Joel's message. His wrenching words cut through time. They are addressed to you and me today, as surely as they were to Israel. God is giving us a chance to reconnect with Him.

HOT READ

Joel ends his message on a high. What special blessing did Joel promise those who remained faithful to God? Joel 2:28-32. That prophecy is meant for you, friend.

⟶ COUNTRY BOY IN THE CITY <

The words of Amos, one of the shepherds of Tekoa—what he saw concerning Israel two years before the earthquake, when Uzziah was king of Judah and Jeroboam son of Jehoash was king of Israel. Amos 1:1.

I was born in another country, but I'm not country—if you know what I mean. Country is pig races and county fairs, one-stoplight towns and dusty overalls, guys named Ned and girls named Betsy. Yep, I'm definitely not country—and that's too bad.

That doesn't mean that I don't know what it feels to be country. My teen years came and went in the eighties on the hardscrabble streets of East Orange, New Jersey. Those were the days of shell-toe Adidas, Kangol hats, belt buckles with your name on it—if you could afford it—and Lee jeans with the stitched seam down the front and back. I was city, baby, or so I thought. The only time I felt country was when I got ready to go to the Big Apple.

We Jersey guys were veggie-thugs compared to the hardened criminals in New York, or at least so everyone thought. Going there, we were warned not to look New Yorkers in the eye or up at tall skyscrapers. There were only two groups of people who did that kind of stuff: tourists and country folk. To be labeled a tourist was bad enough, but to be called "country"? Well, that was a no-no! (But times change. Now all I dream about is being in the country!)

Country folks have always gotten a bum rap from city dwellers. Even way back when the prophet Amos began his ministry, country people had it tough. Amos was from a way-out place called Tekoa, and the only thing worse than that was the way he smelled. He smelled like sheep. (Shepherds tend to smell that way, you understand.) Amos was country—and proud of it!

God called this country guy to the big city to deliver a painful message. What was he supposed to do when he got there? Oh, not much. He just had to walk into the middle of biggest idol worship service ever and declare that God's judgment was soon to come upon Israel. Can you imagine what the city folks thought when they saw Amos coming?

///////// HOT READ /////////

One of the major themes in Amos is Israel's broken relationship or covenant with God. Read Amos 3:3. Are you and God on the same page right now?

——> RIGHTEOUS NATION? <

For I know how many are your offenses and how great your sins. You oppress the righteous and take bribes and you deprive the poor of justice in the courts.
Amos 5:12.

There are many powerful spiritual themes in the book of Amos, and one of those is justice for the poor. To be poor and weak in Judah (the southern kingdom) and Israel (the northern kingdom) was a lot like being poor today.

At the time that Amos was delivering his message, Israel and Judah were extremely prosperous. Israel controlled powerful trade routes that boosted its economy. Judah had successfully regained lost territory, and a building boom was under way. Both nations sported sleek, powerful militaries that were the envy of other nations. Israel and Judah had reached dizzying heights politically and economically, but spiritually they were at an all-time low.

The people believed that their prosperity was a sign that God was blessing them. Have you heard anything like that on TV lately? They judged the quality of their relationship with God based on the amount of their possessions, not on what they did with their possessions. So the rich got richer, and the poor got, well, poorer.

God didn't have anything against the rich people back when Amos was preaching, and He doesn't today. What bothered Him then and now was how the rich got richer. They got their money by stepping on the backs of the poor. They rigged the system to benefit themselves, and they never gave anything to people in need.

If Amos were around today, he'd ask us a few questions: Why is it that approximately 50 million people in the richest country on earth have no medical insurance coverage? Why do the rich give so little financial help to the poor? Aren't the strong supposed to help the weak? Why are the rich pardoned or given probation for crimes that the poor are routinely jailed for? Why are people from certain cultural groups sentenced to death more often than people from other cultural groups? Isn't justice supposed to be blind?

Amos believed that a society couldn't be righteous unless it was fair. And one of the ways that you know if a society is righteous is to watch how it treats its poor and powerless.

//////// HOT READ ////////

What radical tricks did God try to use to wake up His people? Amos 4.

──→ SECOND OPINIONS <

"The days are coming," declares the Sovereign Lord, "when I will send a famine through the land—not a famine of food or a thirst for water, but a famine of hearing the words of the Lord." Amos 8:11.

ver heard the one about the man who developed a dark, painful rash? No. Probably not. But Dr. George Hawkins told this true story.

A man from a rural area came into town for a doctor's appointment. His problem: a severe rash. The nurse took his weight and temperature and had him sit on the examining table. In due time the doctor came in, took his medical history, and, after talking with him, gave him a series of tests. At last the physician reached a diagnosis. He told the man that he needed to get rid of the dog that was causing the allergic reaction—the rash.

As the man got up to leave the office the doctor asked, out of curiosity, if he planned to sell the animal or give it away.

The patient shook his head. "Neither," he said. "I'm going to get me one of them second opinions I've been reading about. It's a lot easier to find a doctor than a good bird dog."

Some people just don't want to hear the truth. The guy with the painful rash believed that he could change the diagnosis by changing doctors. Believe or not, many of us are just like him. God says one thing in the Bible, but we search for a second opinion.

When Israel and Judah refused to listen to God's diagnosis and prescription for their sins, they went after second opinions. King Jeroboam II, an evil king of Israel, hired a false prophet named Amaziah to tell him and the people what they wanted to hear. Amos met him head-on.

"Jeroboam will die by the sword, and Israel will surely go into exile," said the courageous prophet of God before Jeroboam and all those gathered to worship in Jeroboam's sanctuary (Amos 7:11). Amaziah was incensed. Amos was exposing his lies.

"Get out, you seer! Go back to the land of Judah. Earn your bread there and do your prophesying there," Amaziah screamed (verse 12). God must have heard Amaziah, because God gave Amos a frightening message for Israel. Since they didn't want to hear His words, He would stop talking. When we stop listening to God, He just may stop speaking. And that's not a good thing at all.

//////// HOT READ ////////

Amos didn't leave Israel hopeless. Read Amos 9:11-15.

──> SIBLING RIVALRY <

On the day you stood aloof while strangers carried off his wealth and foreigners entered his gates and cast lots for Jerusalem, you were like one of them. Obadiah 11.

t's all bad! Obadiah has absolutely nothing good to say about the nation of Edom, the subject of his very short book. Isaiah gave Israel the hope of one day seeing the Messiah. Jeremiah encouraged Jerusalem's residents to repent and willingly accept the Babylonian exile. Ezekiel, Hosea, and Amos all found something positive to tell people who had totally left God. All had something positive to say—all except Obadiah.

When God has nothing encouraging to say to you, you know you're in trouble. God seemed to single out the nation of Edom for special punishment. Why?

If you've been reading the Bible through with me from the beginning, you'll remember the story of Jacob and Esau, found in Genesis 25-36. You remember how Jacob and his mother Rebekah cheated Esau out of his birthright. When Esau found out what his brother had done to him, he wept bitterly and vowed to kill Jacob. Jacob and Esau later reconciled, but their relationship was never the same. Esau married Canaanite wives and settled in a place called Seir. Another name for Esau is Edom. Esau is the father of the Edomites.

Are you starting to get the picture? Remember the name that God gave to Jacob after he wrestled with the angel? Still no remember? (Dude, you're killin' me! It's Israel.)

The Edomites and Israelites were cousins, but for centuries the Edomites harbored a deep hatred against their cousins for what Jacob had done to their father, Esau. Esau was a mighty hunter, and he passed on this warrior spirit to his descendants. The Edomites attacked the Israelites several times over many years. Needless to say, God was not pleased with them.

"Because of the violence against your brother Jacob, you will be covered with shame; you will be destroyed forever," said God (Obadiah 10). In verse 11 God goes on to say that when Israel was being taken captive, the Edomites took pleasure in their misfortune. They didn't even lift a finger to help. This was the sin that angered God greatly.

God expects us to love our brothers and sisters, even when they've hurt us.

////// HOT READ //////

How complete would be Edom's destruction? Check out verse 18.

——> YOU CAN RUN . . . <

But Jonah ran away from the Lord and headed for Tarshish. He went down to Joppa, where he found a ship bound for that port. After paying the fare, he went abroad and sailed for Tarshish to flee from the Lord. Jonah 1:3.

He's one of the bad boys of the Bible, one of group of slippery characters who did everything possible to avoid God's call. When God called Jonah to go to Nineveh and call the city to repentance, Jonah took off running in the opposite direction. He got on a ship headed for a place called Tarshish. Nineveh was east of Israel. Tarshish was about as far west of Nineveh as one could get. It was a city that was thought to be close to the end of the world. Jonah wanted to get waaaaaay out of town.

What did Jonah know about Nineveh that we do not? Well, for one thing, Nineveh was the capital of the powerful Assyrian Empire and the largest city in the world at that time. Did you get that? God didn't call Jonah to go to a city in Israel. He sent him to the capital city of a foreign nation and told him "cry out" against their sins and call them to repentance.

God cares about all people, even those who don't profess any belief in Him. God wanted to save the people of Nineveh, but Jonah felt that they deserved punishment. He couldn't understand why God would try to save a nation that was a sworn enemy of Israel.

"Nineveh has more than a hundred and twenty thousand people who cannot tell their right hand from their left, and many cattle as well. Should I not be concerned about that great city?" asked God (Jonah 4:11).

The book of Jonah is one of the greatest books in the Bible because it gives a rare view into God's heart. Here we see how much God loves all people—even those we write off as beyond God's mercy. As you read Jonah's book, get past the whale tale. Go deeper. Pay close attention to how patient God is with Jonah, even though Jonah has no such patience for Nineveh. God's heart is splattered all over this awesome book.

////// HOT READ //////

What were the results of Jonah's preaching? Jonah 3. Are you running from something that God is calling you to do? Stop running and let God use you.

——> I'VE GOT THE POWER <

But as for me, I am filled with power, with the Spirit of the Lord, and with justice and might, to declare to Jacob his transgression, to Israel his sin. Micah 3:8.

ne of the great things you've got to love about God is that He never punishes before giving us many opportunities to change. Through His prophets God warned Israel and Judah that they were headed in the wrong direction, that if they continued, destruction would come. Micah, like the other prophets we've been reading about, carries this same message. His prophecies were sent to the southern kingdom of Judah, which, as you know, was made up of two of Israel's original 12 tribes.

The life of a prophet during Bible times was not an easy one. One need only read the book of Hosea to see that. But is it different today? Has spreading God's message gotten easier? I don't think so.

Perhaps you don't remember what happened in April 2007. Some Christian missionaries in the province of Malayta arranged a special service for Muslim "seekers" who wanted to know more about the Christian faith.

When the missionaries arrived at the seeker service, they were kidnapped by five of the young "seekers," who took them to a safe house, where they had stored guns, bread knives, ropes, and towels. The young men knew that what they were about to do would be bloody. The bodies of the three missionaries were later found, and there was evidence that they had been tortured for up to three hours before they died.

Serving God has never been easy, but it helps when we know that God is truly with us—even when He chooses not to intervene. Micah knew that God was with him. He knew that he was filled with the power of God, and not just power. Micah was also filled with justice and might—justice because people with power need to be fair, and might because it takes courage to stand for what it right.

Don't you want to be filled with God's power? I hope you do, because the world sure needs the message that you have to give.

//////// HOT READ ////////

You'd have to know that God was with you to do this: Micah 1:8.

279

——> DIDN'T I SHOW YOU? <

He has showed you, O man, what is good. And what does the Lord require of you?
To act justly and to love mercy and to walk humbly with your God. Micah 6:8.

e was one of my favorite professors at Oakwood College,★ but I wasn't the only student that dug his class. Everyone did! Each semester the hallway around by his classroom was blocked by the chairs that spilled out the door. Students on their breaks would come and stand outside his class to hear him. Pastor E. E. Cleveland was a professor unlike any other.

Why did everyone take his class? Well, if you were fortunate enough to get into his class, you knew you had an A. Since A's were hard to come by, to have a sure one in hand was a gift to your GPA that would never come again. Elder Cleveland taught a class called Fundamentals of the Christian Faith, and he just didn't believe that teaching college kids what it means to be a Christian should be difficult. So he would teach—mostly preach—and tell us exactly what would be on the test. When test time came, the questions were word for word as he'd said. He told us what to expect. The only way you could fail his class was to never show up.

In a very real way, Professor Cleveland was a lot like God.

"He has showed you, O man, what is good," wrote Micah. Both Israel and Judah knew what God expected of them. What was it that the Lord wanted from them? He wanted His people to be known for three things: acting justly, loving mercy, and walking humbly.

All the laws God gave to Israel as they entered the Promised Land—the testing time—could be summed up in these three principles. They were to be fair in the way they apportioned land. Whether rich or poor, all people were to be treated fairly. When someone made a mistake, as far as possible they were to extend mercy. Finally, God wanted them to be known as humble people. God wanted His people to be like Him.

Micah 6:8 is one of the keys to understanding the book of Micah. In the final chapters Micah paints a picture of a God who judges the guilty, forgives sinners, and loves all people.

★ now Oakwood University

⟶ BRING IT ON <

"I am against you," declares the Lord Almighty. "I will burn up your chariots in smoke, and the sword will devour your young lions. I will leave you no prey on the earth. The voices of your messengers will no longer be heard." Nahum 2:13.

e called him Tyson—because he was Tyson. The Tyson I'm referring to is not "Iron" Mike Tyson, the old boxer whom everyone laughs at now. No, this guy was *our* Tyson when Tyson was Tyson. (I know. You're confused.)

The Tyson I'm referring to attended Pine Forge Academy in Pennsylvania back in the late eighties. I happened to be there at the same time. He was huge. Great big biceps and legs like tree trunks—and a mean streak to match. Some guys fooled around with Tyson, but few were crazy enough to actually fight him. My roommate, Gary, was one of the few.

"G, what happened to you?" I shouted as he crumpled onto his bed.

"Man, I just boxed Tyson. That's a big boy! He nearly killed me, yo."

Gary wasn't scared of anybody, but his courage nearly got him killed. I used to box a little back in those days, and I was pretty good. I stayed in my weight class, of course, mixing it up only with my scrawny friends. Tyson heard that I had game and challenged me one day.

"Dwain, let's get it on. You and me." This is how Tyson tested himself. He'd fight anybody with some game. I wanted to be brave, but there was no way that I was going to box Tyson. I had seen what he had done to Gary, and I couldn't even stay with G. That was the end of my boxing career. (That's why I'm writing this book. Boxing didn't work out.)

No matter how bad you think you are, there's always someone bigger, stronger, and meaner. I found that out, and so did a nation named Assyria. During the eighth century B.C., Assyria was the biggest, baddest bully on the block, known for the creative ways in which it tortured its enemies. We read how God sent Jonah to Nineveh, Assyria's capital, to call the nation to repentance. They listened for a while, but then they regressed.

One hundred years later God sent Nahum with a frightening message for Nineveh: "I am against you." I am going to fight you, and when I get done, there will not be anything left of you.

HOT READ

What does Nahum 1:3 tell you about God's nature?

——> WHAT'S WRONG WITH YOU? <

Your eyes are too pure to look on evil; you cannot tolerate wrong. Why then do you tolerate the treacherous? Why are you silent while the wicked swallow up those more righteous than themselves? Habakkuk 1:13.

While surfing the Internet one day I came across an atheist Web site. The opening statement at the top of the home page immediately grabbed my attention. Here's what it said: God, if you truly exist, we have a few (dozen) questions for you. Why don't you answer them for us?

Naturally I kept on reading to see what sorts of questions were posted at the site. Someone wanted to know why men and women have the same number of ribs if God took one from Adam to make Eve. Never thought of that before, I must confess.

But then there were several very deep questions that can't just be brushed away, if for no other reason than the pain hiding just below the surface. This one really touched my heart: "Why do you make your followers suffer so much? Why do they die at the hands of other religions? Can't you put a stop to this? You're omnipotent, right? Can you 'show us your stuff'?" Why do you let all your religious followers die in plane crashes, terrorist attacks, car accidents, famines, floods, hurricanes, tornadoes, etc.? Is this part of 'your plan'?" Good question.

People have questioned God for centuries—even in the Bible. Habakkuk looked around at Judah and couldn't believe his eyes. Violence was everywhere. Justice was nonexistent, people committed open sins, and to top it all off, Judah was surrounded by powerful enemies. Babylon was becoming the world's superpower. The sight made Habakkuk weep.

"God, why do You stand by and do nothing?" asked Habakkuk. He believed in God, but he felt that God was MIA—missing in action. What was God's answer?

"I'm here, Habakkuk. I see it all, but My plan is not yet ready to be unfolded. The righteous don't live by what they see; they live by faith" (see Habakkuk 2:3, 4).

If you ever wondered, "Where is God when I hurt?" you are not alone.

//////// HOT READ ////////

Habakkuk grew in his relationship with God. Habakkuk. 3:17-19. Go ahead and ask God your toughest questions, but never lose your trust in Him. He hears you!

———> " Z " <

Seek the Lord, all you humble of the land, you who do what he commands. Seek righteousness, seek humility; perhaps you will be sheltered on the day of the Lord's anger. Zephaniah 2:3.

God is a team player. How do I know that? The book of Zephaniah told me so. Actually, the background history of the book of Zephaniah told me so.

I don't know about you, but I'd never read the book of Zephaniah before. That's a shame, because I've owned numerous Bibles since I was knee-high to a grasshopper. I had to do a little research on "Z" to find out who he was before I cracked chapter 1. Here's what I found.

Zephaniah was a descendant of King Hezekiah, one of the few good kings of Judah. But after Hezekiah died, the nation went into the tank. Manasseh and his son, Amon, led Israel into deep apostasy and sin. Under their leadership, children were sacrificed to pagan gods. They erected altars to foreign gods right in the Jewish Temple.

Zephaniah grew up in Jerusalem surrounded by sin, yet he was untouched by it. Even more difficult than growing up around sin was the fact that Zephaniah had to go back to many of his family, friends, and neighbors to deliver his message. He was called to be a prophet to his hometown of Jerusalem. Do you have any idea how hard it can be to get your family and friends to take you seriously? Zephaniah probably knew what that felt like.

But Z was not alone in his mission. God knew that he would need help and support. Jeremiah was also prophesying at that time. There's a good chance that Zephaniah would have known Jeremiah. King Josiah was king during Zephaniah's ministry. Zeph's preaching gave force and power to the reforms of Josiah—a teenager who brought Judah back to God.

Might not seem like it now, but God has prepared you for a special mission. It doesn't matter where you came from. It doesn't matter what you came out of. When the time is right, God is going to call you into action. When He does, don't be afraid. God will be with you, and He'll put a team of fellow believers around you to keep you strong.

####### HOT READ #######

Did you know that God sings? Zephaniah 3:17. Zephaniah pointed to a day God would save His people from sin once and for all. On that day God will sing!

——> STRONG TO THE FINISH <

"Go up into the mountains and bring down the timber and build the house, so that I may take pleasure in it and be honored," says the Lord. Haggai 1:8.

When I decided to write a full 365-day devotional, I had no idea what I was in for. I'd written devotional books before, but not the big one. I wasn't sure that I'd had 365 original thoughts since I was born, so coming up with that many under a tight deadline was positively scary.

I started strongly, rattling off entries at a very fast clip. Were they any good? Well, I hope so. I felt that God was leading me for sure. But the more I kept writing, the more difficult the writing got. My job still had to get done. I had a wife to take care of—Yay!—and that's not counting all the stuff I was doing at my church. For a long time I didn't write at all. I was totally overwhelmed by the task.

I needed a jump-start to get back on track, so I went to see my editor, the woman who asked me to write this book. She believes in me. (I still don't know why she does.)

"I know you're going to get it done, Dwain. Yes, sir. There are young people who need this book. There are young people who will be saved by this book. You've got to get it done."

I sat in her office thinking to myself, *I'm going to finish this book—no matter what.* I was already late, but I was determined not to disappoint her any further.

Everyone needs words of encouragement when a tough task looms. When the Jews were released from exile in 538 B.C. and allowed to return and rebuild Jerusalem, they faced many obstacles. We read about some of those challenges in Ezra and Nehemiah. Haggai was among the group of exiles that returned to Jerusalem.

The rebuilding started out great, but over time the people settled into building homes, planting gardens—simply living. They forgot about God's house, because they were too busy hooking themselves up. Haggai—and Zechariah, who'll read about next—stirred the nation to finish what they'd promised God they'd do.

Haggai's words were just what the people needed to hear. They got the job done.

///////// HOT READ ///////

What was happening to the Jews while they were neglecting God's house? Haggai 1:5, 6.

⟶ LOOKING AHEAD <

"Shout and be glad, O Daughter of Zion. For I am coming, and I will live among you," declares the Lord. "Many nations will be joined with the Lord in that day and will become my people. I will live among you and you will know that the Lord Almighty has sent me to you." Zechariah 2:10, 11.

A s I mentioned yesterday, Zechariah and Haggai were both sent by God to wake up the exiles who had returned from the horrible Babylonian captivity. In fact, Zechariah and Haggai both started to share their messages in the same year. These guys were probably running buddies.

There is one very cool aspect to the book of Zechariah that shouldn't be missed: Zechariah received a vision of the Messiah—Jesus—more than 500 years before Jesus' birth! Through Zechariah God pointed to a time that people from many nations would come to know God through Jesus Christ.

As I read this chapter, I started thinking, questioning. Why did God bother to give the message of the coming Messiah to the Jewish exiles when He wouldn't be born for another 500 years? I know God plans ahead, but this was a bit much, don't you think? Then I came across a little story that might explain God's reasoning better than I ever could.

A man approached a Little League baseball game one afternoon. He asked a boy in the dugout what the score was. The boy responded, "Eighteen to nothing—we're behind."

"Boy," said the spectator, "I'll bet you're discouraged."

"Why should I be discouraged?" the kid retorted. "We haven't even gotten up to bat yet!"

I know what you're thinking. *What does that have to do with why God sent the message about the Messiah?* That little boy had something that the returning Jewish exiles didn't have—hope. Remember, they were once the most powerful nation on earth. God Himself fought their battles, but because of their sins, they were conquered and many of them were killed. Out a nation of millions, only about 50,000 people returned from the exile in Babylon.

Why did God give Zechariah that vision? He wanted the small remnant in Jerusalem to know that their best days were ahead. They were done, but Jesus would be coming to the plate.

///////// HOT READ /////////

Read Zechariah 3:1, 2 to see what Satan does to people who try to obey God.

⎯⎯> EVEREST <

What are you, O mighty mountain? Before Zerubbabel you will become level ground.
Zechariah 4:7.

verest. Mount Everest. The most difficult climb any mountain climber could attempt. The highest mountain on earth. To reach the top you've got to climb 29,035 feet. (Just for a little perspective, many planes reach their cruising altitude at 29,000 feet.) The high winds and bone-chilling cold, very steep ascent, extremely unpredictable weather, and a host of other complications make it almost impossible to reach Everest's summit. The mountain has humbled even the most experienced of climbers.

Imagine trying to climb Mount Everest in the dark. That's right, 29,035 feet of pure darkness. Pretty crazy, don't you think? Yet that's exactly what Erik Weihenmeyer did.

"Pushing through brutal cold, savage winds and crushing fatigue at 29,000 feet (8,840 meters)," wrote Tom Foreman from *National Geographic News*, "he reached the top of the world; but he never caught even a glimpse of the famous view. He is the only blind person to ever stand on Everest's peak."

Erik Weilhenmeyer didn't stop there, either. He went on to climb the world's other six highest peaks, and in 2004 he guided a group of blind Tibetan teens up most of Everest. Yep, he's quite a guy.

In Zechariah 4 we met a guy who is also working with not one but several severe handicaps. God tapped Zerubbabel to lead the rebuilding of the Temple in Jerusalem, and almost immediately things started to go south. The people didn't care about the Temple, materials were hard to come by, and powerful enemies threatened the worksite. To Zerubbabel, the task looked like one huge mountain that he could not climb. And he was right.

God called Zechariah near and said, "This is the word of the Lord to Zerubbabel: 'Not by might nor by power, but by my Spirit,' says the Lord Almighty" (verse 6). God's Spirit—not Zerubbabel's strength or ingenuity—was going to get the job done. But God didn't stop there. He promised to level Zerubbabel's mountainous challenge. If God did that for Zerubbabel, He'll do it for you!

///////// HOT READ /////////

If you want to do something great, start with the small stuff. Zechariah 4:10.

——> GROW UP! <

This is what the Lord Almighty says: "You who now hear these words spoken by the prophets who were there when the foundation was laid for the house of the Lord Almighty, let your hands be strong so that the temple may be built." Zechariah 8:9.

agles are astounding birds. They can see another soaring eagle from up to 40 miles away. They cruise at 10,000 or more feet. The can fly up to 44 miles per hour in level flight, and when they dive to nab an unsuspecting fish or rabbit, they can reach speeds of 75 to 100 miles per hour. They grab prey with their long, sharp talons, each of which exerts about 1,000 pounds of pressure per square inch. When they grab, they don't let go.

The eagle has one more trick up its sleeve, and this one always amazes me. Eagle mothers take very good care of their young. They hunt and bring back food for them. They protect them with their lives from other airborne predators. But once the young eaglets get old enough, the mother does something cruel. She picks the oldest of the lot, and pushes it out of the nest. (If I were an eaglet, I would consider this attempted murder.)

As the eaglet careens to the ground, the mother swoops out of the nest, carefully watching the young bird. If the youngster is unable to fly, the mother grabs it right out of midair and takes it back to the nest. (Dude, what if she misses? What if her coordinates are off by a feather or two? It's curtains for the little one!) Father birds also help in this rescue.

God is a lot like a mother eagle. Sometimes He has to give us a push so that we can fly. He did that to the returning exiles from Babylon. The people had successfully built the foundation of theTemple, but then they got sidetracked doing other stuff, and eventually they stopped altogether. God was not "feeling" them at that moment.

What's more, prophets like Haggai and Zechariah had wowed them with the awesome blessings that awaited them once they finished the Temple. The people listened, and listened, and listened some more. But they did nothing.

Finally God said to them, "That's enough listening. Get to work!" It was a rude awakening, but they needed the push. We all do sometimes.

/////// HOT READ ///////

Why do people find it so easy to trust in everything else but God? Zechariah 10:2.

——> ON THE BIG DAY <

On that day I will set out to destroy all the nations that attack Jerusalem.
Zechariah 12:9.

he book of Zechariah closes with several prophecies that can be tough to understand. The overall prophecy concerns the end of time, specifically the Day of
the Lord, when the wicked are judged. The following excerpt from *The Message*
paints a vivid picture for us.

"God's Message concerning Israel, God's Decree—the very God who threw
the skies into space, set earth on a firm foundation, and breathed his own life into
men and women: 'Watch for this: I'm about to turn Jerusalem into a cup of strong
drink that will have the people who have set siege to Judah and Jerusalem stagger-
ing in a drunken stupor. On the Big Day, I'll turn Jerusalem into a huge stone
blocking the way for everyone. All who try to lift it will rupture themselves. All
the pagan nations will come together and try to get rid of it.

"'On the Big Day'—this is God speaking—'I'll throw all the war horses into
a crazed panic, and their riders along with them. But I'll keep my eye on Judah,
watching out for her at the same time that I make the enemy horses go blind. The
families of Judah will then realize, 'Why, our leaders are strong and able through
God-of-the-Angel-Armies, their personal God.'

"On the Big Day, I'll turn the families of Judah into something like a burning match in a tinder-dry forest, like a fiercely flaming torch in a barn full of hay.
They'll burn up everything and everyone in sight—people to the right, people to
the left—while Jerusalem fills up with people moving in and making themselves
at home—home again in Jerusalem.

"I, God, will begin by restoring the common households of Judah so that the
glory of David's family and the leaders in Jerusalem won't overshadow the ordinary people in Judah. On the Big Day, I'll look after everyone who lives in
Jerusalem so that the lowliest, weakest person will be as glorious as David and the
family of David itself will be godlike, like the Angel of God leading the people.

"On the Big Day, I'll make a clean sweep of all the godless nations that fought
against Jerusalem" (Zechariah 12:1-9, Message).

///////// HOT READ ///////

*Are you ready to meet God in peace? Are there sins in your life that you'd like
to confess? Why not do it now? One day God will no longer forgive sin. That
day is coming soon.*

——> LAST CHANCE <

"A son honors his father, and a servant his master. If I am a father, where is the honor due me? If I am a master, where is the respect due me?" says the Lord Almighty. "It is you, O priests, who show contempt for my name." Malachi 1:6.

e've come to the final book of the Old Testament. Give yourself a pat on the back. "You done good!" We're almost two thirds of the way through God's awesome Word, and we can't quit now. Next stop on our journey: the life and times of JESUS! But before we get to Jesus, we have to let Malachi set the stage.

Not much is known about Malachi. He is mentioned nowhere else in the Bible. From the allusion to the Jewish Temple in Malachi 1:10 and the use of various Persian words in his writing, many scholars date his ministry to around 450 B.C., right around the time of Nehemiah. After Malachi, God's voice goes silent. For the next 400-plus years, God says nothing.

Why was God silent following Malachi's ministry? I don't know the answer, but I'll take a wild guess. After Adam and Eve fell into sin in Eden, God tried just about everything to break Satan's hold on humanity and return us to Himself. That's why God called Abraham and promised to make of him a great nation that would help lead the world back to Him. God was true to His word. He raised up Israel, showered it with blessings, gave it a beautiful land, yet Israel "kicked God to the curb." So God punished His chosen people by allowing the Assyrians and Babylonians to conquer, imprison, and even kill them.

Captivity should have been enough to change their hearts, but it did not. Once they were released back to Jerusalem, they started doing the same stuff all over again. Ever done that? The priests stopped teaching and obeying God's Law. Men divorced their faithful Jewish wives and married "exotic" women from other nations, most of whom worshipped idols. They took a piece of wood, used part of it to cook their food, and carved an idol from the other—which they worshipped! Instead of returning their tithes and offerings, they kept God's resources for themselves. Nothing had changed. If I were God, I'd stop talking too. No one was listening.

Malachi's message was God's final plea for his people to fully return to Him.

///////// HOT READ /////////

What kind of sacrifices did the people give to God? Malachi 1:2-8. Didn't God deserve better?

⟶ I DO NOT CHANGE <

"I the Lord do not change. So you, O descendants of Jacob, are not destroyed."
Malachi 3:6.

hy was it that Israel, the descendants of Jacob, were not totally destroyed by their enemies? The answer is found in Malachi 3:6: God does not change.

Everything changes.

Several years ago I went to Miami for a wedding. I remember thinking to myself, *This is going be the trip of a lifetime.* You must understand that I grew up on the East Coast, where thunderstorms and snowstorms were the norm. Visions of Florida's blue skies danced in my head—at least they did until the day of the wedding. A perfect powder-blue sky turned pale-gray. Moments later rain began to fall. My perfect day became one wet nightmare.

Everything changes.

When I married my wife 13 years ago she weighed a whopping 112 pounds. Boy, was she cute! She had a sweet, perky personality and an offbeat style that I just fell in love with. That's my girl! Now she weighs 145 pounds—yep, I just told you her weight, and she's going to kill me.

I guess I better tell you the whole story. As of this writing, my wife is five months pregnant with our firstborn—a beautiful baby boy. I never thought I'd love extra pounds on my honey, but that baby has made her the most beautiful woman I have ever seen. She glows! Sometimes change just takes your breath away.

While seasons may change and times may change, we have one constant on which we can depend, and that's God. Have you ever heard someone say, "God left me"? If you ever hear someone say that, don't believe it. It's just not true. We leave God; God does not leave us. Even though Israel had failed Him many times, God was still there waiting to love them.

Here's what else God said to Israel through Malachi. "'Ever since the time of your forefathers you have turned away from my decrees and have not kept them. Return to me, and I will return to you,' says the Lord Almighty" (Malachi 3:7).

//////// HOT READ ////////

What had separated Israel from God? Malachi 3:8-12.

——> THE GOSPEL ACCORDING TO MATT <

All this took place to fulfill what the Lord had said through the prophet: "The virgin will be with child and will give birth to a son, and they will call him Immanuel"— which means, "God with us." Matthew 1:22, 23.

You may not know it, but 400 years passed by between yesterday and today. There are 400 years between the end of Malachi's ministry and the birth of Jesus. When you flipped the page in your Bible from the Old to the New Testament, you missed a bunch of time, and trust me—a lot has happened. Let's do some catching up, shall we?

If you remember, the Medes and the Persians conquered Babylon on the night of Belshazzar's famous party. In 538 B.C. King Cyrus of Persia allowed the Jewish captives to return to Jerusalem and rebuild it. The Persians fought several wars with the Greeks during the fifth century B.C. until the two signed a peace treaty in 449 B.C. Greece and Persia had decided to stop fighting, but a large threat loomed ahead.

By 275 B.C. Rome had begun to flex its muscles. First the Romans conquered the island of Sicily. Then they slowly overtook Greece, eventually turning it into a province of Rome. When Jesus was born, Rome was the superpower ruling the world. Even Jerusalem was under Roman control and occupation, ruled by a thug called Herod the Great.

Now that we're all caught up, let's get to Matt's Gospel.

Matthew, more than any of the Gospel writers, goes to great pains to prove that Jesus was the Messiah, the Anointed One, the Being to whom all the Old Testament prophecies pointed. This wasn't something that he came up with out of thin air. Jesus had changed his life, and Matt was determined to let the world know—especially his fellow Jews—that Jesus was no ordinary person.

That's why Matthew gives the full genealogy of Jesus. That's why he quoted Isaiah 7:14: "The virgin will be with child and will give birth to a son, and will call him Immanuel."

When Jesus touches your life, as He did Matthew's, you have to tell the world.

####### HOT READ //////

Who prepared the way for Jesus' ministry? Matthew 3:1-4. Did you notice how John the Baptist was dressed? Weird, huh? Did this have anything to do with his message?

——> SPIT ON IT <

Blessed are you when people insult you, persecute you and falsely say all kinds of evil against you because of me. Matthew 5:11.

There's so much to write about today that I don't know where to begin. I thought about focusing on Satan's temptation of Jesus in the wilderness. The whole episode left me with a lot of questions. Why did the Holy Spirit lead Jesus into temptation? And what made the devil think that he could offer Jesus stuff that already belonged to Him? Dude, that doesn't make any sense.

Jesus' temptation tempted me, but then I read Matthew 5:11, 12, and the following story came to mind.

"The Communist soldiers had discovered their illegal Bible study. [As the pastor was reading from the Bible,] men with guns broke into the home, terrorizing the believers who had gathered there to worship. The leading officer pointed his gun at the pastor's head. 'Hand me your Bible,' he demanded.

"Reluctantly, the pastor handed over his Bible, his prized possession. With a sneer on his face, the guard threw the Word of God on the floor at his feet. 'We will let you go,' he growled, 'but first, you must spit on this book of lies. Anyone who refuses will be shot.'

"A soldier pointed his gun at one of the men. 'You first.' The man slowly got up and knelt down by the Bible. Reluctantly, he spit on it, praying, 'Father, please forgive me.' He was allowed to leave.

"A woman was nudged forward. In tears, she could barely do what the soldier demanded. She spit only a little, but it was enough. She too was allowed to leave.

"Quietly a young girl came forward. Overcome with love for her Lord, she knelt down and picked up the Bible. She wiped off the spit with her dress. 'What have they done to Your Word? Please forgive them,' she prayed. The Communist soldier shot her."★

★ dc Talk, *Jesus Freaks,* p. 31.

——> I AM WILLING <

Jesus reached out His hand and touched the man. "I am willing," he said. "Be clean!" Immediately he was cured. Matthew 8:3.

As I read through the book of Matthew, I can't help wondering what it would've been like to watch Jesus in action. Imagine being there when Jesus said, "Do not store up for yourselves treasures on earth, where moth and rust destroy, and where thieves break in and steal. But store up for yourselves treasures in heaven, where moth and rust do not destroy, and where thieves do not break in and steal. For where your treasure is, there your heart will be also" (Matthew 6:19, 20). With that bit of advice Jesus tried to save His listeners a world of hurt and disappointment. Many of them were trying to get as much money as they could.

Jesus gave powerful advice, but nothing moved people like watching Jesus heal the sick—especially people with leprosy. Leprosy was the AIDS of Jesus' time. Those who had it were quarantined and scorned. God Himself had given Israel the rules lepers should follow.

"Now the leper on whom the sore is, his clothes shall be torn and his head bare; and he shall cover his mustache, and cry, 'Unclean! Unclean!' He shall be unclean. All the days he has the sore he shall be unclean" (Leviticus 13:45, 46, NKJV). Who wants to live like that?

The leper who approached Jesus (Matthew 8) took a huge chance. Leprosy is an ugly disease. It damages the sensory nerves so that the sick often injure themselves but don't know it. These injuries, usually to the hands and feet, cause open sores, which get infected. The infection goes through the body, making them even sicker. They may lose fingers and toes.

Can't you see the crowd around Jesus grab their noses and turn away from the gruesome leper? The man saw them, but nothing was going to stop him. This was his moment with Jesus.

"Are you willing to clean me up?" he cried. At that, Jesus walked over and *touched* his sore-crusted body. Right then the leper knew that Jesus was different—He accepted him just the way he was.

"I am willing to clean you up," Jesus said with a smile. "It's done!"

HOT READ

Why did Jesus say that the way to heaven is "narrow" and the way to destruction "broad" (Matthew 7:13, 14)?

——> TRAINING DAY <

Heal the sick, cleanse the lepers, raise the dead, cast out demons. Freely you have received, freely give. Matthew 10:8, NKJV.

ave you read Matthew 9 yet? I know we're moving on to Matthew 10-12 today, but there's something that you absolutely must not miss in Matthew 9. Notice that the first person that Jesus raised from the dead was a young girl. There's a good chance that she was a teenager. Jesus raises young people back to life, friend. No matter how dead you may think you are, no matter how many people have written you off, Jesus can bring you back to life. Believe it!

OK. I just had to get that off my chest. Matthew 9 always gets to me!

But then there's Matthew 10. You can't read this chapter and not get all "tingly" inside. It gives me goose bumps, family.

Here's the setup. Jesus called His disciples together and startled them.

"You guys have been with Me for a while now," He began. "You've seen what God has been doing through Me." They all nodded. The Bible doesn't say it, but I'd bet that Peter piped in, "Oh, yeah! You're one Bad Man, Jesus!" That's what I would've said, and Jesus would have promptly reminded me that there was nothing "bad" about Him. He would be right, of course.

"Now it's your turn, fellas! I told you that the harvest is ripe, but there aren't enough people to pick the grain [see Matthew 9:35-37]. Well, saddle up, boys. It's time to go do some picking." The disciples looked confused. Whatever did He mean?

"I want you to heal the sick, raise the dead, cleanse the lepers, drive out demons, and give people what I have given you." The disciples couldn't believe their ears.

"You mean, do what *You* do?" they chimed almost in unison.

"Yeah," said Jesus. "You've got the power. This is your training day. Use what you've got, and do what God wants."

Friend, God has given you power to make a difference in the world. Don't ever doubt it. You have a special role to play in bringing lost people back to God. If you are willing, God will use you, as He did the disciples.

/////// HOT READ ///////

Was the disciples' witnessing experience going to be easy? Matthew 10:16-19.

——> LOSING KENNY <

When Jesus heard what had happened, he withdrew by boat privately to a
solitary place. Hearing of this, the crowds followed him on foot from the towns.
Matthew 14:13.

enny was a hustler. Not one of those on the street corners of some major
city. No, he was a hustler on the basketball court. Possessed with great size, big
hops (jumping ability), and a nonstop motor (heart), he was tough to handle
around the basket. Kenny had game.

Kenny more than held his own on the basketball court, but he truly shined
off it. We met during my freshman year at Oakwood. He was a smooth, lanky cat
from the Atlanta, who made friends easily and knew everyone. He was always
smiling, always upbeat, and always kind. On top of that, he loved God!

Nights, when we guys returned to our dorm, a Ping-Pong tournament would
break out in the "wreck" room. Kenny and his roommate, Brian, were some of
the biggest talkers around.

"B, I'm 'bout to wax this boy," Kenny would retort to some far-superior
Ping-Pong player. It didn't matter much to Kenny whether he won or lost. What
mattered most to him was that everyone was having a great time, that "the broth-
erhood" was running deep.

After graduation we all went our separate ways and lost track of each other. Now
and then Kenny and I saw each other during Oakwood's alumni weekend or when
I got a chance to visit Atlanta. Whenever we did, it was just like old times. Kenny
had married his college sweetheart, and they had two absolutely gorgeous little girls.

Then one day I received a call from one of my brothers in Atlanta, and almost collapsed at his news. Kenny, the guy with enough life to power a small city,
was dead. For several days I struggled to come to terms with Kenny's death. Why
did God allow his life to be cut short when he was just hitting his stride? I still
don't know why!

Jesus understood what it was like to lose a friend. When Herod beheaded
John the Baptist, Jesus dropped everything, got on a boat, and sailed away to a private place where He could weep for his friend—and Jesus was God. Nothing can
prepare you for the loss of someone you love, but it helps to know that Jesus understands.

/////// HOT READ ///////

Read Matthew 15:29-39. What lesson(s) did Jesus teach the disciples here?

⎯⎯> SHEEP <

What do you think? If a man owns a hundred sheep, and one of them wanders away, will he not leave the ninety-nine on the hills and go to look for the one that wandered off? Matthew 18:12.

They don't have claws or sharp teeth, the stink bomb of a skunk, the speed of a cheetah, the stab of a porcupine, the bite of a snake, the kick of a donkey, the persistence of ants, the horns of a bull, the growl of a lion, or the aggressiveness of a tiger.

Nope. Sheep don't have a whole lot going for them. In fact, their best defense is also their most dangerous trait: sheep are followers. No story makes the point more clearly than one I came across a few years ago.

It was in Istanbul, Turkey, July 2005. Several shepherds were grazing their sheep on a hillside. After keeping the sheep in line all morning, the shepherds decided to take a break to have some breakfast. (Bad idea.) They were chomping down on their grub when one of them noticed something curious. It appeared that the large flock of sheep they'd brought to the hillside was dwindling before their eyes. Then one of the men looked closer and noticed that the sheep were plodding toward a nearby cliff. *What in the world is happening?* they thought in a panic.

The shepherds leaped up and ran toward the sheep. To their horror they saw that the sheep were innocently walking to their deaths. In fact, by the time they arrived, more than 1,500 sheep had walked off the cliff. A mound of dead sheep lay at the bottom of the cliff, and by then the mound was cushioning the fall of the remaining sheep. Can you believe that? It's true!

Of all the animals to which Jesus could have compared you and me, He chose sheep. That's not a "co-inkydink." Jesus knew that, like sheep, humans are prone to wander off and jump off cliffs. Think for a moment. At a time when one in every four teens in North America has a sexually transmitted disease, why do teens keep having sex? That's like jumping off a cliff, don't you think?

Jesus knows this about us, and that's why He promises to drop everything to come find us when we go astray.

HOT READ

What did Jesus say was the secret to greatness? Matthew 18:1-4.

——> THE SADDEST STORY IN THE BIBLE <

When the young man heard this, he went away sad, because he had great wealth.
Matthew 19:22.

Y ou might argue with me about which story in the Bible is the saddest, but you have to agree that Matthew 19's story of the rich young ruler is up there on the list. This guy had everything going for him—a great "rep," deep pockets, a call from Jesus. So what happened?

"Another day, a man stopped Jesus and asked, 'Teacher, what good thing must I do to get eternal life?'

"Jesus said, 'Why do you question me about what's good? *God* is the One who is good. If you want to enter the life of God, just do what he tells you.'

The man asked, 'What in particular?'

"Jesus said, 'Don't murder, don't commit adultery, don't steal, don't lie, honor your father and mother, and love your neighbor as you do yourself.'

"The young man said, 'I've done all that. What's left?'

"If you want to give it all you've got,' Jesus replied, 'go sell your possessions; give everything to the poor. All your wealth will then be in heaven. Then come follow me.'

"That was the last thing the young man expected to hear. And so, crestfallen, he walked away. He was holding on tight to a lot of things, and he couldn't bear to let go.

"As he watched him go, Jesus told his disciples, 'Do you have any idea how difficult it is for the rich to enter God's kingdom? Let me tell you, it's easier to gallop a camel through a needle's eye than for the rich to enter God's kingdom'" (Matthew 19:16-24, Message).

Jesus was known to spend all night healing and helping people. He was never in a hurry. When He encouraged the rich young man to go sell what he had and follow Him, Jesus was willing to wait for him—no matter how long it took to liquidate his assets. It was the invitation of a lifetime, but it was more than the man was willing to do.

What are you willing to give up for Jesus?

HOT READ

Pay careful attention to Matthew 21. Many of the people who celebrated Jesus later called for Him to be crucified.

——> CRUNCH TIME <

Watch out that no one deceives you. For many will come in my name, claiming, 'I am the Christ,' and will deceive many. Matthew 24:4, 5.

runch time. It's the time in the game that someone has to hit the big shot, drive in the go-ahead run, or swat an ace! Jesus knew that His testing time was coming. He'd lived His entire life with the knowledge that His mission on earth would lead Him to a tragic death. What kept Jesus going was knowing that through His sacrifice *everyone* who believed in Him and accepted His sacrifice for their sins would be saved.

While sitting on the Mount of Olives overlooking Jerusalem, Jesus began to prepare His disciples for the trials that both He and they would soon face. He'd hinted to them that He would one day suffer and die, but they didn't believe Him. He even told them that He would go away to heaven, but that one day He come back again to put an end to sin once and for all.

What would be the signs of Jesus' second coming? Matthew 24 details several, but the first one that Jesus chose to mention was "Many will come in my name, claiming, 'I am the Christ, and will deceive many" (verse 5). Jesus must have thought this sign was important, as He gave it first. And that prediction has come true many times. Here are just a few of the people who have claimed to be Jesus.

Jose Luis de Jesus Miranda—organizer of the Growing in Grace church who claims that the resurrected Christ "integrated himself within me."

Luc Jouret—leader of the Order of the Solar Temple and was believed to be the third reincarnation of Jesus Christ. He led his cult in a mass suicide.

Charles Manson—founder of the "Manson Family" who led his commune to murder several people. He's currently serving a life sentence in the California penal system.

Jung Myung Seok—founder of Providence Church, was an international fugitive wanted for rape, among other crimes. He was captured in May 2007.

How would the disciples sniff out the Jesus impostors? They would have to watch! They would have to know God's Word, follow it, and test all would-be Jesus Christs by it.

//////// HOT READ ////////

Read the rest of Matthew 24. Do you believe that Jesus is coming soon? Are you ready? Talk to God right now. Ask Him to show you the areas in your life that need His touch.

——> YOUR WORST DAY <

Then he began to call down curses on himself and he swore to them, "I don't know the man!" Matthew 26:74.

Ever notice that things get better when certain people show up? They don't have to be the best-dressed or the most popular; they're known more for what they have on the inside than what they look like on the outside. Know anyone like that? I do.

On June 9, 2008, newspapers and television stations across the nation reported the story of a hero named Roger Stone. An expert sailor, Stone was serving as a safety officer on a boat participating in a regatta in the Gulf of Mexico. When the boat started taking on water, Stone knew that he had little time to get four sailing students off the boat before it sank.

Stone made sure that the students had life jackets and anything else that would help them survive until they could be rescued. He did what he could for the students, and after spending 26 hours afloat in the Gulf of Mexico, they and another safety officer were found alive. However, Stone's lifeless body was pulled from the sunken vessel.

Roger Stone was the kind of person who would help anyone in need, and that gift cost him his life. His presence made the world a better place to live in. How so? He possessed a God-given ability to put others before himself, an ability to be a blessing by simply *being.* We each have this gift, but few ever use it.

When I think about this awesome story, I can't help thinking about Peter, Jesus' "bigmouthed" disciple. Peter was the one who spoke up before any of the other disciples could speak. He was the daring disciple who stepped out into the water in the dead of night to walk to Jesus (Matthew 14:28). Peter never expected that he would ever deny Jesus, but he did.

Jesus knew that Peter had a blind side—that he was too cocky, too sure of himself. Jesus knew that under the right amount of pressure, Peter would break down and deny Him—not once, not twice, but three times. But Jesus also knew what Peter had on the *inside,* and what a power for good he would become.

Jesus knows our weaknesses—and our heart. That is why we must give all that we are to Him.

///////// HOT READ /////////

Read Matthew 28:1-6. What would have happened if Jesus had not been resurrected?

——> "MR. RIGHT-NOW" <

He got up, took his mat and walked out in full view of them all. This amazed everyone and they praised God, saying, "We have never seen anything like this!"
Mark 2:12.

y wife hates to wait for anything. She's impatient. Of course, she doesn't think she is—people who are impatient never think that they are. Here's a case in point.

One day we were scheduled to meet someone at our home. We were going to leave work and rush home to be sure that we both there, uh, waiting. I drove by the office where my wife works, scooped her up, and headed to the house. We got there about five minutes early. I could see her blood beginning to boil at the idea of sitting still for five whole minutes.

I kept talking to try to keep her calm, but an unexpected development torpedoed my plan. The guy we were waiting on was late, and he didn't even bother to call.

"Where's this guy, Dwain?" she said rather softly. We'd had this patience discussion several times before. I knew this "soft first serve" was just the preamble. A few more minutes of waiting would no doubt lead to some major "hateration"!

"I dunno, sweetheart. He said he'd meet us here at six. He's probably caught up in traffic."

"Aye!" she sighed. "This waiting is killing me." To her credit, she just chilled out. We talked for another 30 minutes or so, and then our friend showed up. Just when I thought she had forgotten the wait, out came "'Bout time he showed up."

If you're at all like my wife, then you're going to love the book of Mark. Mark is one of the coolest books in the Bible, because John Mark, its author, wanted to show that Jesus could respond to any crisis we face in life—immediately. That's the *hot* word to watch for.

Though Mark was not one of the original disciples of Jesus, he was a close friend of Peter's. He wrote this book when Nero, the Roman emperor, was trying to kill all Christians (A.D. 60-65). It was during this time that both Peter and Paul were executed. Under constant threat to his life, Mark still believed that Jesus could do the impossible—immediately.

//////// HOT READ ////////

Not sure what you can do on the Sabbath? Read what Jesus did in Mark 3:1-6.

——> HOMETOWN ZERO <

When the Sabbath came, he began to teach in the synagogue, and many who heard him were amazed. "Where did this man get these things?' they asked. "What's this wisdom that has been given him, that he even does miracles!" Mark 6:2.

There's so much to love about Mark 4-6 that I don't know where to begin. The healing of the demon-possessed man in Mark 5 always gives me chills. It reminds me of the young man who felt that "something" in his bedroom was trying to kill him. After he'd go to sleep, "something" would grab him by the neck and choke him.

After this happened several times, the teen asked Ron, his youth leader, to come and sleep in his room for a night. So Ron went to the teen's home to sleep in his bed. Sure enough, the same thing happened. The force grabbed Ron by the neck, strangling him in his sleep. He awoke yelling the name of Jesus, and the force went away.

I've heard stories like that before and written them off as fiction, but Ron himself—the Ron mentioned above—gave me the blow-by-blow of what had happened that night!

Mark 5 also introduced us to a woman who had a major bleeding problem for 12 years. That's a long time to suffer without a cure, don't you think? I once met a teenager who had to endure daily shots of insulin to control his diabetes. This story reminds me that Jesus sees, feels, and heals. The woman with the blood problem pressed her way to Jesus and managed to nick the hem of His clothes, and she was healed. Got a problem? Use your faith to touch Jesus.

The exorcisms and healings that Jesus performed should have been proof enough that He was no ordinary human being. Most people knew that, but not the people in Jesus' hometown of Nazareth. To them he was nothing more than Jesus, the carpenter's boy.

Mark commented, "He could not do any miracles there, except lay his hands on a few sick people and heal them. And he was amazed at their lack of faith" (Mark 6:5, 6).

Jesus should have been a hometown hero, but instead He was treated like a zero. Sometimes people who know you well try to deny your gifts. Don't let them bother you. Just keep using your talents for God.

///////// HOT READ ////////

Is God's seed falling on fertile soil in your life? Mark 4:13-20.

---> BEHIND THE SEEN <

But when He had turned around and looked at His disciples, He rebuked Peter, say-ing, "Get behind me, Satan! For you are not mindful of the things of God, but the things of men." Mark 8:33, NKJV.

t's takes a brave person to rebuke Jesus. In case you're unfamiliar with the meaning of the word "rebuke," here's what it means: to criticize or reprimand someone, usually sharply. Peter did that to Jesus in front of all of the disciples. Now, that's bold.

Why did Peter do this? Mark gives the answer in Mark 8:31: "He [Jesus] then began to teach them that the Son of Man must suffer many things and be rejected by the elders, chief priests, and teachers of the law, and that he must be killed and after three days rise again." Peter was not ready to hear any talk of death from the Man that he had come to love deeply. Jesus saw through Peter's fierce reply to the being pulling Peter's strings.

Satan was using Peter to take Jesus' mind away from His reason for coming to earth. Jesus came to die for the sins of all humanity, and here was Peter telling him that He was not going to die. This wasn't Peter talking, Jesus concluded, so he met Satan's fire with fire.

" 'Get behind me, Satan!' he said. 'You do not have in mind the things of God, but the things of men' " (verse 33). Translation? Jesus knew that Satan was trying to get Him to care more about His life, the things of everyday living, than His mission and ministry, the things of God. By the way, Satan is also trying to get you and me to do the same thing: to take the easy way out and please our-selves instead of God. But Jesus hadn't finished making His point.

"Then he called the crowd to him along with his disciples and said: 'If any-one would come after me, he must deny himself and take up his cross and follow me. For whoever wants to save his life will lose it, but whoever loses his life for me and for the gospel will save it. What good is it for a man to gain the whole world, yet forfeit his soul?'" (verses 34, 35).

Don't miss Jesus' point. Doing God's will may cost us much, and we have to be prepared to lose our lives. But someone who lose their life for Jesus will joy-fully find it again.

//////// HOT READ ////////

Did Jesus kick Peter to the curb? Mark 9:1-8. What does this tell you about Jesus' patience with people who make mistakes? Jesus saw greatness in Peter.

—> GET OUT <

And as he taught them, he said, "Is it not written: 'My house will be called a house of prayer for all nations'? But you have made it 'a den of robbers.'" Mark 11:17.

ome things just go together. Dwain and Kemba, for instance. It even rhymes. (You may not think that it rhymes, but just wait till you're married for 12 years. Everything starts to rhyme. It's all sweet music!)

Some things don't go together. I once saw a close friend whip up a sandwich. You will not believe what she did. She pulled out two slices of bread and a jar of peanut butter. So far so good. I didn't pay her much attention. After all, who doesn't know how to make a peanut-butter-and-jelly sandwich?

I looked away for a moment and then looked back in her direction. Horror of horrors, she had smeared a thick dab of peanut butter on each slice. Then she did the unthinkable. She pulled out a bag of barbecue potato chips and proceeded to lay down a bed of salty chips on one side of her sandwich. She put the slices together and took a big bite. Watching her do it was like watching a mad scientist in a lab savoring his ghastly creation. Yuck!

Here's something else that doesn't go together: money changers and temples. What would you do if you walked into your church one Sabbath and found a bunch of people yelling and holding up American and Canadian dollars, European euros and Japanese yen? You'd be upset.

That's exactly what when Jesus found when He arrived at the Temple in Jerusalem. Every Israelite male age 20 or older had to pay a half-shekel offering to God. And once a year Jews journeyed from all over the world to attend Passover at the Temple. They brought their offerings, or in the Temple courtyard purchased a lamb to sacrifice. And that's how the money changers came up with an ingenious way to make some quick cash.

They created a Temple coin and charged the pilgrims a high rate to exchange their money for the valuable Temple coin. Worse than that travesty of justice, the priests who ran the Temple did nothing about it. When Jesus saw what the Temple had become, He lost it. He drove out the money-changers violently.

/////// HOT READ ///////

Read Mark 10:35-38. How did James and John's request affect the disciples?

> DESPERATE PEOPLE <

Now the Passover and the Feast of Unleavened Bread were only two days away, and the chief priests and the teachers of the law were looking for some sly way to arrest Jesus and kill him. "But not during the Feast," they said, "or the people may riot." Mark 14:1.

It's hard to believe that religious leaders would be caught plotting murder, but that's the case in Mark 14. The target? Jesus. The hit men? The chief priests at the Temple in Jerusalem.

Last year a *Dateline* NBC special showed videos of several would-be criminals. One guy was determined to rob a liquor store. He fell twice while trying to climb onto the roof of the store, but he pressed on. When he finally got on the roof, it collapsed, and he fell through onto the floor of the store, several feet below. He then packed up bottles of liquor and tried to make his way out of the front doors, which were locked tight. Unable to break through the shatterproof glass doors, he sat down and had a drink as he waited for the police, who were making their way in to arrest him.

That criminal was quite a character, but there were others that weren't nearly as funny. One man had grown tired of having to pay child support to his wife. So guess what he decided to do? He tried to hire a hit man to kill his wife and his kids.

"She's taking me for everything I've got," said the short, pudgy man. "Something's gotta be done about it." The "hit man"—an undercover cop—nodded his head.

"So whaddaya want done? An accident or something like that?" he asked.

"Dead. I want her and the kids dead. The two older ones sleep so hard that they won't feel a thing. You got silencers, right?" The whole conversation had a matter-of-fact quality to it that was surreal. It was like watching a crime drama—not like real life. But before the man could leave the room, the cops swooped in and arrested him. Just think how his ex-wife must have felt!

Desperate people do very desperate things. To get rid of Jesus, the chief priests plotted to kill him—but not because He'd done anything wrong. They wanted to kill Him because He did everything right. It made them look like the hypocrites they were. Jesus knew what it felt like to be hated simply for doing what was right.

////// HOT READ //////

How do you avoid caving in to peer pressure? Mark 15:15.

——> CLOSE EXAMINATION <

Therefore, since I myself have carefully investigated everything from the beginning, it seemed good also to me to write an orderly account for you, most excellent Theophilus. Luke 1:3.

When I was a kid, it was my father who took us to the doctor. We'd walk into his office, sign our names on the registry, and prepare to be poked, prodded—and questioned.

"So, how's it going, Neil?" The doctor usually called me by my middle name.

"Everything's great, Doc."

"Good!" came the quick reply as he tapped my knees, or looked down my throat, or whatever else doctors do. (BTW, why is it that doctors always try to talk to you while they're shoving a stick down your throat?) I always braced myself for his next question.

"Messing with girls yet?" he'd ask softly, his fingers penetrating my ear canal.

"Nope." The doc was cool, but *we* weren't. (My dad was right there in the room. To speak of such things would be suicide.)

My doctor was thorough. When you went to him for a physical, you'd also got a checkup from the neck up. He didn't want to miss anything. Doctors are like that. They're careful to get all the facts and lay them out in the right order. Careful screening of patients helps doctors make the right diagnoses—most of the time.

The writer of the book of Luke—Luke—was a doctor, and a very close friend of the apostle Paul's. They traveled all over the world together spreading the gospel. Luke is also the writer of the book of Acts.

Of the four Gospels—Matthew, Mark, Luke, and John—Luke's is the most accurate and gives the most complete history of Jesus' life. You see, when Luke wrote his book, he didn't have us in mind. He was writing to a new believer named Theophilus. Why? "So that you may know the certainty of the things you have been taught" (Luke 1:4). Luke was sharing the "good news of salvation," which had been shared with him. He did his best to get it right—perfectly right!

////// HOT READ //////

Why did God choose a young, poor female to be the mother of Jesus? Luke 1:46-55. Why didn't God get someone from a more distinguished background?

——> GETTING IT RIGHT <

One of those days Jesus went out to a mountainside to pray, and spent the night praying to God. Luke 6:12.

ave you ever had to make a big decision? And no, I'm not talking about Nintendo Wii or Xbox 360. I'm talking about something big, such as what career you'd like to pursue for the rest of your life. I know, I know. You're only in high school, right? Hey, it's never too early to start talking to God about the big stuff.

Making good decisions is serious business. Did you know that you could get a Ph.D. in a field called decision sciences? For instance, Duke University's Fuqua School of Business offers one of the most highly rated degrees in this field. But I hear you thinking. *I'm not spending four years of college, plus another five years of graduate school, to get a PhD. in making decisions.* I hear you, family! I'm not sure I would either.

If B-School is not your thing, maybe you can follow Charles Foster's Seven Rules for Making Great Decisions. (Yup, he's a Ph.D.) What are those rules?

1. Focus on the most important thing.
2. Turn big decisions into a series of little decisions.
3. Base your decision on self-acceptance.
4. Consider all the good things your decision can bring.
5. Get what you need to make your decision a success.
6. Keep things as simple as possible.
7. Consider all your options.

Pretty good stuff, don't you think? I'd follow those.

The Ph.D. in decision sciences is great, I'm sure, and so is Mr. Foster's Seven Rules for Making Great Decisions. However, if I had to choose only one shot to make a great decision, I'd do it the way Jesus did: I would spend all night in prayer talking to God.

That's what Jesus did the night before He chose the 12 men who would become His disciples. Eleven of those men went on to change the world!

////////// HOT READ //////////

Do you know when to take a break? Luke 4:40-42.

——> NO, HE DIDN'T! <

When the Pharisee who had invited him saw this, he said to himself, "If this man were a prophet, he would know who is touching him and what kind of woman she is— that she is a sinner." Luke 7:39.

how me your friends, and I'll tell you who you are. Have you ever heard that before? *Birds of a feather flock together.* Surely some adult has dropped that one on you a time or two. Well, my wife told me a story that illustrates the truth hidden in those two sayings.

One day when she was 16 or 17, she prepared to go on a date with a boy from her school. She'd just begun going out with guys, and as you might imagine, her parents were not adjusting very well to the change. Usually she'd hang with her girlfriends, but times were "a-changin'."

And somehow she'd forgotten to tell her dad that her date for the evening was Lamar.*

"Sweetheart, who are you going out with tonight?" her father asked softly.

"Lamar. Why do you ask?" came the quick reply.

Her father's voice grew very calm. He never answered her question. Instead he said: "You know this is the last time that you'll be going out with him, right?"

"Yes, Dad." And with that the conversation was over.

She told me that her dad did not want her hanging around Lamar because he had a very bad reputation. Her father did not want Lamar's bad rep to rub off on his little girl. I totally understand his thinking. Dude, I'm so glad Lamar didn't put his paws on my girl.

Yet Jesus hung out with people who had bad reputations. But let's be clear, friends. He was Jesus. He had spent 30 years of his life preparing to minister to everyone that society had to offer. Jesus came to earth to seek and save lost men, women, and children.

Sometimes we think that we are strong enough to be around all kinds of evil influences. We don't think that they can affect us. But they definitely can, and will! Be careful about which person you hang with. You are called to be Christlike, but you are not Christ.

———
* not his real name

//////// HOT READ ////////
What storm in your life do you need Jesus to calm? Luke 8:22-25.

——> DON'T WORRY <

For where your treasure is, there your heart will be also. Luke 12:34.

omeone is targeting you. Yes, *you*. They say you have money to burn, and you spend most of it on luxury items, such as clothing, electronics, and music. They say that you have a powerful influence over what your parents spend their money on because they want to please you. You are a marketer's dream.

Marketers may target you, but if you live by the words of today's text, they'll never catch you.

"Don't fuss about what's on the table at mealtimes or if the clothes in your closet are in fashion. There is far more to your inner life than the food you put in your stomach, more to your outer appearance than the clothes you hang on your body. Look at the ravens, free and unfettered, not tied down to a job description, carefree in the care of God. And you count far more.

"Has anyone by fussing before the mirror ever gotten taller by so much as an inch? If fussing can't even do that, why fuss at all? Walk into the fields and look at the wildflowers. They don't fuss with their appearance—but have you ever seen color and design quite like it? The ten best-dressed men and women in the country look shabby alongside them. If God gives such attention to the wildflowers, most of them never even seen, don't you think he'll attend to you, take pride in you, do his best for you?

"What I'm trying to do here is get you to relax, not be so preoccupied with *getting* so you can respond to God's *giving*. People who don't know God and the way he works fuss over these things, but you know both God and how he works. Steep yourself in God-reality, God-initiative, God-provisions. You'll find all your everyday human concerns will be met. Don't be afraid of missing out. You're my dearest friends! The Father wants to give you the very kingdom itself.

"Be generous. Give to the poor. Get yourselves a bank that can't go bankrupt, a bank in heaven far from bankrobbers, safe from embezzlers, a bank you can bank on. It's obvious, isn't it? The place where your treasure is, is the place you will most want to be, and end up being" (Luke 12:22-34, Message).

////// HOT READ //////

Why did Jesus call the Pharisees hypocrites? Luke 11:42-53.

——> MISTAKEN IDENTITY <

"We ate and drank with you, and you taught in our streets." But he will reply, "I don't know you or where you come from. Away from me, all you evildoers!"
Luke 13:26, 27.

here's nothing quite as embarrassing as mistaking a total stranger for a friend. I tend to pride myself on my ability to remember faces, but not after one embarrassing moment.

It happened at one of those big young adult ministry events that I go to on behalf of *Insight* magazine. I can't tell you how much fun it is to run into old friends from way back. Two winters ago I was in Dallas, Texas, when I caught up with my homie Travis. We hadn't seen each other for more than 10 years. Back in college Travis was the loudest guy I had ever met in my life. Seeing him again brought back great memories and some not-so-great ones—such as the time he decided to wrestle me. He outweighed me by 50 pounds. I held my own for a while, but then he got the best of me. He's a big boy!

At that same event I saw a college friend of mine weaving her way through a crowd of people. I couldn't remember her name, but who needs names? She'll recognize me, and I'll recognize her, and everything will be peachy.

I knew I had to move fast to catch her before she disappeared into one of the many seminar rooms, so I began knocking people over to get to her.

"Excuse me. Pardon me. Sorry. My bad." I did my best to let the people know that I meant them no harm. After a brisk final stride, I finally reached her. Tapping her on the shoulder, I smiled broadly, and said what you say when you can't remember a name. "Hey, girl! How you doin'?" My friend spun around to greet me. She was sure that I was a friend. Why would a guy who didn't even know her part a Red Sea of people just to say hi? But the instant she turned, it was clear I'd made a big mistake.

"Um, I'm so sorry," I stuttered. "I thought you were someone else." She smiled and kept walking. It was so ugly.

Sometimes you think you know someone, and it turns out you don't know them at all. You may know who Jesus is, but does Jesus know you?

////// HOT READ //////

What point was Jesus making in Luke 14:8-11? To whom was He talking?

——> A SINNER'S PRAYER <

I tell you that this man, rather than the other, went home justified before God. For everyone who exalts himself will be humbled, and he who humbles himself will be exalted. Luke 18:14.

Friend, today's Bible reading is really special. I'm so stoked right now that I'm not really sure where to begin. Should I write about the crook that Jesus complimented in Luke 16? I know it sounds crazy, but Jesus told His followers to take a close look at how crooked people in the world use their knowledge to do crooked things (Luke 16:8). His point? In the same way that crooks use their ingenuity and grit to do Satan's work, you should use your ingenuity and grit to do God's work. You can learn a lot from a crook.

What about the leper who returned to thank Jesus for healing him (Luke 17:15, 16)? Jesus had healed 10 lepers, but only one of them bothered to say thank You—and he was a Samaritan. Jesus was a Jew. Jews and Samaritans were like the Crips and Bloods of Jesus' time. There was no love lost between them. The Samaritan was so flabbergasted that a Jew would even stop to help a Samaritan—especially one with leprosy—that he "threw himself at Jesus' feet and thanked him" (verse 16). How can you not love that? That is *hot!*

But I'm amped up over a small parable Jesus told about two men who went to the Temple to pray. One was a Pharisee and the other a tax collector. Tax collectors back in Jesus' time were about as loved as skunks are today. People hated their guts because they worked for the cruel Roman government led by Herod. They'd hike the taxes to make extra money off their own people.

The Pharisee began to pray, and his prayer told you everything you'd ever want to know about him: "God, I thank you that I am not like other men—robbers, evildoers, adulterers." OK, that I can sorta kinda get, but then he added this little nugget: . . . "or even like this tax collector. I fast twice a week and give a tenth of all I get." (Dude, did he just throw most of the world under the bus? Sure looks that way, doesn't it?)

The tax collector knew that he was messed up and in need of help. He refused to even look up at God as he cried out, "God, have mercy on me, a sinner."

Which one of the two men left the synagogue saved that day?

///////// HOT READ /////////

What kind of example are you setting for young kids? Luke 17:1, 2.

⟶ I WISH YOU KNEW <

As he approached Jerusalem and saw the city, he wept over it and said, "If you, even you, had only known on this day what would bring you peace—but now it is hidden from your eyes." Luke 19:41, 42.

've never cried over a city. I have never driven into the city of Philadelphia, where I used to live, and broken down in tears. When Hurricane Katrina destroyed New Orleans, the sight of people huddled on rooftops and wading through waist-high water tugged at my heart. But I didn't cry even then. Have you ever boo-hooed over a city? Chances are you haven't.

As Jesus made His way to Jerusalem, a flood of emotions filled His heart. During most of His ministry Jesus had done His best to avoid the spotlight. He would often tell those He healed and helped not to publicize what He'd done for them. All the glory belonged to His Father. Even so, His fame spread so far that He had to leave Jerusalem for a while, as the Pharisees were ready to put a violent stop to His "act." Now, as Jesus prepared to enter Jerusalem, hordes of people He had helped hailed Him as their king. He rode triumphantly into the city, but He knew that the hour of His trial was just ahead and that He would not escape death.

Jesus paused on a nearby hill as the afternoon sun bathed Jerusalem's beautiful Temple with its golden light. If we'd seen the city right then, we might say it glowed like an enchanted village from one of J.R.R. Tolkien's books. At any rate, the sight filled the crowds with admiration. They looked toward Jesus to see His response, and were perplexed at what they saw. Jesus had grown sorrowful and quiet. Tears rolled down His face. Here's how Ellen White described it.

"It was the sight of Jerusalem that pierced the heart of Jesus—Jerusalem that had rejected the Son of God and scorned His love, that refused to be convinced by His mighty miracles, and was about to take His life. He saw what she was in her guilt of rejecting her Redeemer, and what she might have been had she accepted Him who alone could heal her wound. He had come to save her; how could He give her up?" (*The Desire of Ages*, p. 576).

//////// HOT READ ////////

Read Luke 20:20-26. What kind of citizens should Christians be?

——> SATAN ENTERED JUDAS <

Then Satan entered Judas, called Iscariot, one of the Twelve. Luke 22:3.

I didn't get very far in today's reading before the verse above stopped me cold. Is there a scarier piece of Scripture than this? "Then Satan entered Judas" is quite a sound bite. You can't just run by that one.

Then Satan entered Judas. Those four words explain why Judas betrayed the One who had come to give him eternal life. Most people think that Judas did it for the money. The Pharisees were looking for some way to get rid of Jesus. Everything they tried had failed, but their luck changed when "Satan entered Judas," because after "Satan entered Judas," he "went to the chief priests and the officers of the temple guard and discussed with them how he might betray Jesus" (Luke 22:4). Notice that they didn't go to find him. Judas somehow found them, and I believe it's because—let's all say it together—"Satan entered Judas."

Ancient Roman historians have passed down to us the story of another "Judas" who did his dirty deed not long after "Satan entered Judas." His name was Marcus Junius Brutus, one of the most trusted confidants of the great Roman emperor Julius Caesar. Caesar treated Brutus like a son, but his confidence in Brutus was misplaced.

On March 15, 44 B.C., a band of assassins came to kill Julius Caesar. The emperor fought valiantly, holding off the murderers for a while. But then something happened that made him lose all courage. He looked among the assassins, and there was—you guessed it—Brutus with his dagger drawn. Resigned to his fate, Caesar pulled his robe over his face and said to his close friend, "You too, Brutus?"

There's a little bit of Judas in all of us, so let's not be too hard on the guy. Every time I eat a great meal, get an answer to a prayer—or receive some other blessing from God—and go on sinning, am I any better than Judas? Didn't I have to sell God out to do my sin?

If we leave the door of our lives open to the devil, if we fail to give our hearts totally to Christ, "Then Satan entered Judas" might read something like this: "Then Satan entered me." And there's no telling what we'll do once the dark one comes in.

///////// HOT READ ///////

What was the attitude of those who watched Jesus be crucified? Luke 23:44-49

——> GET A LITTLE CLOSER <

In the beginning was the Word, and the Word was with God, and the Word was God. He was with God in the beginning. John 1:1, 2.

K, let's clap it up, friend. You've made it a long way in God's Word. You deserve something special. How about some ice cream? You know, one of those huge sundaes with three scoops, caramel, chocolate, nuts, sprinkles—all the good stuff. Go ahead!

Well, let's get back to business. You now know that a guy who wanted his fellow Jews to know and believe that Jesus was the Messiah wrote the book of Matthew. You also know that John Mark wrote his book to show that Jesus had supernatural power and when He saw a need, He met it *immediately*. Remember that key word in the book of Mark?

We left Mark and jumped into the Gospel written by Dr. Luke. Luke was a Gentile physician, an outsider, who wrote a meticulous history. Luke's Gospel is the most complete record of Jesus' life. And now we begin the book of John, and it's going to be a blast!

The writer of John is "the beloved disciple," as he referred to himself (see John 13:23; 19:26; 20:2). John wasn't trying to play favorites. He simply had a very close relationship with Jesus. In fact, of all the Gospels, this book is the most intimate. John doesn't worry about presenting all the miracles that Jesus performed. Instead, he chose only eight of them, but they make a powerful point that forms the heart of this Gospel. John's point? Jesus *is* God.

Written toward the end of the first century, roughly 30 to 40 years after the death of Jesus, John's book demonstrates that Jesus was no average person; He was God in the flesh. For instance, John begins by describing Jesus as the Word of God that was poured into a human form and sent to earth. No other Gospel begins in this way—putting Jesus in heaven with God the Father and explaining His role there.

John also unveils Jesus' special relationship with His Father. Furthermore, he highlights the times in Jesus' life that He claimed to be the Son of God. As you read John, mark the "I am" statements that Jesus makes, and you'll see the pattern. No other Gospel has as many of them.

John saw God in Jesus, and he wants you to see what he saw. Enjoy!

/////// HOT READ ///////

Read John 3:1-5. Have you been born again? Have you been baptized?

—> EAT THIS <

"My food," said Jesus, "is to do the will of him who sent me and to finish his work."
John 4:34.

esus was constantly tossing off memorable one-liners, such as the one above. He spoke this one to His disciples, who had left Him resting at a well while they went into town to find food. When they returned, Jesus was on a high. He didn't even look hungry anymore.

Food never controlled Jesus. From His 40-day fast in the wilderness to His arrest and crucifixion, we never hear or see Jesus going berserk because someone forgot to bring lunch. I must confess that much of my life revolves around food. I'm not ashamed to admit it. Be honest. You love to eat too. (You're probably wiping away some crumbs from your lips right now.)

We've been raised to make sure that we get our "three squares" a day—breakfast, lunch, and dinner. Throw in a few snacks between each meal, and you've got a recipe for organ failure. Our bodies literally wear themselves out. According to many health surveys, 60 percent of Americans are overweight—that's putting it mildly—and another 33 percent are obese. Kids and teens aren't doing that much better, either. Sixteen to 33 percent of children and adolescents are obese. Obesity is linked to most health-related deaths in America.

It's hard to avoid the American obsession with food. If you're fortunate enough to live in a city like Philadelphia, you get to see our food addiction close up. Each time that the Philadelphia Eagles miss the Super Bowl—which is most years—the city holds something called Wing Bowl. You heard me right—Wing Bowl.

Professional eaters—yes, there are such people—travel from all around the country to come to Wing Bowl. The rules are simple: Contestants eat as many chicken wings as they can during two 14-minute eating sessions, separated by a short break. Then there's a final two-minute round and tiebreaking rounds, if needed. Last year's winner ate 173 chicken wings. What would Jesus think about that?

Jesus gorged Himself on doing just what God the Father had sent Him here to do.

//////// HOT READ ////////

Read John 5:1-9. Why did Jesus ask this obviously sick man whether he wanted to get well? What role did the paralyzed man have to play in his own healing?

⟶ BRING ON THE LIGHT <

When Jesus spoke again to the people, he said, "I am the light of the world. Whoever follows me will never walk in darkness, but will have the light of life."
John 8:12.

An American traveler was staying overnight with a family in a little Swiss village, and was invited to go to church with them that evening for vespers. It was still twilight when they arrived at the church, and the American noticed that the church had no lights. It was not that the lights weren't turned on. There were no lights to turn on.

The man wondered what they would do when darkness fell. The family he came with had brought a lantern, but it certainly would not light the whole church. Then as he stood at a window and looked outside, he saw lights coming from all directions—almost like fireflies flickering in the gathering darkness. Through the streets of the little village and across the valley and on the opposite hillside, he saw lights in the hands of the people walking to church.

Suddenly he realized that each family was bringing a lantern, and as they entered the church they filled it with light. The walls simply glowed. After the service, he watched the lights going back out into the world, down the streets of the village, across the valley, and up the hills.

"I'll never forget that symbol of what the church really is," he later said. "It's a community of persons, bearing the rich fruit of the Holy Spirit, going forth to light up the world with the really good life of the Lord Jesus Christ. And that's what God wants us to want to be."★

The writer John understood the power of light. During the time in which he lived, lamps were the rule of the day. You couldn't flip a switch and light up a room. You had to pour oil into a small clay lamp and light it. If you ran out of oil, you ran out of light. For many poor people, darkness ruled the night. But Someone was about to light up the night.

"In him was life," wrote John, "and that life was the light of men" (John 1:4). Jesus promised that if we followed Him, we would never walk in darkness.

★ adapted from a story told in www.funnysermons.com

/////// HOT READ ///////

The Pharisees investigated many of the people who were healed by Jesus. Wanna know how to respond to people who doubt your healing? John 9:25.

——> SHEEPSPEAK <

The Jews gathered around him, saying, "How long will you keep us in suspense? If you are the Christ, tell us plainly." John 10:24.

ears ago the *National Enquirer* newspaper—the TMZ before TMZ—had a nifty media campaign. Back then the Enquirer was a trashy tabloid carrying all the latest celebrity gossip. Come to think of it, nothing has changed, but I digress. The media blitz featured commercials with stay-at-home moms, businesswomen, and few men here and there reading *Enquirer* newspapers in different settings.

The ads would give the *Enquirer* spiel, then a booming voice would say, "Inquiring minds want to know!" Then the tabloid reader would look up from his or her newspaper and say, "I want to know!" The whole campaign was cheesy, but it was effective. Back then the *National Enquirer* gave birth to millions of gossipers around the country.

If the *National Enquirer* or TMZ.com existed when Jesus walked the earth, He would've been on the front page every day. People couldn't get enough of Jesus. Crowds followed Him everywhere He went, hanging on his every word and action. All the Jews knew that their history prophesied a Messiah, a Savior who would deliver the Jewish nation. So when Jesus showed up doing a bunch of otherworldly stuff, the gossip heated up. Inquiring minds wanted to know: Was Jesus the Messiah? Some people believed He was, but many did not. Finally when they could take it no more, they asked Him point blank.

"Are You the Messiah or not? Stop playing games and tell us." Jesus' answer exposed the deeper motivations of their hearts.

"I did tell you, but you do not believe. The miracles I do in my Father's name speak for me, but you do not believe because you are not my sheep. My sheep listen to my voice; I know them, and they follow me" (John 10:25-27). Most of the Jewish leaders didn't really want to know who Jesus was.

The answer to their question was right before their eyes. Every miracle answered their question, but they remained unconvinced.

What does Jesus have to do to convince you that He can save you?

∕∕∕∕∕∕ HOT READ ∕∕∕∕∕∕

This is the most powerful "I am" statement ever spoken by Jesus: John 11:25.

——> STAY IN MY LOVE <

As the Father has loved me, so have I loved you. Now remain in my love. John 15:9.

id you see Jesus wash the feet of His disciples (John 13)? Their "dogs" were barking loudly, my friend. There were no closed-toe shoes back in Jesus' day. Sandals were it and the roads were dusty and dirty. There were no mall nail shops either, so—no pedicures. This selfless act of service—doing the job of a servant— sets Jesus apart from all other spiritual teachers and leaders. When was the last time that you heard of a God washing anyone's feet? Jesus is awsome!

After He'd washed the disciples' feet and broke bread with them, Jesus told them that He was going to die. This really upset them. After all, they'd left every- thing to follow Jesus. They couldn't imagine life without Him. *What could Jesus be talking about?* they wondered.

Jesus comforted His disciples with many words, but none more beautiful than those recorded in John 15:1-10. These verses also give us the secret to living a holy, fruitful life.

"I am the Real Vine and my Father is the Farmer. He cuts off every branch of me that doesn't bear grapes. And every branch that is grape-bearing he prunes back so it will bear even more. You are already pruned back by the message I have spoken.

"Live in me. Make your home in me just as I do in you. In the same way that a branch can't bear grapes by itself but only by being joined to the vine, you can't bear fruit unless you are joined with me.

"I am the Vine, you are the branches. When you're joined with me and I with you, the relation intimate and organic, the harvest is sure to be abundant. Separated, you can't produce a thing. Anyone who separates from me is dead- wood, gathered up and thrown on the bonfire. But if you make yourselves at home with me and my words are at home in you, you can be sure that whatever you ask will be listened to and acted upon. This is how my Father shows who he is—when you produce grapes, when you mature as my disciples.

"I've loved you the way my Father has loved me. Make yourselves at home in my love. If you keep my commands, you'll remain intimately at home in my love. That's what I've done—kept my Father's commands and made myself at home in his love" (Message).

//////// HOT READ ////////

What special gift did Jesus promise His disciples? John 15:15, 16.

---> ON HIS MIND <

My prayer is not for them alone. I pray also for those who will believe in me through their message. John 17:20.

ost people believe that the only one of Jesus' prayers that was written down was the famous often-quoted Lord's Prayer. But Jesus prayed constantly. He and His Father were always on the same page. For Jesus, praying was like breathing. He had to do it to stay alive—spiritually.

If you ever want to hear Jesus pray, read John 17. It is simply one of the greatest prayers ever spoken on Planet Earth. What makes it so great? I'm so glad you asked. Well, for starters, we overhear Jesus talking to His Father at a crucial time in His life. Judas had already made the deal to sell Him out to the chief priests. The same night in which He poured out His heart to God with this prayer, Jesus was arrested, tried, beaten, and then hung the next day. So, as you can see, this is no ordinary prayer.

It's also great because Jesus added earnest prayer for His disciples. He asked God to protect them and keep them from the evil one (John 17:11, 15). And Jesus wanted them to experience the joy that He had throughout His life, so He asked God to give it to them in full measure (verse 13).

Just when it seemed as though Jesus' prayer could get no better, He mentioned something that still makes me shout. "My prayer is not for them alone," continued our Savior. "I pray also for those who will believe in me through their message" (verse 20). Please tell me you got the hidden message in that verse. No? OK. Please allow me to give you some good news.

When Jesus prayed for those who would believe in Him because of the disciples' ministry, He was praying for you and me. Friends, we are believers today because of what the disciples did. They went out and shared the good news of salvation with others, and the message kept going until it reached us. We were in Jesus' prayer. We were on His mind just as surely as the disciples were. That makes me shout!

//////// HOT READ ////////

What happened to the people who arrested Jesus when He spoke to them? John 18:4-6. Would you continue to arrest someone who had that kind of power?

⟶ "THIS IS YOUR KING" <

Pilate had a notice prepared and fastened to the cross. It read: JESUS OF NAZARETH, THE KING OF THE JEWS. John 19:19.

t's hard to escape the theme of royalty in the background of Jesus' crucifixion. The Jewish leaders arrested Jesus on the trumped-up charge of blasphemy, which is the act of saying something that disrespects God or sacred things. You see, Jesus "claimed" to be able to forgive sins—something that only God could do (Mark 2:7).

When the Jewish leaders brought Jesus to Pilate to have him executed, Pilate asked, "What charges are you bringing against this man?" (John 18:29).

"'If he were not a criminal,' they replied, 'we would not have handed him over to you'" (verse 30). That's not exactly a clear answer, is it? That's like a prosecutor coming before a judge to try someone. When the judge asks what the charges are, she says, "Take my word for it. Would I bring an innocent man before your court, Your Honor?" (Not!)

Pilate knew that the Jewish charges against Jesus were empty accusations, but he didn't have the guts to anger his Jewish subjects. So Pilate questioned Jesus himself—after having Him beaten. When he asked Jesus if He was a king, Jesus said, "You are right in saying I am a king. In fact, for this reason I was born, and for this I came into the world, to testify to the truth. Everyone on the side of truth listens to me" (verse 37). Jesus' answer cut to the heart of the secular ruler. Pilate knew that Jesus was innocent, but he lacked the courage to free Him.

As Roman soldiers prepared to crucify Jesus, they faced a problem. It was customary to nail to the cross the charges on which a prisoner was convicted. Without any such charge against Jesus, Pilate came up with one that sent the Jewish leaders into a violent range. The soldiers made a sign that said, "JESUS OF NAZARETH, THE KING OF THE JEWS," and they wrote it in Latin, Greek, *and* Aramaic—one of the languages used by the Jews. In a way Pilate was putting his thumb in the eye of the Jews who had forced him into killing an innocent man. He was "dissing" them.

Pilate's "diss" was the truth. Jesus was the long-awaited King of the Jews, and they had just killed their king.

/////// HOT READ ///////

Does the Bible contain all the works that Jesus did on earth? John 21:25.

——> BIRTH PAINS <

But you will receive power when the Holy Spirit comes on you; and you will be my witnesses in Jerusalem, and in all Judea and Samaria, and to the ends of the earth. Acts 1:8.

ey, friend, welcome to the book of Acts. Whose acts will we be reading about? The acts of the apostles—the small band of Christ followers who continued to believe in Jesus after He ascended to heaven.

The author of Acts is someone we've met before. He is a doctor. Can you guess his name? OK, I'll help you. He wrote one of the four Gospels we just read. Now do you know? Of course you do.

Doctor Luke used his powers of observation and meticulous writing style to paint a picture of what the believers went through as they tried to share the gospel of Jesus during a very difficult time. Acts, like the book of Luke, was written to Theophilus, a nobleman who believed in God. Some Bible scholars believe that Theophilus was probably the person funding Luke's writing and helping get his message distributed.

The purpose of the book of Acts is summed up in the latter part of Acts 1:8: "You will be my witnesses in Jerusalem, and in all Judea and Samaria, and to the ends of the earth." Luke wanted to tell the story of how the Christian church got started. That's why there is so much history in Acts. Luke also wanted his readers to see how the early Christians met theological challenges to their newfound faith. He shows us how they defended the faith. Reading Acts is like looking at God's "baby" pictures—the baby being the Christian church.

Finally, Luke captured the power of Christianity in the face of great persecution. Luke was a traveling companion of the apostle Paul. Throughout his life of ministry Paul and the other Christ followers faced fierce persecution by Jews who were trying to stamp out the small Christian sect. Luke gives his readers a blow-by-blow account of life as an early Christian.

If you want to know how Christianity got started, if you want to learn how to stand in the face of death, if you want to see God's power work through ordinary people—Acts is the book!

####### HOT READ #######

Who is the main character of Acts 3? Do you remember Peter's denial of Jesus? Acts 3 shows us why Jesus did not give up on Peter, and why He will not give up on you.

320

——> "FAST AND LOOSE" <

Now a man named Ananias, together with his wife Sapphira, also sold a piece of property. With his wife's full knowledge he kept back part of the money for himself, but brought the rest and put it at the apostles' feet. Acts 5:1, 2.

A few years ago my friend James told me about Ted, one of his coworkers. They knew of each other, but were not actually friends. Since James worked in a part of the company that Ted was interested in, Ted asked to come and talk over some of his career goals.

"Sure," James responded, "come on over anytime." The next day they met and began talking. James told Ted about the opportunities available in his area and other places. Ted was excited about them as he went back to his department. Then a few days later James got a call from someone in yet another department.

"Hey, James," said the caller. "I didn't know you were such a close friend of Ted's."

"Well, uh, I'm not, uh, sure I understand," James stuttered.

"He said he knew you very well and that you guys go way back."

By now James was starting to get upset. He had barely known Ted before their meeting, and what he had known was purely on a professional level. *What is Ted doin?,* James wondered.

After a little research, James found out what Ted was up to. He was "dropping" James' name because he knew that James was respected by his coworkers, especially his bosses. Ted was playing "fast and loose" with the truth to get ahead, and James found him out.

Lies always have a way of coming back to haunt us. That's one of the lessons found in Acts 5 in the story of Ananias and Sapphira. All the believers had pledged to share their possessions so that none of them would lack anything. Ananias and Sapphira also made this pledge, but a funny thing happened when it came time to pay up. They'd just sold some property, and the idea of giving all the proceeds to the church was just too much. They decided to keep part of the money and give the rest to the church.

They never expected to be caught, but they were—by God.

/////// HOT READ ///////

How did Peter and the other apostles respond to the charges leveled at them by the Jewish leaders? Acts 5:27-29.

——> STEPHEN'S STORY <

At this they covered their ears and, yelling at the top of their voices, they all rushed at him, dragged him out of the city and began to stone him. Meanwhile, the witnesses laid their clothes at the feet of a young man named Saul. Acts 7:57, 58.

cts 7 can give you nightmares, especially if you put yourself in the Stephen's shoes for a while. What would it feel like to be dragged out of the city by an angry mob, thrown to the ground, and stoned to death for something good that you did?

Luke tells us that Stephen was "a man full of God's grace and power" and that he "did great wonders and miraculous signs among the people" (Acts 6:8). Aren't those the kind of people you want in a society, the ones who make the community better?

Archbishop Desmond Tutu once told how he found himself in the middle of an angry mob. In the years after the racist government of South Africa fell, pockets of violence broke out as Black mobs searched for White officials who had participated in their oppression. During one such incident a mob captured a police officer, tied his hands behind his back, put a gasoline-filled tire around his neck, and prepared to light it.

Tutu heard what was going on and rushed to stop the violence. Hearing the chants of anger as he drew close, without any care for his life Tutu leaped from his car and ran into the middle of the crowd. "For God's sake," he screamed, "Stop this! No more killing!" He rushed to where the bound man was and pleaded for his life. To Tutu's surprise, the mob relented, but then their anger flared up again. Helpless, Tutu had to leave, and the mob got their man.

Stephen knew what it was like to be killed in cold blood. What was it that drove the Jewish mob to kill him? It was Steven's history lesson. In his defense, Stephen told of Israel's birth, its falling away from God, and the promise of the Messiah. But Stephen also told how Israel had rejected God and killed His prophets—even Jesus Himself (Acts 7:51-53).

At these words the mob began to growl like a dog, bearing their teeth at Stephen. Then they hurried him out of the city and stoned him to death. But even facing death, Stephen remained true!

//////// HOT READ ////////

Who was the powerful official present at Stephen's stoning? Acts 7:57-8:3. What happened to Saul in Acts 9? Paul's turnaround was something that only God could do.

November 11 • *Acts 10-12*

⎯⎯> TELL EVERYONE <

So when Peter went up to Jerusalem, the circumcised believers criticized him and said, "You went into the house of uncircumcised men and ate with them." Acts 11:2, 3.

Acts 10-12 is filled with puzzling passages that can be misunderstood. For instance, by telling Peter, "Do not call anything impure that God has made clean" (Acts 10:15), had God changed His mind about the kinds of meat people might eat? Leviticus 11 lays out a clear diet plan for God's people, and it didn't include meats that God said were unclean. So what did Peter's vision of the sheet and the unclean animals mean? The answer lies in what happened next.

Next God sent Peter to Cornelius, a Gentile who desperately wanted his household to learn about the true God and be saved. The Jews (referred to in Acts as "the circumcised") considered Cornelius and all other non-Jews unclean. They were forbidden even to associate with them. So God used something that Peter understood very well—clean and unclean foods—to prepare him to share the gospel with people from every race and ethnic group. Peter never would have entered Cornelius' home to tell him about their Savior had God not changed the way in which he viewed people.

As Peter shared the gospel with Cornelius and his household, "the Holy Spirit came on all who heard the message" (Acts 10:44). The Jews who were with Peter nearly fell over. They couldn't believe that God would give His Spirit to people who were not Jews. The people began speaking in tongues and praising God (verse 46). The "tongues" or languages they spoke were not the "gobbledygook" languages spoken by some who "get the Spirit" today.

As in Acts 2:4, the people spoke in languages other than their native tongue. God gave them this ability, as He did the disciples in Acts 2, so that they might spread the gospel to people of every nation, tribe, and language.

When the Jewish believers learned that Peter had witnessed to Gentiles, they became very angry. Peter responded by simply telling them about the miracle he had seen.

God wants us to share the good news of salvation with *all* people. Let's get to it!

////// HOT READ //////

When were the disciples first called Christians? Acts 11:26. How did Peter escape from prison? Acts 12:1-12. Never doubt that God can deliver you from anything!

323

——> GROWING PAINS <

"Then some of the believers who belonged to the party of the Pharisees stood up and said, 'The Gentiles must be circumcised and required to obey the law of Moses." Acts 15:5.

ave you ever noticed how hyped up new believers get about Jesus? They attend every service and volunteer for everything. They share their newfound love for Jesus with anyone who'll listen—and even those who don't want to. New believers are special, aren't they?

When Darryl★ decided to give his heart to Jesus, everyone was excited. Family members who had prayed for years that he would quit smoking, drinking, and partying were doing backflips at his baptism. There was not a dry eye in the church that day.

Darryl was on fire for God. You never saw him without his Bible. Instead of club-hopping on the weekends, he witnessed for God. Darryl's flame burned brightly for a few months, but then he met up with a girl he used to kick it with from way back. They started to hook up again, and it wasn't long before Darryl started missing church. Rumors began to spread that he was using again. People at the church talked *about* Darryl, but few of them talked *to* him.

Do you know any Darryls—people who gave their hearts to God and then fell away after a while? In Acts 13-15 we find several Darryls. As Paul and Barnabas traveled around sharing the good news that Jesus had died and risen again, cleansing all sin, many unbelievers gave their hearts to God. These new Christ followers were lit up with the love of Jesus, but they had some baggage. Many of them worshipped Greek gods, such as Diana, Zeus, and Hermes. They also ate strange foods, and let's not even talk about their sexual habits.

The Jewish believers weren't going to receive them until they were ready to keep all the laws given to the Israelites by Moses when they were preparing to enter the Promised Land. (Remember Deuteronomy?) That was an impossible hurdle for a new believer to overcome.

Paul, Barnabas, and Peter fought to lift the Jewish yoke from these new converts. They made their case to the church in Jerusalem, and a compromise was reached. Check out Acts 15:19-28 to see how the conflict was resolved. Gentiles everywhere were overjoyed!

—————
★ not his real name

/////// HOT READ ///////

What was Paul and Barnabas' disagreement? Acts 15:36-41. Is this a good way to solve conflicts between believers?

——> GOT CHARACTER? <

*About midnight Paul and Silas were praying and singing hymns to God,
and the other prisoners were listening to them. Acts 16:25.*

In his book *Talent Is Never Enough,* leadership guru John C. Maxwell tells the story of an old golfer named Bobby Jones. Many consider him the best golfer of all time. Though the game has changed greatly—because of a certain phenom—Bobby Jones was Tiger before the Tiger.

Jones learned the game of golf early. He started playing at age 5 and won his first tournament at 6. By the time he was high school age, he had already won several tournaments, many against adults. Young Bobby Jones seemed well on his way to greatness, except for one fatal flaw: he had a bad temper. Maxwell writes that Jones was nicknamed "the club thrower" because of his penchant for flinging his clubs to oblivion when he missed a crucial shot.

Years later Bobby Jones found his way into a final playoff at the U.S. Open—probably the most respected golf tournament next to the the Masters. He had hit his ball into the rough off the fairway, then, as he prepared to hit his shot, he mistakenly touched the ball. If you watch any golf you know that touching the ball in this way means that you lose a shot. That's huge in a sudden death playoff. No one had seen Jones touch the ball—not even the marshals.

Bobby Jones—the guy who would lose his temper and do anything to win—did something different that day. He promptly told the marshals what he had done. Since they had not seen the infraction, they told him it was his call. He could continue to play as if nothing had happened, or lose a shot. Bobby Jones chose to lose a shot. He lost the U.S. Open that day by one stroke. Jones overcame his anger problem to the point that he became known for his great sportsmanship. Each year the Professional Golfers' Association gives away the Bob Jones Award for Sportsmanship.

Character is formed when we decide to stand for what is right, even when it may cost us much. As you'll read today in Acts 16, Paul and Silas remained true to God even though they were stripped, beaten, and imprisoned. Bloody and broken, they were heard singing and praising God. It takes character to stand in a storm.

//////// HOT READ ////////

Who were the Bereans, and what was their claim to fame? Acts 17:10, 11.

———> "AND PAUL I KNOW" <

The evil spirit answered them, "Jesus I know, and I know about Paul, but who are you?" Acts 19:15.

If you ever find yourself in the middle of an exorcism and a spirit says to you, "Jesus I know, and I know about Paul, but who are you?" that's your cue to "get ghost," friend.

Most of us know that the spirit world is nothing to play with. Scary movies, demonic music, video games, even the "harmless" TV shows about the occult—don't even go near them! Once I was flipping through the channels and came across a promo for *Saw II.* (Yeah, I know it's old, but bear with me.) The amount of disturbing images in that 30-second commercial made me wince. Did God really intend for our minds to be exposed to that kind of stuff?

The spirit world has always a part of the "real" world, though many of us think it doesn't exist. The apostle Paul was forced into "hand-to-hand combat" with demons on a regular basis. Ellen White notes that God gave him special power for this very reason. What kind of power?

"Handkerchiefs and aprons that had touched him were taken to the sick, and their illnesses were cured and the evil spirits left them" (Acts 19:12).

The fame of Paul spread throughout the city of Ephesus, where he had been ministering. Religious leaders saw how the people flocked to Paul, and they started to try to imitate him. *If God's power worked for him,* they reasoned, it would work for them, and the seven sons of a priest named Sceva decided to give the power a try. They found a possessed man, went to his home, and said, "In the name of Jesus, whom Paul preaches, I command you to come out!"

The spirit didn't even flinch. It just got upset. The evil spirit had had first-hand knowledge of Jesus and Paul. But the seven sons of Sceva? They were no-bodies. The spirit then leaped onto them and beat them so viciously that they ran from the man's house naked. (Ouch!)

"Real recognizes real," Lou, my little brother, likes to say. He's right. The demons recognized the real followers of God when they saw them. Sceva's boys were crazy to tangle with a demon, but don't we do the same when we expose ourselves to demonic entertainment?

/////// HOT READ ///////

Read Acts 20:7-12. What happened when Paul's sermon went too long? Did this stop Paul from continuing on? Why was Paul so passionate about sharing the good news?

——> CALLED UP! <

The next morning the Jews formed a conspiracy and bound themselves with an oath not to eat or drink until they had killed Paul. Acts 23:12.

f you've read through the Bible with me so far, you're not surprised by the death threats Paul faced. Prophets who spoke the truth lived under constant scrutiny. But Paul had a secret weapon that gave him courage and kept him centered during the most difficult times in his life: the Holy Spirit. Have you noticed how many times the Bible says that Paul and the other apostles were "full of the Holy Spirit"?

When the Holy Spirit led Paul to denounce the hypocrisy of the Jewish leaders, the high priest Ananias got so angry that he told a guard to punch Paul in the mouth (Acts 23:2). Paul responded, "God will strike you, you whitewashed wall! You sit there to judge me according to the law, yet you yourself violate the law by commanding that I be struck!" (verse 3).

"Under the influence of the Holy Spirit," wrote Ellen White, "Paul uttered a prophetic denunciation similar to that which Christ had uttered in rebuking the hypocrisy of the Jews. The judgment pronounced by the apostle was terribly fulfilled when the iniquitous and hypocritical high priest was murdered by assassins in the Jewish war" (*Sketches From the Life of Paul*, p. 222).

Just as Paul's case appeared hopeless, however, he spied an opportunity. The crowd of Jewish accusers was made up of Pharisees and Sadducees. Paul was a Pharisee and the son of a Pharisee (Acts 23:6). The Pharisees believed in resurrection of the dead, but the Sadducees did not. Paul cleverly appealed to the Pharisees in the group. When they found out that Paul was one of them and believed as they did, they began to fight against the Sadducees. The fight became so fierce that that Roman soldiers whisked Paul away to safety.

The next night God spoke to Paul in a vision. "Take courage! As you have testified about me in Jerusalem, so you must also testify in Rome" (verse 11). Paul was headed to the big leagues.

/////// HOT READ ///////

How did Felix respond to Paul's mighty preaching? Acts 24:22-27. Do you ever put God off until a more convenient time?

——> BLAZE OF GLORY <

Then Agrippa said to Paul, "Do you think that in such a short time you can persuade me to be a Christian?" Acts 26:28.

Friend, if you've skipped any chapters in the book of Acts so far, please don't skip Acts 25-28. Here's a few reasons you don't want to miss these chapters.

In Acts 24 Paul is put on trial for his faith in Felix's judgmental hall. In case you don't know who Felix is, let me clue you in. Felix was a "low-down, dirty old man"! What did he do to earn that title? Felix used a sorcerer named Simon Magus to convince a young drop-dead-gorgeous princess named Drusilla to leave her husband and become his wife. The two of sat terrified as Paul "discoursed on righteousness, self-control, and the judgment to come" (verse 25). Felix and Drusilla knew that they had sinned greatly. Paul's words scared Felix so much that he stopped Paul from speaking. "That's enough for now!" the Roman governor protested. "You may leave. When I find it convenient, I will send for you!"

Riiiiigggggghhhhhhhtttttt!

After two years Felix was succeeded by Festus—no, they weren't brothers. The Jewish leaders asked Festus to let Paul out of jail into their custody—for they were plotting to murder him. Since Paul was a Roman citizen, he appealed to have his case heard in Rome before Caesar. Festus agreed, but decided to get some advice from a higher authority, King Agrippa II, who ruled over the territory on behalf of Rome. His great-grandfather Herod was the man who, in search of the infant Jesus, murdered the innocent babies of Bethlehem. Herod Antipas, his great-uncle, killed John the Baptist, and his father—Agrippa—presided over the death of the apostle James. What chance did Paul have of surviving before King Agrippa II?

Remember the vision God gave to Paul in Acts 23:11? Before Paul's life ended, God wanted him to give his testimony in Rome, and Paul was not there yet. Paul spoke so eloquently before Agrippa that he almost persuaded him to become a follower of Christ (Acts 26:28, KJV).

Paul was then sent to Rome to be tried before the emperor there.

////// HOT READ //////

What did Paul do at Rome? Acts 28:30, 31. The emperor Nero later killed Paul, but before his death Paul testified valiantly before the terrified emperor.

——> ALL IN THE FAMILY <

For all have sinned and fall short of the glory of God. Romans 3:23.

obody likes a braggart. Guys and girls who namedrop about the people they know, the cost of their jeans, their car—nobody likes 'em. (OK, maybe their mommas tolerate them.)

Although he's universally loved today, the great boxer Muhammad Ali once said, "If you even dream of beating me you'd better wake up and apologize." Bragging about his greatness was Ali's way of getting "up" for his fights, and it also had another fringe benefit. It usually made his opponents so angry that they'd lose their head in the ring, make mistakes, and lose the fight. But Ali's boasts didn't work with everyone. A tough Philadelphia fighter named "Smokin'" Joe Frazier cleaned Ali's clock in their first fight. Mr. Invincible was suddenly, uh, "vincible."

Human beings always try to be more than what they are. Even when we know the truth about ourselves, we still try to "fake it till we make it." The book of Romans is Paul's wake-up call to all of us, whether we have a little Ali in us or not.

Paul wrote this letter to a small group of believers in Rome while he was doing ministry in the city of Corinth. Paul had traveled through much of Asia and Greece spreading the then-brand-new gospel of Jesus Christ (Acts 15 and 19). He was planning to move westward to Italy, but before going there, he wanted to send the people a letter that clearly outlined the heart of his beliefs—what it means to be saved (justification) and made holy (sanctification).

Paul began his message by telling the Roman believers how much he longed to visit Rome. He then told them that he was "not ashamed of the gospel, because it is the power of God for . . . salvation" (Romans 1:16). But as Paul continued writing, his main theme became clearer, and it's found in Romans 3:23: *All have sinned and fall short of the glory of God.* Paul then went on to explain just how messed up we humans are, and, folks, the view isn't pretty.

Paul wanted believers then, and believers now, to know that we've got only one thing to brag about—and that's Jesus. Without Him we are toast.

///////// HOT READ ////////

What does Romans 1:18-28 tell you about God's view of homosexuality? How can God love practicing homosexuals yet denounce homosexual acts?

——> YOU GOTTA BELIEVE <

For if, when we were God's enemies, we were reconciled to him through the death of his Son, how much more, having been reconciled, shall we be saved through his life! Romans 5:10.

etter hang on, friend, because Paul is about to take you on a serious ride. For instance, he wants us to get the point that faith in God is our ticket to being justified, or free of sin, and not our own works. How does he make this point? In chapter 4 he tells the story of Abraham. Remember him? God promised Abraham He would create a great and mighty people from him (Genesis 12), but gave Abe the news when he was old and childless. Nevertheless, Abraham believed God, and his faith was "credited to him as righteousness" (Romans 4:22), or rightdoing.

Just as Abraham—often called the father of the faithful—trusted God, we too must trust Him. God doesn't just want to give credit to Abraham for his faith, as Paul wrote, "but also for us . . . who believe in him who raised Jesus our Lord from the dead. He was delivered over to death for our sins and was raised to life for our justification" (verses 24, 25). Paul is saying to you and me, "Guys, you gotta believe God's promises, especially the promise that all who accept the death of Jesus Christ as payment for their sins are saved."

But Paul doesn't stop there. Just because we've been saved from sin doesn't mean that our old sinful natures are going to pack up and go away. A few years ago a teen friend of mine was diagnosed with multiple sexually transmitted diseases. Was he a believer in God? Yep. Did he accept Jesus as his Savior? Sure. None of that stopped him from getting burned, though, because even though he had trusted God to save him, he hadn't trusted God to change his nature.

That's why Paul wrote, "For if, when we were God's enemies, we were reconciled to him through the death of his Son, how much more, having been reconciled, shall we be saved through his life!" (Romans 5:10). Jesus' death is not the only thing that saves us from sin. We must also accept the transforming power of Jesus' life that keeps us from constantly falling back into sin.

There's no such thing as "once saved always saved." It takes faith in Jesus to save us, and faith in Jesus to keep us saved. Does that mean that we don't have to do anything? Our faith in Jesus is demonstrated by our works, by whether we obey Him or not.

///////// HOT READ ////////

Want to know the secret to living strong for God? Read Romans 6:11-18.

——> LAW AND ORDER <

So I find this law at work: When I want to do good, evil is right there with me.
Romans 7:21.

ou've probably heard the one about the dumb criminal in Colorado Springs, Colorado, who decided to rob a liquor store at gunpoint. He told the cashier to put all the cash in a bag. Then, upon further investigation, the crook spied a bottle of Scotch on a shelf behind the cashier.

"Drop that in the bag too," he motioned to the cashier. The cashier refused. "No, because I don't think you're over 21" came the startling reply. The criminal protested, but the clerk was unmoved. Finally the crook pulled out his driver's license and gave it to the clerk. The clerk looked it over, returned the license, and dropped the bottle in the bag. After the criminal left the store, the clerk called the police and gave them a description of the suspect, complete with name, address, height, weight, and eye color.

Dude, even criminals as dumb as the dim bulb who held up the Colorado Springs liquor store know that it's against the law to rob a store with a gun. But somehow that knowledge doesn't stop people from attempting the same crime, and many others, every day of the world. Is there something wrong with the law, or is there a problem with the people who break the law? The people, of course. That's the problem that Paul addresses in Romans 7, the problem of our deeply sinful nature.

Here's how Paul describes the struggle: "For if I know the law but still can't keep it, and if the power of sin within me keeps sabotaging my best intentions, I obviously need help! I realize that I don't have what it takes. I can will it, but I can't *do* it. I decide to do good, but I don't *really* do it; I decide not to do bad, but then I do it anyway. My decisions, such as they are, don't result in actions. Something has gone wrong deep within me and gets the better of me every time" (Romans 7:18-20, Message).

Do we have any hope of overcoming sin? Paul says yes! "Through Christ Jesus the law of the Spirit of life set me free from the law of sin and death. For what the law was powerless to do in that it was weakened by the sinful nature, God did by sending his own Son in the likeness of sinful man to be a sin offering" (Romans 8:2, 3).

####### HOT READ #######

People who live in Christ will overcome all sin (Romans 8:28-32). Believe it!

——> BRING ME YOUR BODY <

Therefore, I urge you, brothers, in view of God's mercy, to offer your bodies as living sacrifices, holy and pleasing to God—this is your spiritual act of worship.
Romans 12:1.

n April 16, 2008, a Canadian newspaper carried the story "Dozens Sacrifice Hair for Tibet." The title of the article spoke to my inner news junkie. I wouldn't try to cut my own hair, and if I did, the results wouldn't be good. One day I decided to give my "locks" a trim and spent the next week bald. That ended my experiment with self-barbering.

The people at the center of the Canadian story weren't practicing to become hairstylists; they were protesting on behalf of relatives in Tibet who were being beaten and killed by Chinese authorities. China and Tibet have had a long-running battle over who owns Tibet. The Chinese claim it as part of China, and the Tibetans say "NOT!" The Chinese have come up with a novel way to wipe out the individuality of their Tibetan neighbors. They built train tracks that lead directly to Tibetan cities, thereby bringing a rush of Chinese laborers and businesspeople. They even offer financial breaks to ethnic Chinese who want to move and live in Tibet. They are transforming Tibet from the inside out.

The Canadian protesters decided to show their solidarity with their loved ones in Tibet by cutting off all their hair. It was one of the few ways that they could draw attention to their cause. Will such an act change the Chinese government's plan to wipe out Tibet's autonomy? Probably not, but every bit of sacrifice helps.

When you believe in something important, you must be willing to sacrifice for it. Paul believed this with all his heart, and he paid the price for his belief. He was beaten several times throughout his ministry—as you've read—yet he continued faithfully serving God. Why was Paul able to remain courageous through it all? He had given his life to Jesus as a sacrifice.

In Romans 12:1 Paul asks us to do the same thing. He asks you and me to present our bodies to God as living, so that God can transform us by making our minds brand-new again! I'm game; are you?

////// HOT READ //////

Why did God reject Israel and open the way for all people to become believers? Romans 11:20-24.

⟶ SAY WHAT? <

Everyone must submit himself to the governing authorities, for there is no authority except that which God has established. The authorities that exist have been established by God. Romans 13:1.

Romans 13 is deadly in the wrong hands. This one chapter has been used by slavemasters to justify some of the most brutal forms of torture known to humanity. It has also been used by governments to oppress people who dare to call them out on the carpet for their wrongs.

If you were a dictator, wouldn't you want verses like these on your side? "He who rebels against the authority is rebelling against what God has instituted, and those who do so will bring judgment on themselves. For rulers hold no terror for those who do right, but for those who do wrong. Do you want to be free from fear of the one in authority? Then do what is right and he will commend you. For he is God's servant to do you good. But if you do wrong, be afraid, for he does not bear the sword for nothing. He is God's servant, an agent of wrath to bring punishment on the wrongdoer" (verses 2-4).

Was Paul—a guy writing to Jewish believers living under Roman oppression—telling them to simply obey the Romans, no matter what? Remember, it was secular governments that persecuted Paul after being egged on by the Jewish priests. If Paul were telling the believers to obey Caesar, the Roman emperor, why then did the Roman emperor later kill Paul?

In Romans 13 the authority Paul is referring to the spiritual authorities leading the church. Paul wanted the Roman believers to see that God is the person who sets up the leaders of His church, and we should follow their lead as they follow Christ. I've been in some churches where members had personal beefs with their leaders and "dissed" them publicly. Paul was saying that we should do our best to work with our leaders. If they do something wrong, we shouldn't blindly follow them. We should deal with them in love, as we would want to be dealt with—not excusing their wrongs, but not destroying them either. We are to give them an opportunity to repent and be restored, the same second chance we would want if we messed up.

Paul's message? God's church should be a place of order that is defined by love.

/////// HOT READ ///////
How should you deal with other members who are weak? Romans 15:1-6.

⟶ YOUR VEGAS IS SHOWING ＜

For I resolved to know nothing while I was with you except Jesus Christ and him crucified. 1 Corinthians 2:2.

f you watch any television, you've probably seen the humorous commercials advertising Las Vegas. They portray regular, everyday guys and gals who go to Las Vegas on vacation and do stuff they wouldn't dream of doing at home. Going back home, they carry a little bit of Vegas on them. The commercials close with the slogan "Your Vegas Is Showing."

Las Vegas is known as a party town, a place people go to become someone else or, some might argue, more of who they really are. Casinos beckon both high rollers and wannabes with promises of instant wealth. Showgirls dressed in skimpy outfits wink wantonly at gullible men. Money and pleasure are Vegas's calling cards.

The Vegas formula is not new. Before Las Vegas ever existed there was a place called Corinth, located on an isthmus of mainland Greece. A bustling business and trade center, Corinth was the place people would go to get their "dirty" on. Most of Corinth's mixed population worshipped Aphrodite, the goddess of love. One thousand young prostitutes worked at the temple of Aphrodite. Corinth's sensuality and luxury was known throughout the then-known world. Have you ever heard Chrysler spokespersons boast about the luxurious feel of the "Corinthian leather" in their cars? The "Corinthian" they're referring to was the Corinth of Paul's day.

But God has faithful believers, even in the most sinful places, and Corinth was no different. Paul spent 18 months in Corinth during his second missionary tour, and a church was born. Paul's letters to the Corinthians are addressed to these new believers. Sadly, they were fighting each other, and many of them had backslidden into behaviors that they'd given up for Christ. And some believers claimed to be followers of Paul; others, of another preacher named Apollos.

When Paul heard what was happening with the believers there, he was alarmed. If you are struggling to walk with God in a sin-saturated environment, 1 Corinthians is for you!

///////// HOT READ /////////

Who was at the center of Paul's preaching? See 1 Corinthians 2:1-5. Why?

—> SAYING AND DOING <

For this reason I am sending to you Timothy, my son whom I love, who is faithful in the Lord. He will remind you of my way of life in Christ Jesus, which agrees with what I teach everywhere in every church. 1 Corinthians 4:17.

ave you ever skipped school? Don't tell me you never wanted to? I loved school most days, but there were times when I wanted out—at least for a day or so. One day I decided to play hookey and found myself dodging truancy officers for most of the day. It's hard to hang when you're watching your back. (Oh, if my parents had found out, I'd be pushing up daisies!)

Truancy officers prowl about looking for kids who should be in school. But who chases down adults when they skip school? Weird question, huh? Yet that's what the community of Yorkshire, England, was wondering when the head teacher—or principal of a local school—called in sick, saying she couldn't come that day. Nothing wrong with that. Who wants to deal with hardheaded kids when he or she is sick? Not me.

But the head teacher wasn't sick. She actually called in sick so she could go on vacation to the Canary Islands. It's hard to tell kids to come to school when the principal doesn't want to.

Friends, examples matter! When people say one thing and do something else, those who look to them or follow them are led astray. Paul reminded the believers in Corinth who had begun to stray, about the example he'd set when he was among them. "I urge you to imitate me," wrote Paul in 1 Corinthians 4:16. Paul had preached Christ to them, but he had also walked as Jesus did. He had modeled for them how to live a life of simplicity in a culture filled with luxury. When he was among them, he had treated all the believers with love and care. Paul knew that his example was even more important than his words. A sermon *lived* is the best kind of all.

The great preacher Charles Haddon Spurgeon had it right when he said: "A man's life is always more forcible than his speech. When men take stock of him they reckon his deeds as dollars and his words as pennies. If his life and doctrine disagree, the mass of onlookers accept his practice and reject his preaching."

####### HOT READ #######

What two problems dominated the church in Corinth? See 1 Corinthians 5 and 6. What solutions did Paul suggest? What can you learn from the tone of Paul's counsel?

——> FOOD FIGHT

No, I beat my body and make it my slave so that after I have preached to others, I myself will not be disqualified for the prize. 1 Corinthians 9:27.

First Corinthians is heating up. In the next few chapters, Paul's messages focus on hot-button issues the Corinthian church was dealing with: the sacredness of marriage and of all sexual relationships and the willingness to sacrifice certain individual rights so that weaker members may be strengthened.

The sexual immorality of Corinth had made deep inroads into the church. Singles were sexually active, and married people were having affairs. (Please don't miss reading 1 Corinthians 6:12-19—Paul's counsel on sexual purity. A must-read!)

Then there was another controversy in the ancient Corinthian church that occupied Paul's attention. Here's what was happening. "When animals were sacrificed to the gods in the heathen temples, part of the animal was given to the officiating priests, who sold the meat. Some of this meat found its way into the public markets."★ The Corinthian believers wanted to know if it was OK to eat meat that had first been offered to idols. What about when they were served it at a friend's home?

You're probably wondering why you should care about this ancient food fight. I understand. But what people eat is often a source of major pressure in the church today. Some vegetarians look down on nonvegetarians, and let's not even talk about how some vegans view dietary matters. Is food important to one's spirituality? Absolutely! We really are what we eat—physically and spiritually. But Paul didn't want the new believers in Corinth to get caught up in who was eating what. He wanted them to think about how what they ate affected the faith of their fellow believers. I'll let Paul speak for himself.

"Be careful, however, that the exercise of your freedom does not become a stumbling block to the weak. For if anyone with a weak conscience sees you who have this knowledge eating in an idol's temple, won't he be emboldened to eat what has been sacrificed to idols? So this weak brother, for whom Christ died, is destroyed by your knowledge" (1 Corinthians 8:9-11). Paul didn't want more knowledgeable believers to cause new believers to stumble by eating things that the new believers felt convicted not to eat.

★ *The Seventh-day Adventist Bible Commentary,* vol. 6, p. 719.

///////// HOT READ /////////

What sacrifices did Paul make to win believers to Christ? See 1 Corinthians 9:24-27.

——> GOD MAKES A WAY <

*No temptation has seized you except what is common to man. And God is faithful;
he will not let you be tempted beyond what you can bear. But when you are
tempted, he will also provide a way out so that you can stand up under it.*
1 Corinthians 10:13.

ne of the most famous verses in the Bible is the one you just read. It's a great
reminder that temptations that seem strong and so overwhelming are not new.
They are common tricks, used by Satan for centuries, to lead adults, teens, and kids
into sin. Furthermore, God carefully weighs all our temptations to be sure that
Satan doesn't load us up with backbreakers that we cannot bear. Even better than
that, God provides us with a way of escape so that we may overcome all temptations to sin. I don't know how you feel, but I for one am glad that God's got my
back on the whole temptations thing.

But as powerful as 1 Corinthians 10:13 is, as encouraging as it is to know that
God has "rigged" temptations for our victory, you must realize that there's one
thing that even God can't do for you. Here's a story that illustrates my point.

In April 2008 a video surfaced on YouTube showing the vicious beating of a
16-year-old girl. Do you remember that? CBS News was one of the news outlets
that reported the crime. "Eight teenagers are under arrest in Florida after police
say they videotaped an attack on a girl and planned to post it on the Web.
Investigators say the suspects started beating the 16-year-old victim after inviting
her to a former friend's house. The girl suffered a concussion, damage to her eye
and ear, and multiple bruises in the attack, which lasted for more than a half hour."

What does that *have to do with temptation,* you ask? The desire to hurt someone
we do not like is a temptation to violence. For some reason the perpetrators of this
violent act—other teenagers—never stopped to consider the harm they were
going to do or the consequences of their actions. God can help us overcome
temptation, but only if we want Him to. When you hear God's "still small voice"
warning you to change course, it's up to you to obey that voice. God cannot make
your choices for you—or mine for me.

/////// HOT READ ///////

**What important principle for overcoming temptation is found in
1 Corinthians 10:12?**

⟶> A BETTER WAY <

And now I will show you the most excellent way. 1 Corinthians 12:31.

f I speak with human eloquence and angelic ecstasy but don't love, I'm nothing but the creaking of a rusty gate. If I speak God's Word with power, revealing
all his mysteries and making everything plain as day, and if I have faith that says to
a mountain, 'Jump,' and it jumps, but I don't love, I'm nothing. If I give everything I own to the poor and even go to the stake to be burned as a martyr, but I
don't love, I've gotten nowhere. So, no matter what I say, what I believe, and
what I do, I'm bankrupt without love.

"Love never gives up. Love cares more for others than for self. Love doesn't
want what it doesn't have. Love doesn't strut, doesn't have a swelled head, doesn't
force itself on others, isn't always 'me first,' doesn't fly off the handle, doesn't keep
score of the sins of others, doesn't revel when others grovel, takes pleasure in the
flowering of truth, puts up with anything, trusts God always, always looks for the
best, never looks back, but keeps going to the end.

"Love never dies. Inspired speech will be over some day; praying in tongues
will end; understanding will reach its limit. We know only a portion of the truth,
and what we say about God is always incomplete. But when the Complete arrives,
our incompletes will be canceled.

"When I was an infant at my mother's breast, I gurgled and cooed like any
infant. When I grew up, I left those infant ways for good. We don't yet see things
clearly. We're squinting in a fog, peering through a mist. But it won't be long before the weather clears and the sun shines bright! We'll see it all then, see it all as
clearly as God sees us, knowing him directly just as he knows us! But for right
now, until that completeness, we have three things to do to lead us toward that
consummation: Trust steadily in God, hope unswervingly, love extravagantly.
And the best of the three is love" (1 Corinthians 13, Message).

——> THE PASSION OF PAUL <

For I wrote you out of great distress and anguish of heart and with many tears, not to grieve you but to let you know the depth of my love for you. 2 Corinthians 2:4.

ey, guys, we're almost to the very end of the Bible. Can you believe it? Keep reading. Let's finish strong, amen?

If you thought the apostle Paul had finished counseling the members of the Corinthian church, think again. Paul just couldn't get the believers in Corinth out of his mind. They were facing several internal challenges that Paul longed for them to overcome. As you read in 1 Corinthians, some members were backsliding, fights were breaking out everywhere, sexual immorality was rampant, and there was a small group within the church who hated Paul's guts.

Like a father weeping over a sick child, Paul cried over the state of the Corinthian church. These members were his "babies." He had led them to Christ, and he longed to see them grow up into Christ. Wouldn't you be concerned if you found out that someone you led to Jesus was beginning to fall back into sin?

Paul was anxious to learn how his first letter to the believers in Corinth had been received. In his second letter he wrote, "Now when I went to Troas to preach the gospel of Christ and found that the Lord had opened a door for me, I still had no peace of mind, because I did not find my brother Titus there. So I said good-by to them and went on to Macedonia" (2 Corinthians 2:12, 13). Paul was anxiously waiting for Titus, a friend and fellow minister, to come with news of Corinth. He was so concerned that when God opened a great opportunity for him to share the gospel in Troas, he couldn't, because his mind and heart were still in Corinth.

Paul had several reasons to be concerned about the believers there. The main one was that a small group in the church questioned whether he was truly an apostle, and demanded to know why he was trying to direct the church by remote control—letters. In the first nine chapters Paul sets out the proof that he is a true apostle. In the last four he makes a withering assault on the small group stirring up trouble. Get ready! Paul is packing some serious heat, and he's about to unleash it on the believers at Corinth—especially the small group of haters.

/////// HOT READ ///////

What did Paul say was proof that his apostleship was from God?
See 2 Corinthians 3:1-6.

——> JARS OF CLAY <

But we have this treasure in jars of clay to show that this all-surpassing power is from God and not from us. 2 Corinthians 4:7.

oes the name Jars of Clay ring a bell? It might. Jars of Clay is a Christian band. I've always loved their name and their music because of the verse from which they chose their name—2 Corinthians 4:7. In his defense of his calling, Paul compared himself and his fellow ministers—Timothy, Titus, Silas, Barnabas, Peter, etc.—to jars of clay holding a precious treasure.

In Paul's day clay jars were not fine china. They were hollow receptacles made out of baked clay. Clay jars were very fragile and would break without careful handling. Paul is saying that human beings are like these "earthen vessels," fragile and easily broken. Have you ever felt broken? Though we are weak, God has given us the privilege of containing the greatest treasure ever known to humanity.

Last year an issue of *Sports Illustrated* told the story of Lee Murray, an English mixed martial artist alleged to have masterminded the greatest cash robbery in the nation's history. The thieves made off with $92 million from a cash depot.

The group managed to get one of the employees of the depot to videotape the layout of the building. They then planned and executed their crime to perfection. How were they caught? They started bragging about the crime and spending the loot like drunken sailors.

But what was most striking about Murray's crime was not just size of the cash haul, but the relative ease with which they accomplished it. The gunmen easily overwhelmed the few guards watching the depot, and without firing a single shot. Great treasures are supposed to be stored under tight security.

Paul believed that one of the proofs that God had called him to ministry was the fact that that God had done great things through him, a very weak vessel containing a great treasure. What treasure was Paul referring to? It's found in 2 Corinthians 4:6: "the light of the knowledge of the glory of God in the face of Christ." The knowledge of God's awesome glory that shone in the face of Jesus Christ, says Paul, is a treasure we all can have! Don't you want it?

//////// HOT READ ////////

What does it mean to be "yoked" with unbelievers? See 2 Corinthians 6:14-18.

——> GIVE TO LIVE, LIVE TO GIVE <

They urgently pleaded with us for the privilege of sharing in this service to the saints.
2 Corinthians 8:4.

uring my early years in college I met a guy named Fred from the French Caribbean island of Martinique. He spoke with a strong French accent that made him tough to understand. One could mistake his words, but not his heart.

Fred was a superior musician. He had studied music before coming to Oakwood. Many days we wiled away our little bit of free time by the piano in our dorm. It was woefully out of tune—a fact that made Fred wince. He would bang keys that should sound a certain way, and when they didn't quite sound the right tone, he would sing it perfectly as he played. Just for kicks I'd describe a nature scene, and Fred would create it musically.

"I'm in a storm, Fred," I'd begin. "It's dark, foreboding. Ominous clouds have snuffed out the moonlight." (English majors are full of hot air.) Fred would listen to me speak, and he'd begin playing. With each chord, Fred would create musical, rhythmical storm. I'll never forget it.

Fred had another gift that was a blessing. He was a generous person with whatever he had. Late at night guys in the dorm would be hungry, going from room to room foraging for food. Fred would share whatever he had. Many times we'd illegally fry up and eat little flour pastries that Fred called johnnycakes. They weren't healthy, but they hit the spot.

The apostle Paul bragged to the Corinthians about the awesome generosity of the believers in Macedonia, the place from which he wrote 2 Corinthians. The people of Macedonia were extremely poor, but when they heard about the deep needs of the believers in Jerusalem, they urged Paul to let them give. They gave what they could, and then some. Their graciousness moved Paul deeply, and he used their testimony to wake up the stingy members of the Corinthian church, who had also pledged to help but were dragging their feet (2 Corinthians 8:7-9)!

Giving is living, and living is giving.

/////// HOT READ ///////

What important warning and promise about giving did Paul give to the Corinthian believers? See 2 Corinthians 9:6-12.

——> MY DEFENSE <

But he said to me, "My grace is sufficient for you, for my power is made perfect in weakness." Therefore I will boast all the more gladly about my weaknesses, so that Christ's power may rest on me. 2 Corinthians 12:9.

The final four chapters of Paul's second letter to the Corinthians is his defense of his ministry, and Paul does not mince words. He begins by stating that he and his fellow ministers are soldiers in a battle, fighting with weapons that are not of this world. Their weapons have divine power to demolish strongholds and anything else that sets itself up against God (2 Corinthians 10:4). Paul is not fooling around!

In chapter 11 Paul goes further, and his words become sharper. Remember, he is addressing a small group of "haters" who have questioned everything he stands for. Their hate made him angry, but he was more upset that their influence was tearing the church apart. In chapter 11, verse 5, he notes that these members had no problem listening to false teachers who came preaching a false gospel. But whenever Paul or one of his group stood up to preach, all hell would break loose. "I do not think I am in the least inferior to those 'super-apostles,'" writes Paul. "I may not be a trained speaker, but I do have knowledge" (verses 5, 6). You can almost hear him ask, "What did I ever do to deserve this kind of treatment?"

Paul pointed to his sufferings as proof of his calling by God. "I have worked much harder, been in prison more frequently, been flogged more severely, and been exposed to death again and again. Five times I received from the Jews the forty lashes minus one. Three times I was beaten with rods, once I was stoned, three times I was shipwrecked, I spent a night and a day in the open sea" (verses 23-25). Paul hated to boast of what he had endured, so he told the believers about a problem, a "thorn in my flesh" (2 Corinthians 12:7) that made his life miserable. We don't know what Paul's problem was, but he wanted it gone! Though Paul prayed for deliverance, God did not take the problem away. Instead, God grave him grace to help him bear it.

People who stand up for God will face challenges, often from other believers. Paul strongly defended his belief in God, and we too must be ready to defend our faith.

/////// HOT READ ///////

What counsel did Paul give the believers? See 2 Corinthians 13:5. Why?

⟶> PERVERTS BEWARE! <

Evidently some people are throwing you into confusion and are trying to pervert the gospel of Christ. Galatians 1:7.

If the title of today's reading started you thinking about dirty old men—or women—you'd better think again. According to one online dictionary, *pervert* means: "to cause to turn away from what is right, proper, or good; corrupt; to bring to a bad or worse condition; debase." As you can see, you don't have to be a sexual deviant to be a pervert. Some would argue that the worst kind of perverts around are those who twist the truth, causing people to be misled. The apostle Paul would probably agree with that statement. I'll explain more later, but permit me a little nostalgia.

Growing up, I attended a church that was very loving in many ways. I still remember the awesome "socials" we used to have. (BTW, do you even know what a social is?) But not everything was great about my church. I also remember how members of the church would shun teens who got pregnant before marriage. Some adults would "put you in hell" for wearing a necklace or an earring. My church taught us that if we obeyed all the do's and don'ts of our faith, we would be saved. They were wrong!

The ancient churches that made up the territory of Galatia during the time of Paul had the same problem that my church had: perverted members. In Paul's day some Jews believed that all new converts to Christianity had to obey the laws given to the children of Israel by God through Moses. You read about those in Leviticus, Numbers, and Deuteronomy—among other places. Prominent Jewish leaders taught that no uncircumcised Gentile could be saved.

The book of Galatians is Paul's letter to them and to all people who believe that you have to abide by a list of do's and don'ts to be saved. Those who pervert God's truth in this way had better not read this book, because there's only one way to be saved, and that's by accepting the sacrifice of Jesus on the cross as payment for our sins.

///////// HOT READ ////////

Does the fact that we cannot do anything to earn salvation mean that we can continue sinning? Check out what Romans 6:1-7 has to say about it.

——> FREE FOR FREEDOM <

*It is for freedom that Christ has set us free. Stand firm, then, and do not let your-
selves be burdened again by a yoke of slavery.* Galatians 5:1.

ou'd probably have a tough time getting filmmaker Sean Langan to visit the
border region between Afghanistan and Pakistan. There's a little conflict going on
there with a group called the Taliban. Osama bin Laden is believed to be their
guest, but who knows.

Mr. Langan traveled to the dangerous region to film *Fighting the Taliban*, a
documentary that was widely acclaimed and put on the short list to win several
awards. He returned to Afghanistan shortly thereafter to do a second documentary
called *Meeting the Taliban*, and boy, did he ever.

Sean Landan was kidnapped by Islamic extremists and held for more than
three months in a dark basement. While there he was subjected to several mock
executions: the captors pretend to kill you, but then laugh it off as a joke. Langan
was mentally and emotionally broken when he was released.

What would you think of Sean Langan if you heard sometime later that he
decided to go back to that hostile border region so that he could be kidnapped and
imprisoned again? The word that first popped into my mind rhymes with pool.
That would be the act of a crazy person, don't you think? Who would want to go
back to prison after being set free? Believe it or not, some Christians do.

Even though Jesus' death has freed us from the penalty of sin, some still
choose to live under the power of sin. Paul argues in Galatians 5 that the freedom
that God gives us is designed to keep us free—from the slavery of sin.

Do you ever feel enslaved by some bad habit or behavior, even though you
have given your heart to God? Don't despair; there is hope. Here's what Paul says
to you and me: "So I say, live by the Spirit, and you will not gratify the desires of
the sinful nature" (Galatians 5:16). Don't stop there. Read the rest of chapter 5 get
the full prescription.

////// HOT READ //////

What is God saying to you in Galatians 6:7-9?

⟶ WHO ARE YOU? <

I pray also that the eyes of your heart may be enlightened in order that you may know the hope to which he has called you, the riches of his glorious inheritance in the saints. Ephesians 1:18.

Identity theft is quickly becoming the signature crime of the twenty-first century. Teams of computer hackers are writing programs that crawl around the Internet looking for vulnerable computers from which to steal information. Some Web sites you visit online have been engineered to lift your vital information without leaving any fingerprints. The culprits could be next door or on the next continent and you'd never know.

But what do you do when your identity is stolen, not by some whiz-kid hacker in Russia, but by someone you love? One victim shared her story on a Web site warning people about the dangers of identity theft. Here's what she had to say.

"I just got back from vacation in Las Vegas and found out that my sister has been using my credit card ($584) and has committed fraudulent crimes under my name. She no longer lives in the same town as me, and I did not order or receive any of the items that were charged. I will not pay for something I didn't order. She is in the county jail serving time for using alias names, and I am prosecuting.

"Also, when I got home last week, I opened all my mail and discovered that I had been denied housing because she had stolen my identity. I was fingerprinted today and am going to fax the information to the Las Vegas police department. Of all the things she has done to me . . ."

I believe there's an even sadder case of identity theft going on right now than the one mentioned above. Satan has stolen the true identity of the Christian church. Somehow God's church has been transformed into one big cash machine in which preachers use members to get rich. If you want to know what God's church is supposed to be like, Ephesians is the book for you.

Paul gives God's intention for the church (Ephesians 1:15-23). He also shares how God intends to accomplish His mission (Ephesians 2:11-3:7). Paul closes with the promise that God will equip His people for victory over evil (Ephesians 3:10-20; 6:12-20).

Ephesians reveals the high and holy purpose to which God called you and me.

HOT READ
Ever wonder what you'd look like without Jesus in your life? Ephesians 2:1-7.

——> WHEN I MOVE, YOU MOVE

Be imitators of God, therefore, as dearly loved children and live a life of love, just as Christ loved us and gave himself up for us as a fragrant offering and sacrifice to God. Ephesians 5:1, 2.

ave you ever felt lost, far from God—as if God moved out of your neighborhood and didn't bother to tell you? Paul knew what if felt like to be far from God, even though he thought he was following God. We learned in Acts that before his conversion Paul relentlessly persecuted Christian believers. At Stephen's murder, Acts 7:54-59 tells us, the people who stoned him laid their cloaks at the feet of a young man named Saul. God later changed that young man's heart (Acts 9), and he followed God everywhere that God went.

In these verses from Ephesians 5, Paul tells us how to walk with God each day.

"Watch what God does, and then you do it, like children who learn proper behavior from their parents. Mostly what God does is love you. Keep company with him and learn a life of love. Observe how Christ loved us. His love was not cautious but extravagant. He didn't love in order to get something from us but to give everything of himself to us. Love like that.

"Don't allow love to turn into lust, setting off a downhill slide into sexual promiscuity, filthy practices, or bullying greed. Though some tongues just love the taste of gossip, Christians follow Jesus have better uses for language than that. Don't talk dirty or silly. That kind of talk doesn't fit our style. Thanksgiving is our dialect.

"You can be sure that using people or religion or things just for what you can get out of them—the usual variations on idolatry—will get you nowhere, and certainly nowhere near the kingdom of Christ, the kingdom of God.

"Don't let yourselves get taken in by religious smooth talk. God gets furious with people who are full of religious sales talk but want nothing to do with him. Don't even hang around people like that. You groped your way through that murk once, but no longer. You're out in the open now. The bright light of Christ makes your way plain" (verses 1-8, Message).

///////// HOT READ ///////

How many times does the apostle Paul mention the word one in Ephesians 4:1-7? How should you treat your parents? Ephesians 6:1. Are you ready to fight? Ephesians 6:10-19.

⟶ PRISON-PROOF ‹

What is more, I consider everything a loss compared to the surpassing greatness of knowing Christ Jesus my Lord, for whose sake I have lost all things. I consider them rubbish, that I may gain Christ. Philippians 3:8.

Friend, if Paul had a group of best friends, they had to be the Philippians. The believers in Philippi were known for their missionary spirit and zeal. In Philippians 4:15 and 16 we read: "Moreover, as you Philippians know, in the early days of your acquaintance with the gospel, when I set out from Macedonia, not one church shared with me in the matter of giving and receiving, except you only; for even when I was in Thessalonica, you sent me aid again and again when I was in need." That's what friends are for, isn't it?

Paul was in prison in Rome when he wrote letters to the Ephesians, the Philippians, the Colossians, and to Philemon. Prison has a way of breaking the hardest of men, but though Paul was in prison, his heart and mind were free. There's not even a hint of fear or sadness in any of his prison writings. When he thought about the Philippians, he "got happy." In fact, the central theme of the Philippian manuscript is how to experience true joy in Jesus Christ no matter what you may be going through. If you happen to be hurting right now, Philippians can show you how to do more than survive. It'll teach you how to thrive!

Because of his boldness in sharing the gospel with the world, Paul lost all his earthly possessions. Yet he considered all his worldly possessions mere garbage when compared to the joy of knowing Jesus Christ. Although he'd been preaching the gospel for many years, Paul still had a hunger to go deeper with God, to know more about Jesus.

"I want to know Christ and the power of his resurrection and the fellowship of sharing in his sufferings, becoming like him in his death" (Philippians 3:10). Maybe I'm missing something, but did Paul just say that he wanted to share in the suffering that Jesus experienced?

Jesus has a way of making His followers prison-proof. Bury yourself deep in Jesus and see what'll happen to you.

///// HOT READ /////

What awesome tips did Paul give the Philippians before saying goodbye? Philippians 4:1-9.

——> COMPLETE <

For in Christ all the fullness of the Deity lives in bodily form, and you have been given fullness in Christ, who is head over every power and authority. Colossians 2:9, 10.

I just checked Google with the question "Who was Jesus?" and my search returned *5 million* different answers. Needless to say, they can't all be right.

Jesus' life, death, and resurrection is one of the most challenging events in human history. People have many strong views about it. Christians say that Jesus was God in the flesh. The Muslims claim that he was a just a prophet—the same as Muhammad or Moses. During the 1970s *Jesus Christ Superstar*, a rock opera, staring "Jesus," ran in playhouses all over North America. In 1973 a film based on the opera was nominated for an Oscar. Who knew that Jesus was into theater and the movies!

If you want to know who Jesus really is, no other book of the New Testament answers that question better than Colossians. Jesus is the star of Colossians. Let me explain.

Colossians is actually a letter written by Paul to the Christian believers in Colossae in Asia Minor. (The Turks and Kurds now live in that area.) But not too long after the founding of the church, strange pagan beliefs started to creep into it. False teachers taught that Jesus was not fully God and not fully human. That's a red flag right there, right? They believed that Jesus was a half-divine being who bridged the gap between God and the world. Doesn't sound too off base, does it? Wait, there's more.

Because Jesus was this "half and half" guy, the teachers believed that He did not have the power or authority to meet all the needs of the Colossians—or of you and me today. And so they taught that to be saved you had to have special mystical knowledge and practice extreme self-discipline. And many people still believe that—that you're saved by what you *know*, or that you need to live on a mountaintop by yourself to truly serve God. Even now, to show thankfulness and/or penitence for sin, every Easter season a number of Filipinos reenact the Crucifixion, including having themselves nailed to crosses. Yikes!

In this letter from prison Paul makes it clear that Jesus created all things (Colossians 1:16), sustains the universe (verse 17), and broke the power of demonic forces at the cross (Colossians 2:15). Paul was saying to the Colossians, You are complete in Jesus. He is all you need to be saved.

/////// HOT READ ///////

How should Christians behave? Check out Colossians 3:1-11 to find out.

——> WORRIED ABOUT THE COMING? <

For the Lord Himself will come down from heaven, with a loud command, with the voice of the archangel and with the trumpet call of God. And the dead in Christ will rise first. 1 Thessalonians 4:16.

Thessalonica was a bustling seaport city in the Roman province of Macedonia. Paul and Silas preached there during Paul's second missionary journey (Acts 17), eventually establishing a church of both Jews and Gentiles. It was more heavily Gentile than Jew, and this posed a problem, as it did in many of the churches started by Paul and his crew.

Remember, Paul was pioneering a brand-new religion called Christianity, one that included *everyone*. Churches of this kind were unheard-of at the time, and the new believers brought some strange belief and puzzling concerns. For example, many of the church members in Thessalonica didn't understand the Second Coming. They thought that Jesus should have come back by then. *When will it happen?* they asked. *What will happen to our family and friends who've already died? Will they be "left behind" at the Second Coming, or will there be some kind of special "rapture" for them?*

Paul answered their questions by explaining that Jesus Himself was coming back to earth and that it would be a huge, noisy event. He said that Jesus was going to raise the dead when He came, and that those who were still alive would "be caught up together with them . . . to meet the Lord in the air" (1 Thessalonians 4:17). Paul also didn't want them to be paralyzed by worry. (To know more about how Jesus will return, read these two letters. Don't be misled by those who believe in the secret rapture and other Second Coming heresies.)

Author E. Stanley Jones wrote in *Transformed by Thorns*, "I am inwardly fashioned for faith, not for fear. Fear is not my native land; faith is. . . . I live better by faith and confidence than by fear, doubt and anxiety. In anxiety and worry, my being is gasping for breath. . . . But in faith and confidence, I breathe freely—these are my native air" (p. 95).

Do you worry about when Jesus will come, about the persecution of the righteous, or whether or not you'll be saved? The antidote to fear is faith in Jesus. Stay alert to the signs of Jesus' soon return (Matthew 24), but don't stress out. Trust God, live each day for Him, and you'll be ready.

//////// HOT READ ////////

What else did Paul say about the Second Coming? 1 Thessalonians 4:17, 18.

——> WORK STOPPAGE <

We hear that some among you are idle. They are not busy; they are busybodies.
2 Thessalonians 3:11.

njoy your life right now, my friend, because once you start working full-time to pay bills, your life is going to change drastically. You'll yearn for days off, vacations, and unexpected work stoppages.

One memorable day we got some unexpected free time at work. I remember the thud with which all the power in the building went out. My computer monitor went blank, the air-conditioning stopped running, the halls and pressrooms were dark, and work came to a standstill. No one knew what had happened, but we all knew that we were suddenly about to get some much-needed vacation time. While we stood around outside—the sun was very warm, as I recall—celebrating the break, upper management was worried about all the money we were losing. Publishing houses don't make money when the presses are suddenly idle.

When the electrical engineers investigated the problem, they found the culprit. A squirrel had gotten into the main electrical transformer. He fried himself when he touched one of the powerful live wires. Poor little guy. He sacrificed himself so that we might get a couple hours away from work. I was sad for him, but happy for myself.

Some work stoppages are welcome, but others are not—such as the one that happened at the church in Thessalonica when certain believers stopped earning a living. Why? They believed that Jesus' Second Coming was imminent. If Jesus is coming soon, why work? Ever heard that before? Furthermore, these believers filled their spare time with gossiping about others. Paul wasn't having any of it. He wrote in 2 Thessalonians 3:10, "If a man will not work, he shall not eat."

Waiting for the second coming of Jesus is not an excuse to stop working. It's not a free pass to stop trying to make the world a better place. God's people must continue to make a difference in the world until He returns, and we fulfill part of that mission in how we approach our work.

///////// HOT READ ////////

**Want a clear description of the events that will precede Jesus' second coming?
Read 2 Thessalonians 2. Knowing this, how should you live your life?**

——> WHO, ME? <

Paul, an apostle of Christ Jesus by the command of God our Savior and of Christ Jesus our hope, to Timothy my true son in the faith: Grace, mercy and peace from God the Father and Christ Jesus our Lord. 1 Timothy 1:1, 2.

What makes a great leader? Toughness? Vision? Courage? Conviction? In his book author Paul Borthwick highlights the qualities of a great leader, outlined by leadership guru Myron Rush. Think about each of these traits carefully.

• You must be willing to stand alone.
• You must be willing to go against public opinion in order to promote what you believe.
• You must be willing to risk failure.
• You must become master of your emotions.
• You must strive to remain above reproach.
• You must be willing to make decisions others don't want to make.
• You must be willing to say no at times, even when you'd like to say yes.
• You must sometimes be willing to sacrifice personal interests for the good of the group.
• You must never be content with the average; you must always strive for the best.
• People must be more important to you than possessions.
• You will have to work harder to keep your life in balance than people do who are not leaders.

Do you have what it takes to be a great leader? If you're not sure, don't worry. Many people whom we consider great leaders had strong doubts about their leadership "skillz." But every great leader starts somewhere. Someone has to believe him or her and give them a chance.

Many scholars believe that Timothy was probably in his 20s when Paul tapped him to lead the church in Ephesus. He faced several daunting odds. Paul had to teach Timothy how to deal with false teachers, how to order the church's worship, how to choose leaders, and how to deal with the different groups of people in the church—some rich, some poor, etc.

Most important of all, though, Paul cautioned Timothy to live a godly life. Timothy was to preach his most powerful sermons by his example. Maybe God is calling you to be a leader in some way. First and 2 Timothy are must reading if you want to know how to lead out for God.

////// HOT READ //////

What qualifications did bishops or overseers of the people have to have? See 1 Timothy 3:1-7. What point was Paul making about the true qualifications for leadership?

——> YOU'RE TOO YOUNG <

Don't let anyone look down on you because you are young, but set an example for the believers in speech, in life, in love, in faith and in purity. 1 Timothy 4:12.

outh often get a bad rap in church. Many adults view them as disrespectful, ungodly, or worse—evil. Let's be honest. Some youth can be evil, but as a general rule, they're not out to destroy the church. But they do tend to lose interest in church when adults dominate the services without giving them much of a chance to participate. I hope I'm not describing your church.

Youth can do great things when given a chance. Just ask Christopher Teel, a kid with a passion to feed the poor. His story was highlighted on thekidshalloffame.com Web site:

"Christopher Teel has tackled several projects over the past six years to alleviate hunger, raise money for a kids' meals program, recruit volunteers for a food bank, and provide food and clothing to migrant workers and low-income Hispanic fathers. Christopher, whose mother struggled to put food on the table when he was young, says, 'I developed a compassion for hungry people of all ages, and a fervor to mobilize the community to address . . . hunger.'

"After learning about the Children's Nutrition Network, an aid program that provides meals and tutoring to underprivileged inner-city youth, Christopher researched the organization and then wrote and presented a proposal to Regis University that resulted in a $3,700 grant. In addition, Christopher mobilized other young people from his school, church and neighborhood to volunteer their weekends, summer vacations, and holidays to work at the Food Bank of the Rockies." Teel was cited by Prudential Corporation as one of America's Top 10 Youth Volunteers of 2002.

The apostle Paul knew that Timothy had special gifts that would bless God's church. "Do not neglect your gift, which was given you through a prophetic message when the body of elders laid their hands on you," Paul wrote (1 Timothy 4:14).

Don't spend your time fighting with older members. Spend your time working for God!

////// HOT READ ///////

How was Timothy supposed to interact with older members? See 1 Timothy 5:1-8. How should Timothy deal with money issues? See 1 Timothy 6:3-10.

——> ONE LAST TIME <

Only Luke is with me. Get Mark and bring him with you, because he is helpful to me in my ministry. 2 Timothy 4:11.

The apostle Paul is one of the superheroes of the Bible. Paul survived numerous beatings. He lived through three shipwrecks. When he finally made it to shore after one wreck, he was bitten by a deadly poisonous snake. Paul shook off the snake, and kept on warming himself by the fire. Jailed many times for preaching the gospel, Paul nevertheless refused to stop. Paul was a biblical superhero.

But friends, even superheroes have rough days. Paul wrote his second letter to Timothy shortly before his death. Unlike his first imprisonment in Rome, when he was essentially under house arrest, this time Paul was put in a dark, cold dungeon. Nero, the emperor of Rome, had begun a terrible persecution of the Christian sect that Paul and the other apostles had worked to build. Paul and Luke were picked up during the sweep.

This letter to Timothy is one of the most emotional pieces of reading in all the Bible, and is believed to be the final message written by Paul. The old spiritual warrior knew that he'd come to the end of the line. He was going to die. "I am already being poured out like a drink offering," he concluded, "and the time has come for my departure" (2 Timothy 4:6).

Before he died, Paul wanted to encourage Timothy to remain faithful—no matter what temptations came his way (2 Timothy 1). He wanted him to be a guy who could "correctly handle the word of truth" (see 2 Timothy 2:15). He wanted him to know the Bible, so that he wouldn't be led astray by the strange doctrines swirling around him. He wanted him to know that "all Scripture is God-breathed and is useful for teaching, rebuking, correcting and training in righteousness, so that the man of God may be thoroughly equipped for every good work" (2 Timothy 3:16, 17). Even as he faced certain death, Paul continued to mentor Timothy.

Paul gave much to Timothy, and in this epistle he asks something in return. As you'll read today, several of Paul's friends had left him, and he simply needed encouragement. He wanted to see Timothy and John Mark one last time to say his final goodbyes.

When people take time to mentor you, do whatever it takes to honor them.

HOT READ

Paul knew that His life had pleased God. Read what he says in 2 Timothy 4:7, 8.

──> FAITH FOR TODAY <

For the grace of God that brings salvation has appeared to all men. It teaches us to say "No" to ungodliness and worldly passions, and to live self-controlled, upright and godly lives in this present age. Titus 2:11, 12.

While 2 Timothy is believed to be the last letter written by Paul before his death, Paul's letter to Titus was written during his first imprisonment—basically house arrest. During this time Paul was allowed to preach and receive visitors.

Titus, a Greek, had been converted by Paul's preaching. Like Timothy, Titus was a young and inexperienced pastor, so Paul offered him some guidelines to help him in his ministry. Paul knew that Titus faced an uphill struggle with the Jewish believers who didn't much care for Gentile believers, let alone having one of them for their pastor.

Titus was in charge of an ornery band of Christians on the Island of Crete, and the Cretans had a bad reputation. Epimenides, a well-known Cretan poet of the third century B.C. (a man regarded as a prophet by his people), wrote, "Cretans are always liars, evil brutes, lazy gluttons." Paul quoted him in Titus 1:12, adding, "This testimony is true" (verse 13). Ouch. He told Titus to "rebuke" false teachers sharply (verse 13).

Paul wanted Titus to preach a message that could transform even the most hardened sinners, and he wanted him to do it boldly. We live in a time that people seem to say only what's politically correct. We don't want to offend people by telling them the truth, and we're definitely not going to tell them when they're wrong. Listen to this counsel from Paul to Titus.

"For the grace of God has appeared, bringing salvation to all, training us to renounce impiety and worldly passions, and in the present age and to live lives that are self-controlled, upright and godly, while we wait for the blessed hope and the manifestation of the glory of our great God and Savior, Jesus Christ. He it is who gave himself for us that he might redeem us from all iniquity and purify for himself a people of his own who are zealous for good deeds" (Titus 2:11-14, NRSV).

The gospel we believe and share with the world has power to help us live right—now!

/////// HOT READ ///////

Do you know anyone who likes to argue a lot? Share Titus 3:9-11 with them.

——> THE FUGITIVE <

So if you consider me a partner, welcome him as you would welcome me. Philemon 17.

Lewis, the great Christian author, once said, "Mankind is so fallen that no man can be trusted with unchecked power over his fellows. Aristotle believed some people were only fit to be slaves. I do not contradict him. But I reject slavery because I see no men fit to be masters."

Lewis was right. No human being is qualified to be master of another human being. But we don't live in a perfect world, and slavery continues today. Zach Hunter, a teenage abolitionist, started an organization called Loose Change to Loosen Chains to help free the more than 27 million people enslaved today. Zach's organization collects loose change—you know, the stuff hiding in the corners of your couch, or sitting on your dresser—and uses it to buy the freedom of people in slavery. Neat, isn't it?

The short book of Philemon is about a slave and his master. In the ancient Roman Empire slavery was a reality. Slaves were openly bought and sold, much as they were in the Americas. And under Roman law runaway slaves could be punished by death. Slave uprisings were put down harshly.

Philemon was a slave owner living in the city of Colossae who accepted Jesus Christ as his Savior. He was so moved by Paul's preaching that he allowed the church in Colossae to meet at his house (Philemon 2). But in spite of his conversion, something happened that pushed Philemon over the edge. One of his slaves named Onesimus stole some money or property from his master and ran away to Rome (verses 10, 18). While in Rome, Onesimus met Paul and was converted to Jesus Christ.

Onesimus wanted to make things right with his master, but he was afraid to return home for fear of what Philemon would do to him. Paul then wrote a letter to Philemon on Onesimus' behalf. Paul asked him to see Onesimus, not as a fugitive slave who swiped his stuff and ran away, but as a fellow "dear brother" in Christ (verse 16).

In his own way, Paul was trying to change how Philemon viewed his slaves. Philemon wasn't ready to give up his slaves, but he could certainly treat them better.

/////// HOT READ ///////

What offer did Paul make to Philemon? (verse 18).

——> BETTER <

In the past God spoke to our forefathers through the prophets at many times and in various ways, but in these last days he has spoken to us by his Son, whom he appointed heir of all things, and through whom he made the universe. Hebrews 1:1, 2.

ey, don't you stop reading now. Keep on going. You can do it! We're almost to the end.

So what's Hebrews all about? Well, the name *Hebrews* refers to people who were direct descendants of Abraham. And the name *Hebrews* is the first key to understanding this deeply theological book. The book itself was written sometime around A.D. 70, when the Romans were killing Christians wherever they could find them. The Romans saw Christianity as a threat to the stability of their empire, so they tried to stamp it out by violently persecuting Christians.

When a Christian was caught, he or she would be offered a chance at freedom. All that was required of the captive was to burn a sacrifice to Roman gods and renounce his or her faith. Most Christians refused, and they died in horrible ways. Long before *Gladiator* brought the barbarity of the Roman Colosseum to light, Christians were fed to wild animals there—as entertainment!

All this persecution led some Jewish Christians to question their new faith. Under the severe trial of persecution, some wanted to go back to the beliefs of their founders. Instead of accepting Jesus' sacrifice for their sins, they wanted to return to the old sacrificial system of killing animals to atone for sin. The writer of Hebrews—and we don't know for certain who that was—wrote this letter to encourage the Hebrew believers (Jews) to trust in Jesus alone to save them.

One of the key words you'll notice in Hebrews is *better.* For instance, the author wanted to show the Jews that Jesus' sacrifice for sin was better than the old system of killing animals; that through His death, *all* sins could be forgiven (Hebrews 7:27). The animals had to be happy to hear that.

Hebrews tells us what Jesus did to save us, and what He is doing now in heaven to keep us saved. This book will challenge you, but don't give up on it. Ask God to help you understand its rich truth.

//////// HOT READ ////////

Read Hebrews 3:1-6. Why did the writer compare Jesus to Moses? How did the Jews view Moses?

——> WHAT A GUY! <

For we do not have a high priest who is unable to sympathize with our weaknesses, but we have one who has been tempted in every way, just as we are—yet was without sin. Hebrews 4:15.

The January 1999 issue of *In Touch* magazine carried this powerful true story. "Cleveland Stroud had coached the Blue Collar Bulldogs for 18 years before his basketball team made it to the state championship. Stroud recalls that 'it was the perfect night' when they won. 'A night you dream of.' He was carried around the gym on the shoulders of his triumphant players and their proud parents. The local paper put his picture on the front page. But the excitement was short-lived.

"Two months after the championship, during a routine grade check, Stroud discovered that one player was academically ineligible. The player had only played 45 seconds during the regional qualifying tournament. Stroud says, 'I thought it was all ruined. I went through a phase where I was really depressed.' He struggled with what to do next. Yet, his commitment to integrity led him to the right decision.

"'Winning is the most important thing for any coach,' he says. 'But your principles have to be higher than your goals.' He reported the error to the league and the Bulldogs forfeited their trophy. When the team lamented their loss in the locker room, he told them, 'You've got to do what is honest, what is right, and what the rules say. People forget the scores of basketball games, but they don't ever forget what you are made of.'"

People don't forget what you're made of. The writer of Hebrews would agree with the old basketball coach. He or she didn't want the Jewish believers comparing Jesus to the high priests who served their descendants centuries before. Not only did Jesus come from heaven, but He experienced more pain, temptation, suffering, and aggravation than any other human. Jesus took this experience with Him to heaven. He is still "touched" by our weaknesses.

Jesus still has the scar in His side from the day of His crucifixion. He still has the marks in His hands from the nails that pierced His flesh. Every time we hurt, His hands tingle and His feet ache. Jesus "feels" us like no one else can. There's no one quite like Jesus.

/////// HOT READ ///////
Did God give Jesus any "breaks" while He was on earth? Hebrews 5:8, 9.

──> NOT GOOD ENOUGH <

This is an illustration for the present time, indicating that the gifts and sacrifices being offered were not able to clear the conscience of the worshiper. Hebrews 9:9.

astor Mike Hamilton of Louisiana told the story of the young man who knelt before a beautiful young woman beside a placid lake. "Darling," he said, "I want you to know that I love you more than life," he began. "I want you to marry me. I'm not a wealthy man. I don't have a yacht, a Rolls-Royce, or lots of money like Johnny Green, but I do love you with all my heart."

The young woman paused for a moment, then said, "Darling, I love you with all my heart too. But before I say yes, tell me a little more about Johnny Green."

Did she really love him with all her heart? Uh, NOT!

Human beings are creatures of habit. We can get used to just about anything if you give us enough time. I had a high school friend who refused to get his athlete's foot treated because he loved to sit on his bed and grind his feet together until little pieces of skin fell off of them. He had gotten used to his athlete's foot.

The ancient Israelites had gotten used to bringing their sacrifices to the Temple and offering them up for their sins. They did it day in and day out until the whole experience became meaningless. The writer of Hebrews pointed out that it would be kinda crazy for the Jewish believers to go back to this system, since it had no power to change people's hearts. People could say they loved God with all their hearts and continue in sin. All they had to do was grab the nearest animal and bring it to the Temple. Their consciences remained unchanged.

Jesus' life, death, and resurrection could do what the killing of sacrifices never could. It could change our sinful hearts. How? Anyone who accepts Jesus as Savior, also gets a bonus: Jesus comes and lives within. As we abide in Him, He then transforms us from the inside out (John 15:1-7).

/////// HOT READ ///////
What does it mean that Jesus is able to save completely? Hebrews 7:25.

——> FAITH <

Now faith is being sure of what we hope for and certain of what we do not see.
Hebrews 11:1.

adies and gentlemen, here's the Bible's Hall of Faith. Not sure what to do with your faith? Here's a tip: Put it all in God, and the world might one day read about you!

"The fundamental fact of existence is that this trust in God, this faith, is the firm foundation under everything that makes life worth living. It's our handle on what we can't see. The act of faith is what distinguished our ancestors, set them above the crowd.

"By faith, we see the world called into existence by God's word, what we see created by what we don't see. By an act of faith, Abel brought a better sacrifice to God than Cain. It was what he *believed*, not what he *brought*, that made the difference. That's what God noticed and approved as righteous. After all these centuries, that belief continues to catch our notice.

"By an act of faith, Enoch skipped death completely. 'They looked all over and couldn't find him because God had taken him.' We know on the basis of reliable testimony that before he was taken 'he pleased God.' It's impossible to please God apart from faith. And why? Because anyone who wants to approach God must believe both that he exists *and* that he cares enough to respond to those who seek him.

"By faith, Noah built a ship in the middle of dry land. He was warned about something he couldn't see, and acted on what he was told. The result? His family was saved. His act of faith drew a sharp line between the evil of the unbelieving world and the rightness of the believing world. As a result, Noah became intimate with God.

"By an act of faith, Abraham said yes to God's call to travel to an unknown place that would become his home. When he left he had no idea where he was going. By an act of faith he lived in the country promised him, lived as a stranger camping in tents. Isaac and Jacob did the same, living under the same promise. Abraham did it by keeping his eye on an unseen city with real, eternal foundations—the City designed and built by God" (Hebrews 11:1-10, Message).

/////// HOT READ ///////

Knowing that we have heroes like the ones you just read about, how should we live our lives? Hebrews 12:1-4. Here's a great reason to be kind to all people: Hebrews 13:1, 2.

——> JOY? <

Consider it pure joy, my brothers, whenever you face trials of many kinds, because you know that the testing of your faith develops perseverance. James 1:2, 3.

elcome to the book of James. The writer of this book is very special, and not just because he wrote a book that got into the Bible. The Bible mentions five different people who are named James, but this James is the brother of Jesus. Josephus, the great historian, reported that James was stoned to death sometime around A.D. 62.

Can you imagine what it was like to have been Jesus' brother? The Jewish leaders hated Jesus, and they had Him put to death. As a Jew whose brother was disliked by the majority of their nation, James knew what it was like to live under pressure. But pressure "ain't all bad."

Geologists tell us that diamonds are formed some 75 to 100 miles below the earth's surface, where temperatures reach between 700° and 1,300° C. Diamonds are formed under immense pressure, and they are brought to the surface by volcanic activity. Pressure forms them, and a firestorm brings them to the surface of the earth. That's why diamonds cost so much. That's why people kill for them. That's why greedy jewelers pay gobs of money to African strongmen and dictators to get their greasy palms on them.

It's been said many times, but people are a lot like diamonds in the rough. We have great potential, but we won't become all that we can be without a little pressure and a few storms.

The book of James is dedicated to helping you become the best you can possibly be. James's advice is very practical. He doesn't get into the high discussions of theology and doctrine. He just tells us how to live the Christian life. He lays out God's commands and encourages us simply to obey and see what happens.

James began his book by telling God's people to count it all joy when trials come their way. James wasn't in love with the trials. But he was in love with what the trials did for his faith and trust in God. He loved the stamina that came from persevering through it all.

If you're having some trials right now, take courage. God is making you into something beautiful.

HOT READ
If you want to know how to treat the rich and the poor, read James 2:1-9.

——> THE FIGHT OF YOUR LIFE <

Submit yourselves, then, to God. Resist the devil, and he will flee from you.
James 4:7.

ome people love a good fight. They don't feel OK unless they're mixing it up—usually with someone they know they can beat. Here's one example of what I mean. Police in a small town in Kentucky began an investigation into video footage showing groups of teenagers fighting each other.

The teens took off their shirts before the fight began. Doesn't sound all that smart, if you ask me. Didn't they know they'd need their shirts to prevent all the scrapes and bruises? Apparently not. The videos show a brutal assault on one of the young men who fell to the ground during the melee. He was beaten until his face was covered in blood. Some guys—and girls—just love a good fight. Sadly, they're fighting the wrong enemy.

I've never been that way. I'm fairly easygoing. You have to really push me to make me fight you. If there's any way that I can walk away from the fray, that's exactly what I'll do. Call me chicken if you want to, but most fights aren't worth the time.

But there's one fight that none of us can escape. No matter how hard we try to get rid of him, Satan is one opponent who never quits. But James has really good news for us. God never quits either, and He's much more powerful than Satan.

James asks a very important question and makes an even more important statement before encouraging us to submit ourselves to God and resist the devil.

"Don't you know that friendship with the world is hatred toward God?" James asks. "Anyone who chooses to be a friend of the world becomes an enemy of God" (James 4:4). You think Satan is a tough enemy, try God.

Submitting to God and resisting Satan will work only when we stop being friends with the world. When we stop dancing to the world's music, watching the world's TV shows, spending more time on worldly social networking sites than we do with God—only then we will be victorious in our battle with Satan.

God has already defeated Satan for us. Satan can hurt us only if we go onto his turf.

HOT READ

Where does all the drama in our lives come from? James 4:1-4.

——> READY <

But in your hearts set apart Christ as Lord. Always be prepared to give an answer to everyone who asks you to give the reason for the hope that you have. But do this with gentleness and respect. 1 Peter 3:15.

he Chinese began building the Great Wall of China more than 2,000 years ago. Later rulers repaired and in some cases rebuilt the wall, and it is massive. Stretching for approximately 4,000 miles, it is the longest human-made structure ever built. Try to imagine a wall that's up to 30 feet high and 25 feet wide, with courts and watchtowers, stretching from New York to San Francisco—and it still wouldn't be as long as the Great Wall.

China had a powerful reason for building the Great Wall. Throughout its history, warrior tribes from Mongolia and other places invaded and toppled Chinese dynasties. The Great Wall was supposed to stop all of that, but it didn't. One story holds that attackers were able to defeat the wall, not by bursting through it, but by bribing the gatekeepers to let them in.

Now, what does any of that have to do with 1 Peter? *Peter wasn't Chinese*, I hear you say. You're right, of course. He wasn't. But like the Chinese, Peter did understand the importance of being ready for attacks that come out of nowhere. He believed that we should be ready at all times to give people a clear reason for the hope we have in God.

Notice, Peter did not ask us to give a deep theological answer as to why we believe in God. He just asks us to tell people what Jesus has done to change our lives, and to be able to do so from Scripture. Also, we must share our testimony with gentleness and kindness.

Aside from the obvious reason that it's good to know what you believe, Peter has another reason for encouraging us to be spiritually ready. It's found in verse 1 Peter 3:16: "keeping a clear conscience, so that those who speak maliciously against your good behavior in Christ may be ashamed of their slander."

/////// HOT READ ///////

How are husbands supposed to treat their wives? See 1 Peter 3:7. How are wives supposed to treat their husbands? See 1 Peter 3:1-6. Is this happening in your home?

⟶ END OF THE LINE <

I think it is right to refresh your memory as long as I live in the tent of this body, because I know that I will soon put it aside, as our Lord Jesus Christ has made clear to me. 2 Peter 1:13, 14.

on't you dare ask God to help me." Those were the reported last words of Joan Crawford, the famous movie star from the 1950s. Crawford spoke them to her housekeeper, who had started to pray aloud for her.

Kurt Cobain, front man of the American grunge band Nirvana, wrote these final words before he committed suicide: "I don't have the passion anymore, and so remember, it's better to burn out than to fade away. Peace, love, empathy."

Contrast the last words of Crawford and Cobain with those of Thomas Edison. You know who he is, don't you? Every time you flip a switch and a light comes on, Edison touches your life. His final words were "It's very beautiful over there." What Thomas Edison saw that made him say that, we have no way of knowing. But I surely like the fact that he seemed at peace with dying.

Until Jesus comes, eventually everyone living will die. But death shouldn't scare us. We know that one day Jesus is going to come again, and the dead in Christ shall be raised back to life to go with Him to heaven (1 Thessalonians 4:16).

Many believe that the book of 2 Peter provides, in essence, the last words of Peter before he was executed by Nero, the emperor of Rome. Peter wrote of his coming death in poetic terms. He knew that he was going to put off the "tent" of his human body, but he refused to sulk or complain. He didn't fill his final letter with hate about his conditions, or things he wished he had done. Rather, Peter warned his readers about the danger of false teachers who were trying to lead them astray.

Peter wasn't concerned for his own life. Rather, he was concerned that the gospel of Jesus Christ would live on in the hearts of his readers. He wanted them to know what they believed and to stand strong for God. That's what Peter was doing when he died.

/////// HOT READ ///////

What will the day be like when Jesus returns to earth? See 2 Peter 3:10-13. What can we do to prepare? See verses 14-18.

⎯⎯> SAY WHAT? <

Dear friends, do not believe every spirit, but test the spirits to see whether they are from God, because many false prophets have gone out into the world. 1 John 4:1.

False prophets come in all shapes, colors, and sizes. I once had some friends who decided to stop going to church. I thought maybe they didn't like the people at church, or the way the pastor preached. As it turned out, I was totally wrong.

"God has given us new light," they told me. "He is revealing Himself to us individually, and we don't need to go to church anymore." They were right that God reveals Himself to each of us, but that didn't change what the Bible says in Hebrews 10:25: "Let us not give up meeting together, as some are in the habit of doing, but let us encourage one another—and all the more as you see the Day approaching." Something important was missing from their new "light."

As I write this, America is captivated by a strange tale unfolding in Eldorado, Texas. Police there raided the compound of the Fundamentalist Church of Jesus Christ of Latter Day Saints, removing more than 400 children whom they believed were being abused or at risk of abuse. The sect practices polygamy. Community elders are encouraged to have several wives, and very young teens (in arranged marriages) may be forced to submit to the elders.

Perhaps you've run into people whose beliefs differ from yours. How do you respond? In 1 John we see that John, "the disciple whom Jesus loved," gives us several clues to help us respond to error. First and foremost, we must test false teachings against the truth. But to do so requires that we know what is truth. "This is the message we have heard from him and declare to you: God is light; in him there is no darkness at all. If we claim to have fellowship with him yet walk in the darkness, we lie and do not live by the truth" (1 John 1.5, 6). John makes clear to us that wherever God is, there is light. If we stay close to God and walk in the light of His Word, we won't be led astray. We can't just talk the talk. We have to walk the walk.

Many people believe that knowing the truth is enough to protect them from false teaching. As you read 1 John, you'll see that knowing and doing go hand in hand.

///////// HOT READ ///////

John places special importance on the transforming power of God's love. But what about our love? What happens if we fall in love with the wrong things? See 1 John 2:15-17.

——> OUT OF SIGHT <

Dear friends, since God so loved us, we also ought to love one another. 1 John 4:11.

love my wife. I miss her when she's gone, and I think she misses me, too. One Saturday afternoon I left her at church and headed home. She was going to hang out on Saturday night with GFs at one of their homes. I wasn't home more than two hours before the phone rang.

"Hey, babe! You made it home OK?" she questioned.

"Yep, I'm here." (Obviously, since I'd answered the phone, but I won't go there right now.)

"Well, I just had to tell you. You shoulda stayed for lunch. Oh, it was so good. There was so much food." Then she described every dish there from the mac and cheese to the parmesan-crusted Boca burgers. She was killing me! She called me again later that night, and then very early in the morning to let me know that she missed me. (Ahhhhhhh!)

Dude, what can I say? My wife loves me, and I'm totally in love with her, too. We'd only been away from each other for a short time, but we were already missing each other. Love just does that to people.

Loving people we cherish is easy, isn't it? But what about those people who get on our last nerve? What about loving them?

In *The Grace of Giving* Stephen Olford tells the story of Peter Miller, a Baptist pastor who was a friend of George Washington's during the American Revolution. Miller lived in Ephrata, Pennsylvania, and pastored a congregation there, but he had one problem—Michael Wittman.

Mr. Wittman "dissed" Miller every chance he could get, to the point that the Baptist minister grew to detest him. But the tables were turned when Wittman was arrested for treason and sentenced to die. The Baptist minister did the unthinkable. Peter Miller traveled 70 miles on foot to plead for the life of his sworn enemy. At first George Washington refused, believing that Miller was interceding on behalf of a friend. But when Miller told him that Wittman was his greatest enemy, George Washington was amazed. He freed Michael Wittman. Together Peter Miller and Michael Wittman returned to Ephrata as friends. Now, that's love!

///////// HOT READ ////////

What kind of love should Christians have for all people? See 1 John 4:7-16.

——> LET 'EM IN OR KICK 'EM OUT? <

If anyone comes to you and does not bring this teaching, do not take him into your house or welcome him. 2 John 10.

've got some great news for you. Today you'll read three chapters of the Bible and knock out three books with one shot. When you finish, we'll be in the final book of the Bible—the mighty Revelation. (Oohh, I'm getting chills just thinking about it, but I digress.)

The final two letters written by the disciple John deal with a controversy that was raging in the city of Ephesus, where he lived. Jewish and Gentile believers were wondering whether or not they should welcome false teachers into their homes.

I know what you're probably thinking. *What kind of weak controversy is that? It's not like they were fighting over abortion or whether gays should be able to marry or not*—two of the hot-button issues of our time. Make no mistake about it, friend—how you treated people who came to your home was a big deal back in Bible times, and it still is today.

There were no air-conditioned motels for people to check in to. You couldn't pull into Subway and order up a veggie sub to go. Traveling from place to place was a long, dusty chore and fraught with danger. To be left out in the streets after dark was to be abandoned to the mercy of robbers. The Christian believers were uncomfortable accepting false teachers into their homes, but this seemed to go against everything in their culture.

John warned them to draw the line at those teachers who openly taught lessons that were contrary to what Jesus taught and lived—those who were "antichrist" (verse 7). These teachers would use the hospitality of the believers just to get into their homes. Then they would begin breaking down the believers' faith in Jesus. However, John is not saying never let people into your house.

Third John takes the opposite tack. Here John focuses on the power of Christian hospitality to smooth the way as we "work together for the truth" (3 John 8).

Today you'll also read the book of Jude. Jude gives an urgent warning against leaders who say they're following God but who live in open sin. It's a must-read for every young Christian!

Enjoy! We're almost done!

/////// HOT READ ///////

How will God deal with leaders who teach false doctrines? Jude 12-15.

──> THE REVELATION OF JESUS CHRIST <

"I am the Alpha and the Omega," says the Lord God, "who is, and who was, and who is to come, the Almighty." Revelation 1:8.

evelation. You've made it to the final book of the Bible. Revelation demands more of the reader than any other book of the Bible. You will need to pray for God's Holy Spirit to help you understand what you're reading. If you don't "get" something, ask your pastor or Bible teacher. Keep studying, and God will lead you to the truth.

To understand Revelation, you've got to understand the time in which this book was written. The writer of Revelation is John the disciple, the son of Zebedee and one of Jesus' closest friends. He's the same guy who wrote the Gospel of John and First, Second, and Third John. John's other works were written while he lived in Ephesus, but the Revelation of Jesus Christ—the book of Revelation—was given to him in vision when he was in exile on a faraway island called Patmos, a Roman territory.

How did John end up on Patmos? He was sent there by the emperor Domitian of Rome. He and John sorta had a falling-out. Domitian was nuts—and that's putting it mildly. He was a power-hungry ruler who rigged the Roman Senate to keep himself in power. When he heard that a man named John was preaching the gospel at Ephesus, he became irate. Why? Well, one reason may have been that the gospel preached by John declared that Jesus is Lord and God. This was in direct conflict to the title that Domitian took as his own—*Dominus et Deus*, or Lord and God. Domitian saw himself as a god, and then some. (Talk about being full of yourself.)

Domitian had John arrested and dropped into a cauldron of burning oil to execute him publicly. But it didn't work. John did not burn. Humiliated, Domitian banished John to a brutal work camp on the island of Patmos. He thought this would stop his message cold, but he was wrong. It was on Patmos that God gave John a vision of the end of the world, when all evil—including Satan—would be destroyed, and Jesus would be revealed in His true majesty and power!

####### HOT READ #######

Read Revelation 1-3. Which one of the churches mentioned describes your church?

——> LOOK INSIDE <

Surrounding the throne were twenty-four other thrones, and seated on them were twenty-four elders. They were dressed in white and had crowns of gold on their heads. Revelation 4:4.

t was one of those houses you dream about—a mansion, really. It had to have about 10 or 15 rooms. Gorgeous marble floors beckoned my wife and me inside. The gourmet kitchen sported not one but two huge ovens. Out back a huge pool sat quietly, its waters begging to be troubled. This house belonged on MTV Cribs, and it had a price tag to match: several million dollars. If the real estate agent had seen the car we'd left parked down the street, he wouldn't have let us in.

The Palos Verdes mansion was beautiful but empty. It was a shell waiting to be inhabited by real people—who had a lot of money. Think about it for a moment. How you feel about the house you live in is not determined just by whether you have nice room, a pool, or a game room. It's about the love, friend. It's about whether there's love in your crib. No matter how beautiful a house, if the people living there are nasty, the house starts to look very "ugg."

In Revelation 4 God gave John a look into the throne room of heaven. The sight is difficult to describe with human words, but John writes, "And the one who sat there had the appearance of jasper and carnelian. A rainbow, resembling an emerald, encircled the throne" (verse 3). The look of the throne room in heaven was vibrant with rich color. God is into color!

But then John kept looking, and another awesome sight captured his attention. Surrounding God's throne were 24 smaller thrones with 24 human beings sitting on them. The fact that there were humans in heaven must have knocked John out of his seat. Where did these guys come from? After all, Jesus hadn't returned to earth as yet.

Many people believe that these 24 elders were some of the people resurrected with Jesus (Matthew 27:52, 53). Whoever they are, they represent great news for us down here. If they can get to heaven, when Jesus comes so will we.

//////// HOT READ ///////

Read Revelation 5:1-7. Why did John weep? John did not want to miss any of God's messages hidden in the scrolls, and he wept at the thought that no human was worthy to break the seal, much less to read the book.

——> A LITTLE MORE TIME <

Do not harm the land or the sea or the trees until we put a seal on the foreheads of the servants of our God. Revelation 7:3.

ou've got to have a few questions by now. You're not alone. If you think you're having a tough time understanding Revelation, imagine how John felt as he watched it all unfold. Remember, God was giving John a view of the end of the world, and the imagery was frightening.

Did you notice the seals of destruction found in Revelation 6? Each seal opened a new event that would occur before the end of the world. The sixth seal said that a great earthquake would rock the earth and that it would followed by a darkening of the sun. Many Bible scholars date this earthquake to that mighty earthquake that rocked Lisbon, Portugal, on November 1, 1755. The shock of this earthquake was one of the strongest seismological disturbances ever recorded—felt from North Africa to the West Indies. As for the sun becoming dark? Do some research on the event that occurred in New York and southern New England on May 19, 1780. Don't take my word for it. Find a research library (such as one at a major university) and read the newspaper accounts of that day.

The things that John saw in vision were not make-believe. Hundreds of years before John's vision on Patmos, the prophet Joel prophesied about these great events (Joel 2:10), as did Isaiah (Isaiah 13:9-11) and Amos (Amos 8:9).

After the frightening opening of the seals and their effects on the earth, John was shown that four angels stood at the four "corners" of the earth, holding the winds of strife (Revelation 7:1). These angels were given power to harm the earth, but just as they were prepared to loose the winds, another angel came in yelling for them to stop.

"Don't do it yet!" the angel screamed. "Not until God's people are sealed in their foreheads." Friends, God is putting His mark on those who belong to Him. Satan is marking those who belong to Him. God has given us a little more time to know Him.

//// HOT READ /////

Note that there are only seven seals, six of which have already been fulfilled. What happens during the seventh seal? Revelation 8, 9. We are almost to these events.

──> SEAL IT UP <

And when the seven thunders spoke, I was about to write; but I heard a voice from heaven say, "Seal up what the seven thunders have said and do not write it down."
Revelation 10:4.

The symbolism found in Revelation 10-12 is difficult to grasp without the book of Daniel. Do you remember when we read Daniel? Daniel, like John, was given a view of the end of the world. Like John, he was overwhelmed by what he saw. He couldn't understand it.

To understand Daniel's and John's dilemma, imagine living sometime during the Stone Age. Imagine standing outside your little mud hut, when off in the distance you see a cloud of dust coming straight at you. A metal object is racing toward you in a blur. When it gets closer, it screeches to a stop. Out pops a human—you think. Its body is strangely clothed. Its hair is clipped close to its head. It walks up to you and hands you the keys to a brand-new Ferrari. Screeching up behind this human is another long, bright object. The human then hops in the other Ferrari and is taken away. What would you think? That's sort of how Daniel and John felt during their visions.

The angel of God told Daniel, "But you, Daniel, close up and seal the words of the scroll until the time of the end. Many will go here and there to increase knowledge" (Daniel 12:4). Why did Daniel have to seal the scroll? Because the events he saw were for a future time.

In Revelation 10 John is in a very similar situation. A mighty angel of God descends from heaven and stands with one foot on the earth and another in the sea. He's carrying a little scroll. (Scrolls were the books of that time.) The angel cried out with a loud voice, and the seven thunders began to speak. As the thunders spoke, Daniel pulled out his pen to write down what he was hearing: "But I heard a voice from heaven say, 'Seal up what the seven thunders have said and do not write it down'" (Revelation 10:4).

The messages of the seven thunders and that of the little book were not for Daniel's or John's immediate time, so God withheld them for a time soon to come upon the earth.

////// HOT READ //////

What do you think are the two witnesses mentioned in Revelation 11? Here's a hint: What do witnesses give in a trial? The Old and New Testaments are the two witnesses, with the power to depose any enemy. People have tried to destroy them, yet they keep on speaking. Please do not miss Revelation 12. The woman is the Christian church, and her Child is Jesus!

⟶ TWO BEASTS AND A DRAGON <

One of the heads of the beast seemed to have a fatal wound, but the fatal wound had been healed. The whole world was astonished and followed the beast.
Revelation 13:3.

orld of Warcraft doesn't have anything on the Bible. Beasts and dragons don't just roam around MMOGs and MMORPGs. Today you'll read about two beasts and a dragon. As you read, notice the specific characteristics of each. John saw the first beast rise out of the sea (Revelation 13:1). In the Bible the term *sea* is used to represent nations of people. For instance, God showed Abraham that his offspring would be numberless like the sands of the sea (Genesis 22). The mouth of this beast speaks blasphemy. What is blasphemy in this context? It is to slander or disrespect sacred things. Each of the beast's heads had a message that blasphemed God. This beast represents an earthly religious power that disrespects the truth of who God is.

The second beast rises from the earth (Revelation 13:11). This beast comes out of sparsely populated territory, and it does so right around the time that the first beast or power was wounded. Many believe that the rise of the United States fits this prophecy perfectly.

Who or what, then, was the first beast? The only power on earth that claimed to stand in the place of God on earth was the Roman Catholic Church. The Roman church dominated much of the world's political and religious life following the fall of the Roman Empire until 1798, when General Louis Alexandre Berthier of France entered Rome, declared an end to the political role of the Roman church, and took the pope prisoner to France. This was the wound written about by John in Rev. 13:3. The wound was later healed in 1929, when a treaty restored power to the pope, and he was allowed to rule over Vatican City. Today Vatican City is considered a nation, complete with its own head of state—the pope—and its own United Nations ambassador.

Just as the Roman church was being wounded, America began to rise on the world's stage. All of this may sound strange to you, but study the prophecies for yourself and let God lead you. God gave John a look at the future so that we would be ready for Jesus' return.

/////// HOT READ ///////

Read Revelation 14:6-13. What do these messages say to you about the final judgment?

——> COME OUT NOW <

Then I heard another voice from heaven say: "Come out of her, my people, so that you will not share in her sins, so that you will not receive any of her plagues."
Revelation 18:4.

Have you noticed that most of the angels written about by John spoke with loud voices? That gives you a hint about how important their messages were. Here's another one of those "loud-mouth" angels, and what he had to say represents God's final warning to His people. Listen carefully to this angel's message. John describes it.

"After this I saw another angel coming down from heaven. He had great authority, and the earth was illuminated by his splendor. With a mighty voice he shouted: 'Fallen! Fallen is Babylon the Great! She has become a home for demons and a haunt for every evil spirit, a haunt for every unclean and detestable bird. For all the nations have drunk the maddening wine of her adulteries. The kings of the earth committed adultery with her, and the merchants of the earth grew rich from her excessive luxuries'" (Revelation 18:1-3).

The angel lights up the world with his message targeted at a mythical woman named Babylon. The Babylon spoken about here represents the world's system of confusion and sin. The angel is giving a final warning to men and women enjoying the pleasures of sin. What's the message? Come out, and do so right now!

One Christian posted this message on a Web site dedicated to testimonies of personal transformations: "I tried to do things my way. It didn't work. Believing that God would accept me if I was moral, I became a very moral but a very lost person. When I met up with a friendly and powerful 'white witch,' I started practicing strange meditation and talking with spirits. I later went along with them in stealing a motor home and robbing an electronics store in an attempt to join up with another cult in California. We were caught in Iowa, and it was then that I realized just how 'lost' I was. I gave my life to God, and He gave His peace to me as He promised in Philippians 4:6, 7."

People are hearing God's call to come out of Babylon. Are you?

///////// HOT READ ///////
How does heaven respond after Babylon is destroyed? Revelation 19:1-4.

──> I SAW IT <

Then I saw a new heaven and a new earth. Revelation 21:1.

f there ever was a guy who needed to see the New Jerusalem, it was John. After viewing all of the destruction we read about yesterday, God showed John a spectacular sight. I want to close with some of what John saw, as paraphrased by *The Message*. This passage encourages me when I'm feeling down, because it reminds me of what's to come.

"I saw Heaven and earth new-created. Gone the first Heaven, gone the first earth, gone the sea. I saw Holy Jerusalem, new-created, descending resplendent out of Heaven, as ready for God as a bride for her husband.

"I heard a voice thunder from the Throne: 'Look! Look! God has moved into the neighborhood, making his home with men and women! They're his people, he's their God. He'll wipe every tear from their eyes. Death is gone for good— tears gone, crying gone, pain gone—all the first order of things gone.' The Enthroned continued, 'Look! I'm making everything new. Write it all down— each word dependable and accurate.'

"Then he said, 'It's happened. I'm A to Z. I'm the Beginning, I'm the Conclusion. From Water-of-Life Well I give freely to the thirsty. Conquerors inherit all this. I'll be God to them, they'll be sons and daughters to me. But for the rest—the feckless and faithless, degenerates and murderers, sex peddlers and sorcerers, idolaters and all liars—for them it's Lake Fire and Brimstone. Second death!'" (Revelation 21:1-8, Message).

John's vision is for all of the starving people in our world. It's for the kid who struggles with his self-esteem, and the mother dying of cancer. It's for the gangbangers in LA and Baghdad. It's for the guy I met at one church who felt as if God had left Him. It's for the HIV-positive guy who posted a video on the Internet explaining why he's spreading the disease to unsuspecting women. If he repents, Jesus' blood covers his sin, and he too can go to heaven.

It's for me.

It's for you.

///////// HOT READ ///////

Are you going to heaven? I'll see you there. Keep the faith and live strong!

1-ON-1 WITH GOD

			MAY								JUNE								JULY	
		Sun	Mon	Tue	Wed	Thu	Fri	Sat	Sun	Mon	Tue	Wed	Thu	Fri	Sat	Sun	Mon	Tue	Wed	
Fri	Sat					1	2	3	1	2	3	4	5	6	7			1	2	
4	5	4	5	6	7	8	9	10	8	9	10	11	12	13	14	6	7	8	9	
11	12	11	12	13	14	15	16	17	15	16	17	18	19	20	21	13	14	15	16	
18	19	18	19	20	21	22	23	24	22	23	24	25	26	27	28	20	21	22	23	
25	26	25	26	27	28	29	30	31	29	30						27	28	29	30	

375

1-ON-1 WITH GOD

FEBRUARY

Sun	Mon	Tue	Wed	Thu	Fri	Sat
					1	2
3	4	5	6	7	8	9
10	11	12	13	14	15	16
17	18	19	20	21	22	23
24	25	26	27	28	29	

MARCH

Sun	Mon	Tue	Wed	Thu	Fri	Sat
						1
2	3	4	5	6	7	8
9	10	11	12	13	14	15
16	17	18	19	20	21	22
23	24	25	26	27	28	29
30	31					

			MAY							JUNE							JULY			
Fri	Sat	Sun	Mon	Tue	Wed	Thu	Fri	Sat	Sun	Mon	Tue	Wed	Thu	Fri	Sat	Sun	Mon	Tue	Wed	Thu
4	5					1	2	3	1	2	3	4	5	6	7			1	2	3
11	12	4	5	6	7	8	9	10	8	9	10	11	12	13	14	6	7	8	9	10
18	19	11	12	13	14	15	16	17	15	16	17	18	19	20	21	13	14	15	16	17
25	26	18	19	20	21	22	23	24	22	23	24	25	26	27	28	20	21	22	23	24
		25	26	27	28	29	30	31	29	30						27	28	29	30	31

Whose side are you on, anyway?

It's the most important decision you'll ever make! This discipleship guide will not only show you how to be a follower of Christ, but also teach you how to become a peer mentor! More than just a baptismal course, this is an exciting way to begin a new life.
0-8280-1711-5. Paperback, 128 pages.

3 WAYS TO SHOP

- **Visit your local Adventist Book Center®**
- **Call toll-free 1-800-765-6955**
- **Online at AdventistBookCenter.com**

Availability subject to change.

REVIEW AND HERALD®
PUBLISHING ASSOCIATION
Since 1861 | www.reviewandherald.com

A STORY OF
COURAGE AND FAITH

Without warning, 21-year-old Mikhail Kulakov was arrested. His crime? Faithful service to God, or, in the words of the KGB, "anti-Soviet activities." Despite unrelenting persecution by his own country, he clung to God's promises. His unforgettable story will astonish, inspire, and humble you.
978-0-8280-2366-5.
Paperback, 192 pages.

3 WAYS TO SHOP

DO GOD AND CHURCH REALLY MATTER?

We don't always feel a need for God—unless we've hit rock bottom. But even if you're well off, well fed, and well educated, life truly is better with God. Nathan Brown considers seven reasons God matters in everyday life, revealing that whether things are good or bad, God makes them better still. 978-0-8127-0436-5. Paperback, 160 pages.